Tradition and Modernity in Arabic Language and Literature

Tradition and Modernity in Arabic Language and Literature

edited by
J.R. Smart
Department of Arabic & Islamic Studies,
University of Exeter

Routledge
Taylor & Francis Group
LONDON AND NEW YORK

First Published in 1996
by Curzon Press

Published 2013 by Routledge
2 Park Square, Milton Park, Abingdon, Oxfordshire OX14 4RN
711 Third Avenue, New York, NY 10017

Routledge is an imprint of the Taylor and Francis Group, an informa business

First issued in paperback 2015

Typeset in Times by LaserScript Ltd, Mitcham

British Library Cataloguing in Publication Data
A catalogue record of this book is available from the British Library

Library of Congress Cataloguing in Publication Data
A catalog record for this book has been requested

ISBN 978-0-7007-0411-8 (hbk)
ISBN 978-1-138-98588-9 (pbk)

Contents

Preface

This volume is a collection of papers presented at the Second Shaban Memorial Conference, held at the University of Exeter in September 1994.

This event was the second in a series of conferences kindly sponsored by H.H. Dr Sheikh Sultan al-Qasimi, Ruler of Sharjah, in memory of Professor M.A.H. Shaban, founder of the Department of Arabic and Islamic Studies at the University of Exeter. This year's conference was run by the Department, the idea being to alternate between it and its sister organisation, the Centre for Arab Gulf Studies, also founded by Professor Shaban, which has been responsible for the first and third in the series. I acknowledge here with deep gratitude H.H. Sheikh Sultan's generosity and patronage of scholarship.

Being the first major conference at Exeter in the literary-linguistic field, the topic chosen was deliberately a broad one, with the aim of attracting a gathering of scholars in a wide variety of Arabic related fields rather than a group of specialists in a narrowly-defined area. In this, the conference was highly successful in its coverage of a multiplicity of topics within the general field of Arabic language and literature, as is reflected in the range of articles in this book.

I have divided the book into three sections, but this is a somewhat arbitrary division and there are many overlapping areas. In this connection I should mention particularly the contributions of Pierre Cachia and Clive Holes, both of which deal with colloquial poetry. I have placed those in the language section on the grounds that they include much material of interest to linguists and dialectologists, but this is in no way meant to imply a lack of poetic merit in the texts they discuss.

As regards technicalities, there arises the perennial question of transliteration. Understandably, coming from a wide variety of sources, many different systems were used. However, these differences were in most cases both minor and slight and I have only interfered where I regarded comprehensibility to be at risk. Exceptions here are again the colloquial-oriented articles which require special symbols for non-standard Arabic sounds. The transcription systems used in these have been explained in the articles themselves, or in footnotes to them.

I conclude by thanking all contributors and, on the home team, especially Dr Rasheed El-Enany, whose wide network of contacts in the international field of Arabic scholarship helped to make the gathering a memorable one. I should also like to thank all those who kindly chaired sessions, and members of the back-up team who helped to ensure that all went smoothly.

Jack Smart,
University of Exeter

Part 1

Poetry

1

Romanticism and Modern Arabic Literature

Jareer Abu-Haidar, S.O.A.S.

Perhaps, in one of the most forceful openings of a literary work of all time, Faust, or Doctor Faust, in Goethe's well-known work, decries the futility of all his studies and endless scholarly endeavours in the following terms:

> I've studied now philosophy
> And jurisprudence, medicine,
> And even, alas! theology – From end to end, with labour keen;
> And here poor fool! With all my lore
> I stand, no wiser than before:[1]

Faust, of course, goes on to say much more than that. But in the same opening verses of the tragedy, he says that he had led other scholars to the same unprofitable pursuits, and that he was not going to rummage in empty words any more.[2]

Having made such an introduction to this paper, the least I should hope for is to avoid rummaging in empty words. Yet, in some respects my quest amounts to an examination or scrutiny of 'empty words', and that is the application of Western critical terms like 'romantic' and 'romanticism' without any qualification to Arabic literature. When these terms were adopted as literary referents in Arabic, particularly in the thirties and forties of the present century, there was little in the Arabic cultural and literary background of that intellectual ferment which, going back to the days of the French encyclopaedists, had brought about the Romantic Movement in the West in the late eighteenth and early nineteenth centuries. There was little of that questioning or self-searching, as to whether it was 'bending over books', or the continuous study of philosophy, jurisprudence, medicine and 'even, alas! theology' which would make people 'wiser than before', or the liberating communion with the world at large, '*Hinaus ins Freie!*' as Faust was to declare.[3]

In the same way, that dichotomy between reason and feeling, or reason and emotion, brought about by the rapid scientific discoveries of the eighteenth century in Europe, had not much preoccupied many of the Arab literati described as 'romanticists' or 'pre-romanticists' in the twentieth century. But it dominated the thinking of Jean-Jacques Rousseau (1712–78) whose thought largely prefigured the trends which came to constitute Romanticism. Rousseau left us his authoritative pronouncement on the controversy: 'If it is reason which makes man, it is feeling which guides him.'[4] The controversy equally preoccupied leading figures in the English romantic movement like Wordsworth and Coleridge, and an older contemporary of theirs, the political philosopher William Godwin (1756–1836).

Little light would be shed on the subject by introducing here a dictionary definition of 'romanticism', and trying to see how Arabic literary works described as 'romantic' would fit into it. A definition can be stretched at will to accommodate any expression of personal sentiment or sense of crisis, or whatever can be presented as romantic colour. It would be more instructive if we could see the Romantic Movement itself at work in the West, sense the undercurrents which brought it forth, and if we could have some clear intimation of how critics in the West viewed both the undercurrents and the outcome. I say 'intimation', because we are dealing here with Arabic literature, and not dealing at length with romantic literature in the West.

In the early chapters of his well-known work, *Science and the Modern World*, (chapters III, IV and V),[5] A N Whitehead views the Romantic Movement in the West as 'a reaction against scientific ideas, or rather against the mechanistic ideas' that scientific discoveries in the seventeenth and eighteenth centuries had given rise to. 'The seventeenth and eighteenth centuries' as Angus Wilson explains, 'were in Europe the great period of the development of mathematical and physical theory . . . The poets, like the astronomers and mathematicians, had come to regard the universe as a machine, obeying logical laws and susceptible of reasonable explanation . . . and they examined human nature dispassionately, in the same lucid and reasonable spirit, to find the principles on which it worked.'[6]

Back in the first half of the eighteenth century, we are told, one of the French encyclopaedists, collaborating with the renowned Diderot, '. . . a medical man and a scientist of note, attempted to dissect and to study man as a pure mechanism.'[7] Diderot, who was perhaps just as interested in the study of the human anatomy, but more intent on improving the human condition, gave little countenance to the enthusiasm of his colleague. More like a prophet than a scientist, he declares: 'All that hurts humankind hurts me' (*Tout ce qui blesse l'espèce humaine me blesse*).[8] To the romanticists, both the universe and the individual human soul were too much of a mystery to be explained by any set of scientific principles or rules. And if they looked for an answer to their intellectual and psychological crises, they did not deem it likely, any more than Faust did, to find an answer in their studies, or the studies and theories of the scientists. The crucibles of the scientists were not expected to provide the required balm. What follows below are a few verses by a well-known Western author and poet who, quite clearly, does not expect such a balm to be the gift of a crucible:

> What profit if this scientific age
> Burst through our gates with all its retinue
> Of modern miracles! Can it assuage
> One lover's breaking heart? What can it do
> To make one life more beautiful, one day
> More godlike in its period?

The verses are by Oscar Wilde (1856–1900),[9] who, chronologically at least, cannot be classified with the romanticists. But it is just as instructive to see the insignificance a crucible acquires in a brief quotation from the poet Shelley. The quotation is in prose, and occurs where the poet is commenting on the acute problems of translation in poetry:

> '. . . it were as wise to cast a violet into a crucible, that you might discover the formal principles of its colour and odour, as seek to transfer from one language into another the creations of a poet.'[10]

There is perhaps a sufficient indication in the preceding pages of how the Romantic Movement in the West constituted a reaction against constricting scientific or mechanistic ideas, when these purported to explain human nature, or the position of man and human society in the universal scheme. While romantic literature in the Arab world contains repeated echoes of resentment, more or less sincere, against materialism, or, more precisely, against devotion to financial gain and the matters of this world, it cannot be equated with its Western counterpart as a reaction against scientific ideas.

It goes without saying perhaps that the return to nature among romantic writers and poets in the West was a close concomitant to the reaction against scientific ideas, or against the prescriptions of Reason or pure intellectualism. The Russian poet Andrei Voznesensky gives what amounts to an injunction: 'Do not touch music with your hands.'

We have already come across Shelley warning us also not to introduce crucibles into nature.[11] Wordsworth, likewise, was not likely to concern himself with atoms and particles of light, when he spoke of the whole earth as being 'Apparelled in celestial light',[12] which gave him intimations of immortality. Wordsworth, we are told, 'was suffering from an emotional collapse or what today would be called a nervous breakdown'[13] when he came under the influence of William Godwin and his theories, outlined in his work *Enquiry Concerning Political Justice*, published in 1793. For Godwin 'social justice would be achieved by the exercise of reason unfettered by emotion or by political, religious or social conventions and institutions'.[14] Wordsworth met Godwin and became 'an ardent disciple' of his. But, as often happens, once the poet was physically refreshed and restored, he was mentally and psychologically restored. He 'rejected Godwin's dichotomy of reason and emotion' in terms which enjoin us to seek guidance primarily from nature, and not from reason or the prescripts of the intellect:[15]

> One impulse from a vernal wood
> May teach you more of man;
> Of moral evil and of good,
> Than all the sages can.
>
> Sweet is the lore which nature brings;
> Our meddling intellect
> Misshapes the beauteous forms of things;
> – We murder to dissect.
>
> Enough of science and of art;
> Close up these barren leaves;
> Come forth, and bring with you a heart
> That watches and receives

The romantic movement in the Arab world did not constitute a reaction against the claims of reason; and the return to nature in a lot of Arabic romantic literature seems quite often to be an exaggerated posture which pictures the poets in particular as being made of a totally different lump of clay from the rest of ordinary mortals. In fact, some titles of *dīwāns* which appeared in the thirties and forties of this century picture some Arab poets as living beyond, or outside nature. Pierre Cachia refers to a collection by Ibrāhīm Nājī which he describes as '. . . characteristically entitled *Beyond the Clouds* (1934) . . .'[16] Contemporary with Nājī's collection was ᶜAlī Maḥmūd Ṭāhā's first collection, also published in 1934 which Mustafa Badawi describes as 'significantly entitled *al-Mallāḥ al-Tāʾih* (The Lost Mariner)'. Badawi goes on to say that this collection was 'characteristically dedicated to "those enamoured of longing for the Unknown, those lost on the sea of life, those who haunt the deserted shore", words that in fact set the keynote to the contents of the entire volume.'[17] Yet, Badawi goes on to say in the same comment on this collection, that the poems in it '. . . reveal a consistently hedonistic attitude to life which Ṭāhā managed to maintain until the end of his life, but perhaps best expressed in his (second) collection *Layālī al-Mallāḥ al-Tāʾih* (nights of the Lost Mariner), published in 1940'.[18]

Edmund Wilson gives us yet another definition of 'romanticism' in his well-known critical work *Axel's Castle* (1931). 'The Romantic is nearly always a rebel', says Wilson. The romanticists he tells us '. . . ask us to be interested in themselves. And they ask us to be interested in themselves by virtue of the intrinsic value of the individual: they vindicate the rights of the individual against the claims of society as a whole – against government, morals, conventions, academy or church'.[19] Are there any rebels among the Arab romanticists, or would one be hard put to it to find one? Among the Arab poets in particular, do we have to wait for al-Sayyāb or Muḥammad al-Māghūṭ to find someone who qualifies as a rebel?

Of course I can go on here to give views of romanticism which run counter to the views outlined above and which assert that it was the successive advances made in science which kindled the imagination of writers and poets, and gave them the incentive to give a free range to their imagination, and to abandon the beaten tracks. But this would leave little space for the discussion of Arabic literature, the focal point of this paper.

When we speak of romantic literature in Arabic, we more often than not seem to be thinking primarily of poetry, although I do not see why we should not speak of the author of *Zaynab* (1913) as a romantic novelist, or speak of Muḥammad Mandūr as a romantic critic. Poetry bulks in Arabic romantic literature, and love poetry bulks above all. Of course romantic poetry is at times described as an expression of 'personal moods in more musical verse', and in this light Arabic love poetry in the earlier decades of this century qualifies as romantic. But love poetry bulks also in the classical Arabic tradition, and ᶜUmar Ibn Abī Rabīᶜa in particular wrote about his personal escapades in the light, more lyrical metres, and in 'a simple, almost conversational style.'[20] Does not ᶜUmar by right qualify as the first Arab romantic poet?

Mustafa Badawi in his recent *Short History of Modern Arabic Literature* treats the poet ᶜAlī Maḥmūd Ṭāhā with some apparent indulgence. 'Although by no means the greatest of the Arab Romantics, ᶜAlī

Maḥmūd Ṭāhā', he tells us, 'deserves a special mention in this context on account of the part he played (unconsciously) in hastening the downfall of the Romantic ideal.'[21] If this were true at all, it would make the application of the terms 'Romantic' and 'Romantic ideal' to Arabic poetry and Arabic literature a mere misnomer or nothing less than a travesty. The Romantic Movement in European literature has been since its inception an ever-widening continuum. Edmund Wilson describes Symbolism, and quite rightly so, as being 'a second flood of the same tide',[22] a second flood of Romanticism. If the Romanticists have enjoined suggestion rather than statement in what we write, 'to intimate things rather than state them plainly was . . . one of the primary aims of the Symbolists.'[23] Mallarmé, the acknowledged prophet of Symbolism, likewise decrees: 'Paint, not the thing itself, but the effect that it produces.' (*Peindre non la chose, mais l'effet qu'elle produit*).[24] Paul Tillich tells us also that 'in . . . Romanticism we have the pre-formation of almost all the ideas of existentialism.'[25] Irving Babbit suggests that Romanticism, like man in Nietzsche's words, is a movement which needs to keep surpassing itself.[26] However, Badawi goes on to say about ᶜAlī Maḥmūd Ṭāhā: 'The modern Arab student or the critic familiar with Western Romantic poetry may find little of profundity in Ṭāhā's imagery and choice of themes, but it must be admitted that in Arabic literature by Ṭāhā's time, such themes or images had not yet become as commonplace as they are now. In fact, it was Ṭāhā himself who, by his exceedingly skilful use of them in his highly musical verse, encouraged a whole generation of younger men among his admirers to imitate them, thereby rendering such themes and images the mere stock-in-trade of facile Romantic poetry.'

One can gather from all this that ᶜAlī Maḥmūd Ṭāhā did not 'hasten the downfall of the Romantic ideal', as Badawi states, but the downfall of 'facile Romantic poetry', the poetry of emotional immediacy or of sheer sentimentalism. I say this because Badawi gives us details about the poet in his *Short History* which do not mark him out as a rebel, or show his poetry to be abreast of a novel original movement. 'In Ṭāhā's work', he says, 'Europe plays a role in some ways similar to that of the exotic and sensuous East in Western Romantic poetry: as Jayyusi put it in volume II of *Trends and Movements* "the charms of the West with its seemingly liberal enjoyment of life, the freedom it allowed to the individual provided a great Romantic appeal to the Arab youths of the forties."' 'Quite rightly', adds Badawi, 'she sees that Ṭāhā's popularity was partly due to the fact that it provided one of the greatest outlets for the emotionally and sexually suppressed youth of the Middle East.'

Of course there is a lot of truth in what both Jayyusi and Badawi say, but one has to remember, in this connection, the simple reality that the Romantic Movement in the West was the product of a crisis of thought, and not a crisis of 'emotionally and sexually suppressed youth.' We have to remember too that the people whose thought or whose ideas prepared the way for the Romantic Movement in France were the same people whose thought and ideas prepared the way for, or inspired the French Revolution.[27] Nor, of course, was the influence of these people, Diderot and Rousseau, for example, restricted to France. While Rousseau is acknowledged as the single most potent influence on the Romantic Movement in France, critics point out that Kierkegaard, Nietzsche, Tolstoy and a great number of Romantic poets in Germany and Britain were in many respects his spiritual heirs.[28] The British historian Lord Acton asserts that 'Rousseau had achieved more with his pen than perhaps any man who ever wrote.'[29]

While it must be admitted that some prominent romanticists practised a form of eccentric coquetry in their 'attempts at uniqueness', I find of little relevance the information Mustafa Badawi supplies about ᶜAlī Maḥmūd Ṭāhā that 'his mistresses tend to be fair, with golden hair', and that 'he chose as romantic settings for his poems Venice, Capri, Como or Lugano.'[30] All these are tourist resorts, as we know, some of them with casinos, and they do not represent a 'return to nature'. Badawi adds as a final assessment of Ṭāhā: '. . . it must be remembered that without Ṭāhā the modernists Nizār Qabbānī and Badr Shākir al-Sayyāb would not have been possible.'[31] I find it difficult to agree with that. Al-Sayyāb, author of the epic poem 'The Blind Prostitute' with its deep compassion is a world apart from Nizār Qabbānī's sensational 'Pregnant', or ᶜAlī Maḥmūd Ṭāhā's *Rākibat al-darrāja* a poem about a young woman he saw riding her bicycle on a visit he paid to Italy.

It is time perhaps that we accepted the verdict of the celebrated Muḥammad Mandūr that the true romanticists of modern Arabic literature, its pioneering romanticists, are the Syro-American authors and poets *Udabāᵓ al-Mahjar*, and no one should seek to minimize their contribution, and its perennial guiding influence. Mandūr had no doubt that these poets and authors, writing in the early decades of this century, were centuries ahead of their contemporaries in the Arab world, and that it was their poetry which would be honoured for all time:

وان شعرهم هو الذي سيصيب الخلود[32]

Muḥammad Mandūr selected for particular comment one of the most perfect and most pure poems ever written in Arabic, the five-stanza poem *'Akhī'* 'brother' or 'comrade' by Mikhāʾīl Nuʿaymah.[33] '*Akhī*' is a war poem. And it might come as a surprise that there are war poems in Arabic written in the early decades of this century. Mandūr chose the poem, as he tells us, for the total absence of a declamatory tone in it. He calls it, together with other works by Nuʿaymah and his colleagues 'whispered poetry' *al-shiʿr al-mahmūs*.[34] I refer to it above as 'a pure poem' using A C Bradley's words, because of the total identity of form and content in it. Because 'we feel it hopeless to convey' its effect 'in any form but its own.'[35] Nuʿaymah wrote it in New York in 1917 upon hearing of the famine in his homeland, Lebanon. Under pretext of an Allied blockade of the Lebanese coasts, the Ottoman authorities had prevented any foodstuffs, clothing or medicines to come into the country, and more than a hundred thousand people, of a population of half a million at the time, died a slow death, without the sound of a single light or heavy gun. The prophetic element in the two opening verses of the poem is quite humbling. The war in 1917 had not ended:

أخي ان ضج بعد الحرب غربي باعماله
وقدس ذكر من ماتوا ، وعظم ابطاله

> Brother, if a Westerner should go on after the war to make too much clamour about his deeds
> Sanctifying the memory of those dead, and glorifying the valour (ruthless valour) of his heroes

It is gratifying to quote these verses, with the knowledge that one is addressing himself to Arabists. Onomatopoeia, of course, exists in all languages. But little represents noise and clamour like the grating together of the two *jīms* in the Arabic terms *ḍajja* and *ḍajīj*. Never also have the emphatic letters *ẓāʾ* in *aẓẓama* and the repeated *ṭāʾ* in *baṭsha abṭālih* been put to such effectual use to represent not only the noise, the drum beats, but also the pomp of a march past.

'If a Westerner should march in pomp after the war', Nuʿaymah says, 'do kneel down in silence with me, brother, in order to mourn the fate of our dead.' The timelessness of the message in 1917, I would like to repeat, is humbling. Even at the expense of sounding as if one is preaching, I would like to point out that only recently the West was still disputing as to whether it should celebrate or simply commemorate the anniversary of the Normandy landings.

What moved the late Muḥammad Mandūr more than anything else in

Nu^c^aymah's poem was that the poet, after inviting his brother to carry a spade and help him bury their dead, goes on to tell his brother that the world is suffering not only the stench of their dead, but also, he says, 'the stench of those of us who are still among the living.' He then asks his brother to help him dig another trench in which to bury those of their people who were still living. Mandūr exclaims at this point that nothing he had read stirs one to life and action, or stirs one out of his torpor like this statement at the end of Nu^c^aymah's poem.[36]

Muḥammad Mandūr goes on with the same heartiness to examine a long self-searching poem by Nu^c^aymah's colleague in America, the poet Nasīb ^c^Arīḍah, a poem entitled '*Yā Nafs*' 'Oh my soul!'.[37] But the poem by ^c^Arīḍah I am going to refer to is yet another war poem written at the same time as Nu^c^aymah's '*Akhī*'. ^c^Arīḍah, who came from Ḥims in Syria, had also heard, of course, of the famine in Lebanon and the harvest it had reaped. What I like about the poem is the same wrath, the same indignation with which ^c^Arīḍah also tries to shake people out of their smugness, or out of their self-complacency. The poem is entitled *al-Nihāya* 'The End'.[38] It starts with what amounts to an injunction, and maintains throughout the same tone of strong and earnest exhortation:

كفنوه !
وادفنوه !
اسكنوه
هوة اللحد العميق

Wrap him in shrouds,
And bury him,
Deep in the abyss of the grave

What ^c^Arīḍah is enjoining people to wrap in shrouds and bury is a whole people *sha^c^b*, the whole of the Lebanese, Syrian, or perhaps even the whole nation to which Syria and Lebanon belong:

ولنتاجر
في المهاجر
ولنفاخر
بمزايانا الحسان
ما علينا ان قضى الشعب جميعًا
أفلسنا في امان !

Let us keep on
In these (Arab) colonies abroad
Plying the trade of our social graces;
What is it to us
If a whole people should perish,
Aren't we feeling snug and secure?

It is, I must admit, Muḥammad Mandūr who guided me to the real value of these two Mahjar poems by Nu^caymah and ^cAriḍah. It is the thrust and the merciless derision with which they try to shake us out of our eternal smugness, asking us to give up outdoing each other with our social graces when people are, literally, being starved to death.

The difference between the Syro-American Arab poets and their contemporaries in the Arab world is that they were not primarily concerned with poetry, but with what they wanted to say through poetry. This term 'concerned with poetry' is not mine. I have borrowed it from the English poet Wilfred Owen. Owen wrote in the preface to his own poems: 'Above all I am not concerned with poetry. My subject is war, and the pity of war. The poetry is in the pity.'[39] When I say that the contemporaries of *Udabā᾿ al-Mahjar* in the Arab world were 'concerned with poetry' I am not, I think, making a false charge, or being unfair to them.

It would be a gigantic task to try to assess fully the far-reaching stir caused by Western romantic literature in the Arab world in the earlier decades of this century. Myth, as we know, constituted an important part of the symbolic language of romantic poetry in the West. When Aḥmad Zakī Abū Shādī published the monthly poetry review *Apollo* in 1932, both the name of the magazine and the figure of Apollo, which dominated the design of its cover, were an indication of the deliberate attempt by the Apollo group to cultivate Greek mythology as the symbolic language of Arabic poetry. In his first editorial, Abū Shādī stressed the international appeal of that mythology, and how much, as he put it, it would lend 'grandeur to the beauty of Arabic poetry and to those who write it.'[40] Of course there was no harm in enriching Arabic poetry with the abiding vitality of Greek mythology. But since this mythology had at no time been part of the Arabic literary heritage, the attempt was destined to be for a long time a studied or an intellectual exercise.[41] The poet and critic Muḥammad ^cAbdul-Ḥai tells us, however, that 'the Mahjar poets . . . found inspiration not in Greek, but in Arab mythologies.'[42] Shelley had expressed a universal experience when he wrote:

We look before and after
And pine for what is not

Nasīb ᶜArīḍah had not read Shelley. But he might well have had on his mind the El Dorado that people seek, or at least fantasize about, and which keeps evading them. ᶜArīḍah, widely read in classical Arabic literature, found a faithful analogue for this eternal longing for 'what is not' in the story of the city of Iram *dhātu 'l-ᶜImād* which appears in various forms in Arabic medieval literature, and which is given added dignity, of course, by a reference to it in *sūrat al-Fajr* (Sūra LXXXIX). Iram, as we know, is the earthly paradise that no one had seen, and in the search for which many caravans had perished. But in one medieval Arabic text at least,[43] Iram, if one allows himself the pun, is more tantalizing than the story of Tantalus in Greek mythology. Scintillating lights are radiated at night from its pillars of gold, its red rubies and various other precious stones. But the minute travellers approach these lights, they move further into the distance, and become like the evasive mirage. ᶜArīḍah utilizes the myth in a poem entitled *ᶜAlā ṭarīq Iram* 'Along the way to Iram'.[44] The poem, as already indicated, epitomizes the story of human life and the perpetual hope, the pining for what is not, which guides it. But it is not a story of philosophical desperation. There is the certainty of a dawn after the night journey to Iram.

Abū Māḍī, another brilliant Syro-American, utilizes yet another Arab myth, the legendary bird *al-ᶜanqāᵓ* (The Griffon) in order to epitomize man's search for happiness.[45] Again there is no philosophical desperation in Abū Māḍī's poem. The popular Sudanese saying asks the question:

اللي يطلع من بيتو حزين يلاقي الفرج وين ؟

'He who leaves his home unhappy, where on earth would he find happiness?'

Abū Māḍī tells us that one cannot find happiness outside his home, nor even in his backyard. That is tantamount to looking for the *ᶜanqāᵓ* which does not exist. Happiness can only be found within oneself.

As Muḥammad ᶜAbdul-Ḥai points out, it was Arab mythology that the Mahjar poets utilized as the symbolic language of their poetry.[46] Perhaps I should not fail to add in this context, that when Mikhāᵓīl Nuᶜaymah asks in the last stanza of his poem '*Akhī*':

أخي من نحن لا وطن ولا أهل ولا جار

Brother, who are we, with no homeland, no kin and no neighbour?

he does not mean that he had no neighbours in New York. He means a neighbour with that noble pre-Islamic Arabic charge or connotation – the neighbour who does not allow those living close to his living quarters to suffer any harm, or to feel unprotected. I say this because words have been bandied about in the past and still get bandied about nowadays, that these brilliant Syro-American writers and poets, thrown into a different culture, had cut themselves adrift from their Arab heritage. These writers and poets did not hit upon an El Dorado in the countries of their *hijra* or their exile, but wherever they found a deep seam of gold in their Arab culture, they knew how to reach for it, and how to utilize it.

Having referred to the poet Abū Māḍī, I should not fail to add another brief comment on his unique contribution to the romantic movement in Arabic poetry. Abū Māḍī wrote Arabic poetry with an ease and melodiousness which many another poet and would-be poet must have envied. We are all aware of how individual verses in classical Arabic poetry were all end-rhymed and end-stopped. It is safe to say that there are no stops, and no obstacles in the flow of a poem by Abū Māḍī. His first *dīwān* to be published in New York in 1927 is entitled *al-Jadāwil* 'Brooks' or 'Streams'. Never perhaps has a title been applied more appropriately. The poetic compositions of Abū Māḍī, whether strophic or in the traditional form, seem to have one stop, and that is at the end. Very much like streams or brooks, their movement is free and tuneful until the end of their course. Few people have succeeded in giving classical Arabic the conversational and confident syntactic flow it attains in Abū Māḍī's poetry. As a gauge of Abū Māḍī's popularity, it is worthwhile mentioning that no other publication in the Arab world went through as many pirate editions as his *al-Jadāwil*. But Abū Māḍī would need a separate article dedicated to his work to do him any justice as a romanticist, as would, of course, the one outstanding and pioneering romantic rebel in modern Arabic letters, Jubrān Khalīl Jubrān. It is easily forgotten that it was back in the first decade of this century, in 1908, that the young Jubrān published one of his earliest works significantly entitled Spirits Rebellious *al-Arwāḥ al-Mutamarrida*. It is now universally acknowledged, of course, that Jubrān was the first purveyor of vitality and a romantic élan to a feebly convalescent Arabic language and literature.

Another relevant note should not be overlooked here. Literary critics in the Arab world, who are so used to rhymes at the end of verses, have had little to say about the rhymes (triple rhymes) which appear at the beginning of the verses in ᶜArīḍah's poem '*al-Nihāya*' quoted above, or about the unprecedented way in which the poet totally transforms the familiar pattern of the poem in Arabic. Rhymes at the beginning of verses were used with equal success by ᶜArīḍah's colleague in the Mahjar, Rashīd Ayyūb, in his strophic poetry.[47] Strophic poetry was extensively written by all the poets of the Mahjar, and it attains at their hands a purity and perfection equal to the best in any other literature. Three quarters of the poems in Nuᶜaymah's *dīwān*, *Hams al-Jufūn* are strophic in form. All of them were written between 1917 and 1926. Yet despite all this, a prominent Arabist, Pierre Cachia, still writes in 1990 that until the appearance of the Free Verse Movement in Iraq in 1949, 'metrical forms going back to pre-Islamic Arabia had reigned unchallenged except for the introduction of some strophic forms in Muslim Spain . . .'[48] The appearance of the Free Verse Movement in 1947, not 1949, as stated in Cachia's work, cannot be seen in the right perspective without reference to what the Syro-Americans were writing in 1917. Apart from '*Akhī*' and '*al-Nihāya*', quoted above, the reader might do well to see other strophic poems such as '*al-Masā*ᵓ' by Abū Māḍī in *al-Jadāwil*, and the *muwashshaḥ*-like poem '*Dhikrā Lubnān*' in Rashīd Ayyūb's *Aghānī al-Darwīsh*.

In the light of what has preceded I choose to describe as 'romantic' any new idea or impulse which can shake us out of our smugness. 'Nothing', it has been said 'is more intolerable than smugness'.[49] People can feel, and snap out of a sense of sloth, inadequacy or ineptitude, but they can go on for ever glorifying in or indulging their smugness. I chose to discuss the two poems by Nuᶜaymah and ᶜArīḍah above because both Nuᶜaymah and ᶜArīḍah addressed their fellow Arabs in 1917 with the tone of wrath and indignation with which their fellow Arabs chose to address themselves fifty years later after 1967. I do not know what Muḥammad al-Māghūṭ meant in more recent times when he said:

سئمتك ايها الشعر ايتها الجيفة الخالدة

'I am sick of you, poetry, you immortal corpse!'

Did he at all mean that we have gone back to being more concerned with poetry than the real substance or perhaps the much needed holy wrath of poetry?

On the other hand, the novel, the short story and, indeed, drama in modern Arabic literature are all drawing quite extensively on the language and experiences of everyday life, and becoming progressively more relevant and more intimately related to life. Does al-Māghūṭ perhaps mean that modern Arabic poetry runs a serious risk of being trapped in a self-imposed cul-de-sac? Does he mean that modern Arabic poetry is in need of a new romantic movement to free it yet again of anything which smacks of embalming, or what amounts, in popular terms, to the flogging of a dead horse?

Notes

1. J. W. von Goethe, *Faust*, tr Bayard Taylor, Sphere Books Ltd, London, 1969, 35.
2. Ibid., 36.
3. See Irving Babbit, *Rousseau and Romanticism*, with a new introduction by Claes G Ryn, Transaction Publishers, New Brunswick (USA) and London (UK), 1991, 25. (This work was originally published in 1919). (Henceforth *Rousseau and Romanticism*).
4. W. D. Howarth et al, *French Literature* from 1600 to the present, Methuen, London, 1974, 54. (Henceforth, *French Literature*).
5. *Alfred North Whitehead, An Anthology*, selected by F. S. C. Northrop and Mason W Gross, Cambridge University Press, 1953, 397–449. (Henceforth *Anthology*.) The three chapters referred to are entitled 'The Century of Genius', 'The Eighteenth Century' and 'The Romantic Reaction' respectively.
6. Angus Wilson, *Axel's Castle, A study in the Imaginative Literature of 1870–1930*, Collins, London and Glasgow, 1931 (Fontana 1961), 10–11. (Henceforth *Axel's Castle*).
7. *French Literature*, 52.
8. Ibid., 52–3
9. *The Works of Oscar Wilde*, ed, G. F. Maine, Collins, London and Glasgow, 1948 (rep 1957), 706. (From the long poem entitled 'The Garden of Eros')
10. I quote this statement by Shelley while fully aware that A. N. Whitehead refers to him on more than one occasion as '. . . the poet, so sympathetic with science, so absorbed in its ideas . . .', just as he speaks of Shelley as using 'the language of accurate science' or the imagery of physical experi- ments. But Whitehead goes on to say that 'The literature of the nineteenth century, especially its English poetic literature, is a witness to the discord between the aesthetic intuitions of mankind and the mechanism of science.' Whitehead says also that 'Wordsworth in his whole being expresses a conscious reaction against the mentality of the eighteenth century'. See *Anthology*, 440, 442 and 432 respectively. See also *The Complete Works of Percy Bysshe Shelley*, eds Roger Ingpen and Walter E. Peck, New York, 1926–1930, vol VII, 114, and Muḥammad ᶜAbdul-Ḥai, *Tradition and English and American Influence in Arabic Romantic Poetry*, Ithaca Press, London, 1982, (henceforth M. ᶜAbdul-Ḥai), chapter VI, where Shelley is quoted at the outset, 83.
11. See n 10 above.
12. *The Poetical Works of Wordsworth*, ed Thomas Hutchinson, A New Edition, revised by Ernest de Selincourt, Oxford University Press, (reprint 1964), 460.
13. Wordsworth and Coleridge, *Lyrical Ballads*, eds R. L. Brett and A. R.. Jones, Methuen, London, (reprint 1986), Introduction, xxxi. (Henceforth *Lyrical Ballads*).
14. Ibid., loc. cit.
15. Ibid., xxxii.

16. *An Overview of Modern Arabic Literature*, Edinburgh University Press, 1990, 20–21.
17. *A Short History of Modern Arabic Literature*, Clarendon Press. Oxford, 1993, 50. (Henceforth, *A Short History*).
18. Ibid., 50–51.
19. *Axel's Castle*, 9–10.
20. H. A. R. Gibb, *Arabic Literature, An Introduction*, The Clarendon Press, Oxford, 1963, 44.
21. *A Short History*, 50.
22. *Axel's Castle*, 9.
23. Ibid., 23.
24. *Mallarmé*, The Penguin Poets, ed Anthony Hartley, (reprint 1970), Introduction, ix.
25. As quoted in M. ᶜAbdul-Ḥai, 182.
26. *Rousseau and Romanticism*, 25.
27. 'The French Revolution itself was the first child of romanticism in the form in which it tinged Rousseau', says A. N. Whitehead. *Anthology*, 450.
28. *French Literature*, 55.
29. Ibid., 54.
30. *A Short History*, 51.
31. Ibid., 51.
32. *Fī 'l-Mīzān al-Jadīd*, 3rd ed Cairo, n.d., 75.
33. Ibid., 69–75. See also, Mikhāʾīl Nuᶜaymah, *Hams al-Jufūn*, 3rd ed, Beirut, 1959, 14–15.
34. Op. cit., 69, 88 and 90.
35. As quoted in M. ᶜAbdul-Ḥai, 100.
36. *Fī 'l-Mīzān al-Jadīd*, 75.
37. Ibid., 75–85.
38. *Manāhil al-Adab al-ᶜArabī, Nasīb ᶜArīḍah*, Beirut, 1950, 10–12.
39. As quoted in *Lyrical Ballads*, Introduction, xxvii.
40. See M. ᶜAbdul-Ḥai, 148, where the editorial of *Apollo*, vol 1, no 1, September 1932, is quoted.
41. One could well say about the Apollo group what Irving Babbit says about many of the neo-classicists, that 'they employed pagan myths, not as imaginative symbols of a high reality . . . but merely as "traditional ornaments" (*ornements reçus*)'. See *Rousseau and Romanticism*, 21.
42. M. ᶜAbdul-Ḥai, 46.
43. *Tuḥfat al-Albāb* of Abū Ḥamīd al-Gharnāṭī (d 1169), which is now available in an excellent translation into Spanish by Ana Ramos (*Tuḥfat al-Albāb* [*El Regalo de los Espíritus*], Madrid 1990). This is the first full translation into a European language.
44. *Manāhil al-Adab al-ᶜArabī* (cf n 39 above), 86–94.
45. The poem appears in *al-Jadāwil*, first published in New York in 1927.
46. See n 43 above.
47. See *Aghānī al-Darwīsh*, Beirut, 1959 (first published in New York in 1928), 68–72.
48. *An Overview of Modern Arabic Literature*, Edinburgh University Press, 1990, 191–192.
49. *Rousseau and Romanticism*, 25.

2

Tradition as a Factor of Arabic Modernism

Darwīsh's Application of a Mask

Ali J. al-Allaq
University of Sana^ca

As a technique, mask has largely been exploited by poets to free their texts from being too dominated by sentiment and lyrical situations.

Mask is, as Abrams says, 'the first person narrator'.[1] Such a technique enables a poem to be detached from its author and stand independently as an artistic work on its own. In Jābir cUṣfūr's words,[2] mask is an 'expanded metaphor' used by a poet to 'furnish his voice with objectivity'. This technique adopts mostly the form of a historical character which talks in the first person.

cAbd al-Wahhāb al-Bayātī defines the mask as follows:[3]

> "The name through which the poet is divested of his own subjectivity"

In doing so, the poet:

> "Transcends the limitations of lyricism and romanticism which have beset most Arabic poetry"

To move from Arabic to Western poetry, Ezra Pound wrote several poems using the mask technique. In his *Homage to Sextus Propertius* and *Hugh Selwyn Mauberley* Pound used this technique to enrich his method of exploiting other poets as masks. Pound's *Homage*, for instance, is based on the Roman poet Sextus Propertius as a mask through which he protests at the monstrous state of society and culture in which he tragically found himself living. These two poems, however, are both to be considered "an ironic survey of Pound's own time and place".[4]

T.S. Eliot also used the mask in several distinguished poems, for example in *The Love Song of J. Alfred Prufrock* and *Gerontion*. In the latter, he used the little old man as a mouthpiece to convey his attitudes and emotions. It is in this poem in particular that Eliot opened "a vein of feeling and imagery that he was not to exhaust for some time to come".[5]

The poem is brimful of remarkable images and ideas of isolation and spiritual senility:

"Here I am, an old man in a dry month,
Being read to by a boy, waiting for rain,
I was neither at the hot gates
Nor fought in the warm rain.
Nor knee deep in the salt marsh,
heaving a cutlass,
Bitten by flies".[6]

In modern Arabic poetry, the use of a traditional character, as a mask, is not only an aesthetic device but also a vehicle for dramatising the feelings and thoughts of the poet. Modern Arab poets profit a great deal from tradition. Time and time again they choose historical characters as masks to display, dramatically and symbolically their dreams, ideas and emotions.[7]

Several prominent poems have been based specifically on the mask, namely Adūnīs's poem *al-Ṣaqr* (The Falcon), al-Bayātī's *ᶜAdhāb al-Ḥallāj* (The Suffering of al-Ḥallāj), Ṣalāḥ ᶜAbd al-Ṣabūr's *Mudhakkirāt al-Malik ᶜAjīb Ibn al-Khaṣīb* (Notes of King ᶜAjīb Ibn al-Khaṣīb) and Saᶜdī Yūsuf's *al-Akhḍar bin Yūsuf*.[8]

To turn to the main focus of this paper, quite recently, Maḥmūd Darwīsh has skilfully utilized a historical character as a mask. In his poem *Aḥada ᶜAshara Kawkaban ᶜalā ākhir al-Mashhad al-Andalusī*[9] (Eleven Stars over the End of the Andalusian Scene), Darwīsh has exploited Abū ᶜAbd Allāh al-Ṣaghīr, the last Arab King of Granada, as a mouthpiece for the poet. This poem, which will hereafter be examined in full, is, I think, a good example of using mask in poetry.

A large number of Maḥmūd Darwīsh's poems have emotionally and intellectually been based on tradition. Time and again Darwīsh derives his poetic symbols and motifs from the past. The poet has made frequent use of Andalusian history, for instance, which, being part of Islamic tradition was, and still is, of great use to Maḥmūd Darwīsh, providing him with a variety of themes, symbols and characters. For example[10]:

بيروت ! من اين الطريق الى نوافذ قرطبة ،

انا لا اهاجر مرتين ،

ولا احبك مرتين ،

ولا ارى في البحر غير البحر ...

ولكني احوّم حول أحلامي

وادعو الارض جمجمة لروحي المتعبةْ ،

واريد ان امشي

لأمشي

ثم أسقط في الطريقِ

الى نوافذ قرطبةْ .

In these lines, as in the earlier phase of his poetic development in general, Darwīsh is considering the Andalusian experience and tradition as a source of refined emotions and a yearning for safer times and places. Thus, so many words and symbols are constantly used to provoke the reader's mind and stir his memories. In other words, Darwīsh does not merely use these Andalusian symbols as a foundation stone on which a poem could structurally be built or developed.

Lately, Darwīsh's poetry has revealed a great sophistication both in thought and structure. In this new poetic stage, traditional motifs and symbols, whether Arabic or Andalusian, are no longer used simply to function as emotional elements or inspiring expressions. The utilizing of traditional factors in Maḥmūd Darwīsh's new poetry is an attempt to take advantage of vital traditional elements, making them a factor of his poetic modernism to embody crucial Palestinian and Arab questions and sources of apprehension.

His well known poem *Aḥada ᶜAshara Kawkaban ᶜalā ākhir al-Mashhad al-Andalusī* is an outstanding piece of work. It is, to an exceptional extent, harmoniously woven with allusions to the past and quotations from tradition.

Darwīsh, unprecedently, exploits Andalusian history not only as a fountainhead of words, phrases or expressions but also as a rich mine of dramatic characters and symbols. In other words, the poet, in this connection, has left behind his lyrical outlook on traditional factors and started to think of them as formal ingredients and structural assignments. Moreover the content and vision in this poem are further consolidated by the influence of these elements.

It is perhaps for the first time that Darwīsh builds one of his most remarkable poems on 'mask' using Abū ᶜAbd Allāh al-Ṣaghīr for this purpose, though it is quite obvious from the title and text that no clear reference is made to the prince himself. Nevertheless, there is something in the text and ideas of the poem that reveals once in a while certain details of the prince in terms of his character, personal traits and destiny. By choosing this figure, Darwīsh tries to stress the similarity between the Andalusian past and the Palestinian and Arab present, which reminds us of Ezra Pound's utilization of Sextus Propertius as a mask. Pound explains clearly why he used the Roman poet by saying that Propertius:

> "presents certain emotions as vital to me in 1917, faced with the infinite and ineffable imbecility of the British Empire, as they were to Propertius some centuries earlier, when faced with the infinite and ineffable imbecility of the Roman Empire".[11]

To put it differently, Ezra Pound draws some analogy between the British and Roman Empires in that they seem to share the same degree of imbecility.

Maḥmūd Darwīsh was, I believe, obsessed with two other 'imbecilic' times, namely the Andalusian era when Abū ᶜAbd Allāh al-Ṣaghīr was confronted with incongruity and inconsistency, and the identical problems faced by the Palestinian in this century.

As far as its title is concerned, the poem focuses heavily on the meaning of *al-Nihāyah* (the ending): *Ākhir al-Mashhad al-Andalusī*. Going beyond the title, deep into the very body of this work, the unpleasant notion of "the ending" can be beheld underneath every single image and phrase. With this in mind the reader is expected to feel the impact of this gloomy idea if, and only if, he has the ability to examine this work from within. Interchangeably, both the poet and his historical personage concentrate upon the substantial significance of the poem. The Andalusian scene, in the past, and the current Arab perspective are, exceptionally, ruled by an agonizing conclusion. But none of this assumes priority over this poetic text. Once the reader feels that one of these two parts of the mask, namely the poet and the historical character, has the upper hand, a moment of anxious balance pieces, once again, these parts together. They are by no means meant to embody unconnectedly either the Andalusian or Arab reality, but to depict these two actualities jointly.

The poem, from the title to the closure, is pregnant with two basic concepts, namely "ending" and "isolation" which are, in iconic connection, analogous with Arab and Palestinian political life which sinks, as the poem suggests, to its end both emotionally and intellectually.

Several examples could be cited to demonstrate such a case. For instance:

... وأنا واحدٌ من ملوكِ النهاية ... أقفزُ عن
فَرَسي في الشتاءِ الأخيرِ، أنا زفرة العربيّ الأخيرة

It is surely apparent that these two lines bring to light the main thrust of the poem. Many more verses and phrases could, again, be quoted to reinforce this concept: *al-Shitā᾽ al-Akhīr* (The Last Winter), *Bāb al-Samā᾽ al-Akhīr*, (The Last Gate to Heaven), *Ṣaqf al-Samā᾽ al-Akhīrah* (The Last Ceiling of Heaven), *al-Masā᾽ al-Akhīr* (The Last Evening), and *al-Adhān al-Akhīr* (The Last Call to Prayer). All these phrases play not only a passionate role but also act as an organic element, tightening the structure and echoing each other throughout the work.

Tradition, in this work, is not confined to the historical character, namely Abū ᶜAbd Allāh al-Ṣaghīr. The poem reflects and makes reference to some Koranic verses and lines of poetry, ancient times and places, cities and civilizations, events and folk customs. Put another way, textuality, which means an allusion to another work, can be lucidly perceived underneath the text.

A direct allusion is made to the Koran: *"Aḥada ᶜashara kawkaban*" which immediately stirs the memory and directs us to the Prophet Yūsuf. Just as the Prince of Granada was betrayed by his people and also disastrously defeated, the Palestinians were let down and, according to the poet's point of view, faced a similar disastrous fate. The poet has, in the title, linked the past to the present on one brutal level, where the historical character and the Palestinians have been dislodged from the entire Palestinian/Andalusian scene and even from its very conclusion.

Using this technique, that is, allusion, Maḥmūd Darwīsh is trying to illustrate a kind of resemblance between Yūsuf and the Palestinian individual who both, as the poem may suggest, were subjected to jealousy and malicious treatment.[12]

Technically speaking, the structure of the mask in this poem develops in conformity with the subject matter to form, ideologically and aesthetically, the final value and setting of the work.

First of all, the number eleven dominates over all the text, not only the main title of the poem but also the poetic form in general. Thus, the poem is divided into eleven stanzas and, taken individually, every single section excluding stanzas 2, 4, 5 and 11, consist of twenty lines and a subtitle of two lines, except the last section, which means that every part is built on the double of eleven.

In harmony with the thematic structure, the mask derives its influence from the parts of the poem as a whole. Without being isolated, formally or emotionally, every strophe has more or less its own nature. Having separate subtitles, nearly all sections of the poem are structured to picture individually certain motive and thematic characteristics. Taking the eleventh part as an example, this trait can easily be manifested. This stanza shows us, for the first time, a title of one word only, *al-Kamanjāt* (The Violins), dislocated from any syntactic relation with neighbouring words which reveal the notion of isolation and singleness. Meditating on this section being the "eleventh" we may rightly conclude that eleven is normally looked upon as "the odd one out", being an odd number compared to the round figure (ten). Thus this section has been prevented from forming an inseparable part of the ten preceding lines. This illustrates the loneliness and segregation which have completely controlled the poem, and forged its ideological and emotional tone. However, the number eleven may, on the other hand, have another significance: it may suggest that it could be the initiation of a fresh start for another ten lines which means, perhaps, another potentiality for the future.

The eleventh part has been totally ruled by nominalism from the title which is formed by one noun, *al-kamanjāt*, to the text which consists of twenty lines starting with nominal clauses:

الكمنجاتُ خيلٌ على وتر من سرابٍ ، وماءٌ يئنُّ
الكمنجات حقل من الليلك المتوحش ينأى ويدنو

الكمنجاتُ وحشٌ يعذّبه ظُفُرُ امرأةٍ مسه ، وابتعدْ
الكمنجات جيش يعمّر مقبرة من رخامٍ ومن نهوندْ

الكمنجات فوضى قلوبٍ تجنّنها الريحُ في قدمِ الراقصةْ
الكمنجات اسراب طيرٍ تفرّ من الرايةِ الناقصةْ

Not only are the subjects in this group of lines controlled by nominalism, but so also are the predicates. There are more examples that could be cited for this purpose; however, let us move to another kind of line:

الكمنجاتُ تبكي على الفجرِ الذاهبينَ الى الاندلسْ
الكمنجات تبكي على العرب الخارجين من الاندلسْ

الكمنجات تبكي على زمنٍ ضائعٍ لا يعودْ
الكمنجات تبكي على وطنٍ ضائعٍ قد يعودْ

It is obvious from these lines that all predicates are in the form of verbal sentences, but subjects remain nominal. The first group and, to a lesser extent, the latter one, reinforce the stagnancy and stillness felt by the poet/his mask in the poem.

If we consider the rhyme scheme and strophic structure, it becomes clear that this section is divided into groups of two lines, that is to say it is made up of couplet form. Being isolated by a solitary rhyme, every couplet reveals individually the sense of isolation and solitude, since it is entirely closed by its rhyme and stands apart from other lines.

It would seem, moreover, that the poem is, structurally, dominated by a certain duality which imposes itself not only throughout the poetic texture, but also on its tone and emotive impact.

What should be emphasized once again is that the influence of this poem has by no means been derived from one factor alone. On the contrary, there are, constantly, two elements which together constitute the poetic impulse of the text.

Turning more directly to a specific example, let us consider the following lines:

الملاءات جاهزةٌ ، والعطور على البابِ جاهزةٌ ، والمرايا كثيرةْ
فادخلوها لنخرجَ منها تماماً ، وعما قليلٍ سنبحث عما
كان تاريخنا حول تاريخكم في البلاد البعيدةْ

وسنسأل انفسنا في النهاية : هل كانت الاندلسْ

ههنا ام هناكَ ؟ على الأرضِ ... ام في القصيدةْ

What I wish to suggest here is that contrasting dual elements govern this stanza: *al-malā^ʾāt* (bed sheets) – visual; *al-ʿuṭūr* (perfumes) – olfactory; *al-dukhūl* (entry), *al-khurūj* (exit); *tārīkhunā* (our history); *tārīkhukum* (your history); *al-qaṣīdah* (the poem); *al-arḍ* (the earth); and *hunā* (here) and *hunāk* (there). This conveys how emotionally and formally dramatic this part is.

Finally, I conclude by saying that this poem is, without doubt, a finely crafted work in terms of structure, texture and imagery. It has tried, and perhaps succeeded, regardless of time and location, to illustrate the suffering of the Palestinians, the Arabs and humanity, rendering the three as intertwined as ever.

Notes

1. M.H. Abrams, *A Glossary of Literary Terms*, 4th ed., New York, 1981, p.131.
2. Jābir ʿUṣfūr, '*Aqniʿat al-Shiʿr al-Muʿāṣir*', Miḥyar al-Dimashqī, in *Fuṣūl*, no.4, 1981, p.123.
3. ʿAbd al-Wahhāb al-Bayātī, *Tajribatī al-Shiʿriyyah*, Beirut, 1968, p.35.
4. A. Alvarez, *The Shaping Spirit*, London, 1972, p.56.
5. George Williamson, *A Reader's Guide to T.S. Eliot: A Poem-by-Poem Analysis*, 2nd ed., London, 1976, p.113.
6. T.S. Eliot, *Collected Poems, 1909–1962*, London, 1977, p.39.
7. ʿAlī Jaʿfar al-ʿAllāq, *Fī Ḥadāthat al-Naṣṣ al-Shiʿrī*, Dirāsāt Naqdiyyah, Baghdad, 1990, chapter 2.
8. For further details on the mask in Arabic poetry as a whole, and al-Bayātī's poetry in particular, see the writer's *The Artistic Problems in ʿAbd al-Wahhāb al-Bayātī's Poetry: A Comparative Critical Study*, (unpublished PhD thesis), University of Exeter, 1983.
9. Maḥmūd Darwīsh, *Aḥada ʿAshara Kawkaban*, Beirut, 1992, pp.7–31.
10. Maḥmūd Darwīsh, *Ḥiṣārun li-Madāʾiḥ al-Baḥr*, 2nd ed., 1985, pp.93–94.
11. Peter Brooker, *A Student's Guide to the Selected Poems of Ezra Pound*, London, 1979, p.151.
12. Yūsuf and his jealous brothers can be regarded as a recurrent theme in Darwīsh's poetry. See, for example, *Wardun Aqall*, 2nd ed., Beirut, 1987, p.77:

« انت سميتني يوسفًا ، وهمو أوقعوني في الجبِّ

والتهموا الذئبَ ، والذئب أرحم من اخوتي ... ابتِ !

هل جنيت على احدٍ عندما قلت إني : رأيت أحد

عشر كوكبًا ، والشمس والقمر ، رأيتهم لي

ساجدين »

3

Tradition and Modernity in Arabic Poetry

The Constant Challenge, the Perennial Assertion

Salma Jayyusi

It is with great pleasure that I stand here today to address this distinguished group of scholars who are all involved in the study of varied aspects of the history and technique of Arabic literature. Scholarship in Arabic literature is branching rapidly, and is becoming more sophisticated with the years as modern critical criteria are applied to it. There is no doubt that the last three decades have produced an admirable number of scholars, both in the Arab world and in the West, who are radically expanding the discipline by painstaking exploration into the background, characteristics and cultural attributes of the old literature; and such exploration will go further and deeper as increasing numbers of scholars are drawn constructively towards a deeper awareness of the original gift Arabic literature has offered to world literature in its long and extremely rich history.

Within the limitless study of Arabic culture and literature, there are some topics which remain constantly pertinent to various periods. Among them is that of tradition and modernity, the theme of our present conference: an age-old topic indeed, but one that continues to preoccupy modern day Arabs and Arabists, and to provide ever new avenues for discussion.

However, the word 'tradition', which once implied a desirable linkage with one's fore-runners, has come, in contemporary times, to carry negative connotations. According to enthusiasts for modernization, tradition has associations with what is hackneyed, shrivelled with use, repetitive and stripped of meaning, with what is unfashionable and embarrassing. Modernization, for them, should be a rebellion against all aspects of an almost totally rejected literary past, the implication being that the output of this past was inferior and should be excised from our modern culture as a gangrenous limb is amputated.

There can be no doubt that the modern poetic revolution had to break loose from those lingering traditions which had stultified the growth of Arabic poetry, searching out a modern means of expression that reflects present-day experience, and using present-day language and imagery. A poet like ᶜAbd al-Muḥsin al-Kāẓimī of Iraq, writing in the first decades of the 20th century, was unable to sever himself either from the traditional language and syntax of classical poetry or from the spirit of that poetry:

ما سلونا آرام نجد ولكن
شغلتنا العلى عن الآرام
وبنفسي تلك الخيام ومن حلّ من الغيد بين تلك الخيام
كل حلو الدلال أبلج كالصبح رقيق الصبا رهيف القوام
لو كذلك الأصنام في الحسن تبرى
جاز عندي عبادة الأصنام

"We have not forgotten the landmarks of Nejd, but high endeavour has kept us from them. I long for the tents [of Nejd] and the maidens who dwell in the tents, each sweet in her coyness, white as the morning, tender in her youth, slender of body. If idols were formed as beautiful, I would find it fitting to adore idols."

In this as in many other passages, al-Kāẓimī is entering the mind of an early mediaeval period, simulating its style and adopting its emphasis. He resorts to evident traditions of language, tone and intention, giving the modern reader a feeling of strange incongruity, of an incompatibility with his or her own experience. There is an impression of unreality, of something being dislocated and totally out of proportion.

However, there are some basic traditions which are subtle and one might say mute, not easily picked up and differentiated, and which, nevertheless, form the backbone of Arabic poetry, the very foundation that supports its edifice.

It is sometimes as important, in the history of poetries, to go back to tradition as it is to renovate and renew. Danger naturally arises when one adopts invariable traditions to the letter, re-entering, as poet or creative writer, the mind of a different period and assuming its particular style, along with its particular concerns and preoccupations. But never to return to tradition would imply perforce that everything in the old literature is to be regarded as deficient, that it contained nothing which is permanently and universally viable; that it was a mere deformity, able to teach us nothing.

Is this true of Arabic poetry?

Contemplating Arabic poetry in the early Middle Ages, one gets the feeling that Arab poets were perhaps *the* poets of the world west of India. The earliest complete poems we have in Arabic, the *mu*^{c}*allaqāt* and other *qaṣīdas*, provide clear signs that Arabic poetry had already somehow assimilated, in greater or lesser measure, the experience of many major poetic trends which later on materialised in major currents and schools in world poetry: the Arabian *qaṣīda* contains the subjective, the nostalgic and the romantic in the overture; then the descriptive, the purely aesthetic, something similar to the notion of art for art's sake, in the passages describing the horse, the she-camel and other desert animals; then the communal, the heroic, the committed in the *fakhr*, *madīḥ* and *ḥamāsa* parts. It also has significant symbolic and archetypal motifs, and existential streaks do exist as well. Indeed, the *qaṣīda* has not yet yielded up all its secrets even to the most positive of critics. Much has still to be explored before we can fully appreciate the great and stunning variety, not just, simplistically, in the matter of theme – thematic variations jump easily to the eye – but, more subtly and artistically, in the different and often opposing modes of the greatest artistic value. Such matters concerning the Arabic *qaṣīda* have not usually been noted by literary historians and critics as major signs of a very early sophistication placing Arabic poetry at the forefront of the world poetry of its time.

Let us then, for the sake of a more accurate comparison, consider the early Middle Ages:

To the **Persians** before Islam, poetry was mere facile versification written to be sung. Only after the Islamic conquests did the Persians adopt, from the Arabs themselves, the grandeur and splendour informing Arabic poetry, and indeed their most famous early poets wrote in Arabic and not in Persian.

Greek poetry, once elaborate and highly creative, had fallen into decline as early as the 3rd century BC.

Roman poetry, highly imitative of Greek, had its Virgil in the 1st century BC, and other major poets too, but Latin poetry had, by the early Middle Ages, become markedly inferior.

Italian poetry only took on real impetus in the late 13th and early 14th centuries, with the rise of Dante Alighieri, before witnessing the genius of Petrarch and Boccaccio later in the 14th.

The earliest **French** poetry dates from the 10th century, and it was only in the three centuries following that the French epics were written, most famous among them being the 11th-century *Chanson de Roland*.

Spanish and **Portuguese** poetry was even more belated. The *Cantar de Mío Cid* was written about 1140, the Galician-Portuguese Cantigas only began towards the end of the 12th century, representing some of the earliest lyrical poetry in the Iberian Peninsula, and achieving their greatest brilliance during the first half of the 13th.[1] The first major Spanish poet (Gonzalo de Berceo) only flourished in the 13th century.

It is **English** poetry that seems to have been most advanced in Christian Europe in the early Middle Ages. The folk epic of *Beowulf* is regarded as the culmination of heroic poetry in Old English verse, being written, probably, some time in the 7th or 8th centuries. Little else survives of such poetry, however, or of the religious Anglo-Saxon poetry of Caedmon and Cynewulf around the 9th century, which was a fusion of history and legend, of pagan and Christian elements. It was only in the 14th century, with the *Canterbury Tales* of Chaucer and William Langland's great social satire *Piers Plowman*, and the works of others contemporary to them, that English poetry came into its own.

Compared to this, it becomes clear that for several centuries the Arabs dominated the world poetic scene, and that Arabic poetry in the early Middle Ages, and perhaps up to the rise of Dante, may have been the richest and most technically advanced in the world west of India. More than two centuries before the rise of the first important Spanish poet in the 13th century, Arabic poetry in al-Andalus had had its golden age. There is great scope for research concerning the residual influence of Arabic poetry on the Sicilian lyrics of the later Middle Ages.[2] In the 11th century, after the end of the two-hundred-year-old Islamic rule, the Norman kingdom of Sicily became a channel of cultural communication between east and west.[3] Such influences, including any possible influences on Dante Alighieri, are either suppressed or at least ignored by scholarship; and although the relationship between the songs of the Troubadours and Andalusī poetry has been discussed, there is much scope for further and more robust research in this area.

Yet, there is a large corpus of writing in Arabic and other languages which has denied the merit of mediaeval Arabic poetry and has indeed attempted to stigmatize it.

The attack on tradition, which should have been directed only towards slavish imitators of the old, has in fact addressed, often viciously, the whole scene of the old poetry and the culture which supported it. Before the 1970s few scholars armed with *modern* critical tools applied themselves to examining the old poetry with sobriety and critical acumen, prepared to recognize true merit where such merit exists. Many older Arabists, unable to assimilate the nuances and the different cultural background of the old poetry, expressed their reservations, sometimes even their dislike of classical Arabic poetry, and quickly found followers among some Arab writers with colonized minds. There was thus created a strong façade of rejection of the old poetry, as an originally bedouin poetry with nothing to offer us in contemporary times. The whole poetic tradition fell into disfavour.

Yet there are periods in the history of any poetry when it becomes necessary to return to traditions for the sake of maintaining a wholesome continuity, or for the sake of regaining the former robustness and drive. Poets who undertake, quite instinctively, to bring alive older traditions cannot simply be termed 'traditionalists', but are sometimes propagators of great genius. In a former essay I wrote on Andalusī poetry, I said that there are three main kinds of successful poet: the propagators, the innovators and the catalysts. The innovators are those who initiate a new and timely trend. They usually come at a time when poetry is in great need of change in a certain direction, which explains their immediate success as they attract followers as if by magic. The catalysts are those who establish a radically new method of writing, and change the direction of poetry, without, however, this poetry being in real need of such radical change. If the appearance of the innovators is inevitable in a dynamic age, that of the catalysts is not, but the latter exploit one or more aspect of the possibilities of their contemporary poetry and change it radically. The propagators are

> . . . those who develop an already established trend to its fullest potential, enriching it and imbuing it with flair and sophistication. Many of the greatest poets of Arab literary history belong to this category, and have preserved their reputation through the passage of years. There is no space here to explore [fully] the underlying reason for this particular phenomenon . . . but something may be said about the poetic situation of their age [when poetry would be] in need not of radical change, but rather of reaching a culmination, of concluding a great beginning, or of halting, through the creation of splendid, original and commanding poetry within an already recognised trend, the waywardness, the adventurism, the overflowing of radical energy and the possible irresponsibility of over-inventive experimentalists.[4]

And it is with the propagators that we are concerned at this point, those who re-assert some basic elements of traditions which are threatened with disintegration. A propagator, however, can also be an innovator who, in his re-establishment of older tradition, is sometimes performing two simultaneous tasks: he is asserting the fact that these traditions have not yet completed their cycle of growth and, being useful for the poetry of the age, should be allowed to re-assert their energy; and he is adding new dimensions to them. This is what Dhū 'l-Rumma (77–117 AH) did in the Umayyad period when, by carrying the older traditions further than the pre-Islamic poets, he revealed beyond doubt their great symbolic and archetypal content.

Some major examples of these timely linkages present themselves here:

The first is that of Ibn Zaydūn (394–463/1003–1071), famous for his exquisite love poems on Wallāda Bint al-Mustakfī, and, in particular, for his famous *nūniyya*:

اضحى التنائ بديلا من تدانينا　　　وناب عن طول لقيانا تجافينا

Ibn Zaydūn is regarded unanimously as the major Andalusī poet. He was born in Córdoba towards the end of the 4th century of the Hijra, and was heir to an already varied poetic history in al-Andalus. He witnessed the civil war, *al-fitna* (499–522/1009–31) and the destruction of Córdoba, then its occupation, just before he died in 463/1071, by his patron, al-Mu^{c}tamid ibn ^{c}Abbād, ruler of Seville. In order to assess his role as a major poet who instinctively felt the need to uphold the best poetic traditions in Arabic, one has to try to examine, very briefly, the situation of Andalusī poetry during his time.

Andalusī poetry never underwent a steady development. The main poetic events were not the predictable outcome of a natural evolution in the art, for Andalusī poetry was dependent, most of the time, on the ready-made, well-entrenched, mature and perfected Eastern poetry arriving in al-Andalus, usually sporadically but sometimes in bulk, as when the literary figure Abū ^{c}Alī al-Qālī came to Córdoba in 330/941 at the invitation of al-Ḥakam al-Mustanṣir with a large number of books of poetry containing the *dīwāns* of many pre-Islamic and Umayyad poets, and such compendiums as *al-Mufaḍḍaliyyāt*, *Shi^{c}r al-Hudhaliyyīn*, and *al-Naqā^{ɔ}iḍ*. His arrival engendered great poetic activity, giving renewed classical nourishment to Andalusī poets always thirsty for further strong linkage with the East. However, in my opinion, this sudden influx of classical Arabic poetry put a stop to a naturally developing intrinsic side-trend within Andalusī poetry; for before this massive new wave of renewed influences, Andalusī poetry had seen some major experiments reflecting a marked development towards extremely simplified diction and a conversational, intimate tone hitherto unknown in Arabic poetry. These we find in particular in the poetry of Yaḥyā al-Ghazāl, whose long life spanned the period from almost the middle of the 2nd century AH through the first half of the 3rd, and in that of Ibn ᶜAbd Rabbihi, the compiler of *al-ᶜIqd al-Farīd*, who was born just before al-Ghazāl died, and lived through the first quarter of the 4th century. He died in 328 AH, five years before the arrival of al-Qālī.

This was, perhaps, the genuine, intrinsic poetry of al-Andalus trying to assert itself. An example of the extreme simplicity of the language is the following piece by al-Ghazāl:

قالت أحبكَ ! قلت كاذبة   غُرّي بذا من ليس ينتقد
هذا كلام لست أقبله   الشيخ ليس يحبه أحد
سيّان قولك ذا وقولك ان الريح نعقدها فتنعقد
أوان تقولي النار باردة   أو ان تقولي الماء يتّقد

She said "I love you"; you're a liar," I said,
"Cheat someone else who cannot scrutinise
these words which I can't accept!
For truly I say, no one loves an old man!
It's like saying 'We have tethered the wind'
or like saying, 'Fire is cold' or 'Water is aflame'.

However, it was soon thrown into confusion and denied a steady development by the intrusion of poetic styles from the East, reflecting not only the great contemporary Abbasid experiments but those of more ancient poets in the old country.

The influx of Eastern poetry continued after al-Qālī, prompting constant poetic activity. By the end of the 4th century the great Abbasid poets of the East had already become legends in al-Andalus. These included not only the poets of the grand style, such as Abū Tammām (188–230/804–845), al-Buḥturī (205–284/822–898) and al-Mutanabbī (303–354/916–966), but also Ibn al-Muᶜtazz (249–296/861–908) and al-Ṣunawbarī (d. 324/939), the poets of the new style of pure description, something loyal to the doctrine of art for art's sake. This was to trigger, in al-Andalus, a very strong trend towards a purely descriptive poetry that would compete with the *qaṣīda* form.

From the mid-4th century onward, we see several conflicting currents in al-Andalus, reflecting the intermittent influence of the varied experiments. A number of poets would resort to the most rhetorical style of the East, foremost among these being Ibn Hāniʾ (320?–362/932?–973) who first studied at Córdoba, memorizing the poetry of the Abbasids and, in particular, that of his immediate contemporary, al-Mutanabbī. When he emigrated to the Fatimids in North Africa, his highly rhetorical style was already set.

Another genre was also becoming very strong in al-Andalus: that of homosexual love poetry, with elaborate examples to emulate in the poetry of Abū Nuwās and other Easterners. Homosexual love poetry was in fact to flourish in al-Andalus. One of its greatest exponents was Ibn Shuhayd, an older contemporary of Ibn Zaydūn, who also excelled in the writing of short descriptive poems of a purely aesthetic nature, but showed little skill in the panegyric.

The whimsical, arbitrary adoption of styles and methods, and the constant readiness to embrace ever more new fashions and conflicting modes, was threatening to become a permanent characteristic of Andalusī poetry. It is clear that poetry in al-Andalus was struggling with the influx of so many poetic methods from the East, but intrinsic tendencies towards poetic simplification were, nevertheless, constantly trying to assert themselves. By the time Ibn Zaydūn began his poetic career, Andalusī poetry was showing signs of veering away from the majesty and grandeur of the well-built traditional *qaṣīda*, which was now losing its commanding sway and grandiose style. We see this with several 5th-century poets, some older and some younger contemporaries of Ibn Zaydūn, such as Ibn Shuhayd, Ibn ᶜAmmār and al-Muᶜtamid Ibn ᶜAbbād, the last two often writing a poetry of personal experience with a rather simplified diction and syntax, and a less imposing structure. The poetic conceit, moreover, had become an established fashion and was threatening to make description[5] for the sake of description[5] a major genre that would submerge the spirit of the *qaṣīda* and its passionate appeal. This meant that the heritage of the Eastern *qaṣīda* was in jeopardy. It was time now, if this heritage was to re-assert itself, for a great poet to rise and restore to Andalusī poetry the balance, the rhetorical command, the eloquence and the majesty of style which characterize the great Arabic *qaṣīda*; and Ibn Zaydūn was that poet. He was a successful propagator of the best traditions of Arabic poetry, with which he connected with ease, writing with an eloquence, a *rhétorique profonde*, a purity of diction which re-asserted the links with the best traditions of Eastern poetry, yet without losing touch with new developments in al-Andalus, particularly the involvement with nature.

However, Ibn Zaydūn rejected the description of nature per se, rather merging his borrowings from nature with his own experience:

> [His] experiment worked as a stop valve for the fashion of pure aestheticism, endeavouring, with obvious success, to halt the profusion of conceits unrelated to a particular experience . . . or to the human condition in general; and, with a craftsmanship that appears to have become, in his poetry, a natural part of his poetic skill, he merged aesthetics with life, showing the possibility of combining the two in a passionate expression of high artistic accomplishment.[6]

His achievement had its successful outcome in the poetry of Ibn Khafāja, born in the middle of the 5th century and living to a ripe old age (451–533/1058–1138), a poet who developed the poetry of nature in many-faceted ways, but also upheld the traditional *qaṣīda* and the panegyric.

* * *

The second example is that of Aḥmad Shawqī (1869–1932). He rose to fame around the end of al-Bārūdī's career, making great use of the older bard's achievement in restoring to modern Arabic poetry its classical strength of diction and form. However, al-Bārūdī (1839–1904), for all his re-discovery and revival of classical Arabic poetry, in reality wrote a verse unsuited to his times, as the Arab world faced an advanced Europe and an oncoming 20th century. His poetry emulated all the qualities of the old *qaṣīda*: form, attitude, tone, language and syntax, and its heroic theme and spirit. With the heritage, on the one hand, of the poetry of verbal niceties and of vacuous poetic exchange rampant throughout most of the 19th century, and the stiffening experiment of al-Bārūdī on the other, Shawqī's role became doubly crucial and difficult. He had to ensure that the strength of form and diction was permanently established, but that poetry should nevertheless move on, in language, theme and concerns, to the modern age. By using the language of his own time while preserving classical strength of syntax and vocabulary, by maintaining the grandeur of the Arabic *qaṣīda* but without al-Bārūdī's martial heroics, and by addressing his audience more in the spirit of a man living at the beginning of the 20th century, he was able to establish the sound basis on which modern Arabic poetry could re-build its edifice of strength and robust technique, so that it would later be able to endure the wildest experiments without losing its potency. Shawqī was one of the greatest propagators in Arab literary history, but he was an innovator too. His classical ties overshadow his innovations in diction, yet these were themselves of major importance, for he wrote in a language that had genuine modern affinities, an achievement hardly ever recognized in the great poet's *oeuvre*. Critics such as Muḥammad Mandūr, Shawqī Ḍayf and Anṭūn Ghaṭṭās Karam blamed Shawqī for not having innovated more drastically. Ḍayf expressed his astonishment that Shawqī, who, as stated in his introduction to his first *dīwān* published in 1898, realized the need for change, failed to introduce any.[7] Mandūr severely blamed him for the fact that 'despite his stay in France at the end of the nineteenth century, when France was seething with literary battles and schools such as Romanticism, Symbolism, Realism and the Parnassian school, he was unable to react to these concepts and come out with a new poetic philosophy in which he combined these [Western concepts] and his vast Arabic culture'. Mandūr seriously thought that, had Shawqī attempted such an amalgamation, he would have 'produced a universal poetry combining a new content and a wonderful structure'.[8] A. Gh. Karam, writing on modern Arabic poetry, also expressed his astonishment that Shawqī had failed to adopt French symbolism when he was in France.[9] Such writings display great naïveté in not recognizing, first, the nature of poetic sensibility, and, second, the crucially important role of the propagators who must go back to traditions as the only means of restoring the viability of the poetry of their day. What Arabic poetry needed at the time was, certainly not an immersion in obliquity, or the injection of new blood from the poetry of a foreign language – that would have further weakened it – but rather to take strength from its own blood, from the particular attributes of robustness, polish and refinement found in classical models of excellence, to return to the splendour and balance of the best in this poetry. Shawqī's sensibility could not and should not have adopted symbolism at the time. After centuries of dissipation and disintegration of its tools, when Arabic verse revolved around itself in a vacuum, as hundreds of poets all over the Arab world wrote a benighted poetry full of embellishments, amusement, politesse and clever exchange, Arabic poetry needed to re-acquire the terse, well-knit phraseology of good, wholesome verse.

* * *

A third example, springing from the very heart of the contemporary modernist experiment, is needed here to show the urge in Arabic poetry to re-assert its strength and spirit by forming a timely linkage with traditions even, sometimes, in periods of great revolutionary change. I am going to speak here of the poet who is most closely associated with the modernist revolution in contemporary poetry: Adūnīs. No one, least of all Adūnīs himself, would ever be likely to think that he has been a propagator of any tradition. A serious innovator, and, in the radically original way he uses images, a catalyst who has changed the metaphorical quality of Arabic poetry for his time and for all times, he is also a propagator of the spirit and vigour of the classical language, retaining for contemporary Arabic poetry, unknowingly certainly at the outset, a strong linkage with some aspects of classical diction.

The language of poetry has been the target of great argumentation in modern times, particularly by poets and intellectuals calling for change and modernization. Adūnīs inherited a long history of abuse of this language and of the Arabic *qaṣīda* in modern times, and witnessed among the group of poets around the *Shi*ᶜ*r* review (founded in 1957) a great 'theoretical' interest in the colloquial. His one-time friend and colleague, Yūsuf al-Khāl, the founder of the *Shi*ᶜ*r* review, firmly believed that the major hurdle to literary modernization was the Arabic language. He exclaimed once, 'We think in one language, speak in another and write in a third.' Contemporary poets and writers in the Arab world were actually indicted by him for not writing in what he called 'the language of the people'. So was the Arabic language itself, which he attacked with relentless zeal, while, ironically, writing all the time in good Arabic himself. The call for writing 'in the language of the people', which he and others sounded with so many ominous overtones, reflects, however, a lack of understanding of the way poetry and poetic diction develop. Al-Khāl gives the examples of Chaucer and Dante, who wrote in the language of the people and launched, respectively, the beginning of English and Italian literature. However, Chaucer and Dante were not heirs to the immensely rich repertoire of poetry and literature to which modern Arabs are heir, a repertoire at least sixteen centuries old, fixed in the subconscious of its people from their childhood, a repertoire, above all, which all Arabs still enjoy with thrill and excitement. In poetry, *al-fuṣḥā* is not an alien, unlived language, but has an immediacy, a functionality and a great passionate appeal for Arabs everywhere.

For all his theorization, al-Khāl was never able to give practical expression to his theories, and his attempt to write in the colloquial, along with that of Saᶜīd ᶜAql (a poet whose hold on classical Arabic is infallible), was abortive. But it is sad to remember how the theories circulated by these and some other poets helped to give the rather innocent and critically naive generation rising in the fifties and sixties a feeling of misachievement, a sense that the Arabic language and its poets were inferior vis-à-vis the great Western traditions of poetry. Adūnīs, living in this climate, proved to be helplessly attracted to ideas imposed by outside critics of Arabic culture or by Arabs who shared their views;

and, unable as yet to discover his own potential, not only agreed with the detractors but went further than they themselves did, attacking the Arabic language and heritage in terms which reflect a strong and irrational bias. He described the Arabic language in which he wrote his ambitious poetry as one which was 'intellectual and abstract'. He also naively echoed Jaques Berque's disparagement of the Arabic language as one that 'descends on life and does not rise from it'.[10] Little did he realize, when he stated this at the Conference of Modern Arabic Literature held in Rome in 1961, the very firm links his own diction had with the great wealth of the classical language. Growing up as an Alawite child, he early studied language, poetry and the religious books in the traditional schools of the remote Alawite mountains of northern Syria, internalizing the literary eloquence of the Qurʾān and the great Shīʿa books, so that these were deeply and (as it turned out) irreversibly inculcated in him.

His genius enabled him, nevertheless, to revolutionize his approach to vocabulary and syntax and his handling of them, turning him into a great adventurer in his treatment of both, without, however, allowing him to deviate from the eloquence, rhetorical sweep and elevated, sonorous tone that characterize much of the Arab poetic heritage he so unabashedly maligned. He could even be wayward in his use of words, and, with his rich repertoire of language (he told me once: 'I have the Arabic language in my pocket'), he invested the contemporary poetic diction with a wealth of metaphysical, mystical and philosophic vocabulary. But, as said earlier, he has not, for all his innovations in poetic diction and syntax, been able to sever those very firm links he has with the classical language. The high tone he preserved has supported his *rhétorique profonde* and the old virility of spirit that totally permeates his verse and prose poetry.

This contradictory stance as innovator *par excellence* and propagator *par excellence* has not, to my knowledge, been broached by critics. For the most part he is either bitterly attacked for his loud and irrational rejection of the Arab cultural heritage, and for other stances and attitudes with which we are not concerned here, or he receives adulation for the positive qualities in his poetic *oeuvre*, and, I suspect, for his age-old eloquence. However, our interest here lies with his role as propagator.

Only a poet advocating the necessity of poetic revolution, preaching the gospel of change and achieving considerable success in forging a new way of writing poetry, could uphold some of the most potent classical traditions with impunity. He called for a complete rupture with tradition in favour of a total modernization of poetry, pulling himself consciously away from apparent traditions of form, theme and syntactic order, and successfully fostering a major revolution in metaphorical representation, but he remained totally at home in the classical poetic language, achieving a firm continuity with a long history of eloquent expression. He also remained, even in his prose poetry, completely at home in the resonant rhythms and loud exhortations of the inherited poetry, and, above all, he remained loyal to many of the inherited attitudes which have characterized the more rhetorical expression of poetry since pre-Islamic times: vestiges from the days of chivalry and the vaunting of valour and grandeur.[12] Attitudes always determine the tone a poet imparts, and Adūnīs's tone, faithful to his outlook of potency, centrality and supremacy, was never able to acquire the low, modest, tender, disturbed, contemplative, or jesting, humorous and sometimes ironic tones of the modernists. He remained trapped in the very inheritance he so adamantly rejected.

What, then, was the actual role played by Adūnīs?

There were taking place, in the fifties and after, several fresh experiments faithful to the modernist prerequisites that the level of language, tone and rhythm in the poem should be free of the loud rhetoric, firm assertions and pronounced rhythmic exuberance of traditional poetry. Such poets as Tawfīq Ṣāyigh and Ṣalāḥ ᶜAbd al-Ṣabūr eminently fulfilled these prerequsites. The latter's linguistic experiment was more radical, for he went diametrically against what was expected in poetic diction, cutting himself off from the 'primal source' of language and using words which were familiar in daily life.[13] His sensitive apprehension of experience and profound empathy with the human condition helped him to create a new sensibility which was making its influence slowly felt in the Arab poetic field. Other experiments took place in Lebanon at the hands of such poets as Unsī 'l-Ḥājj and Shawqī Abū Shaqra, the latter emulating the intonations, the logic, the vocabulary and the rhythms of daily speech in the Lebanese countryside. Other experiments, such as that of Muẓaffar al-Nuwwāb, introduced into poetry words of an abusive colloquial nature. There were signs that the sublime edifice of the inherited language was being threatened, that a genuine change was taking place in the treatment of poetic diction. Helped by a poetry of a high order, Adūnīs's experiment, faithful to the sumptuous linguistic heritage of the Arabs, effectively nipped in the bud any possibility that these mostly successful experiments would spread and become an ongoing trend, or else overshadowed their serious achievement.[14] His poetry also acted as a buffer against the introduction of vulgarities, colloquialisms and over-simplifications, as he imposed his influence on a great number of poets, all over the Arab world, who emulated his style, so preserving an elevated, vigorous language. It is true that many poets were fascinated by his metaphorical revolution and adopted its waywardness, but this would not have happened if this revolution in the use of the metaphor had been forged through a different kind of poetry, a poetry of simple phraseology and humble address. The popularity of his poetry when he himself declaims it from a platform also provides food for thought; for how could such a difficult, complex and often obscure poetry command such popularity among the multi-level audience of the big halls who gather to listen to his sonorous readings? The answer clearly lies in the virile command this poetry continues to assert, in faithful continuity with a long tradition of rhetorical address pulsing with vigour and an exalted tone.

Some critics, on the other hand, might interpret this achievement in an opposing way, claiming that he has halted an intrinsic, naturally developing side-trend within contemporary Arabic poetry.

The appearance of poets like Adūnīs is a phenomenon repeated throughout Arab literary history, with the result that the edifice of the *qaṣīda* or long poem has never crumbled. The assertive presence of the great Arabic poem in the memory of all generations means that, whenever there has been an attempt to engender a serious diversion in Arabic poetry and in the inherited quality of the poetic address, a poetic talent has appeared to rescue the majestic sweep and rhetorical elevation of the classical poem and bring them back to life. The secret probably lies in the immense attachment, persistent, vibrant, pervasive, in the hearts of Arabs everywhere, to the grandeur of the inherited poetry, with its eloquence and its exciting sound, its rhythms that hold equally in prose poetry. We have seen this happen in the prose poetry of Gibrān Khalīl Gibrān, himself a catalyst in modern Arabic poetry, and again in Adūnīs, who has re-asserted the hypnotic influence of Arab poetic rhythms in the two mediums he has used: the verse and the prose poem.

Two years ago, when I was in Cairo, I found myself listening spellbound as ᶜAbd al-Munᶜim Ramaḍān, a young Egyptian poet, read a long love poem. He is one of the poets of the seventies, those who have launched a loud rebellion against the inherited poetry of the Arabs, which, they insist, Egyptian poets should move away from. However, what Ramaḍān was reading was yet another sumptuous poem written in prose, one that has preserved a well-built edifice, a loud rhythmic exuberance and a sonorous tone – all these springing, recognisably, from an older tradition. A year later I was told quite incidentally that Ramaḍān keeps a blown-up picture of Adūnīs in his flat. The tradition endures.

* * *

One of the most obstinate elements within this tradition, which has given it such staying power, is that of tone. This is perhaps the element least addressed in Western poetic criticism, not because it is regarded as the least important, but because tone in English poetry, for example, has not been the problem it undoubtedly is in Arabic poetry. The rise of verse drama in English, soon after the re-establishment of a new poetic idiom by Chaucer and the poets following him, has perforce worked on the elements of language and tone to suit the various dramatic roles. In Arabic we have quite a different history. First of all, the stately edifice of Arabic poetry was not utilized, in classical times, as a dramatic medium. The form of poetry, set in the two hemistich verse and the monorhyme, would in any case have resisted dramatic manipulation, for, with its regulated, accurately spaced measures, it is alien to the way people normally address each other. Had the Arabs sought to write drama, they would perforce have had to find another medium for dramatic expression.

Secondly, poets and the audience for poetry in classical Arabic since *al-jāhiliyya* have retained a predilection for heroic verse, which stipulates an elevated, sonorous and assertive tone. The consecutive periods of poetry have always preserved a high place for the heroic in verse, and when Abū Tammām and after him al-Buḥturī compiled their anthologies, these were both called *Dīwān al-Ḥamāsa*, reflecting how the heroic theme was regarded as paramount. The heroic tone also became part of the *fakhr* theme in the old poetry, and found its way, too, into the poetry of eulogy, i.e. into all those celebrations of the grandeur and glory of king, hero, battle, tribe or the poet himself. Modern revivalists have concentrated on re-establishing much of the poetry dealing with these themes, and the anthologies they compiled and the poems they have selected for modern readers and students of literature have become an integral part of the Arab poetic repertoire internalized by all who have studied them. This has helped to confirm an elevated tone in poetry.

Moreover, the heroic tradition has been reinforced in modern times because of the political situation in the Arab world. One of the major themes in modern Arabic poetry has been that of resistance and defiance vis-à-vis political aggression, and this, again, has encouraged the heroic tone which is so much a part of the old poetic wealth memorized by modern Arabs. Even in the contemporary period, for all the vigorous thrust towards modernization, the embarrassed political situation and the rise of armed resistance in Algeria and Palestine, together with the many-faceted challenges imposed by external aggression against Arab land and integrity, have kept alive the impulse to the heroic.

The prevalence of heroic verse, *fakhr* and eulogy in classical times has also overshadowed interest in less vociferous poetry in classical Arabic. The poetry of women seems to have been neglected, most of it, indeed, being left unrecorded: old reference books note the existence of many women poets, yet we have never seen this rich repertoire of women's verse. The reasons for this absence, which point to intentional omission by the *ruwāt* and the anthologists, lie probably in the fact that women's subject matter would have been naturally different, their tone naturally less assertive and therefore less attractive to the then audience of poetry. This has had its repercussions on the element of tone in poetry, by denying it the mitigating tone of women writing on more intimate themes. Al-Khansāʾ, whose poetry (or at least good examples of it) has been preserved, herself wrote a form of heroic poetry, celebrating her dead brother's heroism and authority in the tribe and resounding with the virile and vaunting spirit of the period. It is of course possible that she was the best woman poet born to the Arabs over all their long history, but I doubt very much that this is the case. We have seen, even in modern times, the way women poets of stature are treated. There is no reason to believe that in older times, when there was even greater reservation concerning women, their work should have been treated differently, and I suspect that Arabic poetry has lost, to its great disadvantage, the output of hundreds of its women poets. As such the virile aspect of poetry has remained a criterion for preservation.

What also helped stabilize the elevated tone in modern times is that the language of the old poetry, in many of its examples, is still quite accessible to modern Arabs; the difference in language is not anything like as great as, for example, that between the language of Chaucer and the modern English language. ᶜAntara's poetry, with its simple and straightforward vocabulary, is perfectly easy to follow still, and so are the poetry of ᶜAmr Ibn Kulthūm, the wise sayings of Zuhayr and a good part of the pre-Islamic odes. From the Umayyad period, the Ḥijāzī love poets, along with much of the poetry of Jarīr, al-Akhṭal and others, are likewise most accessible; and so is much of the verse of the Abbasids and the Andalusīs.

Another reason for the reinforcement of an elevated tone in Arabic poetry relates to technical aspects of the poem: tone has become part of the structure, implicit in the very rhythms of poetry. The relationship of Arab rhythmic structures to tone is a highly important one. The symmetrical, well-measured divisions of the verse encourage a higher tone, particularly given the definitive presence of the rhyme signalling a finale after each verse. I have examined the question of accentual syllables introduced in the forties by Mandūr, who claimed that there are recurrent accents on certain syllables which repeat themselves uniformly. I carried out the study at the Phonetics Laboratory at the School of Oriental and African Studies (London University), with the kind help of the then head of the Linguistics Department, Professor Jack Carnachon, and we found, as I had suspected we would, that accents need not always recur on the same syllables, but that the poet can rather vary his accents according to meaning and other phonetic considerations. However, while stress can be greatly varied and modulated, a kind of higher level of voice still accompanies the verse due to its regular rhythmic structure.

This is not to say that there was no scope for the manipulation of tone in the old *qasṣdas*; rather that, even when the emotional and attitudinal variations within a poem lend themselves to variations in tone, the regular divisions can still work against a fulfilment of tonal variations.

I shall read now the famous *mīmiyya* of al-Mutanabbī addressed to Sayf al-Dawla, which embodies a constant change of emotion ranging from blame to anger, admiration, threat and despair.

The Mīmiyya

Abū 'l-Ṭayyib al-Mutanabbī

THE STEED AND THE WILDERNESS KNOW ME

Calmly passionate:
My heart is on fire for one whose heart is cold
　for whom my body and soul are sick
Why do I hide this love which wastes me away
　while the whole world feigns love for him?
Since we all must love him, let us share his love
　proportionally, according to our love of him.
Matter of fact, conversational:
I've visited him when the Indian swords were sheathed
　and I've seen him when the swords were dripping blood
In each case he was the most gracious of all men
　and the most excellent among the best are his character traits.
The flight of your enemies is victory enough
　encompassing at once triumph and regret
The rumour of your valour made them flee in fright;
　the terror of your name inspired more fear than a mighty army
But you undertook pursuit, even though it was not needed;
　you allowed neither hills not plains to cover them.
Is it not so that when an army flees,

your noble spirit compels you to pursue?
Your task is to defeat them at each encounter
But their own disappearance brings no disgrace on you.
Do you not see victory as victory
till swords fall on heads?
Passionate blame:
O most just of men to all save me alone,
the quarrel is over you, but you are both enemy and judge
I exonerate you from thinking them healthy
those who are merely bloated
What use is eyesight to one
who cannot tell light and darkness apart?
Anger, vaunting, threatening:
The assembly in this hall shall know
that I'm the best man that treads this earth
I am he whose verse the blind man has pored over
I am he whose words the deaf have heard
I sleep through the night not waiting for rhymes to come
while others stay awake and struggle to catch a rhyme.
Look the ignorant! My good humour allowed him to continue his foolishness
Until he was annihilated by hand and mouth alike
If ever you see the lion showing his teeth
Do not suppose the lion is just smiling!
Vaunting:
There is an enemy who seeks my destruction
I felled him charging on a strong-backed steed
Its hind legs galloping are as one, its forelegs too,
he acts as the guiding hand and the spurring foot would have it
And my sword is sharp, I brandished it between two armies strong
until I struck with it while the waves of death were high
Very passionate:
The steed, the night, and the wilderness know me well,
the sword knows me and the spear, the pen and parchment too
I was comrade to the wild beasts in the wilderness
until the mountain peaks marvelled at me!
Sorrow, calm chiding:
Oh! The labour and anguish of parting from you!
After you I shall find all things are nothing
How much I deserved to be honoured by you
if the bond between us were unclouded!
If envious slander had found favour with you

then a wound that pleased you would not ache!
If you had fostered our knowledge of each other
such knowledge for the wise would be a bond
Voice rises in anger; vaunting:
How much you seek to find fault with me, but in vain!
God Himself hates what you do; it's against the spirit of generosity
How alien to my honour are paltriness and meanness
I am the pleiades and they are senility and white hair
Sorrow:
I wish the clouds that hoard up storms in me
would give now my storms to those who have his rains
I see that departure will take me on such a journey
which the strongest of she-camels could not undergo
the moment she leaves Dumair on her lee
those whom we leave behind will grieve indeed
If you leave one who could prevent your going
it's he who has departed.
Contemplation, sorrow:
The most evil of all countries is that where you're wholly without friends
and the worst gain that you make is a tainted one
and the worst thing that my hand could capture
is something where the noblest falcon and the kite are one
Sudden anger:
With what words do the pigmies of verse utter poetry
neither Arabs or foreigners, and yet they're accepted by you!
Calming down:
This is my reproach, yet it is full of love
it is full of jewels, although it's only words!
[translated by S.K. Jayyusi and John Heath-Stubbs]

Tone is one of the most important elements in Arabic poetry, having represented, indeed, a major hurdle for many poets attempting to achieve a modernist address; for, even when the old rhythmic structure had been dismantled and poets wrote their poetry in free verse and in prose, the problem of elevated tone persisted in many experiments. The other crucial element which helped uphold it has been the attitude of the poet, whether he looked at the world as a prophet and leader, or whether he viewed himself as one more victim of the present malaise, or simply as a representative member of the human race. The Arabs have always given a high place to the poet, and continue to idealize his role as a leading spirit among them. The attraction of the platform, moreover, has proved irresistible to many poets who yet aspire to modernity: a situation full of contradictions, since the very use of the platform implies a stipulation that the poet should declaim his poetry, employing a sonorous voice and an elevated address.

However, while the platform continues to attract both poet and audi-ence, and while the most vociferous writings on modernity have faithfully avoided this central issue, a new generation of poets has mushroomed all over the Arab world, from Morocco to Oman, writing a poetry of genuine modernist attributes, yet possessed of a rich vocabulary and powerful phraseology. They are discovering the limitless potential of modern Arabic for connotative subtlety, forgotten meanings and latent metaphoric dimensions, and are also bringing out the many still undiscovered rhythms implicit in the language's immensely rich structural possibilities. What is discarded in their work, quite instinctively I feel, is classical eloquence, rhetorical appeal and tonal elevation; and what is totally abandoned is the role of poet/prophet and poet/admonisher. Immediate heirs to the most radical experiments carried out in Arab poetic history, they seem to have benefited greatly from their predesessors' triumphs and failings, and to have gathered the fruits of experience with a quiet, unpretentious wisdom. They walk with a sure step towards the twenty first century, heralding a new and, I feel, luminous era for Arabic poetry.

Notes

1. See the *Princeton Encyclopedia of Poetry and Poetics*, Princeton, 1974, under 'Galician and Portuguese Poetry'.
2. It is interesting to observe that Italian poetry, which was slow to develop because of the slow development of the Italian language, showed, in the 13th century, two major trends, a religious trend in the north where poets wrote religious narratives, while in the south, 'love songs prevailed . . . It would seem to be a relic of Sicilian popular poetry, as opposed to the literary poetry produced, in close imitation of the troubadours, at the Sicilian court of the emperor Fredrick II. This courtly school . . . has frequently been derided as imitative of an already decadent literature, but such judgment is hardly sound'; see *Encyclopædia Britannica* (vol. 18, 1963), under 'Poetry', p. 109. The interesting point here is that the south, which had enjoyed a flowering lyrical poetic tradition during the Islamic presence, had kept the lyrical tradition. This will be seen in Europe wherever Islamic influences can be suspected to have prevailed. Where none was possible, as in the England of the early Middle Ages, poetry was either heroic or religious, or a mixture of the two. The same seems to apply to German poetry of the same period.

3. See Boase, Roger, 'Arab Influences on European Love-Poetry', in Salma Khadra Jayyusi (ed.), *The Legacy of Muslim Spain* (Brill, 1992), p. 460.
4. Jayyusi, Salma K., 'Andalusi Poetry: the Golden Age', in *The Legacy of Muslim Spain*, p. 354.
5. In 1243 AD Ibn Sa^c^īd al-Maghribī, who lived in the first half of the 7th century AH, produced, while in Cairo, a representative anthology (in honour of his patron Mūsā ibn Yaghmur) consisting mainly of short poems belonging to this genre and called *Rāyāt al-Mubārizīn wa Ghāyāt al-Mumayyizīn* ('The Banners of Champions and the Standards of the Select Ones'). It contains 314 poetic fragments by 145 identifiable poets,and represents only a small part of the original fifteen volumes of the famous *Al-Mughrib fī Ḥulā 'l-Maghrib.*, started by Ibn Sa^c^īd's great grandfather and compiled over the one hundred years preceding the time of Ibn Sa^c^īd.
6. Jayyusi, 'Andalusi Poetry: the Golden Age', pp. 346–7.
7. See *Shawqī, Shā^c^ir al-^c^Aṣr al-Ḥadīth*, Cairo, 1953, pp. 97–100.
8. See *Al-Shi^c^r al-Miṣrī ba^c^d Shawqī*, I, Cairo, 1954–5, pp. 1–3.
9. See 'Madkhal ilā Dirāsat al-Shi^c^r al-^c^Arabī 'l-Ḥadīth, ^c^Āmil al-Thaqāfa', in *Kitāb al-^c^Īd*, ed. J. Jabbūr, Beirut, 1967, pp. 232 & 240.
10. 'Al-Shi^c^r al-^c^Arabī wa Mushkilat al-Tajdīd' in *Shi^c^r* Quarterly, No. 21, Winter, 1962, p.96; also published in *Al-Adab al-^c^Arabī al-Mu^c^āṣir*, the book containing all the papers and responses from the Rome conference, ed. Tawfīq Ṣāyigh, Manshūrāt Aḍwā^o^, 1962. See also my argument with him on this point, pp. 195–7.
11. See his book first produced as a doctoral thesis at the St. Joseph's University in Lebanon, and published in 1973 under the title of *Al-Thābit wa 'l-Mutaḥawwil.* This book contains, in its first two volumes, one of the greatest indictments of the Arab literary heritage in the history of attacks against it, so bearing witness to the divergence between theory (often adopted slavishly and naively from sources believed by the poet to be authorities on the subject) and a practice that reflects a poet's early education and natural affinities.
12. On his egocentric stances and 'his sustained insistence on drawing his own image as that of contemporary man in all the diversity of his experience', see Jayyusi, *Trends and Movements*, II, 746–7, and see what Jabra I. Jabra says about this in 'Al-Tanāquḍāt fī 'l-Masraḥ wa 'l-Marāya', *Shi^c^r*, No. 39, Summer, 1968, pp. 119–23.
13. See footnote 14 below.
14. Much against his own theories about language. In theory, he expressed great admiration for Unsī 'l-Ḥājj's linguistic adventurism, regarding it as the purest linguistic experiment among all the members of the *Shi^c^r* group. On the other hand, his opinion of the language of ^c^Abd al-Ṣabūr was most reprehensible. 'Regarding language,' he says, 'we were absolutely at two opposite poles. I used to wonder when I read his work (as he might have perhaps wondered when he read mine) if it was necessary, in order to get rid of the traditional and inherited and assert a new poetic alternative, to use simple or simplified diction, or the language of daily speech?!' He goes on to say that Arab life exhausts the poet, and so some poets use an exhausted language. 'In a crushed reality' poets sometimes look for similarities between the crushed soul of the poet and a crushed language. 'This is how, at

the artistic level, such poets write with what I call a language below language, so that it can harmonize with this Arab life, which is below life.' See his chapter, 'The Poetics of Harmony' in *The Politics of Poetry* (Beirut, 1985), pp. 132–3.

4

Sundry Observations on the Fate of Poetry in the Early Islamic Period

James E. Montgomery
University of Oslo

Medieval and modern critics have tended to represent the *Mukhaḍramūn* as breathing the same spirit as the poets of the *Jāhiliyyah*, as an uninterrupted continuation of the poetic practice of the latter, a practice unaffected by, indeed oblivious to, the (religious, social and ethical) irruption of Islam. However, 'by analysing early Islamic texts from a literary point of view it has been established that famous *Mukhaḍramūn*, e.g. al-Aᶜshā Maymūn, Labīd, Abū Dhuᵓayb and al-Ḥuṭayᵓa . . . deviated from tradition in several respects, both on the formal and on the conceptual level, thereby anticipating some of the innovative features attributed to Umayyad poets . . . The following aspects have been noted: (a) structural changes in the polythematic ode; (b) the emergence of *ghazal* poetry; (c) individual narrative units, sometimes introduced as similes; (d) a change of attitude towards love and the beloved; and (e) a new experience of time'.[1]

To what extent these represent the influence of Islam (the new *Weltanschauung* and the new social circumstances of life in Arabia) or are to be deemed purely literary phenomena, is a moot point. Basically (a), which is concerned principally with the obsolescence of the *waṣf al-nāqah* (camel description), and (c) should probably be reckoned as primarily literary phenomena, viz. the artistic development of the tradition. Although it should be remarked that (a) was probably actuated by the emergence, in the middle to late *Jāhiliyyah*, of courtly patronage which in turn led to the creation of a professional class of itinerant poets, for whom the *raḥīl* (the desert-journey) would have been of more immediate relevance than the *waṣf al-nāqah* as Bedouin emblem, both as a feature of their lifestyle and as a convincing means of imposing upon the maecenas the urgency of their request for financial compensation. Developments (b), (d) and (e) are interconnected phenomena related to the emergence of the *ghazal* and will not be considered as this paper deals principally with the (tripartite) *qaṣīdah*.[2]

The Koranic Condemnation of Poetry

The locus classicus is the concluding septet of verses in *Sūrah* 26, the *Sūrah* of the Poets (*al-Shuᶜarāʾ*)[3]:

221. *Hal unabbiʾu-kum ᶜalā man tanazzalu l-shayāṭīn<u>*
222. *Tanazzalu ᶜalā kulli affākin athīm<in>*
223. *Yulqūna l-samᶜa wa-aktharu-hum kādhibūn<a>*
224. *Wa-l-shuᶜarāʾu yattabiᶜu-humu l-ghāwūn<a>*
225. *A-lam tara anna-hum fī kulli wādin yahīmūn<a>*
226. *Wa-anna-hum yaqūlūna mā lā yafᶜalūn<a>*
227. *Illā l-ladhīna āmanū wa-ᶜamilū l-ṣāliḥāti wa-dhakarū l-Lāha kathīran wa-ntaṣarū min baᶜdi mā ẓulimū wa-sa-yaᶜlamu l-ladhīna ẓalamū ayya munqalabin yanqalibūn<a>*

221. Shall I impart to you (pl.) those upon whom the *shayṭāns* descend
222. They descend upon every sinful fabricator
223. They listen and the majority of them are liars
224. And the poets, the wayward pursue them
225. Have you (i.e. Muḥammad) not seen that they rave in every valley
226. And that they say that which they do not do
227. Except for those who have faith and do pious /deeds/ and mention Allah often and assist themselves after they have been wronged. And those who wrong will know what a reversal they will suffer (lit., be reversed).[4]

There are many problems with this passage. There is a difficulty with the punctuation of the septet (which my translation leaves unpointed): where does the question, begun in verse 225, end? With verse 226 or with verse 227? If it ends with the former, then the passage becomes a total Koranic condemnation of poetry and verse 227 is a pious formula denoting the proper conduct of the Muslim community. There is evidence to suggest that this was how most early Muslims construed the piece. If the question ends with verse 227, then we have an opposition between poets who are 'all talk and no action' and poets who are pious Muslims and who retaliate when attacked but do not initiate the attack. This would provide a sanction for the Muslim poets who belonged to the nascent community and would imply that vituperative poetry (*hijāʾ*), often conceived of as a weapon inflicting bodily harm in the pre-Islamic period, was wrong unless it was in response to an attack. Three professional poets, all members of the Khazraj tribe of Medina, Ḥassān b. Thābit, ᶜAbd Allāh b. Rawāḥah and Kaᶜb b. Mālik, acted as Muḥammad's court poets and responded to the lampoons of Qurashite poets attacking the Prophet and Islam. Blachère (*Coran*, 214), sees in verse 227 a later, Medinan, accretion from the time when the Medinese poets rallied to the banner of Islam, welcoming them into the community.

Note the clever use in the septet of the language and style of pre-Islamic poetry: *ghawā* meaning, to lose one's way in the desert'; the use of *kull* (222 and 225); [5] *yahīmūna*, a word which originally described madness produced in camels by excessive, burning thirst and used metaphorically by the *Jāhilī* poets;[6] the panegyrical and vaunting commonplace that the true hero does not make empty claims, i.e. not that he is guilty of lying as much as that he is always true to his word. Medieval Muslim exegetes, such as al-Zamakhsharī, for example, were not deaf to the wider implications of the passage (à propos verse 225), seeing in it an allusion to the diversity and illogicality of poetic genres, and modern interpreters have exercised their faculties accordingly. Margoliouth finds in the Qur^ʾānic verses the very encapsulation of the tripartite *qaṣīdah* itself, an encapsulation which, he maintains, developed the force of a critical injunction to compose poetry: 'though the words "they rave in every valley" are probably metaphorical, and mean "they exercise their imagination on all subjects indiscriminately", they can also be rendered "they philander in every valley", and in accordance with this, most poems commence with an erotic situation wherein the poet does what has been described'; 'they regularly commence with erotic passages because the Qurʾān says poets philander in every valley; . . . they proceed to describe their wanderings and their mounts because the Qurʾān says poets are followed by those who go astray, which certainly implies that they go astray themselves; and . . . they proceed to dilate on their achievements, often immoral in character, because the Qurʾān says they say what they do not do'.[7] The notions of 'raving' and 'wandering aimlessly' expressed by the verb *hāma* incited Blachère to speculate 'si la phrase ne fait pas allusion soit à un thème poétique, ou le poète se représente, fou d'amour, allant de tribu en tribu ou d'hôte en hôte pour chercher sa pitance'.[8] Most recently Michael Zwettler has suggested that 'their "wildering in every valley" can also be seen to serve as a slightly disingenuous allusion to the primary structuring topos of the conventional pre-Islamic *qaṣīda* . . . namely the seemingly aimless fictive journey that the poet typically represents himself as making by camel . . .' and brilliantly sees an opposition between 'the rather paltry ruins that the poets 'wildering' fictively takes him past and where he stops (*al-wuqūf* ᶜ*alā l-aṭlāl*) with the incomparably more imposing – and visibly, palpably real – ruins of cities and folk destroyed in punishment for disobedience to God's messengers'.[9]

These questions are not wholly academic, because they led to a divergence of opinion among early Muslims.[10] Despite Gibb's remarks ('the rise of Islam reacted unfavourably at first on the old poetry. Muḥammad himself . . . inevitably adopted a hostile attitude to it, as the chief moral force behind the pagan ideals which Islam had come to destroy. The early Muslim community and the theologians maintained this attitude after him'),[11] the ambivalence which is to be found in the Qurʾān is also, as Kister demonstrates,[12] to be found in the *Ḥadīth*, an indication of the uncertainty entertained by the early community on the legitimacy of poetry, an uncertainty copiously demonstrated in the *tafsīr* of al-Ṭabarī. There is ample evidence for both favourable and unfavourable attitudes to poetry.[13] There was a further dichotomy, one between religious belief and quotidian practice (or religion and everyday life) in view of the fact that in the first century of Islam 'poetry continued to be one of the most favoured preoccupations of Muslim society . . . and even fighting troops on the battlefield showed a vivid interest in it' (Kister 1983: 361). The Bedouins, of course, maintained their deep attachment to poetry throughout this period.[14] The puritanical opposition to verse appears to have been confined to 'pietist circles' and 'literary history shows how small was the community who were guided by such ideas'.[15] Indeed, regional considerations must affect our perception of the extent of the opposition to poetry, together with an appreciation of the degree of 'Islamicization' undergone by any given area or in any given period.[16] Before we can adequately assess the effect Islam had on poetry, we must take a close look at poetry during the Caliphate of the *Rāshidūn*.

The Orthodox Caliphate

It has been maintained that 'this period cut off the line of steady evolution of the poetic art and a wedge was driven between two flourishing poetic periods, the pre-Islamic and the Umayyad. It created a discontinuity which was a shock to the Arab creative talent, making it unsure of its values, its artistic concepts and its traditional roots'.[17] Moreover, it has been maintained that fewer poems have survived from the first century than before and after this period and that the poets are themselves more obscure figures than their pre-Islamic and Umayyad counterparts.

In the first instance, many of the *Mukhaḍramūn* are said to have lived well into the first century: Kaᶜb b. Zuhayr, whose *Burdah* (mantle) *qaṣīdah* is, for many, the supreme poetic celebration of the *Rasūl Allāh*, is said to have been born in the *Jāhiliyyah* and to have died in the

Caliphate of Muᶜāwiyah (AD 661–80); al-Nābighah al-Jaᶜdī, also born in the *Jāhiliyyah*, is said to have died in the Caliphate of Yazīd (AD 680–4); the most conservative estimate of al-Ḥuṭayᵓah's death is given as AD 650, during the reign of ᶜUthmān (see Sezgin, F., *Geschichte des arabischen Schrifttums* (Leiden, 1975), II, 236). The Prophet's poet Ḥassān b. Thābit is last heard of shortly before the assassination of ᶜAlī and his death is fixed to 'a date around 40/659'.[18] Unreliable as these dates may be, there does seem to be evidence to suggest that many *Mukhaḍram* poets spanned the three decades separating the *Jāhiliyyah* from the Umayyad era, thereby producing some degree of continuity. Furthermore, there appear to be few *dīwāns* extant from this period because in many cases it is a question of the work of poets who began their careers in the *Jāhiliyyah* and who have accordingly been classed as essentially pre-Islamic. Indeed, it is also the case that poets who were born in the reign of the Orthodox Caliphs and who lived well into the Umayyad era have been classed as Umayyad poets: Kaᶜb b. Juᶜayl al-Taghlabī is one such poet who was 'probably born during the earliest years of the Hidjra' and who 'if al-Balādhurī is correct . . . lived long enough to write a panegyric of ᶜAbd al-Malik b. Marwān (65/685–86/705)'.[19]

There is no historically compelling necessity to conclude that the *Muᶜallaqah* of Labīd or al-Aᶜshā, for example, or any of the poems in the old style by the *Mukhaḍramūn* were composed before the advent of Islam: the persistence of the ancient traditional values in both the early community and in poetry which combines both Islamic and pre-Islamic elements testifies to the valence of the ancient value-system well into the Umayyad period, and suggests that some of the *Mukhaḍramūn* perhaps undertook artistically to blend the two. There always remains the possibility that a *Mukhaḍram* poem may be consciously and artistically old-fashioned, an example of an 'archaizing' tendency. A poetic tradition rarely, if ever, exhibits a rigorously linear, forward development. Many *Mukhaḍram* productions of a *Jāhilī* flavour may be specimens of post-Islamic composition, especially if the advent of Islam is closely connected with the political rise of the Bedouin ᶜArab.[20]

The social upheavals of this period produced an effect other than the commonly avowed one, viz. the production of unrest and angst in the minds of the perplexed nomads, as they were hurtled from their desert existence and settled in towns on the periphery of the peninsula. The established centres of poetic activity, primarily the territory of Ghassān and Lakhmid al-Ḥīrah, disappeared. They were temporarily replaced by the court circle of Medina, during the Prophet's residence there. The

Orthodox Caliphs, however, despite a reputed interest in poetry, do not seem to have been patrons of poetry. Patronage ensures artistic activity and was not fully re-established on the pre-Islamic scale until Muᶜāwiyah's accession to the Caliphate. With the absence of courtly patronage, the process of the emergence of the panegyric as the most important of the poetic genres, initiated in the sixth century and also evident in the poems in praise of the Prophet, was delayed somewhat, although the *dīwān* of al-Ḥuṭayᵓah shows that panegyrics were, of course, composed in honour of the governors and military commanders of the period. Indeed, in his *dīwān* eulogy considerably outweighs vituperation. Composition of eulogies dedicated to tribal chiefs would also have continued. It is perhaps the lack of a fixed 'court' around which the poets could converge which means that few official, courtly panegyrics have survived: as al-Ḥīrah shows, such courtly patronage also ensures archival activity, the recording of panegyrics in honour of the rulers of the court.

Scholarly opinion has been divided on precisely how far-reaching the influence of Islam on Early Arabic poetry was. The issue is closely connected with that of the co-existence of pre-Islamic and Islamic values and hinges on the researcher's expectations and assumptions. I should like tentatively to suggest that we have two, perhaps three, categories in which to view the relationship between Islam and Poetry.

The Submission of the *Jāhilī* Ode to Islam

Perhaps the most famous poem from this period is *Bānat Suᶜād* composed by Kaᶜb b. Zuhayr in praise of Muḥammad. Its structure is typical of the *Mukhaḍram* style, being 'a tribal ode with *waṣf* [description] and additional *raḥīl* [desert-journey] to the patron' (Jacobi 1982: 9) and comprising 'three well-balanced sections: a *nasīb* centered around similes comparing the beloved's wet mouth to a draught of wine and her flightiness to the shiftiness of the *ghūl*; a journey section that is made up almost entirely of the *nāqa* depiction; and a *madīḥ* in which the warrior virtues of the *rasūlu llāh* are praised in traditional *jāhilī* fashion'.[21]

As the poem refers to a disagreement between the poet and the maecenas, it is to be classed as a panegyrical *Iᶜtidhār* (a Poem of Apology), the classic *Jāhilī* models of which are those addressed by al-Nābighah al-Dhubyānī to the Lakhmid prince al-Nuᶜmān. In may ways, Kaᶜb's *Burdah* ode resembles these poems of al-Nābighah: it is, however, too extreme to claim that it is indistinguishable structurally from them, for Kaᶜb's ode is representative of the *Mukhaḍram* revision of the *waṣf al-nāqah* section and does not contain an oryx bull description, a celebrated passage of al-Nābighah's *Mu^c^allaqah*; it concentrates on the valour of Muḥammad and the Qurashite *Muhājirūn* at the expense of the traditional panegyric emphasis on the generosity of the patron.

The panegyric poet chooses his themes with a view to pleasing (and here appeasing) the patron. It may be something of a surprise to see wine lauded in a *nasīb* addressed to the Prophet. The temporal framework of the *nasīb*, a nostalgic view of an irretrievable past, is significant Su^c^ād, whose saliva is as sweet as wine, is gone never to return. Now that the poet has embraced Islam, both are no longer available to him. If anything, the nostalgic *nasīb* is a swan-song of the *Jāhiliyyah*. Ka^c^b's ode is an impressive synthesis of the traditional and the new and attests to the importance and relevance of the *qaṣīdah* and tribal values to the new religious order. For, as has been pointed out by S. Stetkevych, this ode 'served as a redemption payment . . . for the poet's own life, and . . . as a pledge of fealty marking the poet's transfer of allegiance from the moribund tribal ethos of the Jāhilyyah to the triumphant Prophet of Islam'.[22] It is, of course, hardly surprising that Ka^c^b should represent the *Jāhilī* ethos as moribund, given the nature of the dedicatee and the, personally very dangerous, contextual or situational character of the poem: the political expediency of Ka^c^b's *qaṣīdah* should not be lost sight of. The poet presents the Prophet with a reinterpretation of the ancient *qaṣīdah* tradition rendered subject to the new order of Islam.

A similar reinterpretation of the nostalgic frame of the *nasīb* is found in a poem (a *hamziyyah*, the first in ^c^Arafat's edition) by Ḥassān b. Thābit, the Prophet's poet laureate, celebrating the Muslim conquest of Mecca in January AD 630. This polythematic poem is a combination of *nasīb*, *fakhr* and *hijā^ɔ^* the latter addressed to Abū Sufyān b. Ḥarb of the Umayya, one of the leading citizens of Mecca.

The *nasīb* contains a praise of wine, comparing the saliva of the beloved Sha^c^thā^ɔ^ to a draught of wine, which in turn leads to a boastful description of how the poet's tribe drink wine in the vainglorious, reckless *Jāhilī* manner. This anomalous boast has led some Muslim critics to suggest that verses 1–10 of the poem were composed in the *Jāhiliyyah* and that the rest of the poem originates from after the poet's conversion to Islam.[23]

In this poem of military celebration, the *Mukhaḍram* Ḥassān juxtaposes the two traditions, the pre-Islamic (1 – 10) and the Islamic (11 – 31), the former celebrating his own personal greatness at the court of an erstwhile maecenas and his tribe's former greatness as represented by their aristocratic behaviour: the loss of the beloved, here an obvious emblem of the poet's tribe, represents (not unfondly) the loss of the pre-Islamic ethos. The latter two-thirds of the ode chant the might of Islam, the glories of which now far outshine the petty achievements of pagan yesteryear. As with Ka^{c}b's *Burdah* ode, the *nasīb* is strongly associated with the *Jāhiliyyah*. In a technical sense, too, Ḥassān experiments with the transitions and the structure of the *qaṣīdah*. Wagner (op. cit., 11) finds, however, that this poem contains 'no expressions of belief made for their own sake. They only serve self-praise or the praise of the Anṣār'. In the sense that these religious expressions are so smoothly integrated into the *qaṣīdah* format as to generate an impression of glibness and lip-service, this is of course correct. The poem, however, fits the occasion, which did not call for religious meditation but for vainglorious chronicle, for the resounding celebration of Islam's (re)possession of the Ka^{c}bah. Religious expression was, after all, the preserve of the Qur$^\circ$ān and it seems strange to criticize the poem for not being something which it could never have been and was not intended to be.

The Synthesis of the Pagan and Islamic

The case of the poet Labīd is instructive: 'Labīd, who combines in his work the expression of all that was best in the old Arabian life and who is represented in the *Mu^{c}allaqāt*, lived more than thirty years into the era of the Hijra, but ceased to compose after his adhesion to Islam' (Gibb 1962: 41). This tradition smacks of a later, pious, fabrication and its authenticity has been questioned (see Brockelmann, *EI* 2, V, 584–5).[24] Of crucial importance are the laments (*marāthī*) the poet composed for his step-brother Arbad, apparently struck by lightning some time after a visit to Medina in AD 629. 'It seems to me highly unlikely that the poems represent a burst of intense poetic activity that followed closely on Arbad's death. It seems far more probable that Arbad's death was a topic to which he returned from time to time'.[25] The *Rithā$^\circ$ Arbad* in *^{c}ayn* (Jones 1992: 80–88) is very Koranic. Labīd may have been responsible, or at least, influential, in remoulding the pre-Islamic *marthiyyah* from an emotional outburst-cum-funeral lament to a gnomic and elegiac reflection on the transcience of life and inevitability of death. In two other poems, 'under the influence of Islam . . . he replaces the *nasīb* by pious admonitions. Thus he creates a new artistic form, that of poetical paraenesis on the transitoriness of human life; besides the Ḳur$^\circ$ān, he may of course have been influenced by the Christian preaching in the works of ^{c}Adī b. Zayd' (Brockelmann, op. cit., 584). This activity of gnomic reflection is also, of course, in the pre-Islamic tradition of aphorisms exhorting listeners to *ṣabr* (forebearance) and reflecting on the transcience of life and the inevitability of fate (*al-dahr/ al-manāyā*). Labīd interprets this gnomic heritage in an Islamic context and accords it prominence as a structural unit of the *qaṣīdah*. Indeed, Labīd's *Muᶜallaqah* may plausibly be deemed an attempt to synthesize the two traditions, to combine and interpret what is best in the two traditions, although one can equally argue that in this ode Labīd is 'Islamicizing' the pagan *qaṣīdah*.

The Co-existence of the Pagan and the Islamic: the Permanence of the Jāhilī Ode

To take but one example, a *qaṣīdah* by ᶜAbdah b. al-Ṭabīb (*Mufaḍḍaliyyah* 26) is unashamedly heathen in spirit although it does show traces of Islamic influence in the central *ḥikmah* sequence, the gnomes of which are pious in character. This poem enjoys a development from *nasīb* to *waṣf al-nāqah* (containing an oryx vignette) to *fakhr* and concludes on a festive note with a wine scene. For ᶜAbdah, in this poem, the *Jāhilī* and the Islamic exist side by side in a remarkable equivalence.

The fate of poetry in the early Islamic period is, therefore, complex and, at times, contradictory. The *qaṣīdah* ever displays a vibrancy and relevance which enabled its format to enjoy continued artistic meaningfulness at all stages of the development of Arabic poetry: it is wrong to claim that the composition of poetry came to an abrupt halt, whether it be for religious, artistic or emotional and creative reasons.

Notes

1. Jacobi, R., 'Mukhaḍram', *EI* 2, VII, 516.
2. On the *Mukhaḍramūn* in general, see al-Jābūrī, Y., *Shiᶜr al-Mukhaḍramīn wa-Athar al-Islām fī-h* (Baghdād, 1964) (of which a 2nd edition has appeared: Beirut, 1981), Sallūm, D., *Al-Shāᶜir al-Islāmī taḥta Niẓām Salṭat al-Khilāfah* (Beirut, 1978), 7–56, Jafnā, ᶜAbd al-Karīm, *Al-Shuᶜarāᵓ al-Mukhaḍramūn* (Cairo, 1983). Seminal are the studies of Renate Jacobi: 'The Camel-Section of the Panegyrical Ode', *JAL* XIII (1982), 8–13; 'Die Anfänge der arabischen Ġazal Poesie: Abū Ḏuᵓaib al-Huḏalī', *Der Islam* LXI (1984), 218–50; 'Time and Reality in *Nasīb* and *Ghazal*', *JAL* XVI (1985), 1–17; 'Altarabische Dichtung' in H. Gätje (ed.) *Grundriss der arabischen Philologie*, Wiesbaden 1987, II, 28–31; 'Die arabische Qaṣīde' in W. Heinrichs (ed.) *Neues Handbuch der Literaturwissenschaft- Band 5 – Orientalisches Mittelalter* (Wiesbaden, 1990), 218. See further, Dalgleish, K., 'Some Aspects of the Treatment of Emotion in the *Dīwān* of al-Aᶜshā', *JAL* IV (1973), 97–111.
3. For articles devoted exclusively to these verses, see Shahid, I., 'A

Contribution to Koranic Exegesis', in G. Makdisi (ed.) *Arabic and Islamic Studies in Honor of Hamilton A.R. Gibb* (Massachusetts, 1965), 563–580; idem, 'Another Contribution to Koranic Exegesis: The *Sūra* of the Poets (XXVI)', *JAL* XIV (1983), 1–21; Schub, M., 'Qurʾān 26:224, /ĠĀWŪNa/ = "Fundamentally Disoriented": An Orientalist Note', *JAL* XVIII, 79–80; Zwettler, M., 'A Mantic Manifesto: The Sūra of 'The Poets' and the Qurʾānic Foundations of Prophetic Authority' in J.L. Kugel (ed.), *Poetry and Prophecy. The Beginnings of a Literary Tradition* (Ithaca, 1990), 75–119 & 205–31. For a study of *Sūrah* 26 as a unit, see Martin, R.C., 'Structural Analysis and the Qurʾān: Newer Approaches to the Study of Islamic Texts' in A.T. Welch (ed.) *Studies in Qurʾān and Tafsīr = Journal of the American Academy of Religion* 47.4 (1979).

4. On this type of Qur'anic *tajnis*, see Rippin, A., 'The Poetics of Qur'ānic Punning', *BSOAS* LVII.1 (1994), 193–207.

   I have used the *tafsīr* of al-Ṭabarī, *Jāmiᶜ al-Bayān fī Tafsīr al-Qur'ān* (Bulaq, 1328 H.), al-Zamakhsharī, *Al-Kashshāf ᶜan Ḥaqā'iq al-Tanzīl* (Cairo, 1966), and al-Bayḍāwī, *Anwār al-Tanzīl wa-Asrār al-Ta'wīl* (Cairo, 1925), and have consulted, in addition to the renderings offered in the articles cited in the previous note, the following translations of the Qur'ān: Bell, R., *The Qur'ān Translated, with a Critical Re-arrangement of the Surahs* (Edinburgh, 1937–9), II, 353–62; Blachère, R., *Le Coran* (Paris, 1949–50), II, 197–214; Paret, R., *Der Koran*, (Stuttgart, 1966), 300–9; Ḥamza, S.B., *Le Coran* (Paris, 1972), II, 751–73; Berques, J., *Le Coran* (Paris, 1990), 389–401. Use has also been made of Flügel, G., *Concordantiae Corani*, Leipzig 1842 and Paret, R., *Der Koran: Kommentar und Konkordanz* (Stuttgart, 1971).

5. 'In poetry *kull* followed by an indefinite noun in the genitive singular . . . to denote a number of objects all of which possess this or that quality': Wright, W., *A Grammar of the Arabic Language* (Beirut, 1974), II, 205 = Part Third section 82. D.
6. See Montgomery, J.E., 'Arkhilokhos, al-Nābigha al-Dhubyānī and A Complaint against Blacksmiths – or, A funny thing happened to me . . .', *Edebiyât* 5 (1994), 33 for a discussion of *hāma*.
7. Margoliouth, D.S., 'The Origins of Arabic Poetry', *JRAS* 1925, 418–9 & 443–4.
8. Blachère, R., 'La poésie dans la conscience de la première génération musulmane', *Annales Islamologiques* IV (1963), 94 = *Analecta* (Damascus, 1975), 232.
9. Zwettler 1990: 114 & 240.
10. 'Auf alle Fälle wurde die Stellung des Islams zur Dichtung durch diese Ausnahme ambivalent, und die Ambivalenz setzte sich in der späteren Diskussion fort, die mittels auf den Propheten und seine Genossen zurückgeführter Traditionen (*ḥadīṯ*) ausgefochten wurde' (Wagner, E., *Grundzüge der klassischen arabischen Dichtung* (Darmstadt, 1988), II, 3).
11. Gibb, H.A.R., *Arabic Literature* (Oxford, 1963), 41.
12. Kister, M.J., 'The *Sīrah* Literature' in A.F.L. Beeston et al. (eds) *The Cambridge History of Arabic Literature. Arabic Literature to the End of the Umayyad Period* (Cambridge, 1983), 358–61.
13. Blachère's discussion (1963: 236–7) is instructive as to how the early

generation grappled with the Qur'ānic pronouncement on poetry and provides a useful survey of the evidence pro- and contra-poetry.

14. 'Une masse considérable du monde arabe demeurait attachée à la poésie et à son idéal esthétique. L'entrée en masse dans la jeune communauté d'éléments bédouins d'Arabie centrale et orientale ne peut que renforcer ce courant. Dans ce monde des Nomades, la poésie n'avait cessé d'être en honneur à l'aube de l'Islam' (Blachère 1963: 240).
15. I. Goldziher, *Muslim Studies*, trans. S.M. Stern and C.R. Barber (London, 1967), 56 = *Muhammedanische Studien* (Halle, 1889), 53. See Blachère 1963: 239.
16. Blachère 1963: 239.
17. Jayyusi, S.K., 'Umayyad Poetry' in Beeston 1983: 392.
18. ᶜArafat, W., 'Ḥassān b. Thābit', *EI2*, III, 272.
19. Pellat, C., *EI2*, IV, 315.
20. This aspect of late *Jāhilī* verse is touched upon in Montgomery, J.E., 'The Deserted Encampment in Ancient Arabic Poetry: A Nexus of Topical Comparisons', in *JSS* 40.2 (1995), 289–322, in which I conclude that we can discern 'the emergence of the concept of the Poet as Bedouin Hero, itself allied to the growth of confidence and power of the Arab tribes in their relations with the regal dynasties which hemmed them in to the East and the West'. See also Montgomery, J.E., 'The Cat and the Camel' in M. Mir and J.E. Fossum (eds) *Literary Heritage of Classical Islam. Arabic and Islamic Studies in Honor of James A. Bellamy*, (Princeton, 1993), 144. "the increased prominence accorded to the *jinn* and Bedouin superstition in poems of the middle to late *Jāhilīyah* was a consequence of the political surgence of the Arab tribes in the middle of the sixth century". This construction has been further corroborated by the work of Jan Retsö, "The Road to Yarmuk: The Arabs and the Fall of the Roman Power in the Middle East" in L. Rydén and J.O. Rosenqvist (eds) *Aspects of Late Antiquity and Early Byzantium, Swedish Research Institute in Istanbul Transactions*, IV (Stockholm 1993), 31–41: "The hiring of professional soldiers by the Himyaritic kings from among the tribes created a professional class of warriors all over Arabia. The term Arab was probably originally the designation of this warrior caste . . . In Arabia . . . there must have been circles where it had been realised that foreign intervention and anarchy would continue if no counterweight were created. The ambitions of the warrior caste, awakened by the Himyarite venture, needed a modern ideology if it were to handle the old established antagonists in the North, and in those days ideology was religion" (39–40).
21. Sells, M., '*Bānat Suᶜād*: Translation and Interpretative Introduction', *JAL* 21 (1990),142.
22. Stetkevych, S.P., 'Pre-Islamic Panegyric and the Poetics of Redemption: *Mufaḍḍalīyah 119* of ᶜAlqamah and *Bānat Suᶜād* of Kaᶜb ibn Zuhayr' in S.P. Stetkevych (ed.) *Reorientations/ Arabic and Persian Poetry* (Indiana, 1994), 21.
23. See ᶜArafat, W., *Dīwān of Ḥassān Ibn Thābit* (London, 1971), I, 19. Wagner 1988: 11, refers to the attempt of Sh. Fayṣal, *Taṭawwur al-Ghazal bayna l-Jāhiliyyah wa-l-Islām* (Beirut, 1965), to classify as pre-Islamic the six *nasībs* in the *dīwān* of Ḥassān which contain wine-descriptions.

24. This pious exaggeration of the effect of conversion on prominent heathen poets, is also discernible in the *akhbār* surrounding the dissolute lifestyle of Ḥassān b. Thābit: "sans exclure la possibilité d'une réforme morale du personnage, après sa conversion à l'Islam, il semble plausible que les anecdotes colportées sur Ḥassân se veulent favorables pour la période postérieure à cette conversion à fin de mieux faire sentir les faiblesses du poète dans le paganisme" (Blachère 1963: 234).
25. Jones, A., *Early Arabic Poetry Volume One:* Marāthī *and* Ṣuᶜlūk *Poems* (Reading, 1992), 80.

5

Changing Technique in Modern Arabic Poetry

A Reflection of Changing Values?

Fatma Moussa-Mahmoud
Cairo

Poetry has always played an important role in Arab societies, and its social function was long taken for granted by both poets and their audiences.

The traditional form of classical Arabic poetry which survived for nearly fourteen centuries has been subjected to criticism and experimentation by one generation of 20th century poets after another. Changes involve both form and subject matter; the "pillar" of Arabic poetry, the long recognised norm of good writing, jealously preserved for centuries, has been broken by "new" poets in every region of the Arab World.

The new verse, called free verse because it has discarded the old rule of one measure, one rhyme for the whole poem, was attacked savagely in the fifties and sixties as a dangerous threat to the recognised norms of good writing, and consequently to the traditional values of society. Because classical Arabic is the language of the Qurʾān, all "innovations" in matters of language and literature were actively resisted. In some cases, experimenting with new verse forms and the introduction of new images influenced by Western poetry were equated with heresy and sedition. In no other literature could the problems of versification rouse such heated discussions and even invite formal statements from government bodies. Disputes as to what constitutes good poetry are bandied about in the press; what the poet says and how he says it is a subject for discussion by a wide circle of readers, who are in most cases more conservative in matters of literature than an informed critic. This means that many Arab poets work under pressure to conform technically, as well as ideologically. That a poet should be pressured to conform ideologically is understandable, but that technical innovations in the art of writing poetry should be equated with heresy and sedition is, I think, peculiar to parts of the Arab literary scene, the rise of Arab nationalism in the opening decades of this century having been accompanied by a poetic revival, "a conscious return to the classicism of early mediaeval Arabic poetry".[1]

After centuries of Turkish rule during which Arabic poetry had decayed considerably, degenerating into mere decorative exercises and clever word play, this neo-classical revival produced great poetry in the old tradition, largely untouched by Western examples. However, the poet laureate Aḥmad Shawqī admitted to being influenced by French literature, and even tried his hand at poetic drama in imitation of Western models, but his verse stuck to the traditional form of classical Arabic poetry, the "pillar of verse", or the backbone of Arabic verse, the principles of good writing.

This Neo-classical poetry was soon challenged by young poets and critics of the early decades of this century. Graduates of new secular institutes, the Dīwān group or school as they are often called, were deeply influenced by English romantic poetry of the 19th century. Introducing al-Māzinī's *Dīwān* of poetry in 1913, al-ᶜAqqād attacked the poetry of Shawqī and classical poetics in general. Romanticism ran rampant in Arabic poetry in the first half of the century, under the influence of the *Mahjar* poets who added the influence of Emerson and Whitman to the widespread interest in Shelley, Keats, Victor Hugo and Carlyle. In 1932 *Apollo*, the new poetry review, published by Zakī Abū Shādī in Cairo, became an active forum for new experiments in Arabic versification. Paying lip service to Shawqī, the Appollo society elected him president and he graciously accepted. His death in the same year, soon followed by that of Ḥāfiẓ Ibrāhīm seems curiously fitting to the minds of many writers on the subject. A new voice and a more personal note take over in the poetry of the writers of the forties. Starting with the Dīwān group, critics call for organic unity in a poem and the discarding of conventional diction. Poets experimented with blank verse (calling it free verse), with variation of the rhyme in different stanzas, but one cannot say that any of them "broke the pillar of Arabic poetry".

The real break with the classical tradition started in the mid-century with the New Movement, or the New Poetry, introducing *al-shiᶜr al-ḥurr* (free verse). It was not really *vers libre* as in French, whence Arab critics borrowed the term, but was simply verse liberated from the monorhyme, from the obligation to rhyme at all, and from the regular *ᶜarūḍ* or prosody. The unit of the verse is the *tafᶜīla* or foot, and the number of feet may vary from one line to another. It is now called *tafᶜīla* poetry to distinguish it from the even more radical new waves which appeared on the scene later.

The two now famous seminal poems published independently in 1948 in Baghdad by Nāzik al-Malāʾika and Badr Shākir al-Sayyāb, both graduates of a modern teaching college and clearly influenced by English poetry, have made literary history. A third Iraqi poet, al-Bayyātī, soon contributed *his* free verse to the movement, and ʿAbd al-Raḥmān al-Sharqāwī published his avant-guarde long poem *From an Egyptian Father to President Truman*, a protest in the guise of supplication. The fifties marked the powerful inception of the New Movement in all the Arab capitals of culture and publishing. A new poetry magazine *Shiʿr*, started in Beirut in 1957 and carried the banner of the New Poetry for thirteen years. Ṣalāḥ ʿAbd al-Ṣabūr, Ḥijāzī, Adūnīs and Yūsuf al-Khāl were earlier on recognised as leading figures, and they *did* all break "the pillar of Arabic poetry". All of them expressed a new sensibility and a new diction, often based on the rich variety of their vernaculars, and there was much heated discussion and theorising, which, as mentioned above, spilled over into the daily press.

The rate of change has accelerated tremendously in the last forty years. The range of variation, difference and consensus has become so wide that, for the purpose of this paper, we will concentrate on the Egyptian scene, where the rear guard action of conservative critical opinion concentrated on attacking the values which the New Poetry expressed. The avant-guarde poets were accused of being communists, atheists, and generally subversive to Islam and Arab nationalism. The Higher Council for Art and Literature, which funded state publishing and dispensed state prizes, for years blocked any recognition of the New Poetry. The Committee for Poetry, an organ of the council, regularly referred the New Poetry submitted to it to the Committee for Prose. Strangely enough the chairman of the Poetry Committee, the man mainly responsible for its work, was al-ʿAqqād himself who had, early in his career, attacked neo-classical poetry as out-moded and inadequate for expressing a modern sensibility. His own poetry had been considered modern in a sense, but he had never contemplated breaking "the pillar of Arabic poetry". When the Higher Council for Art and Literature financed the Egyptian monthly poetry magazine in 1964, the members of the Committee for Poetry were scandalised after a number of issues to find that their organ gave much space to free verse and published many critical studies that supported the New Movement. The Committee issued a statement repudiating the policy of the magazine, which summarised its objections to the new poetry. It is thirty years since that statement was issued in 1965, but its arguments regularly surface in studies, reviews and symposiums discussing what is still termed the movement of new verse. Many of these arguments centre round the values represented by new verse.

Some of the more significant passages in the statement run:

> The committee bases its work upon stable principles, because . . . it is a guardian of stable values.
>
> The destruction . . . started by this new movement has begun to reach the Arabic language itself . . . There is a strong connection between language and the national spirit . . . To abandon the language also comes to mean to abandon the greatest cause, the cause of united Arab nationality . . . the conventional form which they want to destroy is represented by masters of classical and modern Arab poetry, therefore their plot is to suppress these masters . . . it is evident that poets who practise what is called new poetry are under the influence of a spirit which is in opposition to Arab-Islamic culture, which has distinguished specific artistic talents through the ages. This renders their writings invalid even when they are banished from the realm of poetry, and are considered as artistic prose, because they allow a foreign element to penetrate into our existence and corrupt it . . . such as the practice of incorporating ideas and symbols derived from non-Muslim religions, . . . such as the ideas of original sin, of the crucifixion and of redemption; also the poets allow themselves to use the word *Ilāh* 'God' in its pagan sense, as though it had not been given a special meaning in Islam, which should be venerated whatever the context.[2]

The new poets were confessedly influenced by Western poets, particularly T.S.Eliot, Saint-John Perse, Baudelaire, Rimbaud, Lorca, Neruda, Aragon, Éluard and Nazim Hekmet. They were in the main current of 20th century poetry, but they had not neglected the best part of the Arabic classical heritage. They were all great readers of poetry and history; Ṣalāḥ ᶜAbd al-Ṣabūr devoted two years (1963–4) to re-reading *all* the heritage of classical poetry.[3] It was probably he who was in the minds of the committee when they issued their statement, for his poetry is full of Christian imagery. He was greatly attracted to Sufism and the protagonist of his first poetic drama, al-Ḥallāj, the Sufi *shahīd* or martyr of the 10th century, is presented as a Christ figure. His mystic call is laced with "subversive" social thinking and he is tried, betrayed and crucified.

The new poets turned to Islamic history and old Arab heroic romances for heroes who represented what they deemed the *true* Islamic values: truth, justice, equality, selfless patriotism and national pride. I take as an example the work of one poet, Amal Dunqul (1940–1983) who started publishing poetry a little before the publication of the document quoted above. His poetry provides good examples of what the Committee objected to, and his work is not widely known outside Egypt. Many poems have titles based on the Bible: *The Last Supper* (1963); a whole volume called *The Testament To Come* with verses, psalms and hymns. One poem is *Spartacus' Last Testament* (1962):

> If you see the child I left on his
> mother's arm with no arm (of support)
> Teach him to bend
> Teach him to bend
> God did not forgive Satan his sin when he said No
> Only the meek
> Inherit the earth in the end
> For they do not hang;
> Teach him to bend.
> There is no escape
> Do not dream of a happy world,
> After the death of every Caesar, a new Caesar,
> After the death of a revolutionary, pain
> without end
> tears in vain [4]

There is also the figure of Khālid ibn al-Walīd, the great Muslim general who never lost a battle, but exercised great humility when Omar demoted him, lest he should become infatuated with his own victories. His famous words on his death-bed are often quoted:

> There is not an inch in my body which is free of wounds and here I am dying in my bed like an old goat. May the eyes of cowards never sleep in peace!

The poem *Death in Bed* (1970) incorporates the words of Khālid and portrays in brilliant images the bitter despair of Arab youth after the defeat of June 1967. Next to Sisyphus a favourite figure in the New Poetry, we have Zarqāʾ al-Yamāma, the Arab Cassandra; her eyes could see very far, but her people would not believe her and scoffed at her warnings. Written on June 13th, 1967, after the terrible defeat of the fifth of June, *Weeping in the Presence of Zarqāʾ al-Yamāma* is the cry of a wounded, defeated soldier, betrayed and bartered by his leaders. The speaker repeats the warning incantation of Zarqāʾ al-Yamāma:

> Why do these camels walk so slowly?
> Are they carrying rocks or iron?

He continues:

Holy sibyl . . .
What use are words now?
You told them of the clouds of dust,
They accused your eyes of weakness.
You told them of moving trees,
They laughed at your prating illusions.
When they were surprised with the naked sword they bartered us
And sought escape.
We are wounded in the heart
Wounded in the heart and tongue,
Nothing left us but death . . .

Using an old Arab legend of a war that went on for forty years between Bakr and Taghlib, he introduces an Electra-like figure refusing to take or give quarter, before her murdered father is vindicated. The treacherous murder of Kulayb by his cousin is the subject of a sequence of poems which Dunqul left unfinished at his death in 1983. The first poem in the sequence is the Testament of Kulayb the murdered prince, written in his blood as he lay dying with the arrow shot by his cousin still in his back. It is addressed to his brother al-Zīr Sālim, the avenger, whom modern poets and dramatists have made absolutely their own.

The *Testament* is in ten sections, each starting with an imperative, "do not compromise," do not accept reconciliation, do not make peace.

Do not make peace
Not if they give you gold
. . .
Such things are not bought
. . .
Will my blood between your eyes turn into water
Could you forget my bloody garment
Would you wear over my blood gold embroidered cloaks?
It is the war
It weighs heavily on the heart.
But behind you is the shame of the Arabs.
Do not compromise
And seek no escape.
Do not compromise, even if the stars warn you
And their priests throw you a prophecy
. . .

I was no invader
I did not draw near their tents
Or steal behind their hills.
I did not touch a fruit from their vines
Or step into their orchards.
My murderer did not challenge me to halt
He walked with me
Shook my hand,
Walked away
But hid in the trees
Suddenly
I was pierced with cold steel between two ribs
My heart shook like a bubble, and burst
. . .
Do not compromise
You have only to will,
You are the only knight of the age
The others are . . . nothing

. . .
Do not compromise
Do not compromise

The second part of the sequence is *The discourse of Yamāma* (the daughter of Kulayb). The story in the old romance quoted by Dunqul (287) goes:

> When delegates came asking for peace, prince Sālim said, "I will make peace if al-Yamāma accepts". Her mother al-Jalīla went in to her, with the wives of the chiefs of the tribe. They all greeted her. Al-Jalīla kissed her daughter and said, "Is it not enough! Our men have perished, things have gone badly with us. Our knights and heroes are dead." Al Yamāma replied, "I will not accept peace, even if none of us are left to fight."

In the poem she cries:

My father . . . I ask no more
I want my father at the castle gate,
In the house of truth,
Erect anew.
I do not ask the impossible, but justice.
Is the land to be inherited by other than its sons?

Will the orchards forget their tillers?
Will the branches deny their roots?

Her lament for her father ends with an invocation to her brother:

My brother will come
Oblivious of the book of inheritance
Oblivious of his royal blood
Of the sceptre of the ivory hand turned into a crow's head,
My brother will come (my heart knows him)

Alienated by her daughter, Jalīla had taken refuge with her own family, and the figure of the infant prince brought up by strangers, unaware of his royal descent and mission, has attracted a number of modern writers, In this poem he represents for his sister "A trinity of hearts", "The precious jewel of sovereignty, justice and love". The poem ends with an image current in modern Arabic poetry, and which the poets of the seventies scoff at, the phoenix rising out of the ashes, a symbol based on ancient Arabian mythology.

Kulayb returns . . .
Like a phoenix with burning feathers
Truth to remain more fair
Her feathers return in the sunlight brighter than ever,
She spreads the wings of the morning
Over cities rising out of memories of destruction.

Phrases of the Qurʾān, allusions and associations from the Holy Book, which have always run through Arabic verse and prose evoking stock responses, their significance long fixed by orthodox interpretation, are now used differently. One of Dunqul's most daring poems is his *Special Interview with Noah's Son*, where the story of the Ark is given a completely new interpretation. There are several references to Noah in the Qurʾān, but a more detailed account is in Sūrat Hūd, verses 25–48. Noah is commanded by God to build the Ark, and the unbelievers scoff at him for building a ship on a high place. He is commanded to take his family to the Ark together with a chosen few who believe in his mission, and a pair of each specimen of God's creatures. When the water begins to rise they all take hastily to the Ark, but Noah's son stands apart:

> She was running in waves as high as mountains, and Noah called to his son who stood apart. He said. "My son, embark with us, and do not remain with the infidels." He replied "I shall take to a mountain to protect me from the water." Noah said "There is no

> defence today from God's orders except those covered by His mercy. The waves separated them, and he was drowned.(vv. 42–43)

When the waters recede Noah reminds God of the son he has lost:

> Noah called upon his God; He said "Please God, my son is surely one of my family and you promised rightly, and you are most just." *He* said, "Noah he is not of your family; he is unrighteous. Do not question what you do not know. I advise you lest you should be one of the ignorant." (vv. 45–46)

The figure of Noah's son has remained that of the unrighteous young man, who spurned the opportunity of salvation offered by his father. As far as I know, no writer in Arabic ever questioned the values of the old Patriarch as opposed to those of the young man. Dunqul gives a modern interpretation, based on the current situation in Egypt, where for more than forty years the best brains and the most skilled technicians have been drained first to Europe and America, then to the new oil-rich Arab states. This, in the sixties, was considered by some as downright desertion of the "homeland"; all should stick to their posts, and work for their country, thus saving their "homeland". Noah's son in the poem stands for this heroic desperation with which the poet identified himself, together with many of his dissenting generation. It is the go-getters who run away; the young man's sarcastic prayer is:

> Blessed are those who ate her bread in goodly times
> And turned their backs on her in adversity[6]

This poem is not one of Dunqul's best, but is his most daring in questioning the orthodox values of his contemporaries. The members of that Poetry Committee back in the sixties were apparently right after all! A poet who dares to break "the pillar of Arabic poetry" will dare to break the "pillar" of any sanctified system of values!

Almost all the members of the old committee are now dead. Their places are occupied by some of those "new" poets and their supporting critics, but the controversy goes on! For Ṣalāḥ ᶜAbd al-Ṣabūr, Ḥijāzī, al-Bayyātī, al-Sayyāb and Dunqul are now *classics*! They are even called "the Establishment". New generations of poets question their theory and practice of poetry and seek a new prosody even more liberated from the *tafᶜīla*. They regard the poetry of the fifties and sixties as "mere statement", which is partly justified by some of the examples in this paper. This new avant-garde in Arabic poetry, described as the movement of the seventies, question the poetic credentials as well as the validity of the values of their predecessors who have now become *the* "established poets".

After a famous battle with the editor of *Ibdā*ᶜ, the Eyptian review for creative writing, the rebel poets of the "seventies generation" brought out their own poetry magazine *Iḍāᵓa 77* (Illumination 77). It was a poorly printed occasional publication which ran for eleven years, bringing out fourteen numbers in all, but it was truly a new poetry *manifesto* declaring in the editorial of its first number (July 1977) that "art does not reflect reality; art creates through its particular language a world of the imagination, parallel to reality". More than a hundred poems by some fifty poets were published by the magazine with occasional editorials, further stressing their difference from the ethos of the sixties.[7] They acknowledged as masters only Adūnīs and M. ᶜAfīfī Maṭar, who "exploded the language from within", giving real poetry a new life.

For them the poetry of the sixties was dead; ᶜAbd al-Ṣabūr's verse was parodied to show the emptiness of the old dream. Ḥijāzī's role as the foremost bard of the community was repeatedly targetted and Amal Dunqul's poetry was written off in the same breath as Shūsha and Abū Sinna, two popular poets who can claim direct descent from the romantic lyrical poetry of the forties.

The poets of *Iḍāᵓa 77* were joined by another group, producing a little magazine called *Aṣwāt* (Voices). All are indiscriminately described as the "seventies generation". They certainly played havoc with the "pillar" of Arabic poetry, destroying it completely; their verse is fragmented, their vision depressed and inward looking, with no respect for traditions, old or new. The reaction of progressive critics, was immediate. "A slap in the face of common taste", wrote al-Naqqāsh in September 1977. M. al-ᶜĀlim, the foremost Marxist critic and a poet *manqué* admitted its importance as poetry of dissent creating a new poetic idiom of its own, but his final verdict in 1989 was "it leaves me cold".[8] For traditional poets and critics this was neither poetry nor prose, it was sheer madness and heresy, an impudent attempt of the "fringe" to occupy the mainstream of poetry.

The accusation of heresy was levelled at some of the best work of these poets, who did not only write "poems of prose" but used the language of the Qurᵓān with its rhythms and stylistic peculiarities for purposes of their own.

The variety of poetry "in prose", ie. non *tafᶜīla* and non *ᶜamūdī* poetry shows in many cases a tremendous command of the language, its copious lexicon and intricate grammar. Deconstructive irony is the pervasive tone of many of the poems of Ḥasan Ṭilib, one of the founders of *Iḍāᵓa 77*, and one of the most persevering and productive of its members. His far-reaching exploration of words, their rhythm and rhyme, and their usage old and new, places him in a category of his own: not the poet as seer, prophet or bard, but the poet as creator, a craftsman, a magician of words and rhythms, almost a god!

In a poem written in Doha 1982, *A Sapphire for Amal Dunqul*, Ṭilib incorporates some lines of a now famous last poem composed by Dunqul in his hospital room on the "whiteness of death", the colour of a dead man's shroud. Ṭilib, evoking the old *muᶜāraḍāt* of classical Arab poets Jarīr and al-Farazdaq, sets his view as to the nature and function of poetry. For the dying poet,

> Poetry is protest
> Words from the heart
> Lifting the people on a wing

For the speaker, poetry is "dark fairness, an effusion of awe, like a sapphire of pure beauty or a violet in a garden".[9]

Ṭilib's poetry has to be read in Arabic, for much of its effect depends on the words themselves, their musical associations and sound rhythms in relation to each other. Accused of being prosaic on occasions, because of the conversational tone of many of his poems, Ṭilib retaliates with clever *taḍmīn* (intertextuality), spinning stretches of verse in imitation of classical poetry from Imruᵓ al-Qays to Ibn al-Rūmī down to Aḥmad Shawqī. In his last collection, *Āyat Jīm* (1992), he boasts in true Arab vein, "what could al-Mutanabbī write if he lived today that I have not already written?" adding six lines of brilliant imitation of a famous *qaṣīda* of al-Mutanabbī.

This post-modernist collage is typical in the work of Ṭilib's generation of the seventies poets. His *Āyat Jīm* finally roused the wrath of the Azhar. The poets of the fifties and sixties had been accused of heresy for introducing new systems of values as well as new poetics, but Ḥasan Ṭilib has gone so far as to compose an *āyah* and call its divisions *sūras*! He skilfully uses the idiom, the rhythm, and the tone of the Qurᵓān. Introducing his subject, the letter *jīm* he wonders why it was not singled out in the Qurᵓān as in the case of *alif*, *lām* or *sīn*. The five sections or *sūra*s present a brilliant reconstruction of Arabic words and images using the letter *jīm*; one could not imagine there could be so many. The third *sūra* is a glaring parody of *Sūrat al-Raḥmān*, using the dual verb and subject in an argument and incantation that no listener can miss.

In the final *sūra*, there is no attempt at versification; it is pure rhyming prose and has to be read in Arabic for the full power of its effect, its stark *muʿāraḍa* (oppostion) to some of the short incantationary *sūra*s that even children can learn to recite without necessarily understanding the meaning (see appendix II). The poem was hailed by Ḥijāzī himself (a very good critic and explicator of poetry), who published parts of it in the *Ahrām* celebrating the solid achievement of yet another generation of poets. *Āyat Jīm* was published by the Egyptian Book Organisation (1992). A protest from the Azhar led to the withdrawal of copies from the stalls of the Book Fair in 1994, a measure leading as usual to a much wider readership of the work.

Notes

1. For details see Salma al-Khadra Al-Jayyusi, *Trends and Movements in Modern Arabic Poetry*, Leiden: Brill, 1977, and S.Moreh, *Modern Arabic Poetry 1800–1970. The Development of its Form and Themes under the Influence of Western Literature*, Leiden: Brill, 1976
2. Translation by S. Moreh, published in *Modern Arabic Poetry . . .* At the time of writing this paper, the original Arabic was not available to me. I have, however, since been able to consult it (as reprinted in *al-Ahrām*, 20th November, 1983). Notably a number of members of the committee were poets of the New Movement of the sixties. The committee asserts that the work of all its members is based on the great heritage of classical Arabic poetry, but conclude:
   "All members believe that adherence to the music of poetry is basic for any poetic form. In this sense all members, both *ʿamūdī* poets and practitioners of free poetry are committed to the Arabic poetic *tafʿīla*. They regard abandoning the *tafʿīla* as equivalent to exiting from the domain of poetry to the world of prose." (my translation)
3. Ṣalāḥ ʿAbd al-Ṣabūr, *Ḥayātī fī al-Shiʿr*, Beirut, Dār al-ʿAwda, 1969.
4. All quotations are from the *Complete Works* published after his death: Amal Dunqul, *Al-Aʿmāl al-Kāmila*, Cairo, Madbūlī, n.d.
5. A leading Egyptian dramatist Alfred Farag had used the legend for the play *al-Zīr Sālim*, written in 1966 and produced in 1967. Dunqul clearly used the play as well as the original *Sīra*, but his vision was different.
6. Full text in Appendix I.
7. Three important editorials of *Iḍāʾa 77* are published in *Alif: Journal of Comparative Poetics*, Cairo, 1991, 98–112. Translation and introduction by Hāla Ḥalīm. This volume of *Alif* (No. 1) is devoted to the experimental poetry of the seventies.
8. Rifʿat Sallām, "Bibliography of the Poets of the Seventies" *Alif* (1991), 178–9.
9. From the Collection *Zamān al-Zabarjad* (The Age of Sapphire), Cairo, Dār al-Ghad, 1990.

Appendix I

A Special Interview With Noah's Son
by Amal Dunqul (1940–1983)

Noah's Flood is upon us

The city sinks slowly under water
Sparrows fly away
The water rises
Over the steps of houses – shops – the post office – the bank
Statues (our Great Ancestors) – temples – sacks of corn
Maternity hospitals – the prison gates – the Wali's office
The passages of fortified barracks
Sparrows fly away
Slowly
Slowly
The geese float on
the water
Furniture floats on the water
A child's toy
The sob of a broken mother
The maidens wave on the rooftops
Noah's flood is upon us
Here are the wise men flying to the ark
The singers – the Prince's groom – the money changers – the Chief Justice (and his page),
The sword bearer and the Dancer of the Temple (happy to have retrieved her wig from the water) the tax collectors – the arms' dealers
The lover of the princess with his bright sweet face
Noah's flood is upon us
Here are the cowards flying to the ark
while I was -----
The youth of the city desperately trying to bridle the rushing stream
Carrying water on their shoulders racing with time
Stacking stones to save scenes of childhood and civilisation
To save the motherland.
The ship master called to me before silence fell,
Save yourself from this soulless city.
I said
Blessed are they who ate her bread in goodly times

and turn their backs on her in adversity!
Glory to us who make a stand.
                (God has erased our names)
We defy death,
And take to a mountain that does
not die
                (they call it the people)
We will not run
We will stay home

My heart criss-crossed with wounds
My heart damned in all texts
Lay now on the wrecks of the city
A putrid rose,
Quiet at hand
Having said "No" to the ark and love the motherland.

Appendix II

السورة الخامسة

الجيم تجرح

أعوذ بالشعب من السلطان الغشيم

باسم الجيم . والجنة والجحيم . ومجتمع النجوم . إنكم اليوم ستفجأون . كم وددتم لو ترجأون . الى يوم لا جيم ولا جيوم . فإذا جد الهجوم . فأجهشت الجسوم . فسجرت الجيم . ومن أدراك ما الجيم . فإذا مزجنا الأجيام مزجا . ثم مخجنا جرجهن مخجا . ثم مججناهن مجا . قل يا أيها المجرمون إنكم يومئذ لفي وجوم . تستنجدون فلا تنجدون. وقل يا أيها الراجون . إنكم يومئذ الناجون . جاءتكم الجيم بما كنتم تستعجلون . ما لكم كيف لا تبتهجون . ولآية الجيم لا تسجدون . وبإعجازها لا تلهجون .

....

الجيم
جل
جلالها

صدق الحرف الرجيم

6

Literacy, Munificence and Legitimation of Power During the Reign of the Party Kings in Muslim Spain

Arie Schippers
University of Amsterdam

In this paper I shall deal with the political situation of al-Andalus (Muslim Spain) during the *Mulūk al-Ṭawā'if* period in relation to the occurrence of munificence towards poets and learned men.[1] The little states rivalled each other in munificence and attracted poets to their courts, Seville especially being a paradise for poets. I want to investigate how poets and learned men of lower class origins or those from ethnic groups and religions other than the Arab and Berber aristocracy, were able to acquire important posts at the courts due to their literary merits. Among the special cases I will study are the political careers of Ibn ᶜAmmār[2] and Samuel han-Nagid.[3] In eleventh-century al-Andalus it was possible to get on in the world by means of skillful poetry and the knowledge of how to write letters in rhymed prose.

Important sources for eleventh century Andalusian poetry are the anthologies compiled by Ibn Bassām (his *Kitāb al-Dhakhīra*)[4] and al-Fatḥ b. Khāqān (his *Qalā'id al-ᶜIqyān*).[5] These books give a good impression of the importance of poetry in eleventh-century Andalus, since they are almost contemporary sources. Later sources include the anthologies compiled by Ibn Saᶜīd al-Maghribī, such as *ᶜUnwān al-Murqiṣāt wa-l-Muṭribāt* (Patterns of verses which make dance and sing),[6] the *Rāyāt al-Mubārizīn* (the Banners of the champions)[7] and the *Kitāb al-mughrib fī ḥulā l-maghrib* (the Relator of extraordinary things about the Jewels of the West).[8] Among the later anthologies worth mentioning are Lisān al-Dīn b. al-Khaṭīb's *al-Iḥāṭah fī Akhbār Gharnāṭah* (the Comprehensive book about the Events of Granada)[9] which is more a biographical poetic anthology than a survey of the events which took place in Granada, and last but not least al-Maqqarī's *Nafḥ al-Ṭīb* (Fragrance of Perfume),[10] which, as we know, was originally meant as a kind of biography of the aforementioned Lisān al-Dīn b. al-Khaṭīb. However, the first part of it is an introduction to Andalusian history and poetry.

The *Dhakhīra* is divided according to geographical regions.[11] Part I comprises Cordoba and surrounding territories, part II the western regions of al-Andalus including Seville, part III includes the Eastern region, i.e. the region of Murcia, Denia and Valencia, and part IV includes an anthology of poets from foreign lands who praised Andalusia. The four main parts of the *Dhakhīra* are split up into sections dealing with individual poets, and in many places narrations of historical events of the eleventh century are inserted, based on the authority of the contemporary historiographer Ibn Ḥayyān.

In most cases Ibn Bassām[12] first lists love poetry (*nasīb*), then laudatory poetry (*madīḥ*), and finally various kinds of descriptive poetry and Lisān al-Dīn b. al-Khaṭīb follows the same system later on in his *Iḥāṭah*. Al-Fatḥ b. Khāqān's *Qalā³id al-ᶜIqyān* more or less copies Ibn Bassām's system. He divides his work into four sections headed by the poet he considered the leader of the group. Part I is devoted to the noble qualities of chiefs of state and their sons, with examples of pleasing stories of their lives, led by al-Muᶜtamid, the king of Seville. Part II deals with the splendours of the vizirs and the poetry of the secretaries and masters of eloquence, starting with Ibn Zaydūn, and Part III deals with judges and scholars, headed by Abū l-Walīd al-Bājī. The fourth part deals with learned literary persons and excellent poets among whom Ibn Khafāja is the most prominent.

Both Ibn Bassām and Ibn Khāqān's works were probably inspired by a nostalgic feeling about the greatness of literary activity in the eleventh century when there were so many kings and high functionaries who were *Maecenates* of poetry. Poetry flourished because of the support provided by the Party kings. Ibn Khāqān writes in his preface: 'When I saw that *adab*, both prose and verse, grew weak and its swords became rusty in their scabbards, and its sparks were full of cinders, I saved what remained of its agonizing spasms and restored to it the spirit which had reached the highest perfection'.[13]

In this climate literature was linked with power and power with literature. The latter is not always the case in other cultures, but in Arabic culture this was true from pre-Islamic times. In Christian Western Europe of the time, most kings were not literate and seldom cultivated knowledge or arts, but rather mainly practised war. Their noblemen also limited themselves to the practice of warfare.[14] In the Arabic situation, the kings legitimized themselves with warfare and poetry, which correspond to the pre-Islamic virtues of bravery and generosity. In Western Europe high posts were occupied by noble families and people belonged to the aristocracy by birth and could not switch from one class to another, whereas in Muslim Spain poets could arise to power from a situation of miserable poverty by means of their poetry. One of the well-known examples of a poor poet who became a powerful vizir, was Ibn ᶜAmmār[15], whose life and works I will dwell upon in the first part of this paper.

In Western Europe non-Christians could not rise to power. In al-Andalus some Jews rose to positions of influence at Muslim courts because of their literacy and poetic talents. The most conspicuous case is Ismaᶜīl (sometimes called Samawᵓal) Ibn al-Naghrīlah known as Shemuᵓel the Nagīd.[16] I will be stressing the impact of literacy upon the acceptance of non-Muslims in high posts in the government of the Andalusian states in the second part of this paper, and in the third part I will deal with a poet-king and his preference of poetry above warfare.

Dealing with Ibn ᶜAmmār's career from poet to vizir, shows how a poet of low origins started to make his living. Usually he was educated in a small village, the taste for poetry being given him by some grammarian who liked verse. Soon after, the poet perfected his skill in a larger town, and then began a life as an errant poet until the moment when he achieved success. Not a few of these errant poets came from the countryside.[17]

Ibn ᶜAmmār (1031–1084) was born near al-Shilb (the present-day Portugese town Silves) of a poor family. The anecdotes that survive about him show us how he arrived in Silves with a mule as his only possession, not knowing if he would have anything to eat that day. Then he received a sack of barley from a merchant to whom he had addressed some verses. Another time, he presented himself before Abū ᶜAbd al-Raḥmān ibn Ṭāhir, the ruler of Murcia, in a long garment of camel hair, with a hair-covering which made him appear ridiculous.

His miserable existence came to an end when he composed a poem ending with the letter *rā'*[18] on the Sevillian ᶜAbbadid king al-Muᶜtaḍid (d. 1068), who had just returned from a successful expedition against the Berber kings of Ronda. As a result of this *rā'iyya* he received a poet's reward and was enrolled in the register of those who were entitled to receive a poet's pension. His relation with al-Muᶜtaḍid's son, the later king al-Muᶜtamid, was to become legendary. Al-Muᶜtaḍid expelled Ibn ᶜAmmār from his kingdom, because he disliked his ascendency over his son. Ibn ᶜAmmār's place of exile was the North of Spain (Saragossa) and, during the course of this exile, he composed various poems, now famous, in which he asked repeatedly to be allowed to come back to Seville. After the accession to the throne by al-Muᶜtamid in 1068 he became the new king's advisor and vizir, but after treacherous behaviour, including conspiracy with the enemy, and even composing an invective poem on the origin of al-Mu^c^tamid's dynasty and his wife Rumaykiyya,[19] he was imprisoned and eventually killed. Although at the end of his life his own treacherous behaviour put an end to his career, we see at least how, in the beginning, he rose to power due to his poetic gifts.

The same holds true for the Jewish poet and learned man Shemuel han-Nagīd who originated from Cordoba, where he received his education. Although he issued from a well-to-do and aristocratic family, it was not easy for a Jew to reach a powerful position at the Muslim courts. However, through his knowledge of Arabic poetry and *adab* he made an impression on the Berber/Ṣinhāja kings of Granada, so that they appointed him as a vizir and – according to Hebrew and Judeo-Arabic sources – as a general of the army.[20] Apparently the importance of knowing poetry and *adab* in al-Andalus was such, that a non-Muslim, even a Jew, could rise to considerable power. In a recent publication, Scheindlin emphasizes how the situation in al-Andalus was an extraordinary one in this respect.[21] He makes a comparison between the Jewish vizirs in al-Andalus with those in the East, saying about one of the first Andalusian Jewish vizirs, Ḥasday ibn Shaprut: 'It is instructive to compare Ḥasday's career with that of his younger contemporary Ya^c^qūb ibn Killis,[22] a courtier in the service of the Fatimid caliph al-Mu^c^izz. Ibn Killis was a Jew who had converted to Islam; while he maintained his personal connections with Jews, he made a point of dissociating himself from Judaism. Ḥasday's case was quite different: not only he was openly Jewish, but he was also a central figure in the Jewish community itself.'

The same is true for Samuel han-Nagīd. Let us quote another sentence by Scheindlin which points at the importance of Arabic culture in their rise to power. He says:[23] 'The Jewish courtiers would not have been able to achieve their public positions if they had not been prepared for them by an Arab education similar to that enjoyed by their Muslim peers.'

The Jewish courtier Samuel han-Nagīd alias Ismā^c^īl ibn Naghrīla,[24] who was also a general, is praised in Arabic sources mainly because of his intellectual activities. The Cordoban historian Ibn Ḥayyān says about him:[25]

> 'This cursed (i.e. non-Muslim) man was a superior man although God did not inform him about the true religion. He possessed extensive knowledge and bore unpleasant behaviour with patience. He paired a solid and wise character with a clear mind and polite and friendly manners. Gifted with refined courtesy, he was able to

flatter his enemies under all circumstances and to disarm their hatred because of his pleasant behaviour. He was a man of extraordinary gifts. He wrote in both languages: Arabic as well as Hebrew. He knew the literatures of both peoples. He went deeply into the roots and basics of the Arabic language and was familiar with the words of the most subtle grammarians. He spoke and wrote Classical Arabic with the greatest ease, and used this language in the letters he wrote in the name of the king. He made use of the usual Islamic expressions, the eulogies of God and Muḥammad, our prophet, and counselled the addressee to live according to Islam. In brief, you would imagine that these letters had been written by a pious Muslim. He was excellent in the ancient sciences, in mathematics as well as astronomy. He also possessed ample knowledge in the field of logic. In dialectics he overwhelmed his adversaries. In spite of his lively spirit, he spoke little and reflected much. He collected a beautiful library. He died on 18th Muḥarram 459. The Jews honoured his bier. They bent their heads in humility. They gathered and wailed openly because of him.'

I now interrupt this notice, which was transmitted by Lisān al-Dīn b. al-Khaṭīb in his *Iḥāṭa* as well as al-ᶜIdharī's *Bayān al-Mughrib* for a while, in order to refer to the education of his son Yūsuf or Yōsef, before continuing to render this passage.

Shemuel han-Nagīd took great care of the intellectual education of his son Yōsef. From the battle grounds he addressed a poem in Hebrew to the little Yōsef, whom he urged to read anthologies of Arabic poetry, because one was only suitable for court life when one knew thousands of lines of Arabic poetry by heart. Thus the poet writes to his young son on this occasion:[26]

'1. Yōsef, receive this book which I have chosen for you from the best of the language of the Arabs.
2. I copied it – while the deadly spear was whetted and the sword was drawn.
3. Whilst Death decreed that one army should be replaced by another one, every time anew.
4. I do not cease teaching you, although Death's mouth is open all around me . . .
5. In order that wisdom may come upon you, for that is dearer to me than discovering my foes defeated.
6. Take it and reflect upon it, and quit the crowds who deride language and speech.

7. Know that the man of understanding is like a tree of sweet fruit whose leaves are healing remedies,
8. While the fool is like the tree of the forest whose limbs and branches will be consumed by fire in the end.'

This endeavour to educate his son in order to prepare him for later statesmanship is also mentioned in the passage by Ibn Ḥayyān quoted above, which I interrupted for a while. It reads: [27]

'[Samuel han-Nagīd/Ismāᶜīl ibn Naghrīla] had encouraged his son Yūsuf, who bore the *kunya* Abū Ḥusayn, to read books. For him he brought together masters and writers from all directions, who instructed him and taught him. The art of writing was also part of this. Thus he prepared him for his first job, namely being secretary of [Buluqqīn], the son of his master, who was the candidate to take [his master's] place. This served as a preparation for the basics of his work. When Ismāᶜīl [Samuel] died on the above-mentioned date, Bādīs approached Yūsuf. Bādīs showed himself to be satisfied with him, as a replacement for his father at [Bādīs'] service.'

But Yūsuf was not as modest as his father in his behaviour. Or, to put it in the terms of the *Bayān al-Mughrib* quoted in *al-Iḥāṭa*:

'[Ismāᶜīll or Samuel] left behind a son, named Yūsuf, who had never known the humility of the *dhimma*, nor the filthy situation in which Jews must normally live. He was a good-looking man, sharp of wit. He started to improve his situation with enthusiasm. He collected taxes and extracted money and appointed Jews to all kinds of functions.'

It was his alleged cooperation with the enemy which brought an end to his life and power.[28] He was murdered in a riot by members of the Ṣinhāja of Granada and crucified at the gate to the town and many other Jews were killed. But then the source speaks about the cultural impact of both:

'The original location of his grave – and that of his father – is known even to-day by the Jews who consecutively transmitted this in their circles. Before the gate of Ilbira, at the distance of a bow-shot, across the road. On his grave is a piece of limestone, roughly shaped. He was famous because of his rank in enjoying a delicate life, his refined behaviour, elegance and literacy. These qualities added to his reputation so that he deserves mention with important intellectuals and unique men. He had the same stature except for his religious beliefs.'

The cultural impact of the clan of the Nagīd was such that the loss of this family was felt as a great cultural loss. Moses ibn Ezra in his *Kitāb al-Muḥāḍara wa-l-Mudhākara* compared this to the loss of the pre-Islamic leader Qays ibn ᶜĀṣim, about whose death the following well-known poetic line was recited:[29]

> 'His Death was not the loss of one person/ but with him the building of a whole people was demolished.//
> (*Mā kāna Qaysun hulku-hu hulku wāḥidin/wa-lākinna-hu bunyānu qawmin tahaddama//*)'

Finally I will deal with one of the poet-kings of the period of the Party-Kings, al-Muᶜtamid b. ᶜAbbād, king of Seville.[30] While the kings in the Christian West had their legitimacy of power mainly as defenders of the Faith, the Muslim kings in al-Andalus associated themselves more with the pre-Islamic or ancient Arab virtues of generosity and bravery. They fell short in defending their faith. In their virtues of generosity and bravery, they deviated from the middle course. They were not only generous towards poets, receiving them in drinking bouts and donating slave-girls to them, but were also generous towards themselves, indulging in drinking wine and making love to slave-girls. As far as their bravery is concerned, they did not fight with their Christian enemies to whom they instead paid tribute, but had continuous wars with each other.

Al-Muᶜtamid (1040–1095) the poet-king of Seville, was a prolific poet and also a valiant king. He ended his life in exile in Aghmāt, where Yūsuf ibn Tashūfīn sent all the Andalusian kings deposed by him around 1091.

He is a good example of a poet king who gained most of his repute as a hero in the battlefields of his time. Nevertheless, he was also a poet who considered poetry to be the most important aspect of statesmanship. Poetry gave the Andalusian king his prestige, although not in the eyes of Ibn Tashūfīn, who did not even know Arabic,[31] and who – according to various contemporary sources – criticised al-Muᶜtamid because of his indulgence in wine drinking and womanising (he occupied himself only with the *ajwafayn*, the two holes, i.e. the belly and the vulva, so relates al-Ḥimyarī[32]), and not devoting enough forces to save Islamic Spain from the threat of the Christian king Alfonso.

The role of poetry in his life was conspicuous. In his adolescence, during his father (al-Muᶜtaḍid's) reign he became a friend of the former errant poet Ibn ᶜAmmār and remembers their life in Silves in a poem ('How many nights I have spent at the barrage of the river in pleasure with a girl like the bending of the river with bracelets').[33] During his father's reign he had to make use of his poetry for political reasons. He lost the city of Malaga, when on expedition against Bādīs of Granada in 1064 and, in order to avoid punishment tried to flatter his father al-Mu^c^tadid by composing a poem which has since become famous.[34]

Likewise poetry played a role in his initial acquaintance with his wife Rumaykiyya.[35] The romantic anecdote is well known. Along the Great River (Guadalquivir) al-Mu^c^tamid and his vizir Ibn ^c^Ammār were playing *ijāza* ('continuing a line of poetry with the same rhyme and metre'). At one point Ibn ^c^Ammār was not quick enough to continue al-Mu^c^tamid's hemistich (*ṣana^c^a l-riḥu min al-mā'i zarad* or 'the wind has spun a coat of mail of water') and a girl who was washing some linen in the river, suddenly appeared with the desired continuation (*ayyu dir^c^in li-qitālin law jamad* or 'What a shield it would be for battle, if it stiffened'). She was the daughter of a muleteer called Rumayk ibn al-Ḥajjāj, and al-Mu^c^tamid immediately wanted to marry her. She subsequently became his wife, was called I^c^timād, and was later famous for her capriciousness.

When he was deposed, al-Mu^c^tamid composed poems about his miserable condition in exile in Aghmāt,[36] but this poetry – although famous in the anthologies – failed to save him from this situation and bring him to power again. This, however, was because the period of the Party Kings had come to an end and the Almoravids rose to power, whereupon the poetic climate deteriorated.

There were political and social reasons for this gradual deterioration of the poetic climate in the courts of al-Andalus. The Almoravid rulers did not have such an interest in poetry, if they knew the sophisticated language of Arabic poetry at all. Monroe describes the arrival of the Almoravids and their effect in the following terms:[37]

> 'The political failure of the refined *mulūk al-ṭawā'if* produced a violent reaction by the urban middle and lower classes. The religious ideals of Islamic universalism were by now strongly opposed to those of secular Arab culture, and with the aid of the Almoravids unity and commercial prosperity for a time replaced the earlier fragmentation and extravagance. The Almoravids were a fundamentalist Islamic brotherhood founded in the upper Senegal in the middle of the eleventh century which soon spread from the western Sudan to the north African coast, from the Atlantic to Algiers. They were Ṣinhājī Berbers, and wore the veil like their modern descendants the Tuaregs. (. . .)'
>
> 'The irruption of the Almoravids had profound and even

> dislocating effects on Andalusian culture. The former were strictly orthodox and they recognized the ᶜAbbasid caliphate of Baghdad. Their government was conducted through the support of the Malikite *fuqahā'* who constitued an intolerant, narrowly legalistic theocracy and imposed a tight control on the free expression of ideas. (. . .)'

'Aristocratic poetry fell out of favour with the loss of royal patronage. Ibn ᶜAbdūn, a secretary under the Aftasid dynasty of Badajoz, wrote a long elegy to mourn the fall of his sovereigns who were murdered by the Almoravids. (. . .)'

'Poets were often forced to entertain less-refined audiences than formerly and so they naturally tended to cultivate the lighter forms. For this reason the *muwashshaḥāt* enjoyed a great vogue at this time.'

To sum up my conclusions, during the period of the Party Kings in al-Andalus, the mastery of Arabic poetry and literature could break through the usual pattern of the layers of society: men and women of poor descent could come to power thanks to their skill in poetry and could become part of the aristocracy. We have seen how Ibn ᶜAmmār – a poor itinerant poet – came to power, or how Rumaykiyya – the daughter of a muleteer – became the wife of a king solely because of their poetic skill. We have also seen how members of a religious minority like the Jews could become influential in the Muslim courts and even acquire the status of vizir thanks to their knowledge of Arabic culture. This special situation came to an end with the arrival of the Almoravids who gave the religious sciences a higher status than Arabic poetry and literature. I do not know whether the period of the Andalusian Party kings is unique in Islamic history or whether there are other periods and countries in which similar situations can be found. However, if we compare al-Andalus with Christian Western Europe, intellectual activities had more status in the former than in the latter. The aristocracy in Christian Western Europe seemed too closed upon itself to make it possible for a poor, literate man to move towards the aristocracy. The survival of the Ancient Arab virtues in al-Andalus during the reign of the Party-kings brought a flourishing period of Arabic literature into existence which even now fires our imagination.

I am grateful that in the present-day Muslim world some of those who are in power take an interest in poetry and Arabic literature just as the Muslim kings of al-Andalus did. Otherwise the present Shaban Memorial Conference would not have been possible.

Notes

1. For this period, see Wasserstein (1985).
2. Lived 422/1031–477/1084.
3. Lived 993–1056. For Samuel han-Nagīd, see *Encyclopaedia Judaica* (1970), Vol. 14, pp. 816 ff.; Ashtor, (1966) II, pp. 26–117; for his name, see Ibn Ḥazm [1899–1903], p. 107 [Ismāʿīl ibn Yūsuf al-Kātib al-Maʿrūf bi-Ibn Naghrala] and p. 121 [Ashmawal ibn Yūsuf al-Lawi al-kātib al-maʿrūf b-Ibn Nafral]; Ibn al-Khaṭīb [1973], p. 435 [Ismāʿīl Ibn Naghralah al-Yahūdī]; al-Zīrī [1955], p.30 [Abū Ibrāhīm al-Yahūdī].
4. ed. Iḥsān ʿAbbās, Ibn Bassām[1979]; See Nykl (1946), pp. 219–227.
5. ed. (Tunis: al-Maktaba al-ʿatīqa, 1966); See Nykl (1946), pp. 219–227.
6. ed. (Cairo: Jamʿiyyat al-Maʿārif, 1286/1869–70; reprint Beyrouth: Dār Ḥammād wa-Muḥyu, 1973).
7. ed. García Gómez (Madrid: Instituto de Valencia de Don Juan, 1942).
8. ed. Shawqī Ḍayf, 2 Vols. (Cairo: Dār al-Maʿārif, 1953–55).
9. ed. Muḥammad ʿAbd Allāh ʿInān, 3 Vols. (Cairo: Maktabat al-Khanjī, 1393/1973).
10. ed. Iḥsān ʿAbbās, 8 Vols. (Beyrouth: Dār Ṣādir 1388/1968).
11. See Nykl (1946), pp. 219–227.
12. See Nykl (1946), pp. 219–227.
13. See Nykl (1946), pp. 219–227.
14. For Christian noblehood, see e.g. Th. Reuter, *The Medieval Nobility: Studies on the Ruling Class of France and Germany from the 6th till the 12th Century* (Oxford, 1979) and A. Borst (ed), *Das Rittertum im Mittelalter* (Darmstadt, 1976).
15. See note 2; and Nykl (1946), pp. 154–62 ; cf. E.I. s.v. Ibn ʿAmmār (vol. III, pp. 705–6).; see also Khāliṣ (1957).
16. See note 3.
17. Pérès (1953), pp. 67–9; Khāliṣ (1957), p. 25; based on Ibn Bassām [1979],II:1, pp. 368 ff..
18. Poem no. 9; cf. Khāliṣ (1957), p. 209.
19. Poem no. 59; cf. Khāliṣ (1957) p. 259.
20. See above note 3.
21. Scheindlin (1992) p. 190.
22. Cf. Shaban (1976), Vol. 2, p. 199.
23. Scheindlin (1992), p. 192.
24. See note 3; cf. also Wasserstein (1993); for his poetry, see Schippers (1994).
25. Cf. Ibn al-Khaṭīb [1973], Vol. 1, pp. 438–9.
26. Cf. Weinberger (1973), p.65; ha-Nagid [1966], p. 66 (poem no. 21).
27. Cf. Ibn al-Khaṭīb [1973], 439–40.
28. Ibn al-Khaṭīb [1973] 439–40; al-Zīrī [1955], p. 54 [10 Ṣafar 459/ 1066]; translation by Tībī (1986), p. 75; Ibn al-Khaṭīb, [1965] p. 233 [465/ 1073 or 469/ 1077]; Hoenerbach (1970), pp. 422, 601, note 13 [9 Ṣafar 459= 30th of December 1066]; Ibn Idharī [1930] pp. 256, 266 [459/ 1066]; Ibn Bassām [1979], I, II, pp. 766–769; Ibn Da'ūd [1967], p. 57 [p.76] [9th of Tebet 4827/1066]; Wasserstein (1985), pp. 208–209; Ashtor [1966], II, pp. 116–117.

29. Line by ᶜAbdah ibn al-Ṭabīb (d. after 20/641), cf. *GAS*, II, 198–199; the famous line is quoted in numerous works, a.o. Ibn Rashīq [1972], II, p. 153; Ibn Ezra [1975], 35b.
30. For his father al-Muᶜtaḍid (407/ 1016–461/ 1069), see Nykl (1946), pp. 129–133; for al-Muᶜtamid (432/ 1040–488/ 1095), see Nykl (1946), pp. 134–154.
31. Cf. al-Maqqarī [1968], IV, p. 355; Norris (1982), pp. 139–141, does not believe in this illiteracy.
32. al-Ḥimyarī, *Al-Rawḍ al-miᶜṭar* and other sources *apud* al-Maqqarī, [1969], IV, pp. 354–377; Wasserstein (1985), p. 289.
33. Al-Muᶜtamid [1952], pp. 11–12.
34. Al-Muᶜtamid [1952], p. 36.
35. Nykl (1946), pp. 139–41; al-Maqqarī [1969], IV, pp. 211 ff.; Al-Muᶜtamid[1952], p. 74.
36. Al-Muᶜtamid[1952], p. 89.
37. Monroe (1974), pp. 33–9

Bibliography

Note: dates between square brackets relate to the date of the *edition* of classical works.

Ashtor, E. (1960–66), *Qorot ha-Yehudim bi-Sfarad ha-Muslimit*, (Jerusalem, 1960–66), I–II.
—— (1973, 1979, 1984), *The Jews of Moslem Spain*, (Philadelphia, Jewish Publication Society, 1973, 1979, 1984), I–III.
Encyclopedia Judaica (Jerusalem, Kether 1970), I–XIII.
Hoenerbach (1970), Wilhelm, *Islamische Geschichte Spaniens*, Uebersetzung des *Aᶜmāl al-Aᶜlām* (Zürich: Artemis, 1970).
Ibn Bassām [1979], *Kitāb al-Dhakhira fī maḥāsin ahl al-jazīra*, ed. Iḥsān ᶜAbbās (Beirut: Dār al-Thaqāfa, 1399/1979), I–IV.
Ibn Da'ūd [1967], *Sefer ha-Qabbalah*, ed. G.D.Cohen (Philadelphia: Routledge, 1967).
Ibn Ezra, Moses (Moshe ibn Ezra) [1975], *Kitāb al-Muḥāḍara wa-l-Mudhākara*, ed. A.S. Halkin, (Jerusalem 5735/1975); – ed. Montserrat Abumalham Mas, (Madrid, Consejo Superior de Investigaciones Científicas, 1985 [I: edición], 1986 [II; traducción] (both quoted according to Bodleiana Neubauer Ms. no. 1974,ff. ab).
Ibn Ḥazm [1899–1903], Abū Muḥammad ᶜAlī ibn Aḥmad, *Al-faṣl fī-l-milal wa-l-' ahwā' wa-l-nihal*, (Cairo, 1317–21/ 1899–1903).
Ibn ᶜIdhari [1948], *Bayān al-Mughrib*, I–II, eds Lévi-Provençal, Évariste, and Colin, G.S. (Leiden 1948²; repr. Beyrouth).
—— [1930], III (Leiden 1930; repr. Beyrouth).
—— [1974], IV, ed. Iḥsān ᶜAbbās (Beyrouth, 1974).
Ibn al-Khaṭīb [1973], Lisān al-Dīn, *Al-Iḥāṭa fī akhbār Gharnāṭa*, ed. Muḥammad ᶜAbdallāh ᶜInān, (Cairo, 1393/1973: I [1973], II [1974], III [1976], IV [1978]).
Ibn al-Khaṭīb [1956], *Aᶜmāl al-Aᶜlām*, ed. E. Lévi-Provençal, E. (Beyrouth, 1956²).
Ibn Rashīq [1972], *Kitāb al-ᶜUmdah*, edited by Muḥammad Muḥyi al-Dīn ᶜAbd al-Ḥamīd (Beyrouth 1972)

Khāliṣ (1957), Ṣalāḥ, *Muḥammad ibn ᶜAmmār al-Andalusī, dirāsa adabiyya tārīkhiyya li-almaᶜi shakhṣiyya fī tārīkh dawlat Banī ᶜAbbād fī Ishbīliya*, (Baghdad, 1957), I (biography), II (edition of the *Dīwān*).
al-Maqqarī [1968], Aḥmad ibn Muḥammad, *Nafḥ al-ṭīb min ghuṣn al-Andalus al-raṭīb*, Beyrouth 1388/1968, ed. Ihsan ᶜAbbas, [I–VIII].
Monroe (1974), James T., *Hispano-Arabic Poetry: a Student Anthology* (Berkeley California, 1974).
al-Muᶜtamid [1951], *Dīwān*, ed. Aḥmad Aḥmad Badawī, a.o. (Cairo 1951).
ha-Nagid [1966], Samuel [Shemuel] Ibn Naghrilah, *Dīwān (Ben Tehillim)*, ed. Dov Yarden (Jerusalem, 1966).
Norris (1982), H.T., *The Berbers in Arabic Literature*, (London/NY, 1982).
Nykl (1946), A.R., *Hispano-Arabic Poetry and its relations with the old Provençal Troubadours*, (Baltimore, 1946).
Pérès (1953), Henri, *La poésie andalouse en arabe classique au XIe siècle* (Paris: Adrien-Maisonneuve, 1937, 1953[2]).
Scheindlin (1992), Raymond P., 'The Jews in Muslim Spain', in *The Legacy of Muslim Spain*, S.Kh. Jayyusi, ed., (Leiden, E.J. Brill 1992), 188–200.
Schippers (1982), Arie, 'Two Andalusian poets on exile: Reflexions on the poetry of Ibn ᶜAmmar (1031–1086) and Moses ibn Ezra (1055–1138)', in *The Challenge of the Middle East*, I.A. El-Sheikh, C.A. van de Koppel, Rudolph Peters, eds (Amsterdam, 1982), pp. 113–21.
—— (1994), *Spanish Hebrew Poetry and the Arabic Literary Tradition*, (Leiden: E.J. Brill, 1994).
Shaban (1976), M.A., *Islamic History, A New Interpretation* (Cambridge University Press, 1976), Vol. 2.
Tibi (1986), Amin T., *The Tibyan. Memoirs of ᶜAbd Allāh b. Buluggin, last Zirid Amir of Granada. Translated from the Emended Arabic Text and Provided with Introduction, Notes and Comments*, Leiden 1986.
Wasserstein (1985), David *The Rise and Fall of the Party-Kings; Politics and Society in Islamic Spain, 1002–1086*, (Princeton, University Press 1985).
—— (1993), 'Samuel Ibn Naghrila ha-Nagid and Islamic Historiography in al-Andalus', in *Al-Qanṭara* 14, pp. 109–126.
Weinberger (1973), Leon J., *Jewish Prince in Moslem Spain: Selected Poems of Samuel ibn Nagrela*, transl. with introduction and notes (Alabama, 1973).
al-Zīrī [1955], ᶜAbdallāh, *Mudhakkirāt al-amīr ᶜAbdallāh, al-musammāt bi-Kitāb al-Tibyān*, ed. E. Lévi-Provençal (Cairo, Dhakhāʾir al-ᶜArab, 1955).

7

The Authenticity of the Poems ascribed to Umayya Ibn Abī al-Ṣalt

Tilman Seidensticker
University of Giessen

Umayya Ibn Abī al-Ṣalt is a personality of some relevance both for religious and for literary history. As for the realm of literature, the poems ascribed to him are markedly different from what else is known of Arabic poetry of the early 7th century A.D. with respect to form and content: the polythematic *qaṣīda* with its typical sequence of topics is missing completely; instead he deals with such subject matters as the creation of the world, the angels' service, the deluge, the resurrection of man and so on. These latter topics, on the other hand, are not likely to be dealt with by a pre-Islamic pagan poet and, as there is no evidence at all that the Ṭāʾifī Umayya was a Jew or a Christian,[1] one has to ask what else he could have been.

From a Muslim point of view, this question is easily answered: he must have been a *ḥanīf*, a member of the small group of monotheists on the Arabian peninsula who followed the monotheism of Abraham. Abraham's belief is attested to in the Qurʾān where it is connected with the Kaʿba in Mecca; according to the Qurʾān, this first monotheism was corrupted later, which fact led to the predominance of *shirk* in Arabia. In Western research, some doubts have been cast on this concept of *Heilsgeschichte* as there is no biblical or extra-biblical evidence of Abraham's connection with Arabia, and these doubts[2] naturally affect the *ḥanīfs*. In 1990, however, Uri Rubin[3] tried to rehabilitate the *ḥanīfs*, arguing that some of them are described as enemies of the prophet Muḥammad and that they therefore can hardly have been invented for apologetic reasons. Convincing as this argument sounds, the problem still remains that the reports on these *ḥanīfs* are contained in quite heterogeneous sources and that Ibn Isḥāq's *Sīra* from which Rubin repeatedly quotes poetry is an unreliable source for poetry even in the eyes of ancient Arab scholars.

The aforementioned characteristics of the poems ascribed to Umayya have drawn considerable attention to this figure. Besides three editions, seven articles and two doctoral dissertations have been devoted to him, 1700 pages altogether, which is quite a lot for someone of whom less than 900 lines have been preserved. But as it seems, this trouble is out of all proportion to the role he plays in modern research. The reason for this neglect is the quarrel about the authenticity of his poetry for, whereas some scholars maintain that there is a hard core of possibly authentic poems of a religious coinage, others are willing only to accept about two dozen uninteresting fragments with non-religious themes. This state of affairs has resulted in a sort of agnosticism: Umayya is simply not mentioned in, for example, *Der Islam* by Watt and Welch[4] or in the first volume of the *Cambridge History of Arabic Literature.*[5] Tilman Nagel, on the other hand, in his monograph on the Qurʾān,[6] goes to the opposite extreme in quoting Umayya's poetry from Arabic sources without worrying about the fact that four of the seven pieces adduced by him are – with good reason – regarded as suspect in the studies on Umayya.

In what follows, I would like to examine the controversy about Umayya once again. First of all, some remarks on his biography, his poetry and its transmission: these facts are more or less undisputed in literature.[7]

Umayya stems from the city of al-Ṭāʾif, situated some 50 miles to the south-east of Mecca in the mountains, and he belonged to the Thaqīf tribe who dominated the area. Through his mother Ruqayya bt. ᶜAbd Shams, he was related to Meccan aristocracy, and close relations to Mecca are also reflected in eulogies on the Meccan celebrities ᶜAbdallāh b. Judᶜān and Ḥarb b. Umayya. An elegy on the Meccans killed at the battle of Badr in the year 2 A.H. is generally accepted as authentic. On the one hand, this poem shows Umayya's political loyalties at that time, and on the other hand, it is the last datable sign of his life. He must have died before the Muslim occupation of al-Ṭāʾif in 8 A.H. because he is not mentioned in the historical reports about this event. A eulogy on the prophet Muḥammad is generally regarded as a forgery, 18 lines in the *mutaqārib* metre composed in an awkward style out of Qurʾānic phrases and in fact hardly suitable to a poet who is supposed to have lived in pagan al-Ṭāʾif until his death.

The well-known philologist Muḥammad b. Ḥabīb, who died in 859 A.D., is said to have collected Umayya's poetry in a *dīwān* and commented on it, and in the 18th century, the compilator of the monumental dictionary *Tāj al-ᶜarūs* still had a copy of this *dīwān* at his disposal.[8] Today, it seems to be lost, but of some consolation to us is the fact that, as can be judged from quotations, it contained some very doubtful poems and thus would not have been of great value in dealing with the question of authenticity.[9] Instead, we have at our disposal three collections of fragments, the first (containing 530 lines) compiled by Friedrich Schulthess in 1911 which is quite voluminous, considering the small number of printed source works available at that time.[10] Second, there is the edition by ᶜAbd al-Ḥafīẓ al-Saṭlī, published in Damascus in 1974,[11] and third, the Baghdad master thesis by Bahja ᶜAbd al-Ghafūr al-Ḥadīthī, published in 1975 (= al-Ḥadīthī [1975]). These editions contain 895 and 857 lines respectively.[12] The lesser part of the poetry in all these editions is devoted to profane topics we are familiar with from Umayya's contemporaries; the greater part bears a religious stamp.

The course of research on Umayya has followed a zig-zag line since he was, so to speak, discovered in the middle of the last century by Alois Sprenger.[13] Sprenger placed him among the group of *ḥanīfs* without, however, discussing the authenticity of Umayya's poems. This question was raised only in the present century by Clément Huart who, in 1904, got off to a dramatic start in his article *Une nouvelle source du Qurān* (= Huart [1904]). As the editor of al-Maqdisī's *K. al-Badᵓ wa-l-tārīkh*, which contains a large number of poems ascribed to Umayya, Huart had noticed that the content of Umayya's poems is often of greater informational value than that of Qurᵓānic passages dealing with the same subject-matter. One of his examples is the story of the extinction of the people of Thamūd who disregarded God's command to give pasture and watering to a female camel consecrated to him but who slaughtered her. In the Qurᵓān, this story is mentioned in five places, and it is the prophet Ṣāliḥ who warns the Thamūd and finally escapes the punishment. Umayya does not mention Ṣāliḥ but gives some details not mentioned in the Qurᵓān: he knows the name of the man who hamstrung the camel and tells us about the camel's young calling down upon the Thamūd the wrath of heaven, and about a girl who escaped and brought the message of the Thamūd's extinction to the neighbouring people of Qurḥ before she died. From additional information of this kind Huart concludes that the common traits between Umayya and the Qurᵓān must go back to Umayya.

Huart's uncritical attitude towards the poems ascribed to Umayya was not accepted in the ensuing period. His article provoked six publications[14] whose authors agreed insofar as they all admitted that poems which do not contain a substantial surplus of information and show a clear lexical agreement with the Qurᵓān are the products of later Muslim forgers. The most important and detailed discussion is Israel Frank-Kamenetzky's Königsberg doctoral dissertation published in 1911 under the title *Untersuchungen über das Verhältnis der dem Umajja b. Abi ṣ*

Ṣalt zugeschriebenen Gedichte zum Qorān. He is willing to accept as authentic, besides pieces or lines without any resemblance to the Qurʾān, free improvisations in Qurʾānic style and in Qurʾānic expressions as well as poems showing isolated reminiscences of the Qurʾān among ideas known from Umayya's unsuspect poems (Frank-Kamenetzky [1911] p. 47). In this way, Frank-Kamenetzky came to consider some 225 lines with a religious subject as authentic.

In a review of Frank-Kamenetzky's book, Theodor Nöldeke, otherwise known to be highly critical of the authenticity of ancient Arabic poetry, puts his view as follows: 'With no. 23 [of the Schulthess edition] begin those poems which we *a potiori* may call "religious" or "pious". At a glance, one is inclined to regard them all as Muslim forgeries. But in some of them, a more thorough study reveals so many strange or even odd traits that we cannot help ascribing them to a poet original in his way, and as several of them resemble each other, there is reason enough to ascribe them to Umayya.' (Nöldeke [1912] p. 163). Nevertheless Nöldeke accepts a smaller number of lines as genuine than does Frank-Kamenetzky.

In order to give examples of the poetry in question, I would like to quote from two poems. The first one deals with the annunciation to Mary and the birth of Jesus; as it is quoted to show a case of obvious use of the Qurʾān, I have picked out only five lines out of a total of 17.

Umayya 38/1.4.9.11–12 SCHULTHESS = 79/1.4.9.11–12 AL-SAṬLĪ = 119/1.4.9.11–12 AL-ḤADĪTHĪ (from al-Maqdisī, *Badʾ*, line 4 also in Yāqūt, *Muʿjam al-Buldān*):

1. *wa-fī dīnikum min rabbi Maryama āyatun*
   munabbiʾatun wa-l-ʿabdi ʿĪsā bni Maryamī
   'In your religion is an announcing sign from the Lord of Mary and of the servant Jesus, the son of Mary.'

   With this compare the following quotations from the Qurʾān: *wa-li-najʿalahū* [i.e. *ʿĪsā*] *āyatan li-l-nāsi*: Qurʾān 19/21; *wa-jaʿalnā bna Maryama wa-ummahū āyatan*: Qurʾān 23/50; *qāla* [i.e. *ʿĪsā*] *innī ʿabdu llāhi*: Qurʾān 19/30; *lan yastankifa l-masīḥu an yakūna ʿabdan li-llāhi*: Qurʾān 4/172; *ʿĪsā bnu Maryama*: Qurʾān, passim.

4. *wa-laṭṭat* [i.e. *Maryamu*] *ḥijāba l-bayti min dūni ahlihā*
   taghayyabu ʿanhum fī ṣaḥāriyyi Damdamī
   'She dropped the veil of the tent before her people, hiding from them in the deserts of Damdam.'

Cf.: *idhi ntabadhat min ahlihā makānan sharqiyyan fa-ttakhadhat min dūnihim ḥijāban*: Qurʾān 19/16–17.

9. *fa-qālat* [i.e. *Maryamu*] *lahū* [i.e. *li-l-malʾaki*] *annā yakūnu wa-lam akun baghiyyan wa-lā ḥublā wa-lā dhāta qayyimī*
'Mary said to the angel: Whence shall this be, as I am not a whore, not pregnant and not married?'

Cf.: *qālat annā yakūnu lī ghulāmun wa-lam yamsasnī basharun wa-lam aku baghiyyan*: Qurʾān 19/20; *qālat rabbi annā yakūnu lī waladun wa-lam yamsasnī basharun*: Qurʾān 3/47.

11. *fa-sabbaḥa thumma ghtarrahā fa-ltaqat bihī*
ghulāman sawiyya l-khalqi laysa bi-tawʾamī
'The angel praised God and then came over her unexpectedly, and she conceived from him a well-proportioned boy, no weakling.' *sabbaḥa* said of angels: Qurʾān, passim.

12. *bi-nafkhatihī fī l-ṣadri min jaybi dirʿihā*
wa-mā yaṣrami l-raḥmānu mil-amri yuṣramī
'by his breathing into her breast through the bosom of her garment, and what the Merciful decides is decided.'

Cf.: *ka-dhālika llāhu yakhluqu mā yashāʾu idhā qaḍā amran fa-innamā yaqūlu lahū kun fa-yakūnu*: Qurʾān 3/47; *wa-kāna amran maqḍiyyan*: Qurʾān 19/21.

The last two lines show that the Qurʾān is not only quoted or paraphrased but occasionally interpreted in agreement with the *tafsīr*. Whereas in the Qurʾān the creative breath seems to come directly from God (*wa-Maryama bnata ʿImrāna llatī aḥṣanat farjahā fa-nafakhnā fīhi min rūḥinā*: Qurʾān 66/12), the commentators of the Qurʾān, apparently from a desire to avoid anthropomorphism, make Gabriel, at God's command, breathe into Mary's garment, which is what Umayya's line seems to imply.[15]

The second example does not contain any borrowings from the Qurʾān at all; it consists of two fragments (taken from an ensemble completely composed of fragments) both showing the same rhyme and probably belonging together. The first fragment is quoted in several sources, the oldest of which date from the 3rd/9th century. Variant readings abound, and the text is difficult to understand. I therefore give the sources, the text in Arabic characters and the critical apparatus in an Appendix.

Umayya 25/10–14 SCHULTHESS = 10/10–14 AL-SAṬLĪ = 23/1–3.5–6 AL-ḤADĪTHĪ:

10. 'God made the earth kneel down like a she-camel to be covered by the water until every fire drill was lent (as there was no more dry wood).[16]

11. 'The earth is our refuge and was our mother, in it are our graves, and on it we are born.'

12. 'On it, there are angel-servants[17] on its summits, held in custody standing, their jugular veins trembling (with strain).'

13. 'And God built upon them (heavens) one covering the other and smooth, which do not vanish nor bend.'

14. 'And if you tried to drive a louse over its back, the louse would drop from what is not matted.'

The second fragment is preserved only in al-Maqdisī's *K. al-Badʾ wa-l-tārikh* (Umayya 25/32–37 SCHULTHESS = 10/32–37 AL-SAṬLĪ = 23/21–26 AL-ḤADĪTHĪ; again, there are some difficult passages:

32. *yantābuhu l-mutanaṣṣifūna bi-suḥratin*
fī alfi alfin min malāʾika tuḥshadū
'The servants (i.e. the angels, or: those appealing for justice) come to him (i.e. God) consecutively at the beginning of dawn among a million of gathered angels.'

33. *rusulun yajūbūna l-samāʾa bi-amrihī*
lā yanẓurūna thawāʾa man yataqaṣṣadū
'Messengers traversing the heavens at his command who do not mind that those who have been broken to pieces (or killed) remain (dead).'

34. *fa-humū ka-awbi l-rīḥi baynā adbarat*
rajaᶜat bawādiru wajhihā lā tukradū
'They are like turning wind: he has hardly turned his back when his fore-runners return and cannot be driven away.'

35. *ḥudhdhhun manākibuhum ᶜalā aktāfihim*
ziffun yaziffu bihim idhā mā stunjidū
'Their shoulders have scanty feathers, on their shoulder blades there is plumage which carries them swiftly when they are asked to help.'

36. *wa-idhā talāmīdhu l-ilāhi taᶜāwanū*

ghalabū wa-nashshaṭahum janāḥun muᶜtadū
'And when God's angel-servants assist each other, they are victorious, and a well-prepared wing strengthens them.'

37. *nahaḍū bi-ajniḥatin fa-lam yatawākalū*
lā mubṭiᵓun minhum wa-lā mustawghidū
'They rise with the help of wings without being indifferent (to their duties), are neither sluggish nor weaklings.'

In these fragments, there is not much reminiscent of the Qurᵓān. Of course, the concept of God as the cause of rain in line 10 is compatible with the Qurᵓānic message, but the comparison is not Qurᵓānic, nor are the angelology and cosmology and the concept of 'mother earth' in the remaining lines. Although there was some disagreement in borderline cases, research in the time prior to World War I generally accepted poems like this one as genuine.

The confidence that at least some of the poems ascribed to Umayya might well be authentic was shaken by Tor Andrae, a historian of religion and for a time bishop of Linköping, and it seems to be due to his influence that nowadays nobody in the Western world dares to be serious about Umayya. In his book *Der Ursprung des Islams und das Christentum*, published in 1923–5, Andrae devoted seven pages to Umayya, focussing his attention on those cases in which Umayya seems to display a greater extent of knowledge than the Qurᵓān. He managed to adduce passages from commentaries to the Qurᵓān which, for their part, contain more information than Umayya's poetry.[18] In dealing with the extinction of the Thamūd, we have heard that Umayya on the one hand does not mention the prophet Ṣāliḥ but on the other hand knows the name of the evil-doer who hamstrung the camel, tells of the camel's young crying for punishment and is informed about a girl who escaped and brought the message of the catastrophe to the neighbours before she died. Andrae quotes a report from al-Ṭabarī's commentary to the Qurᵓān which contains details about the evil-doer's origin and of the sacrilege and mentions that the girl's father was called al-Silq (Andrae 52f. [200f.]/59f.). He quotes two more examples of this kind and then concludes that the poems ascribed to Umayya must be pseudepigraphic versifications stemming from the exegetes called *quṣṣāṣ*, whose contribution consisted in providing more detailed reports on Qurᵓānic narrative themes. They sometimes were renegades of Jewish origin or at least had Jewish informants.

Andrae's scepticism has made a lasting impression on scholarship. In the entry on Umayya in the first edition of the *Encyclopaedia of Islam*, for example, Andrae's 'noteworthy arguments' are mentioned; Brockelmann accepted Andrae's views as well as Blachère who, in his *Histoire de la littérature arabe*, is willing to accept as genuine only the poems dealing with profane matters.[19]

Yet, in 1939, Joachim W. Hirschberg cast his vote against Andrae. Hirschberg, in his Cracow doctoral dissertation entitled *Jüdische und christliche Lehren im vor- und frühislamischen Arabien*, tries to show that there is reason enough to assume that Umayya had drawn his information from pre-Islamic Haggada and therefore is independent of Islamic exegesis; as a matter of fact, he is able to adduce Jewish texts which no doubt can corroborate this theory (Hirschberg [1939]). Regrettably, his monograph is somewhat ill-constructed, and certain arguments are not very convincing. Johann Fück wrote a gruff review,[20] and Hirschberg's contribution was dismissed.

Nevertheless, the material he presents is very useful. One of Andrae's three examples for Qurʾānic exegesis as a source for pseudo-Umayya is a report on the sacrifice of Abraham's son which goes back to al-Suddī. Here, the son asks his father to fasten his shackles so that he will not wince. This is exactly what Umayya reports:

Umayya 29/15 SCHULTHESS = 62/15 AL-SAṬLĪ = 87/7 Al-ḤADĪTHĪ

(fa-ajāba l-ghulāmu . . .) wa-shdudi l-ṣafda an aḥīda ᶜani l-sikkīni ḥayda l-asīri dhī l-aghlālī
'(And the son answered:) "and fasten the shackles because I might dodge the knife, as does the captive caught in chains."'

In the Qurʾān, on the other hand, these details are not mentioned. Hirschberg (1939) (p. 126f.) quotes several pre-Islamic Haggadic passages which give the reason for these requests: according to Talmudic regulations, a sacrificial animal must not twitch when slaughtered; if this happens, the sacrifice is not valid.[21] There are some other cases where Hirschberg adduces Haggadic material which explains certain lines of Umayya that are otherwise difficult to understand. To give just one more example: without giving any explanation, Umayya mentions that the sun has to be forced to rise in the morning:

Umayya 25/47 SCHULTHESS = 10/29 AL-SAṬLĪ = 22/12 Al-ḤADĪTHĪ

laysat (i.e. *al-shamsu) bi-ṭāliᶜatin lahum fī rislihā illā muᶜadhdhabatan wa-illā tujladū*
'The sun rises for them slowly only after it has been punished and flogged.'

The Haggadic reports tell us that the sun would rather not rise because it is ashamed that mankind adores it (Hirschberg [1939] p. 91).[22]

Summarizing Hirschberg's contribution, we can note that there are some pre-Islamic Jewish sources which might very well represent Umayya's background. Parallels between Umayya and Muslim exegesis do not therefore prove that 'Umayya' is forgery based on the latter; they can just as well be explained assuming that both are dependent on the same tradition. Moreover, we cannot exclude the possibility that Muslim *tafsīr* presents Haggada-like reports on the Qurʾān *and* Umayya even in cases where the latter's name is not mentioned. As for Umayya's possible informants, it is interesting to read in al-Balādhurī that there were Jews living in the district of pre-Islamic Ṭāʾif; according to him, they were expelled from Yathrib and the Yemen.[23]

So far, we have heard about two stages in research: the first one took place in the years 1904 to 1912 and was devoted to editing and sorting out cases of obvious dependence on the Qurʾān, the second one consisted of Andrae's sceptical attack with its aftermath in the statements of Brockelmann and Blachère and in Hirschberg's answer, which was presented in insufficiently clear terms and therefore inadequately taken note of by other scholars. The third and so far last phase of scholarly preoccupation with Umayya took place in the seventies in the Arab world. The editions of al-Ḥadīthī and al-Saṭlī mentioned above contain introductions of 150 and 330 pages respectively. While al-Ḥadīthī gives only a general statement on the question of authenticity,[24] al-Saṭlī explains in detail which poem he considers for what reasons as a) genuine or forged very well, b) questionable but not definitively forged or c) definitively forged. In this, he follows a comparatively sceptical course. In some cases, he is overly critical, for example when he summarily dismisses the *kāmil* 'poem' rhyming in *-dū* (Nr. 25 ed. Schulthess/Nr. 10 ed. al-Saṭlī) from which we quoted above. The 50 line 'poem' consists, to say it again, of several fragments collected from a number of sources. These 50 lines are rejected altogether because he regards line 15 and line 27f. as containing purely Islamic elements. In line 15, the seventh heaven is called inaccessible, in line 27f. shooting stars are explained as missiles launched in order to chase away eavesdropping devils (*shayāṭīn*). Al-Saṭlī quotes reports from al-Ṭabarī's commentary on the Qurʾān which state that the heavens were not regulated in the time before the prophet Muḥammad; he furthermore points to the fact that in Qurʾān 72/8–10 (which speaks about some demons, *nafarun mina l-jinni*) this 'shooting star myth' is told as something unheard of by the *jinn* (al-Saṭlī [1977] p. 190f.). Even if we accept this argument, one could still ask whether the possibly Islamic origin of lines 27f. (which are transmitted in isolation) must necessarily affect the status of the remaining fragments bearing the same rhyme and metre.

Nevertheless, a comparison of his results with those reached by Frank-Kamenetzky is quite interesting. The latter came, as we have heard, to consider 225 lines with a religious thematic as genuine, while al-Saṭlī regards only 104 lines out of a larger number on religious matters as authentic. The most important point is that these 104 lines, with the exception of six, are regarded as authentic by Frank-Kamenetzky *as well*. As al-Saṭlī arrived at his results more or less independently of Frank-Kamenetzky, this shows that there must be criteria which can be objectivized.

However, we have not heard the last of Umayya. Laudable as the editions of al-Ḥadīthī and al-Saṭlī are, they contain incomplete or erroneous explanations, do not give all variant readings and could be enlarged with the help of the numerous editions of primary sources published since the seventies. Further, the possible motives of forgeries should be examined.[25] Finally, neither al-Ḥadīthī nor al-Saṭlī has made use of the analysis of Frank-Kamenetzky and the material presented by Hirschberg. The task of an authoritative edition and translation and a balancing of all arguments about authenticity against each other still has to be carried out. What I have tried to show is that there might well be some authentic material among the nearly 900 lines ascribed to Umayya. Also there is a very early testimony to Umayya's fame as an author of a special sort of poetry, namely a line by Surāqa al-Aṣghar who died about 700 A.D.:

(wa-dhkur Labīdan . . .) wa-Umayyata l-baḥra lladhī fī shiᶜrihī ḥikamun ka-waḥyin fī l-zabūri mufaṣṣalī
'(Remember Labīd . . .) and Umayya, the "sea" (of knowledge) in whose poetry are pieces of wisdom like a detailed revelation (or: book?) in the Psalter.'[26]

Appendix: Umayya 25/10–14 SCHULTHESS = 10/10–14 AL-SAṬLĪ = 23/1–3.5–6 AL-ḤADĪTHĪ

V. 10–11: Jāḥiẓ, *Ḥayawān* III 363 ult. – 364, 1

V. 11–14: Jāḥiẓ, *Ḥayawān* V 437, 8 – 438, 2; al-Shantamarī, *Sharḥ abyāt al-Īḍāḥ* (?), manuscript of the Oriental Library, St. Joseph's University, Beirut (as quoted by Power [1906] p. 204, footnote 9)

V. 11–12: Baghdādī, *Tilmīdh* 222, 4f.
V. 10: Jāḥiẓ, *Ḥayawān* III 365, 10; b. Qutayba, *Mushkil* 68 pL.; *Lisān al-ᶜarab* 3, 218 b 7f. (*sfd*) = *Tāj al-ᶜarūs* 2, 380, 3 (*sfd*) = Lane 1370 a (*sfd*)
V. 11: b. Qutayba, *Mushkil* 76 ult.; Thaᶜlabī, *Qiṣaṣ* 7, 17; *Mukhaṣṣaṣ* 13, 180 apu.; Qurṭubī, *Jāmiᶜ* I 112, 9
V. 12: *Qāmūs*, Turkish translation (as quoted by Fleischer [1885] I 62, 19)
V. 14: b. Qutayba, *Maᶜānī* 633, 4

١٠ وَالأَرْضُ نَوَّخَهَا الإِلٰهُ طَرُوقَةً　　لِلْمَاءِ حَتَّى كُلُّ زَنْدٍ مُسْفَدُ
١١ وَالأَرْضُ مَعْقِلُنَا وَكَانَتْ أُمَّنَا　　فِيهَا مَقَابِرُنَا وَفِيهَا نُولَدُ
١٢ فِيهَا تَلامِيذٌ عَلَى قُذُفَاتِهَا　　حُبِسُوا قِيَامًا فَالْفَرَائِصُ تُرْعَدُ
١٣ فَبَنَى الإِلٰهُ عَلَيْهِمُ مَخْصُوفَةً　　خَلْقَاءَ لا تَبْلَى وَلا تَتَأَوَّدُ
١٤ فَلَوَ انَّهُ تَحْذُو الْبُرَامَ بِمَتْنِهَا　　زَلَّ الْبُرَامُ عَنِ الَّتِي لا تَقْرَدُ

.10 نوّخها Jāḥiẓ *Ḥayaw.*, b. Qut. *Mushkil* : صيّرها *Lisān, Tāj*, Lane *

.11 مقابرنا Jāḥiẓ *Ḥayaw.* III, b. Qut. *Mushkil*, Thaᶜl. *Qiṣaṣ*, Qurṭubī *Jāmiᶜ*:
معاقلنا Jāḥiẓ *Ḥayaw.* V, Shant. *Sharḥ* : معايشنا *Mukhaṣṣaṣ* :
مقامتنا Baghd. *Tilmidh* *
وفيها Jāḥiẓ *Ḥayaw.*, b. Qut. *Mushkil*, Thaᶜl. *Qiṣaṣ*, Shant. *Sharḥ* :
ومنها *Mukhaṣṣaṣ* *

.12 فيها Jāḥiẓ *Ḥayaw.*, Shant. *Sharḥ* : وبها Baghd. *Tilmīdh, Qāmūs*
تلاميذ على قذفاتها Jāḥiẓ *Ḥayaw.*, Baghd. *Tilmīdh, Qāmūs*:
تلامذة على قدمائها Jāḥiẓ *Ḥayaw.* variant:
تلامذة على قذفاتها Shant. *Sharḥ* *
حبسوا Jāḥiẓ *Ḥayaw.*, Baghd. *Tilmīdh, Qāmūs*
حسر ، خسرا Jāḥiẓ *Ḥayaw.* variants : حسرى Shant. *Sharḥ* *
فالفرائص Jāḥiẓ *Ḥayaw.*, Baghd. *Tilmīdh, Qāmūs* :
والفرائض Shant. *Sharḥ* *

.13 مخصوفة Jāḥiẓ *Ḥayaw.*, Shant. *Sharḥ* : محصوفة Jāḥiẓ *Ḥayaw.*. variant *

* Jāḥiẓ *Ḥayaw.* variant فلا : Jāḥiẓ *Ḥayaw.*, Shant. *Sharḥ* لا

: Jāḥiẓ *Ḥayaw.* variant يحدو : Jāḥiẓ *Ḥayaw.* تحدو .14

: Shant. *Sharḥ* Ms. يخد

* b. Qut. *Ma^{c}ānī* يجد : ed. Schulthess (conj.) يجدو : Shant. *Sharḥḥ* تجد

: Jāḥiẓ *Ḥayaw.*, Shant. *Sharḥ*, b. Qut. *Ma^{c}ānī* البرام

* Jāḥiẓ *Ḥayaw..* variant البؤام

* Shant. *Sharḥ* لمتنها : Jāḥiẓ *Ḥayaw.*, b. Qut. *Ma^{c}ānī* بمتنها

: Jāḥiẓ *Ḥayaw.* variant لبنى وألفاها : Jāḥiẓ *Ḥayaw.* زلّ البرام عن

* b. Qut. *Ma^{c}ānī* صعدا لألفاها : Shant. *Sharḥ* لبنى وألقاها

Abbreviated Literature

Andrae (1923): Tor Andrae, *Der Ursprung des Islams und das Christentum* (Uppsala/Stockholm, 1926 [originally published in *Kyrkhistorisk Årsskrift* 23 [1923] pp. 149–206, 24 [1924] pp. 213–92, 25 [1925] pp. 25–112])/ *Les origines de l'Islam et le Christianisme*, transl. Jules Roche (Paris, 1955)

Bustānī (1942): Buṭrus al-Bustānī, 'Umayya b. a. al-Ṣalt al-Thaqafī, *al-Mashriq* 46 (1942) 201–20

Fleischer (1885): Heinrich Leberecht Fleischer, *Kleinere Schriften*, 3 vols. (Leipzig, 1885–8)

Frank-Kamenetzky (1911): Israel Frank-Kamenetzky, *Untersuchungen über das Verhältnis der dem Umajja b. Abi ṣ Ṣalt zugeschriebenen Gedichte zum Qorān*, (Diss. Königsberg: Kirchhain N.L., 1911)

al-Ḥadīthī (1975): Bahja ^{c}Abd al-Ghafūr al-Ḥadīthī, *Umayya b. a. al-Ṣalt. Ḥayātuhu wa-Shi^{c}ruhu* (Baghdad, 1975)

Huart (1904): Clément Huart, 'Une nouvelle source du Qorān', *Journal Asiatique*, Sér. 10, 4 (1904) pp. 125–67

Ḥusayn (1927): Ṭāhā Ḥusayn, *Fī al-Adab al-Jāhilī* (Cairo, 1927; here used in the 12th ed. 1977)

Lane: Edward William Lane, *Arabic-English Lexicon*, 8 vols. (London, 1863–93)

Nöldeke (1912): Theodor Nöldeke, 'Umaija b. AbiṣṢalt', *Zeitschrift für Assyriologie* 27 (1912) pp. 159–72

al-Rabī^{c}ī (1979): Aḥmad al-Rabī^{c}ī, 'Umayya b. a. al-Ṣalt', *al-Balāgh* 7, 10 (1979) pp. 38–44

Rubin (1990): Uri Rubin, '*Ḥanafiyya* and *Ka^{c}ba*. An inquiry into the Arabic pre-Islamic background of *dīn Ibrāhīm*', *Jerusalem Studies in Arabic and Islam* 13 (1990) pp. 85–112

al-Saṭlī (1977):, ^{c}Abd al-Ḥafiẓ al-Saṭlī, '*Umayya b. a. al-Ṣalt*', (Damascus,[2] 1977)

Vallaro (1978): Michele Vallaro, 'Umayya ibn Abī ṣ-Ṣalt nella seconda parte del "*Kitāb az-Zahrah*" di Ibn Dāwūd al-Iṣfahānī (manoscritto di Torino)", *Atti della Accademia Nazionale dei Lincei. Memorie. Classe di Scienze morali, storiche e filologiche* 22, 4 (1978) (p. 423–8)

Arabic Sources

Baghdādī, *Tilmīdh* ᶜAbd al-Qādir al-Baghdādī, *Risālat al-Tilmīdh*, ed. ᶜAbd al-Salām Muḥ. Hārūn, *Nawādir al-Makhṭūṭāt* (Cairo,² 1973) pp. 217–25

Jāḥiẓ, *Ḥayawān* a. ᶜUthmān b. Baḥr al-Jāḥiẓ, *K. al-Ḥayawān*, ed. ᶜAbd al-Salām Muḥ. Hārūn, 7 vols. (Cairo 1938–45)

Lisān al-ᶜarab Jamāl al-Dīn a. al-Faḍl Muḥ. b. Mukarram al-Ifrīqī, *Lisān al-ᶜArab*, 15 vols. (Beirut, 1955)

Mukhaṣṣaṣ a. al-Ḥasan ᶜAlī b. Ismāᶜīl b. Sīda, *K. al-Mukhaṣṣaṣ*, 17 vols. (Būlāq, 1898–1903)

Qurṭubī, *Jāmiᶜ* a. ᶜAbd Allāh Muḥ. b. Aḥmad al-Qurṭubī, *al-Jāmiᶜ li-Aḥkām al-Qurʾān*, 20 vols. (Beirut, 1985 [repr.])

b. Qutayba, *Maᶜānī* a. Muḥ. ᶜAbd Allāh b. Muslim b. Qutayba, *K. al-Maᶜānī al-Kabīr fī Abyāt al-Maᶜānī*, 3 vols. (Hyderabad, 1949–50)

b. Qutayba, *Mushkil* id. *Taʾwīl Mushkil al-Qurʾān*, ed. al-Sayyid Aḥmad Ṣaqr (Cairo, 1954)

Tāj al-ᶜarūs a. al-Faḍl Muḥ. Murtaḍā b. Muḥ. al-Zabīdī, *Tāj al-ᶜArūs*, 10 vols. (Bengasi, n.d. [repr.])

Thaᶜlabī *Qiṣaṣ* a. Isḥāq Aḥmad b. Muḥ. al-Thaᶜlabī, *K. Qiṣaṣ al-Anbiyāʾ al-Musammā bi-l-ᶜArāʾis* (Cairo, ²1951)

Notes

1 Cf. the discussion in Huart (1904) pp. 135 f.; al-Ḥadīthī (1975) pp. 57–64; al-Rabīᶜī (1979) pp. 40–2; al-Saṭlī (1977) pp. 55–68. That Umayya at some time of his life adopted Islam is quite unlikely. Schulthess (1911) p. 7 f. seems at least willing to take this into consideration, but was rejected by Power (1912) p. 183*–190*; cf. Vallaro (1978) p. 430 f. footnote 45; Rubin (1990) p. 96; al-Saṭlī (1977) p. 40. In the years 1993 and 1994 I read papers on Umayya at the Oriental Institutes of the universities of Berlin (FU, Semitistik – Arabistik), Kiel and Hamburg. I would like to thank those present on thos occasions, as well as the participants in the 2nd Shaban Memorial Conference for their comments and suggestions.

2 Inaugurated by Christian Snouck Hurgronje in his doctoral dissertation *Het Mekkaansche Feest*, generally accessible in id., *Verspreide Geschriften*, vol. I (Bonn/Leipzig, 1923).

3 Rubin (1990) pp. 85–112.

4 W. Montgomery Watt and Alford T. Welch, *Der Islam* I (Stuttgart etc., 1980).

5 A.F.L. Beeston et al., *Arabic Literature to the End of the Umayyad Period* (Cambridge etc., 1983).

6 *Der Koran. Einführung – Texte – Erläuterungen* (München, 1983).

7 The most extensive treatment of Umayya's "biography" is al-Saṭlī (1977) pp. 33–85 (Addenda p. 697); cf. also al-Ḥadīthī (1975) pp. 46–70; Schulthess (1906) pp. 72–6; Power (1906) pp. 208–10.

8 See al-Saṭlī (1977) pp. 86–92 (and in addition the reference in Power [1912] p. 146 footnote 1). On a collection of 300 of Umayya's poems in a 'book' *(kitāb)* by Jarīr b. Ḥāzim al-Baṣrī or his son Wahb b. Jarīr cf. ᶜAbd

al-Malik b. Qurayb al-Aṣmaᶜī, *Fuḥūlat al-shuᶜarā'*, ed. Charles Torrey, *Zeitschrift der Deutschen Morgenländischen Gesellschaft* 65 (1911) p. 500/ed. Muḥammad ᶜAbd al-Munᶜim Khafājī and Ṭāhā Muḥammad al-Zaynī (Cairo, 1953) p. 33.

9 See Schulthess (1906) p. 72 and Saṭlī (1977) pp. 121–4.

10 Schulthess (1911). Additional material was published by Power (1912).

11 A second edition was published in 1977 which contains an appendix (pp. 673–95) with seven poems or fragments (46 new lines) (= al-Saṭlī [1977]).

12 Independently of al-Saṭlī and al-Ḥadīthī, Vallaro (1978) published material not contained in Schulthess's edition from Ibn Dāwūd's *K. al-Zahra* which is, however, included in the edition of al-Ḥadīthī and the second edition of al-Saṭlī. Vallaro abstains from developing his own ideas about the issue of authenticity while confessing that he instinctively feels more attracted by Andrae's critical approach (Vallaro [1978] pp. 471f.).

13 *Das Leben und die Lehre des Moḥammad nach bisher grösstentheils unbenutzten Quellen bearbeitet* (Berlin, 1861–5), vol. I, pp. 76–81 and 110–19.

14 Schulthess (1906); Power (1906); Schulthess (1911), introduction; Frank-Kamenetzky (1911); Nöldeke (1912); Power (1912).

15 Cf. Thomas J. O'Shaughnessy, *The Development of the Meaning of Spirit in the Koran* (Rome, 1953) p. 63.

16 This is the explanation given in *Lisān al-ᶜarab* (and *Tāj al-ᶜarūs* and Lane), cf. the quotations given for line 10 in the Appendix. A different explanation is proposed by b. Qutayba, *Mushkil* p. 69, lff.; he takes the two woods used to make fire as the parents and the fire as the child. A third explanation is given by Schulthess [1911] p. 85 in his translation *'bis jedes (kleinste) Feuerholz begattet war'*, obviously implying that the rain makes the wood grow (cf. his footnote 6). But *zand* means the fire drill and not the plant from which it is taken, and *asfada* means 'to make cover', not 'to cover'.

17 Cf. *talāmidhu l-ilāhi* in line 36 below.

18 Andrae (1923) p. 48 [196] – 56 [204]/55–63.

19 *Enzyklopaedie des Islām*, vol. IV (Leiden/Leipzig, 1934) p. 1080 b (H.H. Bräu); Carl Brockelmann, *Geschichte der arabischen Litteratur*, Erster Supplementband (Leiden, 1937) p. 55; Régis Blachère, *Histoire de la littérature arabe* (Paris, 1952–66) p. 305f.

20 *Orientalische Literaturzeitung* 44 (1941) col. 76f.

21 The following line reads: *innanī ālamu l-maḥazza wa-innī lā amassu* (or *amassa?) l-adhqāna dhāta l-sibāli.* On the interpretation cf. Schulthess' translation (Schulthess [1911] p. 93); H. Reckendorf's remark in *Orientalische Literaturzeitung* 15 (1912) col. 214; al-Saṭlī (1977) p. 442, footnote 5. Even if this line gives a reason for the son's request (which is not sure), this would not make Hirschberg's explanation superfluous.

22 Similar reports are found in Islamic sources, cf. Frank-Kamenetzky (1911) p. 42 footnote 3 (from p. 40); Hirschberg (1939) p. 91; al-Saṭlī (1977) p. 366 footnote 2.

23 Aḥmad b. Yaḥyā al-Balādhurī, *K. Futūḥ al-Buldān*, ed. M.J. de Goeje (Leiden, 1866) p. 56 line 10.

24 On p. 127, he accepts as probably genuine those poems in which there are

traces of the *ḥanīfiyya* and the holy books of the Jews and Christians, whereas he dismisses poems showing influence of the Qurʾān and written in pallid style. This is acceptable in general, but there will be room for considerable disagreement where the classification of single poems is concerned.

25 So far, the following motives have been mentioned: the tabooing of imitating the Qurʾān (Power [1912] p. 190*f.; Werner Caskel, *Ġamharat an-nasab. Das genealogische Werk des Hišām ibn Muḥammad al-Kalbī*, vol. 2 [Leiden, 1966] p. 570b); attempts to improve the esteem of the tribe Thaqīf, unpopular by the role of al-Mughīra b. Shuʿba, Ziyād b. Abīhi, ʿUbaydallāh b. Ziyād, al-Ḥajjāj and others (Nöldeke [1912] p. 161 footnote l; Bustānī [1942] p. 210); attempts to make Umayya a Muslim (Power [1912] p. 190*f.); attempts to fabricate a pre-Islamic monotheism on the Arabian peninsula (Ḥusayn [1927] p. 145).

26 Cf. al-Rabīʿī (1979) p. 42; al-Ḥadīthī (1975) p. 50; Nāṣir al-Dīn al-Asad, *Maṣādir al-shiʿr al-jāhilī* (Cairo, 1982), p. 230. Cf. also S.M. Husain, 'The poems of Surâqah b. Mirdâs al-Bâriqî – an Umayyad poet', *Journal of the Royal Asiatic Society* (1936) p. 610, 8f.

8

The Hunt in the Arabic *Qaṣīdah*

The Antecedents of the *Ṭardiyyah*

Jaroslav Stetkevych
University of Chicago

Arabic poetry is a poetry of a very clearly circumscribed repertory of themes. With much formal rigour these themes are distributed over the Arabic poem's (*qaṣīdah*'s) three structural 'sections', – the *nasīb* (elegiac-lyrical prelude), the *raḥīl* (desert journey), and the *fakhr* (self-exaltation) or *madḥ* (encomium) – themselves very clearly circumscribed and defined as components of a quite architectonic construct. These structural sections then determine not only the kind of themes they accept but, even more importantly, they impose or, as it were, pre-determine the moods that will rule over the repertory of poetic themes by 'modulating' them – and that will ultimately give those themes their abiding semanticity. Because of the very rigorous structural system that is thus engendered, Arabic poetry is, necessarily, a poetry that in its praxis of achieving individual, and original, works of art expands, or rather 'impends', toward the interior – its own interior. It is formally, structurally, and thematically highly inward looking and capable of its own 'private' exaltations and self-absorbed refinements – and these exaltations and self-absorptions are also its limitations. This comes to the fore especially in that poetry's formal, and indeed formalist, confines, which do not allow it much room for a loosening, or dissipation, of perspectives, or of idiosyncracies other than the idiosyncracy of genre, nor of formal exploratory manoeuverability outside those established confines – all these being the things which in modern literary-critical parlance we have come to call 'creative poetic freedom'. To look for such notions of 'poetic freedom', however, would be in the case of the classical Arabic sense of form no less than anachronistic.

A further particularity and specificity of classical Arabic poetry is that not only are its themes, genre-variants, and moods in their extreme internal rigour and sustained pre-selectivity poetically 'radical' and 'central' (having become unavoidable, indisplaceable, and nonreplaceable), but that, ruled by some even more central and radical imperative, they all cluster together, ordered with much self-conscious formalist neatness, into the single and formally singular system of poetic expression called the *qaṣīdah*.

In this, Arabic poetry is not only specific and capable of self-definition: it may be said to be unique among the major poetries known to us. In so full a sense and to such a degree of formal comprehensiveness, Arabic poetry, in the form of the *qaṣīdah*, thus experiences its true canon-setting classicism between the pre-Islamic and the mid-Umayyad periods. There it is all and many, all in one. It speaks of the totality of experience each time a poet speaks through it.

Therefore, too, for the purposes of discussing the genre-genesis and the genre quality of the Arabic hunting poem, the *ṭardiyyah*, we have to turn to the basic formal questions harboured in the fully structured pre-Islamic Arabic *qaṣīdah*. For the genre-formation of the Arabic hunting poem is in all respects an outgrowth of the themes contained in, and in their semiotics and purport defined by, specific structural parts, or sections, of the *qaṣīdah*. The structural specificity of those parts or sections will be not only the point of departure for the subsequently born genre-poem, the *ṭardiyyah*, but it will also determine much of the referential semantics of the *ṭardiyyah* as a total poem and, within it, the nature, behavior, and variety of the animals that constitute its 'object', that is, the quarry.

For that we have to remind ourselves that in the structurally fully articulated classical Arabic *qaṣīdah* the subject of the hunt is divided with the utmost formal rigour between two of its three paradigmatic sections (that are also its, the *qaṣīdah*'s, thematic and modal units). These are, firstly, the poet's liminal 'desert journey' (*raḥīl*) section and, secondly, the celebratory, or self-celebratory, section of the poet's re-entry into, or return to, his reconstituted sense of self and community (*fakhr*, both individual and tribal; and/or *madḥ*).[1] This structural differentiation has its drastic thematic consequences, inasmuch as in the properly classical *qaṣīdah* one must indeed speak of two *different* hunts: the hunt of the animal panels in the *raḥīl* section, which may be terminologically qualified as *ṣayd* or *qanṣ*, and the hunt of the third, 'reintegrative' structural section, which may only be viewed as, and thus be termed, a *ṭard*, that is, a 'chase on horseback'. This latter terminological specification also tells us that the subsequent – post-classical – independent genre of the *ṭardiyyah* must in some primary, or even paradigmatic, sense be relatable to the original thematic and structural section of the *qaṣīdah* in which there takes place a 'chivalrous chase'. By the same token, the designation of the post-classical genre-poem as a *ṭardiyyah* will tell us that between it and the hunting scenes of the liminal *qaṣīdah* section of the *raḥīl* there must exist a 'substrative' difference of meaning – that is, a difference that draws upon the deepest affinities of semiotic polarity: a paradox.

First of all, in the *raḥīl* section the protagonist is not the hunter but the hunted animal itself. This animal is for the most part an oryx bull or cow, a wild ass, or, more rarely, an ostrich; and from its encounter with the hunter it must emerge victorious, unless the poem in which this type of hunting scene figures is an elegy, for only then is the quarry – still a protagonist – a tragic figura.[2]

The hunter himself in the *raḥīl*-framed scene of the hunt is invariably a personification of despondency and failure, as well as of a distinct social destitution. In brief, he is not only poor but also fated to be unlucky; and there is almost an air of wrong to his very pursuit of his quarry. He is, as it were, a poacher, as though he had no real right to intrude into the realm of the animal world itself.

This stripping of the *raḥīl* hunter even of his skill-acquired chances at success in the hunt, or, what is more, of his entitlement to sustenance, has as its primary reason the fact that in the hunt panels of the classical *raḥīl* the hunted animals stand formally as similes of the poet's precious mount, his she-camel (*nāqah*), while the she-camel herself is none other than an archaic, totemic expression of the poet's own indomitable *anima* – or his quite Frazerian 'external soul'.[3] Behind the twofold mask, the poet is thus himself the tried and tested, ultimately redeemed by the singular prowess of the victorious quarry. Together, therefore, the she-camel and her own similes or personifications – the oryx, the wild ass, the ostrich – constitute the broad allegory of the desert-crossing poet's own liminality, in which he survives as long as she survives, as long as they survive.

For that reason, only in the Bedouin elegy, where the allegory becomes one of death, not of life, not only does the 'substitute' animal die, but it *must* die. Such is the symbolic logic of the hunt in the *raḥīl*. The representational realism of the hunt in the *raḥīl*, including the specific sociology of the hunter, has led literary criticism astray much too often, however, into not looking beyond the well-crafted image framed quite panel-like, and thus thought to be detachable from the semiotics of the structure of the *raḥīl* and its functionality therein – this in disregard of the fact that the *raḥīl* is no more than a constituent part of the only truly sufficient frame and structure which is the *qaṣīdah*. Thus the hunt in the *raḥīl*.

As for the hunt which takes place in the 'third', or reintegrative, structural section of the classical *qaṣīdah*, that is, *fakhr* (self-exaltation) or *madḥ* (encomium), in it there must as a rule be no further reference to the she-camel and the 'animal panels'; for the liminal journey is now over, and the poet is no longer traveling alone in a danger-filled desert. Instead he finds himself again in his tribal community, or at a patron's 'court'. There he must engage in and practice certain given and firmly established customs and social, or communal, rituals. These communal acts are then either celebratory, such as banquets, homages, etc., or expressedly and, as it were, iconically heroic, such as the gallant hunt.

This other hunt must thus, almost in all respects, be fundamentally different from the hunt in the *raḥīl*. First of all, in it the protagonist is no longer the quarry but – manifestly – the hunter himself. As such he must be the victor, and as such he must also be endowed with all the attributes of gallantry, skill, and heroic demeanour. Indeed, he must quite paradigmatically represent, or embody, the champion of the community. Another decisive and, one should say, iconic characteristic of this type of the hunt scene is that in it the hunter, gallant and heroic in his total appearance, is always, and necessarily, a *horseman*. Such a hunt is thus distinctly a 'chivalrous hunt'; and, by terminological definition, it is a *chase*, thus a *ṭard*. A third difference is the rigourous rule regarding the type of hunting weapon the respective hunters are assigned.

The despondent and wretched 'poacher' of the *raḥīl*-hunt may use only the bow, never a spear or javelin. With his bow he hides either behind a hill or dune, or in a hunter's blind (*qutrah*, pl. *qutar*), from behind which he shoots his ever-failing arrow: thus in the hunt of the wild ass. If his quarry is the oryx bull or cow, he relies furthermore on his dogs, which are doomed to be equally unsuccessful.

By contrast, the huntsman-as-horseman, who, in the fullest sense figures as the 'chivalrous hunter', may never use bow and arrow, which would be beneath the dignity, or the heroic code and quality, of a horseman and a hunter. His weapon is the javelin or the spear alone, never a bow.

These are matters of almost unfailing semiotics that rule explicitly the *matter* of the hunt in the classical Arabic *qaṣīdah* and which, implicitly, through their structural efficacy, determine much of the formal and thematic semantics of the *qaṣīdah* as a whole. Above all, in their ritualized quality, they transcend the literalist levels of the *qaṣīdah*'s meaning.

As our hermeneutical backdrop and as examples of the two essential paradigms of the theme of the hunt in the classical Arabic *qaṣīdah*, we shall quote from three poets.

1. For the *raḥīl*-framed occurrence of the 'wild ass' panel the example will come from the already *mukhaḍram* (of the generation bridging the late pre-Islamic and early Islamic periods) poet Rabīᶜah Ibn Maqrūm.
2. For the panel of the oryx (cow), also structurally and thematically part of the *raḥīl*, it will be from Labīd Ibn Rabīᶜah of the *Muᶜallaqāt*.
3. The paradigm of the theme of the 'chivalrous hunt', strictly non-*raḥīl*, will, compellingly, be from the *Muᶜallaqah* of Imruᵓ al-Qays.

Rabīᶜah Ibn Maqrūm's hunt scene of the 'wild ass' occurs in the *Mufaḍḍaliyah* no. 38, vv. 6–19. Its obligatory framework is the 'description' of the poet's mount, his she-camel: the poet has turned away from the melancholy site of an abandoned encampment. As dictated by Bedouin custom and, above all, by poetic canon, the poet mounts his singularly endowed riding animal, which is a she-camel. To her he gives free rein to carry him off (v. 6). The characteristic, and again strictly canon-imposed epithetic representation of the she-camel[4] follows (vv. 6–8): she is of the light color of good breed, strong, one that never tires. Her flesh is compacted. Quite as a male, she is resilient, never emitting a groan of complaint.

It is at this point of descriptive exaltation that, as the she-camel's representational enhancement, there is introduced the simile of the onager stallion with his three onager mares. This simile, in its ekphrastic[5] and altogether panel-like self-containment, then leads to, or rather integrally enframes, the scene of the hunt:

8. To me she was like a cross-girded,
   Slender-bellied onager, white on his sides,
   coarse, mean-demeanored.
9. Three mares, thinned out like spear shafts,
   He wards off from water,
   even as they burn with thirst.
10. He had let them graze on rocky hills till the herbage
   around water pockets
   All wilted and the simoon beset him.
11. So parched they stood,
   contracted eyes toward the sun,
   Fearful of succumbing.
12. And when he clearly saw that the day had expired,
   And he felt dense darkness coming on,
13. He thrust them into the midst of night,
   himself by their side,

A fierce biter, driving them on by constant nipping.
14. And with the light of morning he took them
Down the paths that led to waterholes,
whose dense overgrowth they cleared,
15. Whose water swelled over, greenish black,
the colour of the nightly sky,[6]
Its pearly bubbles outshining the stars.
16. But there, at the water, stands Qays Abū ᶜĀmir,
For a while he gives them hope and respite.[7]
17. In his hand, arched, a Ḥirmī bow:
Of those of single bough, that rustle and twang.
18. The arrow slender, the point sharp,
The arrowhead's mounting soaked with blood.
19. And yet he missed them, and off in flight all went,
Well-nigh bursting from their very skins from fright.[8]

As the sister paradigm of the onager hunt, the hunt of the oryx in Labīd's *Muᶜallaqah* (vv. 36–54) is equally illustrative. Here the simile/panel of the oryx cow already follows an extended panel of the onager. Any direct 'description' of the poet's she-camel is, therefore, far behind us (vv. 22–24), at the very outset of the *qaṣīdah*'s *raḥīl* section. And, as regards that main referent of comparison, which is the she-camel, Labīd's oryx cow, in its own ekphrastic panel, is thus a 'twice-removed' simile, one of comparison beyond her comparison with the onager. The poet, therefore, begins this second-level simile/panel:

36. Is she [my camel mare] like this [i. e., the onager] or
like the oryx cow,[9] her calf the wild beasts' prey . . .?

This oryx cow is, furthermore, introduced not so much through an epithetic 'description' as through an intense dramatization: her calf has fallen prey to wild beasts. Bereft, from stony tract to stony tract, from dune to dune, she roams, calling her calf, lowing. But ashen predators, have long since caught up with the half-weaned calf, 'for fate's arrows never miss their mark' (v. 39).

As a thematic unit, however, this scene, the poem's verses 36–39, through which the oryx cow is introduced into her panel, constitutes no more than a preamble to the more strictly paradigmatic core of the oryx panel. It resolves the problem of the radical symbolic identification of the animal that is to become the object of the hunt: that animal, the oryx, must be, as it were, ontologically alone, perceptively, if not 'psychologically', lonely, and existentially solitary – the total *Einzelgänger*.

Being an oryx cow, not a bull, Labīd's oryx/mother had thus first to lose her calf. Only then could she become the iconic 'persona', the embodiment of iconic solitariness required by the archaic symbolic canon ruling the oryx hunt. This is of the essence to the oryx paradigm, as it is – to the same degree – of the essence to the wild ass paradigm that the wild ass be always gregarious and earthy, or, more precisely, the stallion/leader of his own herd/family.

Only in being solitary is the oryx in the *raḥīl* panel of the classical (Bedouin) *qaṣīdah* ready to face the dread-instilling dark, stormy night that precedes the morning of the hunters and the struggle with the unrelenting hounds. This innermost core of the oryx panel in which the animal, all alone, faces the trials of the almost cosmic sense of the darkness of the desert night and of the immediacy, and then reality, of danger, is the true, formally and thematically distilled paradigm of the oryx and its hunt (vv. 40–52). Thus we turn to Labīd's oryx cow in her solitude:

40. She waited through the night beneath a cloud
    that shed an unremitting rain
    And let a ceaseless downpour fall
    upon the dense-grown dunes.
41. Uninterrupted raindrops fell on her spine's track
    In a night whose stars were veiled by clouds.
42. She took shelter in the hollow of a contorted tree
    Set apart upon the edges of the dunes whose drift-sand slopes.
43. And in the first watch of the night her lustrous face
    Gleamed like the diver's pearl, its string drawn forth.
44. Till, when the dark dispelled and dawn shone forth,
    Her hoofs slipped on the early morning's rain-soaked earth.
45. Bewildered, she searched doggedly among Suᶜāᵓid's puddles
    Seven full nights coupled with their days.
46. Until, hope's stores exhausted, and udder, once milk-swollen,
    Neither from suckling nor weaning now gone dry,
47. She heard with dread the buzz of human voice
    That frightened her from unseen side – for mankind is her bane.
48. Then early in the day she ventured forth,
    fearing for head and tail,
    Dangers from behind and from in front
49. Until when the hunters in despair of bow and arrow
    Set on her their rawhide-collared, flop-eared hounds.
50. They overtook her, and she returned their charge

With a horn like a Samharī spear in point and shaft
51. To ward them off, for she knew
If she did not repel them she would die.
52. Fetch was first to fall, smeared all in blood,
Then Blackie was left for dead where he had charged.
53. On this one when sun's shimmerings
dance in full forenoon light,
And the hillocks don the cloaks of the mirage
54. I attend my own heart's needs . . . .
[trans. Suzanne Pinckney Stetkevych]

Returning to the poet's she-camel and desert journey, verses 53 and 54 are no longer part of the oryx hunt. Beyond the hunt, they lead to their closure not only the animal similes and panels but the *qaṣīdah*'s now structurally complete *raḥīl*.[10]

Opposite these two thematic hunt paradigms lodged, we shall be reminded, as complex similes, or rather as allegories, in the *raḥīl* section of the *qaṣīdah*, there stands the paradigm of the 'chivalrous' hunt of the third, re-integrative section of the *qaṣīdah*'s total structure. It is found in one of its fullest forms in Imruʾ al-Qays's *Muᶜallaqah* (vv. 53–70). It also provides the genre of all subsequent hunt poetry (*ṭardiyyāt*) with its characteristic, micro-paradigmatic opening motif of 'setting out' (*wa qad aghtadī wa ṭ-ṭayru fī wukunātihā*):

53. I would ride forth early, the birds still in their nests,
On a steed sleek and swift, a shackle for wild game, huge.

Verses 54 to 62 follow with the 'description' of that extraordinary horse as it carries the gallant poet-hunter towards his goal, the quarry. Once engaged in the chase, the horse appears:

63. As if the blood of the herd's front-runners upon his throat
Were henna juice upon an old man's combed and hoary head.
64. Then there appeared before us an oryx herd
as if its cows were virgins
Circling round a sacred stone in long-trained gowns.
65. They turned about like alternated onyx beads upon the neck
Of a child nobly uncled in the clan from dame and sire.
66. Then he let us catch the herd's lead runners
And outstripped those that lagged in an unbroken cluster.
67. One after the other, he hit a bull and cow,
And yet was not awash with sweat.
68. Then the meat cooks kept on cooking

both meat laid upon the rocks
To roast well-done, and meat quick boiled in cauldrons.
69. And our glance, in the evening, almost failed before him,
To whatever spot the eye was raised, dazzled it dropped.
70. At night he remained, his saddle and bridle upon him,
All night he stood beneath my eye, not loosed to graze.
[trans. Suzanne Pinckney Stetkevych]

Thus the hunt ends – in truly chivalrous fashion – with a banquet and, as the night falls, with the final praise, or rather apotheosis, of the horse of the poet-as-chivalrous-hunter.[11]

Although the paradigmatic patterns and the structural framework of the hunt scenes in both respective sections of the *qaṣīdah* remain established as a canon, the idea must not be entertained that such a conception of the hunt, with its restricted number of protagonist-participants engaged in a pre-ordained agon, is a perpetually static one within some frozen formalist bounds; or, for instance, that the motival and ritual-symbolic border between the failed hunt of the *raḥīl* and the successful chase in the third section of the *qaṣīdah* is entirely inflexible. Rather the opposite has been true, or sufficiently well represented, even in early pre-Islamic poetic praxis.

Thus ᶜAbīd Ibn al-Abraṣ, one of the oldest pre-Islamic poets, will with great poetic skill and sure control of the formal poetic canon weave back and forth across the paradigmatic divides of the two types of the hunt. In his much-celebrated *qaṣīdah* of forty five verses, which opens:

Abandoned by its people lies Malḥūb,
Then al-Quṭabiyyāt, then al-Dhanūb,[12]

after a she-camel *raḥīl* through a desert that fills the heart with dread, the poet makes an abrupt exit out of that *qaṣīdah* section (the *raḥīl*) and introduces us to the poem's third and final section, which is in its entirety (vv. 32–45) a chase on horseback. He begins that section after the clearest of formal and experiential closures: *Fa dhāka ᶜaṣrun* (v. 32), 'That was a time long gone', or 'That was the time that was!' Then he rides off on a tall, long-bodied mare: . . . *Wa qad arānī/taḥmilunī nahdatun surḥūbu*. Thereafter, however, the poet does not speak to us of his hunt directly. Let us remember that in a hunt/chase the poet himself is expected to be the hunter-protagonist. Instead, in an extended simile strikingly modelled on the hunt panel proper of the *raḥīl*, the poet 'digresses' into a substitution for his horse of an 'ever-pursuing' eagle (*liqwatun ṭalūbu*), in whose nest lie the desiccated hearts of his prey (v.

35). This falcon, or eagle, is not the wretched and despondent hunter of a *raḥīl* panel after all. It sets out for the hunt in the early, cool morning (*fa aṣbaḥat fī ghadāti qurrin* [v. 37]) entirely in the 'heroic' time and manner in which, as we know, the paradigm of the 'setting out' of the heroic hunter on his steed or mare must occur (e. g., Imruᵓ al-Qays's *wa qad aghtadī*). And soon it has sighted on a wide barren plain a swift fox – its prey. The description of the 'chase' follows, ending in the *victory* of the bird of prey and the *defeat* of the hunted fox (vv. 41–45). Thus, through this transfer of the agents in the hunt, ᶜAbīd Ibn al-Abraṣ introduces two significant changes into the paradigm of the 'chivalrous chase': first of all, the poet is not the direct protagonist of the chase; and second, neither is the poet's horse the agent. Instead, in a manner that clearly and knowingly strains the paradigm, the agent/protagonist is the fierce bird of prey. Then, however, the paradigm, and with it the entire post-*raḥīl*, heroic and integrative section of the *qaṣīdah* is saved in its purport and semiotics in a highly circuitous manner by still producing the 'victory' of the now very complex 'hunter'.

The equally pre-Islamic al-Ḥārith Ibn Ḥillizah al-Yashkurī, too, is aware of the possibility of this thematic variant.[13] In his hunt on horseback he likens his mount to a falcon (*ṣaqr*), whose apprehended quarry is a dove. Thus, from the hunter to the horse to the falcon, only a figurative substitution of the protagonist of the chase has taken place.

Symbolically and formally of much greater significance in the development of the Arabic poem of the hunt is, however, a famous hunt/chase scene in a *qaṣīdah* by Zuhayr Ibn Abī Sulmā.[14] This poem opens with some of that poet's most hauntingly lyrical lines:

> The motley throng departed, unmindful
> of those they forsook,
> As your own journey's fare they left you
> longing for the roads they took.
> The slave maids brought in the tribe's camels
> and they packed to leave:
> Right into the noontime their hubbub
> wouldn't cease.

In the equestrian hunt/chase scene of this early, still strictly Bedouin poem the horse is introduced first of all in a tone, and in a 'pose', strongly akin to the more familiar apotheotic depiction of the horse carrying the poet-as-tribal-champion. That horse is, however, soon replaced by the simile of the sand grouse (*qaṭāh*), and it, the *qaṭāh*, is pursued, that is, 'hunted'/'chased', by a falcon. Quite significantly, the true protagonist of this poem's gallant hunt on horseback thus becomes the *qaṭāh*, which stands not only for the horse, but for the poet/hunter himself; and it, as the hunted prey, must, and does, escape its pursuer. The necessity of its escape from its hunter/pursuer is dictated, even on the surface of things, by the metaphoric fact that it represents the heroic poet's majestic horse. However, what is operative in the fuller sense of the resulting structural and semiotic interdependencies in this scene is the result of the tension between analogy, which is the reflection of a structural and thematic code, and contrast, which is the breaking of the code – or, as it were, the formal paradox enhanced by, and built into, the analogy. Altogether it is a 'clash' between the two faces of two stubborn paradigms: of the liminal hunt panel of a *raḥīl* and of the structurally implied celebratory hunt on horseback – for in the latter the function of the horse is an aggressive-active one: that of the *hunter* and not of the *hunted*. Zuhayr's horse has thus been replaced, implicitly, by the classical-canonic she-camel/*nāqah*, and formally, by the dictate of the canon, according to which it must bear the consequences.

To make that variant even more evident, or 'prefigured', and to bring out Zuhayr's self-consciousness and awareness of its being such a variant, we note that Zuhayr does not begin the chase scene with the otherwise quite obligatory *wa qad aghtadī* of 'setting out with the dawn'. Instead, he chooses the opposite time of day, the evening: *wa qad arūḥu* (v. 10). Such a parallelism in antipositions of structural semiotics, themes, and styles does not appear to be merely 'coincidental'. Rather it looks like the product of the style-consciousness of a superior poet. When Zuhayr introduces, instead of an unmediated theme of the horse, the simile of the sand grouse/*qaṭāh*, we expect the 'unusual' to take its course – especially since the *qaṭāh* begins to appear with much semiotic transparency quite in the manner in which Labīd Ibn Rabīᶜah in his *Muᶜallaqah* – wholly paradigmatically – represents the oryx cow in a *raḥīl* hunt panel proper: she has lost her suckling calf to predators, and in that state of bereavement is faced with the fearsome hunter and his hounds. Zuhayr's *qaṭāh*, too, has been driven away from the water hole, while her sister has fallen into a bird-trap (v. 13). This grouse is then described succinctly, but with forceful plasticity: she is black and smooth like those stones which the Bedouins place into their cups when in times of scarcity they are forced to measure out the precise level of water. Like those stingy cups of the Bedouins, such is also the soil from which the grouse gleans her livelihood. No good plants grow there (v. 14). This sturdy bird is not spared for one moment. She is attacked by a hawk which itself had been able to escape from every trap set for it (v. 15). The encounter is thus between equals. Between heaven and earth they play out their game of skill – one does not escape, the other does not overcome (v. 17). But, extending its avid talons and beak, the falcon remains in pursuit (v. 20) – until the grouse seeks refuge at a water hole in a dense growth of roots and plants (v. 22): quite as the calf of a full-uddered cow hides underneath its mother (v. 23). The hawk now realizes the uselessness of its endeavour. In a show of frustration, which remains nonetheless a proud gesture, it soars up to the top of a hill and from its promontory overlooks the plain below. It is of added interest, and a warning to our ways of reading especially pre-Islamic Arabic poetry, that the final image of the promontory is in Zuhayr's poem expressedly that of a place of sacrificial offering, although on its imagist level it speaks merely of the redness of the rock of the promontory itself or of the bloodied feathers of the proud bird of prey (v. 24).

Here the hunt panel ends quite abruptly, and what follows (vv. 25–33) is the poet's missive and threat to a hostile tribe. But in this, too, that is, in the *qaṣīdah*'s final 'political' section, there lies the hermeneutical key to the inversions of the paradigmatic hunt themes and the playing out of the variations of their motifs. For Zuhayr Ibn Abī Sulmā's final explicit threats and admonitions to his tribe's foes suggest that their fate is bound to be quite like the fate of that poetically so jarringly misplaced falcon of the hunt scene. Thus verse thirty three, the poem's closure:

Surely there will reach you from me
words most foul
That will remain [on people's tongues]
as grease stains rich Coptic cloth.

A further observation is to be made here. The strange fragility and vulnerability of the metaphoric protagonist in Zuhayr's poem's hunt scene, that is, of the *qaṭāh*, already points toward the nurturing in the Arabic poetic hunt of altogether more lyrical strains which, come the subsequent epochs of sensibility – the Umayyad and the ᶜAbbasid – will reveal still another face of the many faces of the hunt, that of the melancholy hunt of love and of the presence in it of the sand grouse/*qaṭāh*.[15] So too, aside from that characteristically melancholy variant of the hunt of love, other motival elements and metaphorizations of the 'chase of love', mostly based on the inversion of roles between hunter and quarry, make their early appearance in Arabic poetry. Thus, from among the poets before Islam, we find such motifs in Imruᵓ al-Qays,[16] al-Muthaqqib al-ᶜAbdī,[17] al-Muraqqish the Elder,[18] Muᶜāwiyah Ibn Mālik;[19] from the Umayyad period, in al-Akhṭal,[20] Jarīr,[21] Qays Ibn

Dharīḥ,[22] Majnūn[23]; or, among the ᶜAbbasids, in Ibn al-Rūmī,[24] al-Mutanabbī,[25] Mihyār al-Daylamī,[26] and many, many more.

All this said, we have still to state with theoretical firmness that these are not the readily furnished 'origins' and formulations of the Arabic genre of the hunt poem, that is, of the *ṭardiyyah*, but rather its formative, or call them procedural, 'beginnings'. This distinction I refer to Kathryn J. Gutzwiller's most insightful discussion of 'The Formation of a Genre'.[27] Following her views, themselves much influenced by the Russian Formalists and the Prague Linguistic Circle, the birth of a genre ought to be viewed not so much as the beginnings of a form but rather of a process, thus not of actual 'birth' but of transformation; and that that process is part of a rehierarchization and revision of existing elements. In order to produce a genre, however, this rehierarchization must have its 'independent function' that moves toward the outside of the form-awareness of a pre-existing rule of form and toward its ultimate disengagement from it.

Transposing this formalist reasoning to our Arabic case, therefore, the formalist process which ultimately leads to the development of the genre-poem of the hunt, that is, of the *ṭardiyyah*, ought to be identified as an 'outward-movement' out of a 'prior' strong awareness of a 'form', a 'thematic range', and a 'diction' – an awareness which, however, also implies a counter-current – of the semiotics of the internal hierarchization of these elements. For only out of the semiotic lingering-on of the formal 'language' of that underlying internal hierarchization (as matrix) will the process of the formation of the new genre, if successful in its rehierarchization, emerge as a new formal entity of aesthetically 'knowable' confines. For the Arabic hunt poem/*ṭardiyyah*, such a semiotic and formal/structural matrix is necessarily (and singularly) the thematically fully structured, classical *qaṣīdah*. The *ṭardiyyah* develops as much with it as against it.

As we know from the historical fortunes of the form of the *qaṣīdah* itself, the outgrowth of the independent hunt poem/*ṭardiyyah* from it took place almost as a process of omission. For by the end of the Umayyad period the survival of the archaic poetic hunt paradigms within the *qaṣīdah* could no longer be sustained. The subject of the hunt did not 'separate' itself from the *qaṣīdah* – it was left out. It became an outcast from a form and a structure which no longer had room, or understanding, for what had once been its great thematic paradigms of the hunt – especially of the hunt as the liminal experience of the *raḥīl*.

As the Umayyad period was running out and the ᶜAbbasid one was setting in, the fully structured classical *qaṣīdah* was undergoing changes of significance – especially of significance to our topic. From ternary structure, the now predominantly epideictic and courtly *qaṣīdah* was rapidly changing into a binary form. And even if a *raḥīl* section was occasionally retained, it was invariably a *raḥīl* of *himmah*, not of *humūm*, thus not of 'care' but of 'aspiration' and 'purpose'. In it, very much in the manner in which Ibn Qutaybah has formulated it, there was room only for the direct journey of the supplicant poet intent upon reaching the presence of the patron.[28] The experiential liminality of the Bedouin poet, as it is structurally embedded in the *raḥīl*,[29] and his existential stance, were no more. Those, however, had been the matters of which the Bedouin poet had spoken through his animal panels and allegories of the hunt.

If the Bedouin *raḥīl* had undergone such changes, so too had changed the third section of the *qaṣīdah*. In its new courtly and celebratory role as undiluted eulogy of the patron, there was no room for the poet's self-assertion and self-glorification through his 'chivalrous' hunt as the champion of his tribe/community. Thus it was the *qaṣīdah* itself that had changed and could no longer accommodate the two 'archaic' forms of the hunt under its structural roof.

Such is, however, only a formalist assessment. For, as the *qaṣīdah* was changing, or had to change, so, too, were changing the semiotics of a new concept of community, state, and power, those factors that touched most directly upon the functionality of the 'third' section of the *qaṣīdah* – and the *qaṣīdah* itself was no more than changing according to those new dictates of state and power. And, furthermore, the subject of the hunt in Arabic poetry, in its turn, appeared no longer to have to lean on the *qaṣīdah* for its old supportive, and indeed comprehensive, meaning-giving form and circumstance. As it became its own 'poem of the hunt', the subject of the hunt now had a new master: the newly opened-up Umayyad, and then ᶜAbbasid, world of the court. What it all meant from the literary-critical point of view is another matter. Yet, a new genre was needed, and a new genre was born.

In Arabic poetic genre history, this birth of a new formal body may be seen almost as a case of the proverbial cutting of the umbilical cord. And yet, viewing the development at a closer range, the *ṭardiyyah* poem, with all its thematic and formal linkages to the *qaṣīdah*, had at first cut surgically only one, indeed, the most external of ties with the matrix – namely that of the propriety of the classical *qaṣīdah* canon of rhyme and meter. Thus, when the first Umayyad *ṭardiyyāt* were actually achieved, they were set to the meter of *rajaz*, considered then, and thereafter, as falling outside the classical pale. These poems were also made to rhyme as hemistich-length verses throughout, thus producing a drastically shorter verse length. The resulting form – in this most technical sense – was an '*urjūzah*'. The *ṭardiyyah* poets had thus opted for the least canonical and the most 'popular', metrically relaxed and, one could, with foresight, have said, 'folkloric' type of prosodic system available at that time to the Arabic poet. There are paradoxes in such a choice of prosody for precisely a 'courtly' genre, but this is almost another 'matter', whose solutions reach too far and too wide past our immediate purposes.[30]

Notes

1. I am presuming here familiarity with, and acceptance of, the now not-so-recent application of the van Gennepian experiential formula of the 'rite of passage' to the classical Arabic *qaṣīdah*, as expounded in Suzanne Pinckney Stetkevych, 'Structuralist Interpretations of Pre-Islamic Poetry: Critique and New Directions', *Journal of Near Eastern Studies* 42, no. 2 (1983): 85–107; 'Al-Qaṣīdah al-ᶜArabiyyah wa Ṭuqūs al-ᶜUbūr: Dirāsah fī al-Bunyah al-Namūdhajiyyah', *Majallat Majmaᶜ al-Lughah al-ᶜArabiyyah bi Dimashq* 60, no. 1 (1985): 55–85; *The Mute Immortals Speak: Pre-Islamic Poetry and the Poetics of Ritual* (Ithaca and London: Cornell University Press,1993), 3–54; and Jaroslav Stetkevych, *The Zephyrs of Najd: The Poetics of Nostalgia in the Classical Arabic Nasīb* (Chicago and London: The University of Chicago Press, 1993): 40–49.
2. ᶜUthmān ᶜAmr Ibn Baḥr al-Jāḥiẓ, *Al-Ḥayawān*, ed. ᶜAbd al-Salām Muḥammad Hārūn, 8 vols. (Cairo: Muṣṭafā al-Bābī al-Ḥalabī, 1965–69), 2:20.
3. On Frazer's 'external soul', see James George Frazer, *The Golden Bough: A Study in Magic and Religion*, 1 Volume, Abridged Edition (New York: Macmillan Publishing Company, Collier Books, 1963), Chapters LXVI/LXVII (pp. 773–802).
4. See the discussion of the rigourous canonic aspects of the representation of the Bedouin poet's riding animal – both as necessarily a she-camel and as nameable only epithetically – in Jaroslav Stetkevych, 'Name and Epithet: The Philology and Semiotics of Animal Nomenclature in Early Arabic Poetry', *Journal of Near Eastern Studies* 45, no. 2 (April 1986): 89–124.
5. In a strict and literalist sense, the term 'ekphrasis' introduced as a possible designation of the pre-Islamic *qaṣīdah*'s extended similes of the *raḥīl* section, may, at a first glance, appear misplaced. It should be obvious, however, that my tying ekphrasis interpretively to the term 'panel', implicitly pre-qualifies the formal identity of the 'frameable' extended animal similes of the *raḥīl*'s she-camel 'figura'. This in itself ought to be understood as a hermeneutical procedure to facilitate the transition of a specific poetic material – the ekphrastic animal panels – from its inherent 'temporality' of narration-as-representation to 'spatiality' and 'plasticity'. The formal concept of 'panel' refers itself at first to something that suggest the concrete, visual, and tactile. Only then does it permit, or suggest, the possibility of abstraction and figuration. In the history, or evolution, of

plastic representation, however, the plastic arts themselves, as much in painting as in sculpture, have been the ones to have first attempted to cross the limits of the spatial/plastic and the temporal/verbal – precisely through the spatial/temporal ambiguity proper of 'panels'. *Ut pictura poesis* thus reflects the restlessness and fluidity of the border-regions of the two arts with full bi-directionality. For a discussion of ekphrasis precisely in its multidimensionality, see Murray Krieger, *Ekphrasis: The Illusion of the Natural Sign* (Baltimore and London: The Johns Hopkins University Press, 1992).

6. In its pre-Islamic semantics the colour *akhḍar* was 'green', but not merely green. It could also be a hue such as 'black', 'blackish', 'metallic blackish gray', and 'metallic dark green', such as would be a dark oxidation of copper or bronze; and even 'tawny' and 'brownish'. It was, however, never a hue of blue, although, poetically, it served to render the colour of the nightly sky. This latter meaning becomes important to our understanding of the image in Ibn Maqrūm's poem's verse 15, for in it we necessarily perceive an allusion to and projection of the Bedouin pastoral visualization of the 'pasture of the sky' as the 'green' nightly firmament. See Jaroslav Stetkevych, *The Zephyrs of Najd*, p. 156.
7. This motif of a 'respite' of hope, and even enjoyment (*tamattuᶜ*), before the onset of tragedy is characteristic not only of Arabic poetic hunting scenes but also of mythopoeia in the Qurʾān, such as that of the fall of the ancient people of the Thamūd, and the further exegetic and narrative elaborations of that legendary material. This topic I discuss more extensively in my monograph, *The Arabian Golden Bough: Myth, Scripture, and Mythopoeia* (forthcoming).
8. Abū al-ᶜAbbās al-Mufaḍḍal Ibn Muḥammad al-Ḍabbī, *Dīwān al-Mufaḍḍaliyyāt*, Commentary by Abū Muḥammad al-Qāsim Ibn Muḥammad Ibn Bashshār al-Anbārī, Vol. 1, Arabic Text, ed. Charles James Lyall (Beirut: Maṭbaᶜat al-Ābāʾ al-Yasūᶜiyyīn, 1920), 355–58. Unless otherwise specified, all translations are mine.
9. Here the oryx cow is, once again in accordance with the classical Arabic *qaṣīdah*'s semiotic canon of 'description', represented epithetically, not directly by its primary denotant. See Jaroslav Stetkevych, 'Animal Nomenclature', pp. 106–08.
10. For a translation and discussion of the full poem, see Suzanne Stetkevych, *The Mute Immortals Speak*, pp. 13–14/3–54.
11. For a full translation and discussion of the poem, see Suzanne Stetkevych, *The Mute Immortals Speak*, pp. 254–56/241–85. Further on the subject of the apotheosis of the chivalrous hunter's horse, see Jaroslav Stetkevych, *The Zephyrs of Najd*, pp. 34, 251–52 n.82.
12. ᶜAbīd Ibn al-Abraṣ, *Dīwān* (Beirut: Dār Ṣādir/Dār Bayrūt, 1964/1384), 23–30 (rhyme *-ūbu*).
13. *Al-Mufaḍḍaliyyāt*, pp. 515-18 (no. 62), (rhyme *-jī*).
14. Zuhayr Ibn Abī Sulmā, *Dīwān*, Redaction and commentary by Abū al-ᶜAbbās Aḥmad Ibn Yaḥyā Ibn Zayd al-Shaybānī Thaᶜlab (Cairo: al-Dār al-Qawmiyyah li al-Ṭibāᶜah wa al-Nashr, 1384/1964), 164–83 (rhyme *-ku*). For other aspects of my discussion of these lines, see Jaroslav Stetkevych, 'Name and Epithet', pp. 115–16.

15. Here the model should be the beautiful *Ru^c^āt al-layli* ('Oh herders of the night') poem attributed to the 'love-maddened' ^c^Udhrī poet Majnūn (Qays Ibn al-Mulawwaḥ). See Majnūn Laylā, *Qays Ibn al-Mulawwaḥ al-Majnūn wa Dīwānuh*, ed. Shawqiyyah Ināljiq (Ankara: Maṭba^c^at al-Jam^c^iyyah al-Tārīkhiyyah al-Turkiyyah, 1967), 74. See this poem's English translation and discussion as otherwise reflecting an Arabic pastoral genre, in Jaroslav Stetkevych, *The Zephyrs of Najd*, pp. 161–63.
16. Imru^ɔ^ al-Qays, *Dīwān*, ed. Muḥammad Abū al-Faḍl Ibrāhīm, 3rd. ed. (Cairo: Dār al-Ma^c^ārif bi Miṣr, 1969), 155 (vv. 8–9).
17. *Al-Mufaḍḍaliyyāt*, p. 303 (no. 28, v. 2) (rhyme *-duhā*).
18. *Al-Mufaḍḍaliyyāt*, p. 461 (no. 46, v. 8) (rhyme *-īdu*).
19. *Al-Mufaḍḍaliyyāt*, p. 698 (no. 105, vv. 3–5) (rhyme *-ābā*).
20. Al-Akhṭal al-Taghlibī, *Dīwān*, ed. Īlīyā Salīm al-Ḥāwī (Beirut: Dār al-Thaqāfah, 1968), 659 (vv. 1–2 [rhyme *-lī*]).
21. Jarīr [Ibn ^c^Aṭīyah Ibn al-Khaṭafā^ɔ^], *Dīwān*, 2 vols., Commentary by Muḥammad Ibn Ḥabīb, ed. Nu^c^mān Muḥammad Amīn Ṭāhā 3rd ed. (Cairo: Dār al-Ma^c^ārif, 1986), 2: 777 (vv. 16–19 [rhyme *-mā*]).
22. Qays Ibn Dharīḥ, *Dīwān* [*Qays Ibn Dharīḥ: Shi^c^r wa Dirāsah*], ed. Ḥusayn Naṣṣār (Cairo: Dār Miṣr li al-Ṭibā^c^ah, 1960), 69.
23. Majnūn Laylā, *Dīwān*, p. 36.
24. Ibn al-Rūmī [Abū al-Ḥasan ^c^Alī al-^c^Abbās Ibn Jurayj], *Dīwān*, 6 vols., ed. Ḥusayn Naṣṣār (Cairo: Maṭba^c^at Dār al-Kutub, 1393/1973), 5: 2091 (rhyme *-mu* [vv. 5–7]).
25. Abū al-Ṭayyib al-Mutanabbī, *Dīwān*, 4 vols., Commentary by Abū al-Baqā^ɔ^ al-^c^Ukbārī, eds. Muṣṭafā al-Saqqā^ɔ^, Ibrāhīm al-Abyārī, ^c^Abd al-Ḥafīẓ Shalabī (Cairo: Maṭba^c^at Muṣṭafā al-Bābī al-Ḥalabī wa Awlāduh, 1391/1971), 3: 251 (rhyme *-lu* [esp. vv. 6–7]).
26. Mihyār al-Daylamī, *Dīwān*, 4 vols. (Cairo: Maṭba^c^at Dār al-Kutub al-Miṣriyyah, 1344/1925), 1: 221 (rhyme *-ḥu* [vv.7–9]).
27. Kathryn J. Gutzwiller, *Theocritus' Pastoral Analogies: The Formation of a Genre* (Madison, Wisconsin: The University of Wisconsin Press, 1991), 10–11, 199–200.
28. For a discussion of the rhetorical and epideictic theory of the *qaṣīdah* according to Ibn Qutaybah, see Jaroslav Stetkevych, *The Zephyrs of Najd*, pp. 6–16. For *humūm/himmah*, see same, pp. 21, 23, 27, 30, 40.
29. See Suzanne Stetkevych, *The Mute Immortals Speak*, pp. 7–8, 26–33, 270–73; and Jaroslav Stetkevych, *The Zephyrs of Najd*, pp. 42–45.
30. Manfred Ullmann has answered as many of these questions of 'matter' as he has thrown open and created. His *Untersuchungen zur Ragazpoesie: Ein Beitrag zur arabischen Sprach- und Literaturwissenschaft* (Wiesbaden: Otto Harrassowitz, 1966) is here of great value.

9

ᶜAbbāsid Panegyric

The Politics and Poetics of Ceremony Al-Mutanabbī's ᶜĪd-poem to Sayf al-Dawlah

Suzanne Pinckney Stetkevych
Indiana University

The dominant genre of the classical Arabic ode throughout the Islamic period, indeed down through the neo-classical poets of the first half of the twentieth century, was the panegyrical *qaṣīda*, that is, the poem of praise to the ruler or patron.* The present paper takes as its working premise the need to establish a poetics appropriate to the evaluation of this body of poetry that was intimately and functionally bound up in courtly politics and ceremonial. The paper focuses on a *qaṣīda* whose ceremonial function and historical circumstance are explicitly recorded both within the poetic text itself and in the commentaries of the scholiasts upon it, al-Mutanabbī's panegyric rhymed in the letter *dāl* presented to the Ḥamdānid prince Sayf al-Dawlah on ᶜĪd al-Aḍḥā 342/953. My argument will be that ceremonial and ritual are not accidental or circumstantial, but rather constitute essential and formative elements of the poem; and further, that the ceremonial and ritual aspects that are quite explicitly perceptible in this particular *qaṣīda* are equally present and formative in other poems in which they may have heretofore eluded our detection. In this respect the present study builds upon my earlier work in Arabic poetry (Stetkevych 1991: part 2; 1993; 1994; 1996; unpub.) as well as work in other fields on ceremony and art (see MacCormack 1981; Cannadine and Price 1987; Connerton 1989; Sanders 1994).

The historical, ritual, and ceremonial dimensions of this *qaṣīda* are given in all the major al-Mutanabbī commentaries and are as well extricable from the poetic text itself. As al-Maᶜarrī tells us, al-Mutanabbī composed this poem in the month of Dhū al-Ḥijjah 342 as a panegyric and an ᶜĪd al-Aḍḥā (10 Dhū al-Ḥijjah 342A.H.= 15 April 954 A.D.)

* The research for this study was assisted by an award from the Joint Committee on the Near and Middle East of the Social Science Research Council and the American Council of Learned Societies with funds provided by the National Endowment for the Humanities.

greeting. He recited it to Sayf al-Dawlah in his parade ground *(maydān)* in Aleppo, beneath his tribune (*majlis*), while both of them were mounted on horseback. Al-Maᶜarrī then adds, describing the contents of the poem, that al-Mutanabbī mentions in it Sayf al-Dawlah's capture of the son of the Byzantine general, and boasts of himself and his poetry (al-Maᶜarrī 1986: 3:372; see al-Barqūqī 1986: 2:3; al-ᶜUkbārī 1936: 1:281; al-Wāḥidī n.d.: 539; al-Yāzijī 1964: 179).

For our own analytical ends we can extrapolate the following from these descriptive remarks: This poem is not, in the traditional terminology, merely an 'occasional' poem, that is, it does not merely describe a specific event or incident. It is, rather, performative: the act of recitation of the poem itself to the *mamdūḥ* (patron) fulfills two obligations or performs two functions: the praise of the ruler – a topic we will come back to – and the ᶜĪd greeting. As I will discuss in more detail further on, these are twin acts of political and religious homage. The first can be viewed as a declaration of political allegiance. The second is of a more explicitly religious nature, the obligatory ᶜĪd greeting which amounts to a formal recognition of the legitimate Islamic rulership of the *mamdūḥ* and the withholding of which would constitute an act of sedition (*fitna*). For both we can say, paraphrasing Connerton, that the poem effectively brings these attitudes and obligations into existence by virtue of the 'illocutionary act' (Connerton 1989: 58; see Austin 1962: 98–100 and passim).

Most striking and ultimately most revealing of the conceptual substructure of the poem is the remark that al-Mutanabbī recited it to Sayf al-Dawlah when they were both on horseback. It is well established that in classical Arabo-Islamic protocol and ceremonial the inferior dismounts to show respect for his superior (Sanders 1994: 22). This remark then – whether we take it as historical fact or literary semiosis – can only mean one thing: viz., that al-Mutanabbī styles himself Sayf al-Dawlah's equal.

The poet thus simultaneously offers praise and greeting and therefore, as the rules of ritual exchange (see below) and, more specifically, the Islamic prescriptions for returning the greeting require, justifiably anticipates a counter of equal or greater value. For example, of the return of greeting we read in the Qurᵓān 4:87: 'When someone extends a greeting to you, reply with a better greeting or return the same greeting, for indeed God takes account of everything'; so too the *ḥadīth*:

> ᶜImrān ibn Ḥusayn reported that a man came to the Prophet and said, 'Peace be upon you', to which he responded, and then said,

> when the man sat down, 'Ten'. Another man came and said, 'Peace and God's mercy be upon you', to which he responded, and then said, when the man sat down, 'Twenty'. Another man came and said, 'Peace and God's mercy and blessings be upon you', to which he responded, and then said, when the man sat down, 'Thirty'. (Wensinck 1962: 4:215 [Abū Dāwūd *adab*: 132])

Into this we must then integrate al-Maᶜarrī's brief descriptive remarks, that the poet mentions Sayf al-Dawlah's capture of the Byzantine general's son and boasts of himself and his poetry. As I hope to show, this combination of praise and boast is the poetic structural equivalent of the *mamdūḥ* and poet both being mounted on horseback. Further, I will attempt to demonstrate how the historical event of Sayf al-Dawlah's military victory over the Byzantines becomes through the ritualizing capacity of the *qaṣīda* incorporated in the cyclical-mythical pattern of the Islamic liturgical calendar, and thereby projected both backward and forward in time – i.e., it is monumentalized, commemorated, and, hence, immortalized. In light of these remarks I would like to turn to the poem itself.

قال المتنبّي يمدح سيف الدولة ويهنّئه بعيد الاضحى

١. لِكُلِّ امْرِئٍ مِنْ دَهْرِهِ مَا تَعَوَّدَا   وَعَادَاتُ سَيْفِ الدَّوْلَةِ الطَّعْنُ فِي العِدَا
٢. وأنْ يُكْذِبَ الإرْجافَ عَنْهُ بِضِدِّهِ   وَيُمْسِي بِمَا تَنْوِي أعَادِيهِ أسْعَدَا
٣. وَرُبَّ مُرِيدٍ ضَرَّهُ ضَرَّ نَفْسَهُ   وَهادٍ إلَيْهِ الجَيْشَ أهْدَى وَمَا هَدَى
٤. وَمُسْتَكْبِرٍ لَمْ يَعْرِفِ اللّهَ سَاعَةً   رَأى سَيْفَهُ فِي كَفِّهِ فَتَشَهَّدَا
٥. هُوَ البَحْرُ غُصْ فِيهِ إذَا كَانَ سَاكِنًا   عَلَى الدُّرِّ وَاحْذَرْهُ إذَا كَانَ مُزْبِدَا
٦. فَإنِّي رَأَيْتُ البَحْرَ يَعْثُرُ بِالفَتَى   وَهَذَا الّذِي يَأتِي الفَتَى مُتَعَمِّدَا
٧. تَظَلُّ مُلُوكُ الأرْضِ خَاشِعَةً لَهُ   تُفَارِقُهُ هَلْكَى وَتَلْقَاهُ سُجَّدَا
٨. وَتُحيِي لَهُ المَالَ الصَّوَارِمُ وَالقَنَا   وَيَقْتُلُ مَا تُحْيِي التَّبَسُّمُ وَالجَدَا
٩. ذَكِيٌّ تَظَنِّيهِ طَلِيعَةُ عَيْنِهِ   يَرَى قَلْبُهُ فِي يَوْمِهِ مَا تَرَى غَدَا
١٠. وَصُولٌ إلَى المُسْتَصْعَبَاتِ بِخَيْلِهِ   فَلَوْ كَانَ قَرْنُ الشَّمْسِ مَاءً لأوْرَدَا
١١. لِذلك سَمّى ابنُ الدُّمُسْتُقِ يَوْمَهُ   مَمَاتًا وَسَمّاهُ الدُّمُسْتُقُ مَوْلِدَا

١٢. سَرَيْتَ إِلَى جَيْحَانَ مِنْ أَرْضِ آمِدٍ   ثَلاثًا لَقَدْ أَدْنَاكَ رَكْضٌ وَأَبْعَدَا
١٣. فَوَلَّى وَأَعْطَاكَ ابْنَهُ وَجُيُوشَهُ   جَمِيعًا وَلَمْ يُعْطِ الْجَمِيعَ لِيُحْمَدَا
١٤. عَرَضْتَ لَهُ دُونَ الْحَيَاةِ وَطَرْفِهِ   وَأَبْصَرَ سَيْفَ اللَّهِ مِنْكَ مُجَرَّدَا
١٥. وَمَا طَلَبَتْ زُرْقُ الأَسِنَّةِ غَيْرَهُ   وَلَكِنَّ قُسْطَنْطِينَ كَانَ لَهُ الْفِدَا
١٦. فَأَصْبَحَ يَجْتَابُ الْمُسُوحَ مَخَافَةً   وَقَدْ كَانَ يَجْتَابُ الدِّلاصَ الْمُسَرَّدَا
١٧. وَيَمْشِي بِهِ الْعُكَّازُ فِي الدَّيْرِ تَائِبًا   وَمَا كَانَ يَرْضَى مَشْيَ أَشْقَرَ أَجْرَدَا
١٨. وَمَا تَابَ حَتَّى غَادَرَ الْكَرُّ وَجْهَهُ   جَرِيحًا وَخَلَّى جَفْنَهُ النَّقْعُ أَرْمَدَا
١٩. فَلَوْ كَانَ يُنْجِي مِنْ عَلِيٍّ تَرَهُّبٌ   تَرَهَّبَتِ الأَمْلاكُ مَثْنَى وَمَوْحَدَا
٢٠. وَكُلُّ امْرِئٍ فِي الشَّرْقِ وَالْغَرْبِ بَعْدَهَا   يُعِدُّ لَهُ ثَوْبًا مِنَ الشَّعْرِ أَسْوَدَا
٢١. هَنِيئًا لَكَ الْعِيدُ الَّذِي أَنْتَ عِيدُهُ   وَعِيدٌ لِمَنْ سَمَّى وَضَحَّى وَعَيَّدَا
٢٢. وَلا زَالَتِ الأَعْيَادُ لُبْسَكَ بَعْدَهُ   تُسَلِّمُ مَخْرُوقًا وَتُعْطَى مُجَدَّدَا
٢٣. فَذَا الْيَوْمُ فِي الأَيَّامِ مِثْلُكَ فِي الْوَرَى   كَمَا كُنْتُ فِيهِمْ وَاحِدًا كَانَ أَوْحَدَا
٢٤. هُوَ الْجَدُّ حَتَّى تَفْضُلُ الْعَيْنُ أُخْتَهَا   وَحَتَّى يَكُونُ الْيَوْمُ لِلْيَوْمِ سَيِّدَا
٢٥. فَوَا عَجَبَا مِن دَائِلٍ أَنْتَ سَيْفُهُ   أَمَا يَتَوَقَّى شَفْرَتَيْ مَا تَقَلَّدَا
٢٦. وَمَنْ يَجْعَلِ الضِّرْغَامَ لِلصَّيْدِ بَازَهُ   تَصَيَّدَهُ الضِّرْغَامُ فِيمَا تَصَيَّدَا
٢٧. رَأَيْتُكَ مَحْضَ الْحِلْمِ فِي مَحْضِ قُدْرَةٍ   وَلَوْ شِئْتَ كَانَ الْحِلْمُ مِنْكَ الْمُهَنَّدَا
٢٨. وَمَا قَتَلَ الأَحْرَارَ كَالْعَفْوِ عَنْهُمُ   وَمَنْ لَكَ بِالْحُرِّ الَّذِي يَحْفَظُ الْيَدَا
٢٩. إِذَا أَنْتَ أَكْرَمْتَ الْكَرِيمَ مَلَكْتَهُ   وَإِنْ أَنْتَ أَكْرَمْتَ اللَّئِيمَ تَمَرَّدَا
٣٠. وَوَضْعُ النَّدَى فِي مَوْضِعِ السَّيْفِ بِالْعُلاَ   مُضِرٌّ كَوَضْعِ السَّيْفِ فِي مَوْضِعِ النَّدَا
٣١. وَلَكِنْ تَفُوقُ النَّاسَ رَأْيًا وَحِكْمَةً   كَمَا فُقْتَهُمْ حَالاً وَنَفْسًا وَمَحْتِدَا
٣٢. يَدِقُّ عَلَى الأَفْكَارِ مَا أَنْتَ فَاعِلٌ   فَيُتْرَكُ مَا يَخْفَى وَيُؤْخَذُ مَا بَدَا
٣٣. أَزِلْ حَسَدَ الْحُسَّادِ عَنِّي بِكَبْتِهِمِ   فَأَنْتَ الَّذِي صَيَّرْتَهُمْ لِي حُسَّدَا
٣٤. إِذَا شَدَّ زَنْدِي حُسْنُ رَأْيِكَ فِي يَدِي   ضَرَبْتُ بِنَصْلٍ يَقْطَعُ الْهَامَ مُغْمَدَا
٣٥. وَمَا أَنَا إِلاَّ سَمْهَرِيٌّ حَمَلْتَهُ   فَزَيَّنَ مَعْرُوضًا وَرَاعَ مُسَدَّدَا
٣٦. وَمَا الدَّهْرُ إِلاَّ مِنْ رُوَاةِ قَلائِدِي   إِذَا قُلْتُ شِعْرًا أَصْبَحَ الدَّهْرُ مُنْشِدَا
٣٧. فَسَارَ بِهِ مَنْ لاَ يَسِيرُ مُشَمِّرًا   وَغَنَّى بِهِ مَنْ لاَ يُغَنِّي مُغَرِّدَا
٣٨. أَجِزْنِي إِذَا أُنْشِدْتَ مَدْحًا فَإِنَّمَا   بِشِعْرِي أَتَاكَ الْمَادِحُونَ مُرَدَّدَا

٣٩. وَدَعْ كُلَّ صَوْتٍ بَعْدَ صَوْتِي فَإِنَّنِي   أَنَا الصَّائِحُ الْمَحْكِيُّ والآخَرُ الصَّدَى

٤٠. تَرَكْتُ السُّرَى خَلْفِي لِمَنْ قَلَّ مَالُهُ   وَأَنْعَلْتُ أَفْرَاسِي بِنُعْمَاكَ عَسْجَدَا

٤١. وَقَيَّدْتُ نَفْسِي فِي ذَرَاكَ مَحَبَّةً   وَمَنْ وَجَدَ الإِحْسَانَ قَيْدًا تَقَيَّدَا

٤٢. إِذَا سَأَلَ الإِنْسَانُ أَيَّامَهُ الْغِنَى   وَكُنْتَ عَلَى بُعْدٍ جَعَلْنَكَ مَوْعِدَا

TRANSLATION

Al-Mutanabbī's *dāliyya* to Sayf al-Dawlah on cĪd al-Aḍḥā, 342/954

[Note: In text and commentary I have followed primarily al-Macarrī 1986: 3:372–86; with further reference to al-Barqūqī 1986: 2:3–16; al-cUkbārī 1936: 1:281–92; al-Wāḥidī n.d.:529–35; al-Yāzijī 1964: 2:179–85. In trying to achieve a readable and appealing English translation I have followed the spirit over the letter of the Arabic poem.]

1. Each man becomes accustomed to what fate allots him,
   and Sayf al-Dawlah's custom is to strike the foe,
2. To belie mendacious rumour by true deed,
   hereby gaining from his foes' malevolence greater felicity.
3. Many wished him harm only to harm themselves;
   many guided armies against him only to surrender them to him.
4. Many an arrogant infidel who denied Allah
   saw H/his sword in H/his hand, then swore his creed.
5. He is the sea. Plunge into it for pearls when it is calm;
   but when the tempest churns its foam, beware!
6. I have seen the true sea throw its rider,
   but when this one fells his foe, it's by design.
7. To him the kings of the earth submit;
   whether they flee from him and perish, or approach him prostrate.
8. The cutting blades and spear-shafts revive his wealth,
   but his smile and generosity soon slay what they revive.
9. Acute, his wit is vanguard to his eye;
   his heart discerns today what his eye perceives tomorrow.

10. To reaches remote and arduous he leads his horsemen;
    were dawn's first gleam a waterhole, he'd lead them there.
11. So the Domesticus' son called the day of his capture death;
    while the Domesticus called it his birth.
12. You journeyed to the River Jayḥān from Āmid in just three nights;
    the gallop brought you near to one, far from the other.
13. The Domesticus fled and gave you his son and all his armies;
    but it wasn't to be praised for generosity he gave.
14. You stood between him and his life, obstructing his view;
    in you he beheld God's swordblade bared.
15. The blue speartips sought only but him;
    but his son Constantine became his ransom.
16. So out of fear he came to wear the monk's hair shirt,
    when once he'd worn the lustrous weave of mail.
17. Penitent he paces with crozier the convent grounds,
    he whom the sleek red roan's best pace had failed to please.
18. He did not repent until the battle-charge had gashed his face
    and the stirred up battle-dust inflamed his eye.
19. If monkery could save men from ᶜAlī;
    kings would take to monasteries singly and in pairs.
20. And every man, after the Domesticus, both east and west,
    would ready for himself a black hair-cloth robe.

21. To you a joyous 'Īd whose 'Īd you are!
    and 'Īd to all who invoke Allah, sacrifice, and celebrate the 'Īd!
22. And may 'Īds ever after be your garb,
    surrendering worn garments and given garments new!
23. For this day among the days is like you among mankind:
    as you are unique among men, it is among the days unique.
24. It is fortune that makes one eye sharper than its twin,
    that makes one day the master of another.
25. How amazing the ruler whose sword you are!
    Does he not fear the two edges of the sword he's girt?
26. He who makes the lion his hunting falcon
    will soon find his lion hunting him!

27. I consider you pure forbearance in pure power;
had you wished your forbearance could have been a blade of Indian steel.
28. Nothing kills noble men like forgiveness;
but who would vouch for a noble man who's mindful of a favour?
29. When you honour a man of honour, you own him;
when you honour an ignoble, he's impudent.
30. Generosity put in the place of the sword is
as harmful to high rank as putting the sword in generosity's place.
31. But you surpass all men in judgment and wisdom
just as you surpassed them in rank, soul, and lineage.
32. Your deeds are too subtle to contemplate;
so what's concealed is left and what is clear is apprehended.

33. End the envy of my enviers by humbling them;
for it was you who made them envy me.
34. When you brace my forearm with your high esteem
I will strike them with a sword that even sheathed splits skulls.
35. I am nothing but a Samharī spear you bore;
an adornment when displayed; terrible when aimed.
36. Time itself is a reciter of my odes;
I compose a poem, then time recites it.
37. Recluses rush out to bruit it abroad;
with it the tuneless raise their voice in song.
38. Reward me for every poem recited to you;
for what the panegyrists bring is but my poems repeated.
39. Leave off every voice but my voice;
mine is the uttered cry, the others, echoes.
40. The night-journey I have left to him of meagre means,
and by your bounty I have shod my steeds with gold.
I [hereby/will] quit . . .
I [will] shoe my steeds . . . .
41. I have bound myself to your protection out of love,
for he who finds beneficence is bound with a firm bond.

I [hereby/will] bind . . . .

42. When a man asks his days for wealth and you are distant,
    they make reaching you his promised goal.

Analysis

The *qaṣīda* is in the metre *ṭawīl* (*fa^cūlun mafā^cīlun* x 2) and rhymed in the letter *dāl*. This rhyme the poet exploits to the fullest. In the first place, he appropriates the by now traditional poetic plays (*jinās*) on the root *ᶜ-w-d* (return), whence the words *ᶜīd* (annually recurring holiday) and *ᶜāda* (habit) (see al-Barqūqī 1986: 2:3,8; Lane 1968: s.v. *ᶜ-w-d*), a custom he will repeat himself, under quite contrary circumstances, in his renowned *ᶜĪd* invective (*hijāʾ*) against Kāfūr (see Stetkevych 1996). In the second place, one of the most striking features of this poem is al-Mutanabbī's extended and structurally functional development of *jinās* on the metathetic permutations of this root. Indeed, we will be able to structure our analysis of the poem around this sophisticated etymological play. Hence we can divide the poem into the three following structural-etymological components which we will present briefly before proceeding to a more detailed analysis of the poem.

Part I (vv. 1–20) derives from the play of *ᶜāda* (habit, custom), from *ᶜ-w-d* (return), with *ᶜaduww* (enemy), from *ᶜ-d-w*, a root whose meanings encompass run, cross, transgress, be hostile. This part is constructed on the theme of Sayf al-Dawlah's *habit* of striking the *enemy* (v. 1). Here the metathetic antithesis of *ᶜ-w-d*, denoting repetition and cyclicality, as opposed to *ᶜ-d-w*, denoting crossing and transgression, is extended to establish an antithesis between the Islamic ruler, i.e., ᶜĪd celebrant, and Byzantine Christian enemy, *ᶜaduww*, the military transgressors and aggressors against Islam who would cut off the repeated celebration of the ᶜĪd.

Part II (vv. 21–32) resolves the opposition of Part I into identity: not only does the poet extend his greeting to Sayf al-Dawlah on the ᶜĪd, but identifies his patron with the ᶜĪd itself (vv. 21–23). In purely practical military and political terms, we can say that without Sayf al-Dawlah's successful campaigns against the Byzantines the population of Aleppo would not be celebrating ᶜĪd al-Aḍḥā, but rather, in accordance with the *cuius regio eius religio* principle then in effect, at the very least the public celebration of the ᶜĪd would have been suppressed. Thus it is the emir's *ᶜāda* of Part I that qualifies him for Islamic rulership, indeed makes him the embodiment of Islam. This therefore provides for a legitimization and definition of Islamic rulership. Shockingly, for any poet other than al-Mutanabbī anyway, the ensuing *madīḥ* (panegyric) section seems to indicate that Sayf al-Dawlah should rise up against the

Caliph, the idea apparently being that the more victorious Islamic conqueror is the more legitimate ruler.

After Part I concerning the relation of the *mamdūḥ* (patron) to the enemy and Part II his relation to his subjects on the one hand and his overlord, the Caliph, on the other, Part III (vv. 33–42) now turns to the relation between poet and patron, and to the power of poetry – specifically al-Mutanabbī's. The etymological permutation this time comes at the end (v. 42), where the *mamdūḥ* is termed the *mawᶜid* (promise, appointed time or place), from *w-ᶜ-d* (promise), of all who would seek bounty.

Thus al-Mutanabbī virtually generates the entire structural and semantic, as well as acoustic, framework of the poem from this extended metathetic etymological play. For the poet the roots *ᶜ-w-d* (return, habit), *ᶜ-d-w* (hostility, transgression), and *w-ᶜ-d* (promise) do not bear arbitrary meanings nor are their metathetic relations accidental, rather, in al-Mutanabbī's hands, they exemplify in a most striking manner Gian Biagio Conte's description of poetic language:

> In literary discourse . . . the poetic overrides the communicative function, so that the arbitrary nature of the linguistic sign disappears to become fully motivated by the internal system of the poetic word. The relation of signifier to signified, irreversible in prose where signification is conventional and accessible only via the signifier, is, in poetry, a reciprocal two-way movement in which even the signified can recall its signifier.
>
> In other words, the elements that make up poetic discourse (both forms of expression and forms of content) are systematically related in so far as they are all coherently *guided* by a single poetic intention. Each is distinguished by belonging to a composite organic system in which the relationship between signifier and signified is so intimate as to be reversible. The world of contents evoked by the poem corresponds coherently to the verbal texture in which it is expressed, as if one were inherent in the other. (Conte 1986: 75–76).

Part I

The explicit theme of Part I is military victory, but we are not dealing here with battle description. Instead the poet deploys a rhetorical strategy through which Sayf al-Dawlah's campaign of Jumādā al-Ākhirah 342/September–October 953 in which he routed the Byzantine General (Domesticus) Bardas Phocas and captured his son, Constantine, (for historical sources see Blachère 1935: 169; Canard 1950) becomes paradigmatic of the emir's habitual and customary defeat of the Infidel and thereby proof of the Islamic legitimacy of his rule. The opening verse states a *ḥikma* (aphorism) and then exemplifies it, i.e., it moves from the general and axiomatic to the specific and hypothetical. The rhetorical effect of the juxtaposition is to confirm, by association as it were, the hypothesis. This is followed by a more extended repetition of the pattern as the general praise of the patron's virtue and prowess in subjugating the enemy (vv. 1–10) is followed by the specific exemplum of his most recent campaign (vv. 11–20).

But let us tarry a bit at the two opening lines, for they introduce concepts essential to understanding the classical Arabo-Islamic concept of nobility and, therefore, of fitness to rule. 'Nobility' in both senses was understood to be essentially military in character and, again in both senses, to be inherent and inherited (see Connerton 1989: 85). The customs (*ᶜādāt*) of Sayf al-Dawlah are the 'embodied experience' (Connerton 1989: 93) of noble deeds. Connerton's remarks on 'the force of habit' are helpful here. Building upon Dewey's demonstration of the power of good habits by analogy to that of bad, Connerton notes the large role that desire plays in habitual behavior, that habits compel us toward particular courses of action, that habits are affective dispositions, that 'habits have power because they are so intimately a part of ourselves' (Connerton 1989: 94). Again, a habit is

> an activity which is acquired in the sense that it is influenced by previous activity; which is ready for overt manifestation; and which remains operative even when it is not the obviously dominant activity . . . . The term habit conveys the sense of operativeness, of a continuously practiced activity. It conveys the fact of exercise, the reinforcing effect of repeated acts. (Connerton 1989: 94)

One can only note with what striking etymological precision the Arabic term *ᶜāda* conveys the concept that Connerton is trying to get across. In other words, the striking of the foe and defeating false rumours by true deeds are not merely 'second nature', but the true nature of Sayf al-Dawlah.

The dominant theme of the verses of general praise (vv. 1-10) is the submission of the enemy to Sayf al-Dawlah and to Islam. Particularly effective in this regard is verse 4 in which the *double entendre* generated by the ambiguity of the pronominal antecedent, 'H/his sword in H/his hand' (see Yāzijī 1964: 1:179) has the effect of identifying Sayf al-Dawlah's military prowess with divine might, and hence submission to one constitutes submission to the other (Islam in its original meaning of *islām*/submission) (see also v. 7).

Also of note is verse 8 which plays on the archetypal topos of the ancient Near Eastern king as bringer of life and bringer of death. In this verse a charming conceit and antithesis (*ṭibāq*) reveals the reciprocity between these two functions: it is only through the ruler's military might that he can acquire the wealth to be magnanimously disbursed to his subjects. Hence war *revives* his wealth while his generosity *kills* it. The proper deployment of these two pillars of rulership is a subject the poet will take up once more (v. 30).

With verse 11 comes the transition from general to specific, or, more precisely, from the description of the *ᶜāda* of Sayf al-Dawlah to the enactment of that 'embodied experience'. The events referred to here are corroborated in the historical sources (Blachère 1935: 169; Canard 1950)). Al-Mutanabbī does not, however, give a 'battle description' – the common misnomer of military passages in Arabic poetry that reflects an equally common misconception – rather he wrests from the historical event those elements that can serve as exempla of Sayf al-Dawlah's *ᶜāda*. Thus, for example, the principle established in verse 7, that the kings of the earth submit to Sayf al-Dawlah, whether by fleeing or surrendering, is embodied in the flight of the Domesticus and the capture of his son. The Domesticus' retreat from the field of battle to the monastery, the exchange of coat-of-mail for haircloth robe, amounts to renouncing the active aggressive for the passive submissive. Al-Mutanabbī is thus quite correct in evaluating it as an act of cowardice and defeat, not of (Christian) religious devotion. Our Byzantine sources indeed inform us that it was standard for disgraced military and political figures to be relegated to monasteries.

The rather fanciful hypothetical flight of cowering (Christian) kings into monasteries then serves as a rhetorically powerful transition to the triumphant celebratory Islam of the coming section. The final verse (20) of Part I, while completing the apodosis of the preceding verse, provides a formal closure through the repetition in *wa-kullu -mriᵓin* (every man) of the *li-kulli -mriᵓin* of verse 1. The antithesis of defeated Christianity and triumphant Islam is subtly restated, for the Christians' preparation of black hair-cloth robes with their association of withdrawal, mortification of the flesh, and mourning provides the antithesis of the celebratory function of garb associated with the Islamic ᶜĪd al-Aḍḥā. The latter is of two types, first the donning of new garments by the general Muslim populace and second, for the actual pilgrims to the *ḥajj*, the exchange of the stark ritual garment, the *iḥrām*, for profane (and far more colorful) costume after the sacrifice on ᶜĪd al-Aḍḥā, both types symbolizing new life, rebirth, purification (see the discussion of verse 22).

We can now observe how al-Mutanabbī's exemplary employ of the military campaign of 342/953 allows the historical event to be subsumed into the repetitive cycle of Sayf al-Dawlah's *ᶜāda*. In Part II of the poem we will witness, through the etymological identification of Sayf al-Dawlah's *ᶜāda* with the ᶜĪd, the subsequent subsuming of the historical event into the Islamic liturgical calendrical cycle.

Part II

Numerous studies of ritual and ceremonial tell us that calendrical holidays, such as the new year, celebrate above all the restoration of order after chaos (see, e.g., Wensinck 1923; Gaster 1977; Connerton 1989: 65; Bloch 1987: 276–80) and that court ceremonial constitutes primarily the symbolic embodiment or recognition of the social, and indeed cosmic, hierarchy (Cannadine and Price 1987: 1–5; Kuhrt 1987: 44; Bloch 1987: 278). In this *qaṣīda*, then, inasmuch as it is both *madīḥ*, as I claim a literary form of court ceremonial, and *tahniᵓa bi-l-ᶜīd*, the liturgically obligatory greeting on the calendrically recurring holiday, both of these concepts should find expression. As I will be arguing, al-Mutanabbī in fact fuses both elements – the restoration of order after chaos and the recognition of the social/cosmic hierarchy – in this *qaṣīda*. This he does quite simply by his claim that in vanquishing the Christian Byzantines Sayf al-Dawlah has restored Islam and has thereby established his legitimate Islamic rule.

In all respects verse 21 is the pivot-point of the poem. Through a repetitive insistence on the word *ᶜīd* itself and its verbal form *ᶜayyada* (II to celebrate the ᶜĪd), al-Mutanabbī anchors the poem both acoustically and semantically. What begins as an ᶜĪd felicitation to the emir concludes, through the role reversal of emir and ᶜĪd, in identifying the two: the emir is an ᶜĪd to every Muslim (see al-Barqūqī 1986: 2:7–8). We can take this to mean that Sayf al-Dawlah's rule is recognized and his victories celebrated by all Muslims. In this way, we can say for the present ceremonial *qaṣīda* what Maurice Bloch has said of the ritual of the royal bath in 19th century Madagascar, that it 'links the cosmic and political order and in this way legitimates the latter' (Bloch 1987: 284). Similarly we can say that in identifying the emir, and more precisely his habitual military victory, with the ᶜĪd, al-Mutanabbī has established between the two what Connerton has termed in his analysis of Nazi commemorative ceremonies, a 'mythic concordance' (Connerton 1989:

43). Moreover, inasmuch as the ᶜĪd is performing the ritual greeting to the emir, it would seem that their relationship is, respectively, that of subject to ruler. The identification of the ᶜĪd and the emir then forms the basis for the extended metaphor of verses 22–24.

The metaphorical complexity, even confusion, of verse 22 is such that commentarists differ in their vocalization and hence precise interpretation of it. Whichever reading we follow, the role reversal of verse 21 seems still in effect here in the poet's benediction, itself another common category of performative speech, which basically conveys the idea of 'Many happy *returns* of the day'. The poet styles the ᶜĪds as the *mamdūḥ*'s garment. Hence, following the customary Islamic practice on ᶜĪd al-Aḍḥā, each year the worn garment, here the previous ᶜĪd, should be replaced with a new garment, i.e., ᶜĪd. The poet's evocation of the ᶜĪd custom of donning new garments in symbolic celebration of spiritual renewal and rebirth serves as an expression of Islamic triumph, an antithesis to the Christians' garments of renunciation and mortification, in brief, defeat, of verses 16 and 20. At the same time, though in an enlarged cultural arena, the association of this custom with the ruler in al-Mutanabbī's verse echoes the ancient Babylonian ritual of the annual divestiture and revestiture of the king (Kuhrt 1987: 33).

In what we cannot help but read as an inverted simile, verse 23 explains the socio-political hierarchy that places the emir above his subjects by analogy to the priority of the ᶜĪd among the days. In so doing it establishes the emir at the top of the social hierarchy: the emir is to the general Muslim populace as the ᶜĪd is to the other (profane) days of the year (see al-Barqūqī 1986: 2:8–9). Expanding on this *primus inter pares* explanation of rulership, the poet in verse 24 attributes this to fortune – just as a person has two seemingly identical eyes, but one is sharper than the other. Within the ensuing political passage of this poem, this could be interpreted as a challenge to the caliphal sovereignty of al-Muṭīᶜ lil-Lāh based on lineage at a time when military and political control of ᶜAbbāsid lands were in the hands of the Būyid emirs and their rivals – not least among them the Ḥamdānids – and Sayf al-Dawlah was virtually independent.

Having established the hierarchical position of Sayf al-Dawlah vis-à-vis his subjects, al-Mutanabbī then moves up the scale in verses 25 to 30 to present the emir's standing with regard to his presumptive liege-lord, the caliph. This section probably reflects less upon the audacity of al-Mutanabbī than on the debility of the 4th c. Hijrah Caliphate. Playing as he did in verses 4 and 14 on the emir's name (Sayf al-Dawlah = Sword of the [ᶜAbbāsid] Dynasty), the poet expresses his amazement that the

Caliph is not afraid of the sharp edges of the sword with which he is girt (v. 25); like using a lion in place of a falcon for hunting, the danger is that it will turn on the hunter and make him its prey. The point of this parable, occurring as it does precisely in that part of the poem that is concerned with the socio-political hierarchy, is that something is out of order. Verses 27 through 30 then present the emir's predicament as the poet sees it. What is of interest in the course of the present argument is that it is articulated in terms of the norms of reciprocal behavior that serve to define rank and position in the hierarchical system. The two cardinal virtues then are forbearance (*ḥilm*) and power (*qudra*), by which the poet intends possessing power and knowing when and how to use it. Within the system of hierarchies one establishes and preserves one's position through the appropriate exercise of these virtues. What the poet suggests in the second hemistich of verse 27 is that Sayf al-Dawlah's restraint toward the Caliph, presumably out of respect for his exalted rank, might better have been replaced by military aggression.

Verses 28 through 30 serve as a definition of the rules of nobility, here understood as the reciprocal definition of ranks within a hierarchy of such ranks. Status within the hierarchy is negotiated and regulated through rituals of exchange, which in this context encompass a variety of symbolic and ceremonial forms, such as physical and verbal expressions of dominion and obeisance, dominance and submission, e.g., greetings, gestures, as well as material (gift) exchange. Marcel Mauss's formulation of ritual exchange applies equally to material and ceremonial (symbolic) exchange and is central to our understanding the establishment and maintenance of the Arabo-Islamic courtly hierarchy. He writes:

> Between vassals and chiefs, between vassals and their henchmen, the hierarchy is established by means of these gifts. To give is to show one's superiority, to show that one is something more and higher, that one is *magister*. To accept without returning or repaying more is to face subordination, to become a client and subservient, to become *minister*. (Mauss 1967: 70)

Further, 'No less important is the role which honour plays in the transactions . . . . Nowhere else is the prestige of the individual as closely bound up with expenditure, and with the duty of returning with interest gifts received in such a way that the creditor becomes the debtor' (Mauss 1967: 35). It is within this conceptual framework that Roy Mottahedeh's important discussion of the bonds of obligation entailed by *niᶜma* (benefit) (Mottahedeh 1980: 72–78) should be read. Thus, 'Nothing kills noble men like forgiveness' (v. 28) means that when you excuse a noble rather than demanding or expecting of him reciprocal noble behavior, his rank is lowered with regard to yours.

The poet then complains that the times are such that you can hardly find anyone who recognizes a favour, let alone realizes his obligation to repay it (= gratitude). Verse 29 states with elegance and simplicity the basic rule of nobility, i.e., that its principles of reciprocity and obligation function only among nobles, or, in other words, adherence to these rules defines nobility – '*noblesse oblige*'. When you commit an act of generosity to a noble, he will acknowledge the debt incurred and his obligation to repay it, that is, he will feel grateful and 'obliged'. A bond of loyalty is thereby established. Conversely, such generosity conferred upon an ignoble will elicit only insolence or contempt – he will claim he was owed it all along, or that he has cleverly taken advantage of you. The point is that the ignoble value material gain over honour. In sum, we can say that a man's response to an act of generosity defines his position in the hierarchical scale.

Along the same lines verse 30 implies that the maintenance of high rank requires not merely the possession of the two foremost forms of power, viz., military and economic might, but also their proper deployment. We must first remark that the latter in Arabic poetic and political terms means above all the power to give, generosity. In the poetic canon these are mythopoeically expressed as the power over life and death, the basis of the charming conceit and wordplay of verse 8.

Of particular interest is the role these verses (27–30, or esp. 28–30) play within this *qaṣīda*. For they perform two simultaneous functions, each one connected to a particular dimension of the poem. The first is the one already discussed, that is an elegant and concise definition of the courtly code on which the social structural hierarchy is founded. As such, these verses will remain rhetorically and morally compelling to all who subscribe to that system of values and, in turn, will serve to prop and propagate such values. In this respect they contribute to the lasting appreciation of the poem as it functions within the courtly culture of the Arabo-Islamic military aristocracy, and further as a 'cultural artifact' or work of art beyond the limits of that culture.

The second function applies in a much more immediate manner to the circumstances of the poem's composition. For, in the context of the poem, these verses must be read in light of verse 25 and 26. Thus, in what amounts to incitement to insurrection, the poet suggests that the emir has, in the case of the Caliph, confused or misplaced his greatest virtues, forbearance and might or generosity and power (vv. 27-30). Thus, where we might expect to find an expression of obeisance and allegiance to the upper echelons of the Islamic political hierarchy, we find in al-Mutanabbī's *qaṣīda* to Sayf al-Dawlah the presentation of a Realpolitik, and an instigation to correct, as it were, a hierarchy that does not reflect the true distribution of power. More to the point, the fact that al-Mutanabbī could present such a poem in itself testifies, as do the historical accounts (see, e.g., Canard *EI2*; Cahen *EI2*), to the debility of the caliphate under the Būyid emirate. What is of crucial importance is that we realize that al-Mutanabbī is fully backing the Arabo-Islamic courtly concept of nobility, that is, military aristocracy, as the principle for the construction and maintenance of the socio-political hierarchy. What he is criticizing is a malfunction that has led to 'disorder' in that system. Al-Mutanabbī's call then is for a restitution of the proper order, an order that to him seems properly to be based on military prowess and the concomitant magnanimity that it allows for.

In both its general and specific dimensions, al-Mutanabbī's call for restitution of a rightly ordered hierarchy can be understood in formal terms as expressing the ancient Near Eastern pattern of annual recurring rituals (new year festivals) in which what is celebrated above all is the restitution of order after chaos. Sayf al-Dawlah's identification with the ᶜĪd then takes on two aspects: first, with regard to the Byzantine Christian enemy, his military triumph marks the restoration of the proper cosmic and political order after the 'chaos' of Infidel aggression.

Second, with respect to the political hierarchy within the Islamic world, the poet calls for the restitution of what he sees as the proper 'order' of the political hierarchy which has been 'disorder' by the subordination of Sayf al-Dawlah to a liege-lord who is his inferior. In more immediate terms, perhaps what we are seeing in this *qaṣīda* is an expression of the tension between the true military aristocracy and the figurehead hereditary caliphate.

Verses 31 and 32 serve as a sort of double closure of Part II. With regard to the more immediate argument, they express the poet's deference toward the emir's better judgment in not rising up against the Caliph – this due to Sayf al-Dawlah's superiority over all men in opinion, judgment, rank, soul, and lineage, which render many of his deeds unfathomable and unchallengeable. With regard to the broader structural lines of the *qaṣīda*, these two verses provide a closure to the *madīḥ* section grounding allegiance to the emir and the legitimacy of his rule in his superior virtue, and establishing a principle of unquestioning obedience to him. I should note that my reading of these two verses is somewhat more contextual and political than that of the commentarists who remark on them as general praise for the virtues and generous deeds of Sayf al-Dawlah. The net effect, in any case, is the poet's reaffirmation on the ᶜĪd of the legitimacy of the emir's rule and of the social hierarchy that his rule embodies.

The role of the poet and the ceremonial function of panegyric are such that what the poet says in his *qaṣīda* is understood to be paradigmatic for the polity as a whole, i.e., for all the emir's subjects. Furthermore, as an expression of the principles upon which the Arabo-Islamic social structure is erected, the poem is paradigmatic for the relation of all Muslim subjects to their rulers. Again, it is these two aspects that explain the *qaṣīda*'s immediate ceremonial function, i.e., why it was presented to and accepted by Sayf al-Dawlah as a ritual ᶜĪd greeting in 342H., and why it has been preserved as part of the Arabo-Islamic cultural heritage ever since.

If, as we have stated above, the force of Part II is to subsume the historical event or exemplum into the cyclical liturgical calendar through the identification of the *ᶜāda* of Sayf al-Dawlah and the ᶜĪd, then the final step remains to be taken, that is, the *qaṣīda* must serve as the vehicle for the perpetuation of Sayf al-Dawlah's place in the Islamic liturgical calendar. Thus the *qaṣīda* goes far beyond its immediate ceremonial function on the particular day of its first recitation. It will have failed in its poetic and liturgical purpose if it is not found to be so strikingly beautiful that it is itself, like the ᶜĪd, perpetually repeated. In Part III then we turn from the relation of the emir to his subjects and liege-lord to his relation with the poet, and to the poet's, or poem's, capacity to project Sayf al-Dawlah's glory into the future.

Part III

To begin to understand the final section of the *qaṣīda*, which deals, above all, with the role of poet and poetry, we must examine further the functional aspect of poetry as it relates to poetic form. First of all, we should keep in mind that the poet's presentation or recitation of a *qaṣīda* to the ruler is one of the primary insignia of power in Arabo-Islamic rulership. To receive homage in this tradition-honoured way is an expression of legitimate rulership. In this respect, the ritual and ceremonial aspects of the *qaṣīda* come to the fore. By this I mean those genre-defining characteristics of the *qaṣīda* that are fixed, what I have termed the 'liturgical' characteristics. Thus the established monorhyme and metres, diction, tropes, themes, structure, etc. of the *qaṣīda* are *necessarily* fixed, for their function is to create a trajectory back in time, re-enacting, as it were, the autochthonous and originary Arabic and Islamic acts of homage. In this respect the *qaṣīda* functions as a commemorative ceremony of the twin authenticities or twin legitimacies of Arabo-Islamic rule. For the *qaṣīda* is at once the re-enactment of the panegyrics of the Jāhiliyyah, of which we might cite al-Nābighah al-Dhubyānī's *dāliyya* to the Lakhmid king al-Nuᶜmān ibn al-Mundhir as a renowned example, and thus legitimates the Arabicity, whether genetic or cultural, of the ruler who through this ritual of *imitatio* receives it. At the same time, through the Prophet Muḥammad's co-opting of the pre-Islamic *qaṣīda* as a rite of homage to himself as the embodiment of Islamic rulership, the recitation of *qaṣīda* to ruler likewise re-enacts events of such 'mythic' significance as the submission and homage of Kaᶜb ibn Zuhayr to the Prophet through the recitation of his renowned *Qaṣīdat al-Burda* (Stetkevych 1994). Thus I would argue that the fixed, i.e., liturgical, aspects of the *qaṣīda* are necessary to establish its ritual cognation with, not so much specific originary poetic acts of homage, as an entire cultural poetic heritage composed of liturgically cognate *qaṣīda*s (see further Stetkevych unpub.).

With regard to the *mamdūḥ*, the presentation of the *qaṣīda* then identifies him, ritually at least, with every other Arabo-Islamic ruler, past or present, who has been or will be, the recipient of a *qaṣīda*. We can grasp this more clearly if we extend our analogy to commemorative rites: just as every Christian who celebrates the mass or takes Holy Communion thereby identifies with every other Christian, past or present, or every Jew who celebrates Passover, or every Muslim who performs the sacrifice of ᶜĪd al-Aḍḥā, etc. (see Connerton 1989: 41-71), so too the *mamdūḥ* who participates in the *qaṣīda*-presentation ritual becomes thereby ritually or even mythically identified with every other Arabo-Islamic ruler or, in a more abstract sense, with legitimate Arabo-Islamic rulership. That is, repetition, at least symbolically, constitutes identity.

But the *qaṣīda* is not merely a ritual or liturgical text. For however great the formal strictures on the Arab panegyric poet, his mandate was above all to be original and beautiful. That is, in order to establish the *qaṣīda* in the classical corpus and thereby immortalize the renown of the *mamdūḥ*, the poet had to produce a poem that falls generically within the tradition – this is to achieve the backward trajectory necessary for the legitimation both of the ruler and *qaṣīda* – and at the same time a work so striking and compelling in its originality that it establishes its own place in that tradition – this is to achieve the forward trajectory.

This forward trajectory is of two types: the first is what we might call 'passive perpetuity', that is, the poem is memorized, recited, written down; the second, 'active perpetuity', that is, that the poem has true generative force within the tradition, a force that spawns borrowings (*sariqa*/plagiarism) and imitations (*muᶜāraḍa*/counter-poems)(for a discussion of various types of *imitatio*, ranging from plagiarism to rivalrous emulation, in the Arabic and Persian traditions, see Losensky 1994). It is in this projection backward and forward of a unique literary work that the *qaṣīda* distinguishes itself from liturgy, and in this respect too that there is no substitute for the artistic work of compelling beauty and originality. The poet is not merely invoking or intoning the sanction of time-honored rituals of homage, he is constructing a monument to a particular *mamdūḥ* that will itself stand for all time. It is with this aesthetically dependent aspect of poetry in mind that we can begin to understand Part III of the poem.

In our opening remarks, we noted that al-Mutanabbī, in reciting this *qaṣīda* while he and his patron were both mounted, presented himself ceremonially as Sayf al-Dawlah's equal. In Part I we witnessed in Sayf al-Dawlah's defeat of the Byzantine Christians the restitution of the proper cosmic order, that is, of Islam triumphant. In Part II we observed that the poet is concerned primarily with the restitution of the proper order in what we might call the domestic sphere, i.e., the relationship of the emir Sayf al-Dawlah to the Caliph. In Part III, likewise, the concept of restoration of a proper order comes to the fore. Here the poet is concerned first with his rank among the other poets of the Ḥamdānid court and second with his rank vis-à-vis the emir. All of this is expressed in terms of the ritual exchange between poem and prize, *qaṣīda* and *jāʾiza*, through which the patron expresses his valuation of a particular poem and poet, both in themselves and with regard to others, in objectively quantifiable terms.

Given the brusque imperatives that punctuate Part III of the poem (the beginning of vv. 33, 38 & 39), I think it is appropriate to speak in terms of the poet's demands. These should be understood as originating in the ancient Near Eastern tradition of the supplicant presenting his plea before the ruler and therefore, as part of a ritual or ceremonial demonstration of the ruler's justice, mercy, and magnanimity. As we know from studies of ritual exchange (Mauss 1967; Stetkevych 1994; 1996), this is virtually a form of entrapment, for the ruler would lose face and status if he did not respond to the plea in the most gracious and magnanimous of terms.

On the other hand, what is probably the main point in the ceremonial context is that the poet's plea, which the patron can fulfill on the spot through the simple granting (another performative act) of a prize –

dirhams, dinars, horses, slave-girls, are the common currency – offers the patron the opportunity to give a concrete demonstration of his justice, generosity, etc., thereby establishing a paradigm of the relation of the Arabo-Islamic ruler to all of his subjects (see Stetkevych 1996). Thus in a performative sense the poem incorporates the poet-patron and subject-ruler relationship. If al-Mutanabbī presents himself more as an equal than as a supplicant, it is because of his extraordinary, though, as the centuries have proven, correct, estimation of his poetic powers.

Al-Mutanabbī's first demand (v. 33) is for Sayf al-Dawlah to rid him of the jealousy of his rivals at the Ḥamdānid court by humbling them. This verse has a certain rhetorical twist to it in that one would first expect the dispelling of jealousy to be achieved by his giving as generously to them as he has to al-Mutanabbī. Quite the contrary, al-Mutanabbī means that Sayf al-Dawlah has been too generous with them, till they imagined they were as deserving as al-Mutanabbī and waxed envious. It was, the poet implies, Sayf al-Dawlah's unwarranted generosity, that is, raising them above their true rank, that is responsible for their envy. The situation then is precisely that of the misplaced generosity described in Part II, verse 29.

Conversely (v. 34) Sayf al-Dawlah's 'good opinion' (*ḥusnu raʾyika*) of al-Mutanabbī, by which he means high estimation of and lavish reward for his poetry, would allow the poet to subdue his enviers. The metaphor employed here is of particular note since the image of the sword that slays even when sheathed expresses with great force and precision the implicit or potential power of the great poet – that his rivals dare not challenge him – what we otherwise know as the principle of deterrence. The weaponry metaphor continues in verse 35 where it serves again to express with conciseness and precision the double symbolic and practical nature of the panegyric poet and his poetry. Like a Samharī spear that serves to adorn – that is, as one of the insignia of power – the warrior-ruler when displayed and to strike terror in his enemies and awe in his followers when aimed, the mere presence of so renowned a panegyric poet adorns the court of his patron as a symbol of power and prestige – only the heroic can attract poets and only the magnanimous can retain them – and when his poetic powers are unleashed in panegyric to Sayf al-Dawlah they create a portrait of the *mamdūḥ* so formidable that it amazes his followers and confounds his foes. This interpretation is at variance with that of the classical commentarists, such as al-Maᶜarrī, who says rather that the spear displayed refers to al-Mutanabbī's poetry at court and the aimed spear refers to his going to battle with Sayf al-Dawlah (al-Maᶜarrī 1986: 3:384). In my view the latter reading weakens the metaphor and is somewhat outside of the immediate poetic context, especially of verse 34 in which the blows involved are clearly poetic ones.

Verses 36 and 37 express the dissemination and circulation of al-Mutanabbī's poetry, and hence the *mamdūḥ*'s renown, both chronologically, in what we have termed the forward trajectory of the *qaṣīda*, and geographically. The first employs a metaphysical conceit that personifies *dahr* (time, fate) itself as a reciter and transmitter of al-Mutanabbī's verse. The basis of this verse is the pre-Islamic transmission of the originally orally preserved *qaṣīda* tradition through *ruwāt* (s. *rāwī*), reciters or transmitters, who memorized a poet's verse and passed it down orally generation after generation. So compelling is al-Mutanabbī's poetry that recluses rush out to bruit it abroad and, in a miracle on the order of making the blind see, with it the tuneless raise their voices in song. These verses thus express what I have termed above the 'passive perpetuity' of poetry, that is, the power of the poem to captivate and capture an audience and thereby be incorporated permanently into the poetic canon.

In verse 38 al-Mutanabbī restates the demand of verse 33, now explicitly both claiming his reward and justifying it. Here the poet claims what I term the 'active perpetuity', the power of the poem to generate other poetry, whether in the illicit form of plagiarism (*sariqa*) or the licit form of 'rivalrous emulation' (*muᶜāraḍa*) (see Losensky 1994). Al-Mutanabbī claims payment for all the panegyrics presented to Sayf al-Dawlah, since the other court panegyrists are merely repeating, i.e., plagiarizing, his poetry. This demand is reiterated metaphorically in verse 38 where al-Mutanabbī calls on Sayf al-Dawlah to reject all poetry but his, since his is the actual, uttered voice, the others', mere echoes.

We can thus observe in this *qaṣīda* how both the poet and the patron employ the element of ritual exchange implicit in the ceremonial presentation of the *qaṣīda* and conferral of the *jāʾiza* (prize) as a means to negotiate and regulate rank and status, much as Sanders has claimed for ceremonial generally (Sanders 1994: 37). For the purpose of the prize as explicitly stated here is to raise al-Mutanabbī to his deserved rank. The humbling of his jealous rivals should likewise be understood in material terms. Al-Mutanabbī's plea or demand is for Sayf al-Dawlah to restore him to his proper position as the foremost of the poets of the Ḥamdānid court and to put his jealous rivals 'in their place'. In the poet's call for the restoration of proper poetic and courtly hierarchy after the chaotic frenzy of impudent and inferior rivals Part III shares with Parts I and II the ancient Near Eastern new year theme of restoring order after chaos.

Al-Mutanabbī seals his *qaṣīda* with three verses (40–42) that serve as closure in a more immediate sense to Part III and in a more extended sense to the poem as a whole. The controlling image of these verses is that of the panegyrist who journeys from court to court until he finds a patron worthy of him, i.e., who rewards him generously, and to whom he therefore feels bound by ties of loyalty and obligation. It is noteworthy though that this closure is expressed in broad terms so as to be paradigmatically applicable to any of the liege-lord's subjects, or nobles. Thus al-Mutanabbī describes himself (v. 40) as having left the night journey to the impecunious and having settled permanently with Sayf al-Dawlah who has shod the poet's steeds with gold (referring, according to al-Maᶜarrī's commentary, to an actual incident when Sayf al-Dawlah conferred upon the poet a steed shod in golden horseshoes, Maᶜarrī 1986: 3:385).

But gift exchange, as Mauss has told us, involves above all the forging of bonds, and it is the bonds of love and loyalty toward his patron that al-Mutanabbī declares in verse 41. It is of note here that the nature of this bond is explicitly bound up with the concept of nobility and honour propounded in verse 29: he who finds beneficence a bond is *ipso facto* a noble. The two verses (40 & 41) taken together thus constitute a declaration of allegiance or homage, at once, I believe, *bayᶜa* (oath of allegiance) and *shukr al-niᶜma* (gratitude for benefit, obligation) (see Mottahedeh 1980: 50–54, 72–78). As the alternative translations indicate, verses 40 and 41 can be read as constative, 'I have quit . . . I have bound . . . .' or as performative (here with a contractual force), 'I [hereby] quit . . . I [hereby] bind myself . . . .' or even 'I will quit . . . . I will bind' (see Austin 1962: passim; Wright 1967: 2: 1–3). For the poet in recognizing Sayf al-Dawlah as his liege-lord, i.e., what is meant by 'I have bound/bind myself to your protection', thereby is bound to compose panegyric virtually exclusively for him (or others at his liege's court). The poet's payment of homage, i.e., the poem itself, in return for protection and beneficence thus ceremonially embodies the social contract upon which the Arabo-Islamic rulership was founded.

The closing verse (42) in one respect recapitulates the two preceding verses, but the change from the first to the third person moves the discourse from the specific to the general, from the personal to the universal, particularly as 'a man' (*al-insānu*) of verse 42 is synonymous with the 'everyman' (*li-kulli -mriʾin*) of the opening (v. 1). Finally, the closing word *mawᶜid* (promise, pledge, appointed time or place), the noun of place of our final metathetic permutation, *w-ᶜ-d* (promise) has the effect of recapitulating the entire *qaṣīda* and projecting it into the future. First it recalls Sayf al-Dawlah's *ᶜāda*, the habit built up through repeated exercise until it is bodily incorporated (and that habituation itself suggesting futurity), of striking the enemy/Infidel so that he has become the embodiment of Islam triumphant (Part I). Second, it recalls the calendrically repeated ᶜĪd, now identified with Sayf al-Dawlah, that celebrates the cyclical restoration or restitution of Islam triumphant and of the Arabo-Islamic cosmic and social hierarchy and whereby the historical is incorporated into the mythical (Part II). Third, the reciprocal bond established by the exchange of panegyric and prize implies a reciprocal promise or pledge, i.e, it is contractual and is understood to *bind* the two parties to a *future* course of action, specifically, to continued panegyric on the part of the poet and continued prizes on the part of the patron. Thus *mawᶜid* suggests that now that the poet has delivered his panegyric, the payment has become due (Part III). Finally, if we look more closely, we perceive a subtle use of the personification of the abstract and concomitant abstraction of person in this verse. For if our usual understanding is that men make promises and the course of time fulfills them, here, 'the days' (*al-ayyām*), synonymous with *dahr* (time, fate), make the promises and Sayf al-Dawlah fulfills them. Thus Sayf al-Dawlah becomes not merely the fulfillment of the hopes of every supplicant, but the fulfillment of the promise, the goal, of time.

To conclude briefly, I hope that this study has succeeded in demonstrating its critical premise, i.e., that the aesthetics of the *qaṣīda* are intimately bound up with the multiplicity of ceremonial, ritual, political, social and economic functions that it performs. Far from detracting from the *qaṣīda*'s aesthetic worth, our appreciation of these functional aspects increases our understanding and enhances our estimation of the Arabic poetic art.

Bibliography

Austin, J.L., *How To Do Things with Words* (Cambridge: Harvard University Press, 1962).

al-Barqūqī, ᶜAbd al-Raḥmān, *Sharḥ Dīwān al-Mutanabbī* 4 vols (Beirut: Dār al-Kitāb al-ᶜArabī, 1986).

Blachère, R., *Un poète arabe du IVe siècle de l'Hégire (Xe siècle de J.-C.): Abou -ṭ-Ṭayyib al-Motanabbî* (Paris: Adrien-Maisonneuve, 1935).

Bloch, Maurice, 'The ritual of the royal bath in Madagascar: the dissolution of death, birth and fertility into authority' in Cannadine and Price, *Rituals of Royalty*.

Cahen, Cl., art. 'Buwayhids' in *Encyclopaedia of Islam* 2d ed.

Canard, Marius, *Extraits des sources arabes* part 2 of A.A. Vasiliev, *Byzance et les Arabes: II la dynastie macédonienne (867–959)* Henri Grégoire and

Marius Canard (eds) (Brussels: Éditions de l'Institut de Philologie et d'Histoire Orientales et Slaves, 1950).
Canard, M., art. 'Ḥamdānids' in *Encyclopaedia of Islam* 2d ed.
Cannadine, David, and Simon Price (eds) *Rituals of Royalty: Power and Ceremony in Traditional Societies* (Cambridge: Cambridge University Press, 1987).
Connerton, Paul, *How Societies Remember* (Cambridge: Cambridge University Press, 1989).
Conte, Gian Biagio, *The Rhetoric of Imitation: Genre and Poetic Memory in Virgil and Other Latin Poets*, trans. Charles Segal (Ithaca, N.Y.: Cornell University Press, 1986).
Gaster, Theodor, H., *Thespis: Ritual, Myth, and Drama in the Ancient Near East* (New York: Norton: 1977).
Kuhrt, Amélie, 'Usurpation, conquest and ceremonial: from Babylon to Persia' in Cannadine and Price, *Rituals of Royalty*.
Lane, Edward William, *An Arabic-English Lexicon* 8 vols (Beirut: Librairie du Liban, 1968).
Losensky, Paul E., '"The Allusive Field of Drunkenness": Three Safavid- Moghul Responses to a Lyric by Bābā Fighānī' in Stetkevych, *Reorientations*. [= 1994]
al-Maᶜarrī, Abū al-ᶜAlāᵓ, *Sharḥ Dīwān Abī al-Ṭayyib al-Mutanabbī, 'Muᶜjiz Aḥmad'* 4 vols, ᶜAbd al-Majīd Diyāb (ed) (Cairo: Dār al-Maᶜārif, 1986).
Mauss, Marcel, *The Gift: Forms and Functions of Exchange in Archaic Societies*, trans. Ian Cunnison (New York: Norton, 1967) (*Essai sur le don, forme archaïque de l'échange*, 1925).
MacCormack, Sabine G., *Art and Ceremony in Late Antiquity* (Berkeley and Los Angeles: The University of California Press, 1981).
Mottahedeh, Roy P., *Loyalty and Leadership in an Early Islamic Society* (Princeton, N.J.: Princeton University Press, 1980).
Sanders, Paula, *Ritual, Politics, and the City in Fatimid Cairo* (Albany: State University of New York Press, 1994).
Stetkevych, Suzanne Pinckney, *Abū Tammām and the Poetics of the ᶜAbbāsid Age* (Leiden: E.J. Brill, 1991).
Stetkevych, Suzanne Pinckney, *The Mute Immortals Speak: Pre-Islamic Poetry and the Poetics of Ritual* (Ithaca, N.Y.: Cornell University Press, 1993).
Stetkevych, Suzanne Pinckney, 'Pre-Islamic Panegyric and the Poetics of Redemption: *Mufaḍḍalīyah 119* of ᶜAlqamah and *Bānat Suᶜād* of Kaᶜb ibn Zuhayr' in eadem, *Reorientations* [= 1994].
Stetkevych, Suzanne Pinckney, (ed) *Reorientations: Arabic and Persian Poetry* (Bloomington, Indiana: Indiana University Press, 1994).
Stetkevych, Suzanne Pinckney, 'Abbasid panegyric and the poetics of political allegiance: two poems of al-Mutanabbī on Kāfūr' in Stefan Sperl and Christopher Shackle (eds) *Qaṣīda Poetry in Islamic Asia and Africa* (Leiden: E.J. Brill, forthcoming 1996).
Stetkevych, Suzanne Pinckney, 'The Qaṣīda and the Poetics of Ceremony: Three ᶜĪd Panegyrics to the Cordoban Caliphate' unpublished paper presented at conference on Languages of Power in Muslim Spain, Cornell University, Nov. 1994.
al-ᶜUkbārī, Abū al-Baqāᵓ, *Dīwān Abī al-Ṭayyib al-Mutanabbī, al-musammā bi al-Tibyān fī Sharḥ al-Dīwān* 4 vols, Muṣṭafā al-Saqqāᵓ, Ibrāhīm al-Abyārī, and ᶜAbd al-Ḥafīẓ Shalabī (eds) (Beirut: Dār al-Maᶜrifah, 1936).

al-Wāḥidī, Abū al-Ḥasan ᶜAlī ibn Aḥmad, *Dīwān Abī al-Ṭayyib al-Mutanabbī wa fī athnāᵓ matnih sharḥ al-imām al-ᶜallāmah al-Wāḥidī* Friedrich Dieterici (ed) (Cairo: Dār al-Kitāb al-Islāmī, n.d.)
Wensinck, A.J., 'The Semitic New Year and the Origin of Eschatology' *Acta Orientalia* 1 (1923) pp. 158–99.
Wensinck, A.J., et al. *Concordance et indices de la tradition musulmane* (Leiden: E.J. Brill, 1936–62).
Wright, W., *A Grammar of the Arabic Language* 3d ed. 2 vols (Cambridge: Cambridge University Press, 1967).
al-Yāzijī, Nāṣīf, *Al-ᶜArf al-Ṭayyib fī Sharḥ Dīwān Abī al-Ṭayyib* 2 vols (Beirut: Dār Ṣādir/Dār Bayrūt, 1964).

10

Najīb Al-Ḥaddād's Essay on the Comparison of Arabic and European Poetry

Geert Jan van Gelder
University of Groningen

The essay by Najīb al-Ḥaddād that I intend to discuss here was recently described, by Sasson Somekh, as "his famous article".[1] I must confess that I myself, not a specialist in modern Arabic literature, was not aware of its existence until I saw the article reproduced in facsimile in the Cairene journal *al-Fuṣūl* of 1984,[2] taken from the journal *al-Bayān* in which it was originally published in 1897. That the essay did and still does enjoy some fame is evident from the fact that al-Manfalūṭī incorporated it in his anthology *al-Mukhtārāt*, forty years after its publication,[3] and that *Fuṣūl* recently, in 1992, reproduced it once more, this time taken from al-Manfalūṭī's anthology, with a short introduction by Midḥat al-Jayyār.[4] Surprisingly, it seems that he as well as the editors of *Fuṣūl* were unaware of the fact that the essay had already appeared in the same journal eight years earlier.

Najīb al-Ḥaddād, a nephew of Ibrāhīm al-Yāzijī (son of Nāṣīf al-Yāzijī), was born in Beirut in 1867, but in 1873 his family moved to Alexandria, and the rest of his short life was spent in Egypt. He worked as a correspondent of *al-Ahrām*, founded or led several literary journals, wrote poetry, plays and *qiṣaṣ*, and translated and adapted prolifically from the French (Corneille, Racine, Molière, Voltaire, Victor Hugo, Alexandre Dumas père, Lamartine, Shakespeare, Walter Scott; the last two from French translations). He died in Alexandria in 1899, shortly before his 32nd birthday.[5] Especially with his plays and adaptations he contributed to the popularity both of drama and of European literature at the turn of the century. In this field he had predecessors; in another he seems to have been something of a pioneer.

Traditionally, Arabic literary criticism and theory were self-contained and self-centred, almost totally uninterested in other literatures. One was aware of the existence of Greek or Persian poetry; the former was left unread, the latter must have been known at least to the several critics who were themselves Persian or had some knowledge of the language, but this is hardly noticeable in their works. Nobody went as far as to compare the literature or the poetry of two different literary traditions.[6] The nineteenth century changed all this. After some decades of adaptation and translation from European literatures, it was time to make an attempt to stand back and reflect on the differences between the two literary traditions. Shortly before the end of the century it was Najīb al-Ḥaddād, having himself served as one of the stones in the bridge between Europe and the Arab world, who was the first, it seems, to write an essay on comparative literature in Arabic. He was soon followed by others, such as Sulaymān al-Bustānī, in his preface to his verse translation of the *Iliad* (1904), and Rūḥī al-Khālidī in his erudite and strange book with the rather odd title *Tārīkh ᶜilm al-adab ᶜinda l-Ifranj wa-l-ᶜArab wa-Victor Hugo* (also 1904) – the title will appear less odd in a minute.[7] Al-Ḥaddād's *Muqābala bayn al-shiᶜr al-ᶜarabī wa-l-shiᶜr al-ifranjī* has been praised by Salma Jayyusi, who speaks of the "good modern critical insight" of the author,[8] and by Sasson Somekh, who describes the essay as "a systematic and illuminating analysis of the distinctive qualities" of European and Arabic poetry.[9] A dissenting voice comes from Jan Brugman, who dismisses it as being little more than "a description of French prosody and hardly a comparison (*muqābalah*) of European and Arabic poetry".[10] I do not agree with either side, admirers or detractors, as I hope will become clear. Both Jayyusi and Somekh give a short summary of the essay; I shall now provide my own, somewhat longer, résumé, with the addition of a few comments, followed by an evaluation.[11]

"Poetry is the art that conveys thought from the world of sense-perception (*ḥiss*) to the world of imagination (*khayāl*), words that shape the subtlest feelings[12] of the heart in the most splendid likeness, reality that may don the clothes of figurative speech, a great theme (*al-maᶜnā l-kabīr*) brought forward by thought in the moulds of concision . . .' [257/126]. Al-Ḥaddād begins in the grand style, with *sajᶜ* and all. Poetry is found in every civilized and uncivilized nation; man is a poet by nature just as a bird sings. The author has been fond of poetry since early childhood. He has read much French poetry, and, in French translation, also Classical Greek and Latin, English, German and Italian poetry. "Someone whose wish cannot be opposed", as the standard expression goes, has asked him to write the present essay on the comparison of Arabic and European poetry. It is a difficult task, one that requires a good knowledge of the various languages in order to appreciate the qualities of the different kinds of poetry. Since the author is not competent except in French and Arabic, he will leave matters of linguistic eloquence, *al-faṣāḥa l-lafẓiyya*, out of consideration and restrict himself to a discussion of *al-maᶜānī l-shiᶜriyya*, "poetical meanings", or themes and motifs, which are an indication of the poet's share of nobility and wisdom (*al-nubl wa-l-ḥikma*).

He is aware [259/129] that conveying poetry in the form of prose seriously diminishes the value of the poetry, especially when this has been translated from its original language in the first place. The harm done by this latter aspect, however, is mitigated to some extent since the various European languages are so similar to one another in their ways of expression. This is, he maintains, because all these poetical conventions derive from the same source, which is their ancestral language: Latin. (This will surprise speakers of Greek, English and German). Consequently, the beauty of the original is only marginally affected by translation into French. Another reason why the use of translation is not a very serious drawback is that the Europeans are, on the whole, far more concerned with *maᶜnā* than with *lafẓ*, anyway, due to the poverty of their languages. Where the Arabs have ten or more different ways at their disposal to convey the same idea, the Europeans have merely one or two.

Before embarking on a comparison of the two poetical traditions, the author compares the ideas on the origin of poetry current in the two cultures [260/131]. Spokesman for Europe is "the greatest French poet" of the time, Victor Hugo, who had died in 1885, twelve years before the publication of al-Ḥaddād's essay. The source, not mentioned by al-Ḥaddād, is Hugo's preface to *Cromwell* (1827), where he sketches the prehistory and history of poetry in three periods.[13] First came the age of the ancients (*al-ᶜahd al-ᶜatīq* or *ᶜahd al-awwalīn*), in which lyric poetry was created in the form of hymns, spiritual songs, prayers or invocations, by a pastoral society knowing neither laws nor wars. In the second age, the age of fables or myths (*ᶜahd al-khurāfāt*), families grew into tribes, tribes became nations; states emerged, wars arose. These changes are reflected in the epic, heroic poetry of this age, which produced Homer. Al-Ḥaddād's terminology is a little confused, for *ᶜahd al-khurāfāt*, used for the second age, is obviously derived from Hugo's *ère fabuleuse*, which in Hugo's system is the first rather than the second age; whereas *al-ᶜahd al-ᶜatīq*, the oldest stage, looks like a translation of Hugo's *les temps antiques*, which stands not for the oldest but the second stage. The confusion might be partly due to the fact that whatever might be called "epics" in classical Arabic literature, either legendary pre-Islamic narratives or the popular "romances' such as *ᶜAntar* or other *siyar*, counted as *khurāfāt* for educated Arabs. The third age came when Christianity arrived from the East and took over from paganism. The old myths were dispelled, a true civilization arose, and with it came an awareness of the two lives: earthly life and the Hereafter. Poetry moved from *wahm* to *ḥaqīqa*, from delusion to reality or truth. That this third age is associated with drama, to complete the triad lyric – epic – drama, is not mentioned by al-Ḥaddād, although it was in fact Hugo's main point. One might think that al-Ḥaddād believed, correctly, that the universality of this triad is questionable and its application to Arabic literature fraught with problems. But of course al-Ḥaddād believed no such thing. There is another reason why he does not say so and I shall come back to it.

The rather unhistorical but optimistic vision of poetry's past and present contrasts strangely with Thomas Love Peacock's scathing "Four Ages of Poetry", which antedates Hugo's essay by eight years. Hugo's ideas had obvious attractions for al-Ḥaddād, himself a Christian, who apparently takes it for granted that Hugo's little fable represents a truth generally acknowledged by the Europeans. Yet he does not apply Hugo's model to the history of Arabic poetry. Unlike the Europeans, the Arabs took their language and their poetry from no other nation, nor has any other nation adopted the poetry of the Arabs, says al-Ḥaddād [263/134], blithely disregarding the effects of the Arabo-Islamic conquests. The only distinct transition that may be discerned in the history of Arabic poetry is that from *badāwa* to *ḥaḍāra*, from bedouin to urban poetry, with a concomitant refinement in diction. Otherwise its composition, in terms of its prosody and themes, remained much the same. Still the *diyār*, campsites, are being described and the *aṭlāl*, the remains found there, wept over. The earliest poetry is concerned with personal events and emotions such as love, complaint or *ḥamāsa* (martial fervour), all this rendered without fictional additions or exaggerations. When they praised a man they praised him for what he was worth, no more. The simple fare of the Bedouin made place for the luxury and extravagance of later times; the poetry of the *muwalladūn* is characterized by exaggeration, *ifrāṭ*, in meaning and diction, while fantasy, *khayāl*, takes the place of the original realistic presentation, *ḥaqīqa*.

In short, European poetry, in Hugo's view, moved from fables to Truth, whereas Arabic poetry, in al-Ḥaddād's view, moved in the opposite direction, from truth to fantasy. Some kind of juggling is involved with the various meanings of *ḥaqīqa*: either Truth with a capital T, the antonym of nonsense or falsehood (*bāṭil*), or "veridical, non-figurative expression", the opposite of *majāz*. It is likely that al-Ḥaddād was not aware of this juggling. The result seems obvious, even though al-Ḥaddād refrains from making the point explicitly: Arab poets would do well to turn to European poetry, in order to retrieve the lost Truth.

The differences between European and Arabic poetry are of two kinds: matters of *lafẓ* and *maᶜnā*. *Lafẓ*, however, seems to be restricted here to prosody. In spite of his earlier announcement he proceeds [265/137] with a brief exposé of European prosody, which is in fact French prosody; it does not occur to al-Ḥaddād that the Greeks or the Germans might have different conventions. His description of metre (*wazn*) is marred by the fact that Arabic traditionally lacks a good equivalent of the concept "syllable". Instead of *maqṭaᶜ*, now the usual term, he employs the word *hijā'*, plural *ahjiya*, which strictly means "spelling" (without a plural) but had already been used to mean "syllable".[14] These syllables are called *aqdām*, "feet', says al-Ḥaddād, who apparently does not understand that a foot is composed of syllables. European prosody is based on syllable count only (al-Ḥaddād ignores stress, which plays no part in traditional Arabic metrics); therefore it is much easier than quantitative Arabic prosody; European poets have much more freedom to arrange words within a line. The absence of monorhyme is explained by the scarcity of words in their language. It is strange, says al-Ḥaddād [266–67/139], that in spite of their easy rhyming conventions they still complain of the difficulty of making verse; one of their greatest poets, Voltaire, called it "a heavy burden" to find a rhyme. They also have blank verse, *shiᶜr abyaḍ*, popular especially with the English, who took it from Latin. In some poems they even jump from one metre to another, "like in some obsolete kinds of *muwashshaḥa* that nobody uses any longer in our days amongst us" [267/140].[15]

As for the content, *al-jiha l-maᶜnawiyya*, of their poetry, they stick to realism, *yaltazimūna l-ḥaqā'iq fī naẓmihim iltizāman shadīdan*, unlike the Arabs who are so fond of hyperbole and exaggeration. In their aversion to far-fetched imagery they resemble the pre-Islamic Arab poets. It is remarkable, says al-Ḥaddād [268/14–42], that European poetry in full civilization thus resembles the earliest, "uncivilized" Arabic poetry. But in Arabic poetry both kinds, the realistic and the hyperbolic, are possible, in European poetry only the former, so that in a sense Arabic poetry has more to offer in his view. This view presupposes that hyperbole (*ghuluww*, *ighrāq*, *ifrāṭ*, *mubālagha*) is in itself a good thing, even though it has often been seen as a defect by many, and not only in the last century, judging by the longstanding debate on this matter.[16] In any case, continues al-Ḥaddād, the mannerism, hyperbole, verbosity and figurative overload of Arabic verse affects only some modes and themes, such as amatory and panegyric verse, where the poets let their imagination run free, helped by the unlimited potentialities of the Arabic language with it richness in forms, eloquent expressions, lofty diction, abundant metaphors and metonymies. In other modes and themes they do not exceed the bounds of nature and truthfulness; in this respect they resemble the Europeans.

The convention of introducing a poem with *nasīb* is unknown to the Europeans. They dislike vaunting poetry, *fakhr*, traditionally one of the major Arabic modes but in this day and age largely abandoned apart from exceptional circumstances, such as when one is forced to use it in a polemic. The Europeans are superior to the Arabs in the telling of stories in verse, which they count as the highest form of poetry. They are right in this: it is a better sign of creativity than the composition of a *dīwān*ful of *qaṣīda*s and short poems [269–70/143–44]. It is a demanding form, requiring much thought and inventivity to arrange the story, connect its parts, express different emotions and see things from different viewpoints. They surpass us, the Arabs, in the description of a situation (*ḥāla*) or an event (a battle, duel, lovers' meeting, shipwreck etc.), we surpass them in depicting things (a lion, horse, palace, handsome young man or woman). One may compare, for instance, Hugo's description of the Battle of Waterloo – no Arab could do it like that, and al-Mutanabbī's depiction of a lion – no European could equal it [270–71/145].

No lines by al-Mutanabbī are quoted, but he refers obviously to the *lāmiyya* that was compared with another piece on a lion, by al-Buḥturī, in al-Qāḍī al-Jurjānī's monograph on al-Mutanabbī, *al-Wasāṭa*,[17] and in *al-Mathal al-sā'ir* by Ḍiyā' al-Dīn Ibn al-Athīr.[18] It is interesting that here, too, al-Mutanabbī's poem figures in a comparison (Ibn al-Athīr speaks of a *mufāḍala*); moreover, Ibn al-Athīr, in another work, extensively compared and contrasted two passages on a wolf by al-Buḥturī and al-Sharīf al-Raḍī, in which he declares the former to excel in the description of the situation (*ḥāl*), whereas the latter is superior in the description of the animal itself.[19] In short, the same contrast that al-Ḥaddād discerns between European and Arabic poetry.

Al-Ḥaddād briefly mentions a few other differences: according to him the Europeans do not have the figures of speech and thought (*badīᶜ lafẓī* and *badīᶜ maᶜnawī*) of the Arabs, nor are they capable of expressing one motif in numerous ways like the Arabs can, as he argued before. Summing up, he observes that the Arabs have adopted the best elements of European poetry, whereas the Europeans have not taken anything from Arabic poetry. Consequently, Arabic poetry is superior, since it combines the best of two traditions and has the advantage of possessing as its medium the most perfect language in the world, as even the Europeans acknowledge (al-Ḥaddād quotes words to that effect from the Larousse Encyclopaedia). But "every girl admires her father", he concludes, admitting that he is naturally biased, being Arab himself; a phrase left out of the version in al-Manfalūṭī's *Mukhtārāt.*

The primary aim of any extended comparison in the Arabic literary tradition, whether it is called *mufāḍala*, *munāẓara* (the most common term for the "literary debate") or *muwāzana* (as in al-Āmidī's celebrated comparison of two poets entitled *al-Muwāzana*), is to establish which is the better one. Not surprisingly, Najīb al-Ḥaddād's essay concludes with a summing-up and a verdict; not altogether surprisingly, this verdict turns out to be gratifying to its intended audience, the Arab intellectuals and writers. It would be naïve, however, to assume that al-Ḥaddād's real and only motive was to establish the superiority of his own literary tradition.

It seems to me that al-Ḥaddād's essay has been praised for the wrong reasons. I do not think that it can be described, as did Somekh, as "a systematic and illuminating analysis of the distinctive qualities" of the two literary traditions, for it is not particularly systematic and it illuminates the author's limited knowledge more than anything else. Nor do I believe, as does Somekh, that the essay may serve as an example of the fact that even "those poets and intellectuals who were very much at home with European literature never dared, in the early stages of the *Nahḍa*, to urge Arabic poetry to expose itself to the influence of western poetic concepts".[20] On the contrary, I would like to argue that the main point and the ultimate aim of the essay is precisely to urge the exposure of Arabic poetry to European ideas on poetry. Al-Ḥaddād, wisely, did not attempt to prove that Arabic poetry is inferior, thus antagonizing his readership. For once, the conclusion is not at all what al-Ḥaddād is driving at, even though it may seem so at first sight: the main point is slyly made in passing. This is that Arab poets would do well to turn their hands to making verse drama of the European model. Verse drama is the highest form of poetry for the Europeans, and they are right in thinking so, says al-Ḥaddād, who adds that the Europeans are superior in this to the Arabs. The inescapable conclusion would seem to be that Arabic poetry is inferior to European poetry, for surely it is the highest form that should be decisive. Of course al-Ḥaddād does not draw this conclusion. He observes that the genre of verse drama has already been introduced into Arabic literature and mentions his nephew Khalīl al-Yāzijī, Ibrāhīm's younger brother (1858–1889), the author of *al-Murū'a wa-l-wafā'*, a verse drama written in 1876, performed in 1878 and published in 1884.[21] But in this genre, he says, "we have not yet reached the level of the Europeans, their perfection and mastery".

Seen in the light of al-Ḥaddād's oeuvre as a whole it is clear that the

Muqābala should be read, not as a comparison between two different literary traditions in which Arabic is the winner, but as a comparison between the old *qaṣīda* and verse drama. Here the latter is clearly the victor, supported by Victor Hugo and his high reputation. Al-Ḥaddād is rather outspoken at times, for instance when he declares a verse drama to be a better indication of creativity than a *dīwān*ful of *qaṣīda*s and short poems. But, very sensibly, he did not want to rub it in too firmly. That is, I believe, why he did not state explicitly, in his account of Hugo's three ages of poetry, that drama represented the last and highest stage but left this for his reader to conclude; and that is why he turned the essay ostensibly into a boastful comparison in order to lull reactionary opposition. After all, drama was still being regarded, as Mustafa Badawi puts it, "not as serious literature but as a commercial entertainment of ephemeral value and of a morally doubtful nature".[22] Al-Ḥaddād uses what is obviously a fable, *khurāfa* (Hugo's theory of the ages of poetry), to raise the status of the fictional story, traditionally called *khurāfa*, while calling it, with Hugo, a fable, *khurāfa*, transformed into Truth.

Notes

1. S. Somekh, in M. M. Badawi (ed.), *Modern Arabic Literature* (Cambridge, 1992), p. 38.
2. *Fuṣūl* 4:2 (1984) pp. 257–71, taken from *al-Bayān*, 7, 8 and 9 (September – October 1897).
3. Muṣṭafā Luṭfī al-Manfalūṭī, *Mukhtārāt* (Cairo, 1937), pp. 126–46.
4. 'al-Adab al-muqābal wa-bidāyat al-adab al-muqāran fī l-dirāsāt al-ᶜarabiyya al-ḥadītha: al-Shaykh Najīb al-Ḥaddād wa-Muqābalatuhu bayn al-shiᶜr al-ᶜarabī wa-l-shiᶜr al-ifranjī', taᶜlīq wa-taqdīm: Midḥat al-Jayyār', *Fuṣūl* 10:3–4 (no. 32, 1992) 245–59 (al-Ḥaddād's article on pp. 249–59).
5. On his life and works, see C. Brockelmann, *Geschichte der arabischen Litteratur, Supplementbände* (Leiden, 1937–42), ii, 762, iii, 268; P. G. Sadgrove, art. 'Nadjīb b. Sulaymān al-Ḥaddād' (1992), *Encyclopaedia of Islam*, New Edition (Leiden, 1960–??); Khayr al-Dīn al-Ziriklī, *al-Aᶜlām* (Beirut, 1986), viii, 12; ᶜUmar Riḍā Kaḥḥāla, *Muᶜjam al-mu'allifīn* (Damascus, 1957–61), xiii, 79, Jurjī Zaydān, *Tārīkh ādāb al-lugha al-ᶜarabiyya*, iv (Cairo, 1937), 213–14; Rufā'il Nakhla, *al-Mukhtārāt*, vol. ii (Beirut, 1931), 197–206; Jacob M. Landau, *Studies in the Arab Theater and Cinema* (Philadelphia, 1958), 110–13; Salma Khadra Jayyusi, *Trends and Movements in Modern Arabic Poetry* (Leiden, 1977), (i,) 64–5. I have not seen ᶜĀdil al-Ghaḍbān, *al-Shaykh Najīb al-Ḥaddād 1867–1899* (Beirut & Cairo, 1953), Idwār Sāmī Sabānikh al-Yāfī, *Najīb al-Ḥaddād al-mutarjim al-masraḥī* (Cairo, 1976), or the chapter on al-Ḥaddād in Isḥāq Mūsā al-Ḥusaynī, *al-Naqd al-adabī al-muᶜāṣir fī l-rubᶜ al-awwal min al-qarn al-ᶜishrīn* (Cairo, 1967), mentioned by Jayyusi (op. cit., p. 315).
6. Among the few exceptions is the brief remark by Ḍiyā' al-Dīn Ibn al-Athīr

at the end of his *al-Mathal al-sā'ir* (Cairo, 1959–n.d., iv, 12), on lengthy works of epic poetry found in Persian but not in Arabic literature.

7. On al-Khālidī and his book, see e.g. *EI*[2] s.v. (S. Moreh). The most recent edition was prepared, with an introduction, by Ḥusām al-Khaṭīb (Damascus, 1984).
8. Jayyusi, *Trends and Movements*, i, 64.
9. Somekh, in Badawi (ed.), *Modern Arabic Literature*, p. 38.
10. Jan Brugman, *An Introduction to the History of Modern Arabic Literature in Egypt* (Leiden, 1984), p. 331.
11. Page references given in the summary give the pagination of the *Fuṣūl* reproduction of 1984, followed by the pagination of al-Manfalūṭī's *Mukhtārāt* reproduced in *Fuṣūl* in 1992.
12. *adaqq al-sha*ᶜ*ā'ir*; the version published in al-Manfalūṭī's *Mukhtārāt* (henceforward referred to as M) has *araqq* instead of *adaqq*. *Sha*ᶜ*ā'ir* seems to serve as a plural of *shu*ᶜ*ūr* rather than of *sha*ᶜ*īra*, "rite".
13. There are several editions; a useful separate edition, obviously meant for schools, is Victor Hugo, *Préface de Cromwell*, avec une Notice biographique, une Notice historique et littéraire, des Notes explicatives, une Documentation thématique, des Jugements, un Questionnaire et des Sujets de devoirs, par Michel Cambien, (Paris, 1972) (*Collection Classiques Larousse*).
14. See R. Dozy, *Supplément aux dictionnaires arabes* (Leiden, 1927) s.v., with a reference to Humbert, *Guide de la conversation, ou Vocabulaire français-arabe* (Paris & Genève, 1838).
15. Instead of *mahjūra* M has *madhkūra*.
16. See especially J. Christoph Bürgel,' "Die beste Dichtung ist die Lügenreichste": Wesen und Bedeutung eines literarischen Streites des arabischen Mittelalters im Lichte komparatistischer Betrachtung', *Oriens* 23–24 (1974) pp. 7–102.
17. al-Qāḍī ᶜAlī Ibn ᶜAbd al-ᶜAzīz al-Jurjānī, *al-Wasāṭa bayn al-Mutanabbī wa-khuṣūmihi*, ed. Muḥammad Abū l-Faḍl Ibrāhīm & ᶜAlī Muḥammad al-Bijāwī (Cairo, n.d.), pp. 130–32; al-Mutanabbī, *Dīwān*, ed. F. Dieterici (Berlin, 1861), pp. 224–31 (esp. lines 17–43).
18. ed. Aḥmad al-Ḥūfī & Badawī Ṭabāna, vol. iii (Cairo, 1962), pp. 284–7.
19. Ḍiyā' al-Dīn Ibn al-Athīr, *al-Istidrāk fī l-radd* ᶜ*alā risālat Ibn al-Dahhān* . . ., ed. Ḥifnī Muḥammad Sharaf (Cairo, 1958), pp. 70–3.
20. Somekh (as in note 1), p. 38.
21. Brockelmann, *GAS* S II, 767. Khalīl al-Yāzijī had been the founder of the magazine *al-Bayān* in which al-Ḥaddād's *Muqābala* was published.
22. Mustafa Badawi, *Modern Arabic Literature and the West* (London, 1985), p. 199.

Part 2

Prose and Drama

11

Arabic Influences in the Literature of Nineteenth and Early Twentieth Century Britain

C. Edmund Bosworth
University of Manchester

First-hand acquaintance in Britain with Arabic literature, as opposed to knowledge via translations, often at second or third-hand, really dates back to the mid-seventeenth century and to the generations of outstanding pioneer Arabic scholars filling the newly-founded chairs of Arabic at the Universities of Cambridge and Oxford, such as Edward Pococke and his son of the same name, Abraham Wheelock and Simon Ockley. But despite the interest in the historical, scientific, ethical and philosophical monuments of Arabic literature evinced by these scholars, the true spirit of Arabic literary achievement could not be apprehended in the West, nor could it have any significant influence on the indigenous literatures there, until the most characteristic expression of the Arabic literary genius, poetry, began to be known. There were many obstacles to an acceptance, and, even, to a comprehension of this poetry, with its peculiar conventions and its multiplicity of allusions. Régis Blachère rightly described Arabic poetry as 'a secret garden', entry to which requires not only profound linguistic expertise but also an empathy with the entire thought-world of Islam, its religion, history and culture. It was the Welsh judge, administrator and scholar Sir William Jones (1746–94) who achieved a proficiency, remarkable for its time in the languages of ancient India and of the Persian world, and who also brought Arabic poetry to the wider attention of British readers, even if it is now clear that he was not a profound Arabic scholar. In 1772, at the age of 28, there appeared his *Poems, Consisting Chiefly of Translations from the Asiatick Languages*, in 1774 a work in Latin, *Poesos Asiaticae commentariorum libri*, on ancient Arabian poetry, and in 1782 his English prose translation of the seven *Mu^{c}allaqāt*, for which he had consulted some of the best native Arabic commentaries, including those of al-Tibrīzī and al-Zawzanī.[3] It was not until over a century later that C. (later Sir Charles) J. Lyall, an Indian Civil Servant, endeavoured very successfully to convey the metrical feel of the quantitative measures of this poetry; Lyall eschewed rhyme, but pointed out that the Arabic metre *ṭawīl*, for instance, already existed in English prosody as a form of anapæstic metre, and that an English poem like Robert Browning's *Abt Vogler* (though quite uninfluenced, so far as we know, by Arabic models) contains many lines which (substituting of course stress for quantity) perfectly fulfil the requirements of an English *ṭawīl*, metre:

> Ye know why the forms are fair, ye hear how the tale is told.
> . . . .
> Existent behind all laws, that made them and, lo, they are!
> . . . .
> And there! Ye have heard and seen: consider and bow the head.

Yet despite Sir William Jones' pioneering efforts, the form and themes alike of Arabic poetry, so alien to the epic or lyric traditions of poetry in the West, were long in having much effect on nineteenth century English literature. For one thing, whilst Germany had its twin geniuses Goethe, himself no orientalist but the author of the extremely influential *West-östliche Diwan*, drawing upon translations made by the Austrian orientalist Joseph von Hammer, and Friedrich Rückert, equally skilled in Arabic, Persian, Turkish and Sanskrit, the English-speaking world had no poet of first rank who was literate in Arabic and so able to penetrate into the 'secret garden'. Translations made at this time were mainly by academic orientalists, who cast them into the literary moulds of contemporary verse or, in some cases, used archaising forms which they imagined as more suitable to the venerable nature of the Arabic poetry. A cursory glance at those translations by various scholars, from Jones onwards, collected in the anthology *Arabic Poetry for English Readers* by W.A. Clouston (Glasgow 1881) – whose obscure compiler himself knew no oriental languages – displays this clearly; with the exception of a fine translation of al-Būṣīrī's celebrated *Burda* ode by Sir James Redhouse, the famous Turkish and Arabic lexicographer and scholar, it is hard to discern that these translations are from Arabic at all and not by minor poets of the later 18th and early 19th centuries.

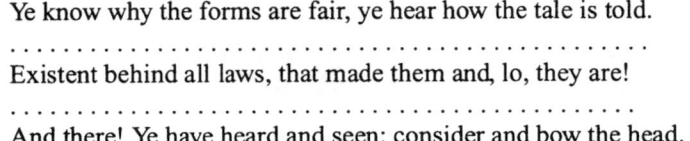

Nevertheless, it was to be expected that the Arabic and Islamic worlds would have an attraction for the poets of the Romantic period, with their love of the exotic and recherché, and the very limited number of translations available of Arabic poetry and romances had a certain subordinate influence. Thus Percy Bysshe Shelley (1792–1822) produced in 1821 a poem *From the Arabic, an Imitation*, based on a passage in the romance of the pre-Islamic Arab poet and hero ᶜAntara b. Shaddād and author of one of the *Mu^c^allaqāt*; two years previously, the Scotsman Terrick Hamilton, who had been employed by the East India Company and who later became Oriental Secretary at the British Embassy in Constantinople, had published a translation of the first third or so of the *Sīrat ^c^Antar* as *Antar, a Bedoueen Romance,* and Shelley utilised this. Two decades later, Alfred (later Lord) Tennyson (1809–92) wrote his poem *Lockesley Hall*, concerning which his son Hallam subsequently wrote in his *Memoir*, 'I remember my father saying, that Sir William Jones's prose-translation of the *Moâllakât*, the seven Arabic poems . . . hanging up in the temple at Mecca, gave him the idea of the poem'. Certainly, the opening couplets recall the topos of the *nasīb* of an ancient Arabic *qaṣīda*, that of the poet grieving over the traces of the former encampment of his departed beloved (*al-wuqūf ^c^alā 'l-aṭlāl*):

> Comrades, leave me here a little, while as yet 'tis early morn:
> Leave me here, and when you want me, sound upon the bugle-horn.
> 'Tis the place, and all around it, as of old, the curlews call,
> Dreary gleams about the moorland flying over Lockesley Hall;

Similarly, the poet's subsequent musing as he gazes out towards Lockesley Hall, his beloved's home, echoes the Arabic poet's description of his journeys through the desert by night to his inamorata:

> Many a night I saw the Pleiads, rising thro' the mellow shade,
> Glitter like a swarm of fire-flies tangled in a silver braid.

Moreover, Tennyson attempted, with considerable success, to imitate the long distichs of the Arabic *qaṣīdas* – as Sir Charles Lyall was, as I have mentioned, later to do – by his use of trochaic couplets, with eight stresses per line; Sir William Jones had conveniently produced a Roman-script transliteration of the Arabic to accompany his *Mu^c^allaqāt* translation.

Not long afterwards, in 1859, Edward Fitzgerald (1809–83) published his renderings from the Persian of ^c^Umar Khayyām's *Rubā^c^iyyāt*, which after a slow start achieved an extravagant success and might have been expected to stimulate a taste for Islamic poetry and other literature of a kind, in particular for that which expresses a world-weariness, a fatalistic and even cynical view of life, in tune with the later Victorian climate of religious doubt and uncertainty seen, for instance, in the poetry of Matthew Arnold, Arthur Hugh Clough and Tennyson himself. Within the Continent of Europe, the Austrian scholar Alfred von Kremer's researches into and translations of the eleventh-century Syrian author Abū 'l-^c^Alā' al-Ma^c^arrī (1889) stimulated an interest in scholarly circles in the pessimistic philosophy of the blind poet, although at the same time it caused a distortion in the assessment of this writer, who was in reality not so far from the mainstream of Islamic thought and was certainly not a *poète maudit* eight or nine centuries before the appearance in Western Europe of that literary phenomenon.

It is indeed the case that the strain of philosophical pessimism in certain Arabic and Persian poets appears in later Victorian England in the shape of the traveller, diplomat and writer Sir Richard Burton (182–90), who had a profound knowledge of both the written literatures and the spoken tongues of the Arabic, Persian and Indian worlds and who lived much of his life in India, the Middle East and the Mediterranean lands. Best known in English literature as the translator of what was for its time, a daringly frank version of *The Thousand and One Nights*, and, in the minor genre of erotic literature, of an English rendering, via an earlier French translation, of Shaykh al-Nafzawī's *al-Rawḍ al-ᶜAṭīr* "The Perfumed Garden", Burton was also the author of a long English poem which he entitled *The Kasídah of Haji Abdu El-Yezdi, a Lay of the Higher Law*. This was in form a poem of 268 couplets, and just as Fitzgerald had at first published his *Rubāᶜiyyāt* translation anonymously, so Burton in 1880 published *The Kasídah* in a limited edition as the work of a friend of his, the learned Persian Ḥājjī ᶜAbduh al-Yazdī, who 'evidently aspires', wrote Burton himself in his *Notes* to the poem, 'to preach a Faith of his own, an eastern version of Humanitarianism, blended with the sceptical, or as we now say, the scientific habit of mind'. Hostile as Burton was to all forms of established religion, the fatalistic atmosphere of the whole poem was evidently aimed – although its presenter vehemently denied that *The Kasídah* was only an inferior *Rubáiyát* – at a public which had grown to appreciate a mood of gentle melancholy and resignation in the face of Fate like that attributed to ᶜUmar Khayyām and which now, rightly or wrongly, inevitably regarded such attitudes as typically Islamic. Yet it is very probable that Burton was also familiar with the pre-Islamic Arabic poets who often expressed similar sentiments in the politically-troubled sixth century AD before the rise of the firm faith of Islam and whose poetry often contains such motifs as *dhamm al-dahr* 'railing against Fate' and regret for the changes brought by the *ṣurūf al-zamān* 'vicissitudes of Time'. *The Kasídah* enjoyed a certain popularity, with sixteen editions in 40 years, and is often now to be found on the shelves of second-hand bookshops, but it only succeeded in introducing to the West and in popularising just one of the many component themes – and that a subordinate one – of Arabic poetry, and it is now only of literary-historical interest.

The influence of the East and of Arabic literature in particular is discernible in the nineteenth century in the general diffusion of a highly-coloured picture of supposed oriental life, one often based at least in part on what purported to be the mediaeval Baghdad portrayed in *The Thousand and One Nights*, stories from which had come into English literature in one form or another since the fourteenth century. This view of the East was much more widely diffused than the more scholarly one to be gained from the more classical manifestations of Arabic literature, and this was only to be expected in a period when there were few British authors, certainly before Burton's time, who were really literate in Arabic. It was more in France that interest in the Arabs and the Arabic world was shown, in the artistic sphere by Delacroix, Goupil-Fesquet, Gérôme, Guillaumet, Vernet and the other 'Orientalist' painters, and in the literary one by figures of the Romantic Revival such as Victor Hugo and Gérard de Nerval, clearly as a reflection of increasing French colonial interest in North Africa, Egypt and the Levant. German writers like Goethe, August von Platen, Rückert and Adolf Friedrich von Schack were as much interested in Persia and its literature as in the Arabs (although the latter author did play a great role in making the Arabic poetry produced in Sicily and al-Andalus available to Western non-specialists), whilst for British writers, the Indian subcontinent had, for obvious imperial reasons, an attraction rivalling that of the Middle East.

A vague knowledge of oriental life, or what was believed to be such, affected some early nineteenth century English poets, as the titles of several of Lord Byron's poems show (*The Giaour, a Fragment of a Turkish Tale*; *The Bride of Abydos, a Turkish tale*; *The Siege of Corinth*; etc.), but is more clearly observable in prose and poetic prose. The Irish poet Thomas Moore's *Lalla Rookh* (1817) is a mixture of prose and verse, in that a prose frame, on *The Thousand and One Nights* pattern, provides the setting for four verse tales set in Persia and India nominally but, in fact, in the vague, generalised oriental atmosphere just mentioned. *Lalla Rookh* nevertheless proved extremely popular, and Moore was very proud of his creation; it was even very speedily translated into Persian. Moore had immersed himself for a preparatory period in the works of earlier authorities on the Islamic East, such as the historical-biographical *Bibliothèque orientale* of Balthasar d'Herbelot (1625–95) and the works of Sir William Jones. He boasted that 'Although I have never been in the East myself, yet every one who *has* been there declares that nothing can be more perfect than my representations of it, its people, and life, in "Lalla Rookh" '; but as H.A.R. Gibb drily observed, 'his poem merely transports the accents of Scott from his native land to India'. Indeed, Sir Walter Scott's mediaevalism and his brilliant use of local colour in both his novels and in his poems and ballads well illustrate the contemporary enthusiasm for the East and for the Arab world. Scott's poem *The Vision of Don Roderick* (1811) deals with the semi-legendary story of the last Visigothic king of Spain on the eve of the Arab invasion of 711, a theme also treated by his contemporaries Robert Southey (*Roderick, the Last of the Goths*, 1812) and Walter Savage Landor (*Count Julian*, 1812); and his novel *The Talisman* (1825), one of two *Tales of the Crusades*, is set in the Holy Land at the time of Richard Cœur-de-Lion and the Ayyūbid sultan Saladin, with many skilful descriptions of Islamic daily life and religious practices. The same spirit pervades Benjamin Disraeli's half-political, half-romantic novel *Tancred or the New Crusade* (1847), in which the hero Tancred, Lord Montacute, travels through the Levant, to Sinai and Jerusalem and through the mountains of Lebanon and Syria in order, as we would now say, to find himself, becoming involved in the intrigues there of Muslims, Maronites and Druze; Disraeli must, however, have relied for the local colour here on the accounts of several early nineteenth-century English and Continental European travellers in these regions, such as John Lewis Burckhardt, William Hamilton, James Silk Buckingham, etc., plus his own observations from the year 1830–1 which he spent in the Levant, rather than on direct Arabic material.

It is really only with the last years of the nineteenth century and the early twentieth one that a specifically Arabic influence, based on first-hand knowledge of the Arab world and on a deeper sympathy and understanding of it than previously, is discernible. The English poet and writer Wilfred Scawen Blunt (1840–1922), who was an ardent champion of the Arabs in Egypt during the proconsulship of Sir Evelyn Baring, later Lord Cromer, produced together with his wife Lady Ann Blunt in 1903 *The Seven Golden Odes of Pagan Arabia*, the first attempt since Sir William Jones' time at an English literary version of the complete *Muᶜallaqāt* Lady Ann seems to have been responsible for the Arabic scholarship, aided by certain native Egyptian scholars for the work of translation, whilst her husband put it into poetic shape; but though it was praised in the literary world, *The Seven Golden Odes* was never reprinted after publication.

A few years later, in the Edwardian and early Georgian periods, a much more talented poet than Blunt, James Elroy Flecker (1884–1915), was to bring his Arabic, Persian and Turkish scholarship and his experience in the British consular service at Istanbul and Beirut to bear on his composition of poems with Islamic themes and translations of poetry from the three great Islamic languages. Flecker was the son of an

Anglican clergyman, but had East European Jewish blood on both sides of his parentage. He did not get a high enough degree at Oxford – only a modest Third Class Honours in Classical Greats – to open the way to top jobs in either government service or academic life, to both of which he aspired at various times. But in 1907 he entered the Levant Consular Service, and began learning Turkish, Arabic, Persian and Russian at Cambridge under the Director of Studies for the Consular Department course, the great Persian scholar E.G. Browne, passing out at the end with First-Class Honours. Flecker already knew of Burton's *The Kasídah*, and as an Oxford student had written out long extracts from it in his copy-book, noting that 'Aflāṭūn = Plato, and Arisṭū = Aristotle'. By 1910 he was in Istanbul for attachment to the consulate in the Ottoman capital, and in the next year was appointed Vice-Consul in Beirut, remaining there, apart from spells of sick-leave, until the outbreak of the First World War but dying the next year from tuberculosis.

It was not that Flecker became in thrall to the East, as so many other British persons did at that time (such as T.E. Lawrence, whom Flecker met in Beirut). He had been educated, like most of his generation, in the Greek and Roman classics, a process calculated to turn out Philhellenes rather than Turcophiles (although as the line from David Urquhart to Sir Mark Sykes and Aubrey Herbert shows, these last were not wholly lacking). Also, he was already suffering from the debilitating disease which was to kill him. Hence in such poems as 'Brumana', written at the mountain resort above Beirut where he was convalescing, he imagines hearing in the pines of Mount Lebanon the sound of the pines of the Dorset heathlands which he knew, and implicitly contrasts the harsh, clear light of the Levant with the more diffuse light and the lawns shining in the rain of England.

Nevertheless, in the fairly modest body of poetry which he published in Britain between 1907 and 1915, he drew for one vein of inspiration on Islamic literary models. In his translation from the Persian Sufi poet Jalāl al-Dīn Rūmī, 'The Lover of Jalalu 'ddin', he brilliantly blends the sensuousness, the atmosphere of bacchic celebration and the mystical piety of the genre of poetry exemplified in the *Mathnawī*. The early eighteenth century Ottoman Turkish poet Aḥmed Nedīm provided the opening lines for his 'Saadabad', an elegant and evocative poem called into existence by a boating trip with his future wife up the Sweet Waters of Europe outside Istanbul, where the tulip-loving sultan Aḥmed III had had a summer palace.

Flecker was enchanted by the bazaars of Damascus, which he visited from Beirut at Christmas 1911, and that city provided the inspiration for

'The Gates of Damascus', a poem concerning which Flecker's biographer and nephew John Sherwood has written that it 'marks the high point of Flecker's achievement in the oriental mood, since it combines powerful and concentrated ideas with an assured and free manipulation of the Persian-style internal and external rhymes', and a work which Flecker himself described to his diplomat friend Frank Savery as 'my greatest poem'. It gives, after an introductory quatrain, the songs of the city's four gates: the Gate of the East, leading across the desert to Baghdad and Diyarbakr, for many a road of death, where travellers see their hopes shattered; the Gate of the West, leading across Lebanon to the Mediterranean, a way redolent of mystery but also of potential danger; the Gate of the North, which conveys traders to Aleppo, impelled by their expectations of material gain; and the Gate of the South, that taken by the pilgrims to the Holy Places in Arabia, where those faithful devotees, after enduring hardships en route, will be amply rewarded by cleansing of the body, redemption of the soul and a mystical union with God. This last, Flecker avers in his poem, is the only safe way through life – a conclusion, John M. Munro has noted, somewhat at variance with the poet's normal sensuousness and hedonistic view of life.

But it is in his poetic prose drama *Hassan*, in full, *Hassan, the Story of Hassan of Baghdad and How He Came to Make the Golden Journey to Samarkand, a Play in Five Acts*, that Flecker most extendedly and brilliantly displays his debt to the Orient. In origin, Hassan was a comic pantomime figure, based on some Turkish tales which Flecker was reading in Corfu in 1911 when preparing for a consular examination in that language, but he was also reading at that time the French translation by J.C. Mardrus of *The Thousand and One Nights*, and this last must have influenced his placing the drama of Hassan in the Baghdad of Hārūn al-Rashīd rather than in Turkey.

The play tells the story of a middle-aged sweetmaker and confectioner of Baghdad, Hassan, who becomes embroiled in events on a level far above his modest station when he unwittingly rescues the caliph from a conspiracy planned against him. He accordingly attains to Hārūn's patronage and to a sumptuous life-style in the palace environs, but is thereby compelled to witness from the royal shadow the arbitrary acts of violence and sadism inflicted by the caliph. In the end, his revulsion is so great that he resolves to leave this artificial way of life and to accompany the former court poet Ishak, equally disgusted at the events he has had to witness, as a wandering dervish. Their journey to the East and to their goal, the remote city of Samarkand, is the theme of the drama's concluding song, 'The Golden Road to Samarkand'. The leitmotiv of the play is thus, basically, the clash between over-refined aesthetic feeling and the simple, unimaginative ways of ordinary life, a clash which, in this instance, can only be resolved by renunciation of an effete and spiritually unsatisfying mode of existence. In other words, Flecker seems to imply, such doctrines as that of art for art's sake, fashionable amongst artistic and literary circles in Britain during the 1890s and the Edwardian era, are not enough as a basis for man's true fulfilment in life. Yet somewhat paradoxically, this view is once again at variance with much of what Flecker had himself stood for in his poetic career; perhaps one should take into account the effects of his mortal disease in bringing him to a more spiritual view of life's meaning.

Throughout the play, Flecker achieves a remarkable evocation of mediaeval Islamic atmosphere by the use of inflated, ornate language and poetic exaggeration, faithfully rendering the spirit and, at times, the actual phraseology, of classical Arabic *adab* literature. The first British production of the play at London in 1923, eight years after the author's death, with incidental music by Delius and choreography of the ballet sequences by Fokine, must have been an outstanding experience for the audience (who allowed it to run for 281 performances); certainly, English poetic literature has produced nothing since that time with any comparable Arabic or Islamic inspiration.

Notes

1. For the background here, see the papers by P.M. Holt reprinted in his *Studies in the History of the Near East* (London, 1973), pp. 3–63.
2. See his 'Un jardin secret: la poésie arabe', *Studia Islamica* 9 (1958),pp. 5–12, reprinted in his *Analecta* (Damascus 1975), pp. 223–30.
3. A.J. Arberry, *Oriental Essays. Portraits of Seven Scholars* (London, 1960), pp. 5–2, 55; *idem, The Seven Odes. The First Chapter in Arabic Literature* (London, 1957), pp. 7–13, 24–6; Sarah Searight, *The British in the Middle East* (London, 1969), pp. 184–5; Garland Cannon *The Life and Mind of Oriental Jones, Sir William Jones, the Father of Modern Linguistics* (Cambridge, 1990), pp. 34–50, 188–9.
4. Translations of Ancient Arabic Poetry, *Chiefly Pre-Islamic, with an Introduction and Notes* (London, 1885), Introd. pp. xlix-l.
5. One might cite here the *Specimens of Arabian Poetry from the Earliest Time to the Extinction of the Caliphate, with Some Account of the Authors*, by J.D. Carlyle, Professor of Arabic at Cambridge (Cambridge, 1796) (I am grateful to Dr Richard Hitchcock for showing me his copy of this book).
6. At pp. 319–41, 462–7.
7. Cf. Norman Daniel, *Islam, Europe and Empire* (Edinburgh, 1966), pp. 48–61, on exoticism as a component of nineteenth-century English and French literature.

8. See Fawn M. Brodie, *The Devil Drives. A Life of Sir Richard Burton* (London, 1967), pp. 276–9. In fact, as Daniel notes, *op. cit.*, p. 56, *The Kasidah* is empty of intellectual content, and the idea that all faiths are equally true, or untrue, is hardly a startling discovery.
9. See now on this whole topic, Peter L. Caracciolo (ed.), *The Arabian Nights in English Literature. Studies in the Reception of The Thousand and One Nights into British Culture* (London, 1988) (I am grateful to Professor Fatma Moussa-Mahmoud for this reference).
10. See Mary Anne Stevens, 'Western Art and its Encounter with the Islamic World 1798–1914', in *eadem* (ed.), *The Orientalists: Delacroix to Matisse. European Painters in North Africa and the Near East* (Royal Academy of Arts, London, 1984), pp. 15–23.
11. Ch. 'Literature', in Sir Thomas Arnold and Alfred Guillaume (eds.), *The Legacy of Islam* (London, 1931), p. 207; Searight, *The British in the Middle East*, pp. 178–9.
12. See Kathryn Tidrick, *Heart-Beguiling Araby* (Cambridge, 1981), pp. 4–2.
13. See Arberry, *The Seven Odes*, pp. 27–30; Tidrick, *op. cit.*, p. 112.
14. See on Flecker's life and career in general, John Sherwood, *No Golden Journey, a Biography of James Elroy Flecker*, (London, 1973), and for the Oriental influences in his work, C.E. Bosworth, 'James Elroy Flecker: Poet, Diplomat, Orientalist', *Bull. of the John Rylands University Library of Manchester* 69/2 (Spring 1987), pp. 359–78.
15. The Collected Poems, *with an Introduction by J.C. Squire* (London, 1916), pp. 179–81.
16. *Ibid.*, p. 87.
17. *Ibid.*, pp. 160–2. For this poem, and for some translations which he made from the early fifteenth-century Ottoman poet Nesīmī, Flecker drew on E.J.W. Gibb's classic *A History of Ottoman Poetry* (London, 1900–9).
18. *Ibid.*, pp. 15–7; Sherwood, *op. cit.*, pp. 149, 170.
19. *James Elroy Flecker* (Twayne's English Authors Series, Boston, Mass., 1976), p. 70.
20. For the poetic process involved in the genesis and composition of *Hassan*, see Sherwood, *op. cit.*, pp. 20–11, and Munro, *op. cit.*, pp. 102–12.
21. See the analysis of the play in *ibid.*
22. See Sherwood, *op. cit.*, pp. 223–5, and *idem*, 'James Elroy Flecker and Hassan', in *The Times Saturday Review*, 11 August 1973.

12

Tradition and Modernity in the work of the Tunisian writer al-Mas^c^adī

J.C. Bürgel
University of Berne

Maḥmūd al-Mas^c^adī[1] (b. 1911) was first presented to the western public by M. Férid-Ghazi in an article on contemporary Tunisian literature published in 1959.[2] Ten years later, G.E. von Grunebaum in his magisterial "*Studien zum Kultur- und Selbstverständnis des Islam*" praised him enthusiastically as an author, in whose work the problem of acculturation, meaning the fusion of Eastern and Western literary styles, tradition and modernity, was solved in an unparalleled manner.[3] And again eight years later, R.C. Ostle tackled some aspects of his work, mainly highlighting the element of parody and satire in the language of *The Dam*.[4] In 1981, S. Ballas published an article in Arabic on the existentialist dimension of the play "The Dam".[5] I myself translated this play into German[6] and published an article about it interpreting the dam as a symbol of rebellion against fate.[7] Furthermore, in 1987, I gave a lecture in Warsaw, where I discussed the whole literary output of al-Mas^c^adi under the heading of the search for the absolute.[8] Meanwhile, al-Mas^c^adī's work has found its way into a number of manuals on contemporary Arabic or Tunisian literature.[9]

The blending of tradition and modernity in al-Mas^c^adī's writings has already been focused upon both by Arab and Western cities, however, mainly with regard to his style. In my paper, I shall rather dwell upon aspects of the contents and the structure.

1.

Maḥmūd al-Mas^c^adī, who was born in 1911 and studied at the Sorbonne, is considered to be the Nestor of modern Tunisian literature. His fame is, however, to some degree also due to his very successful political career. He was a leading member of the Neo-Dastūr Party and he occupied a number of posts in the Ministry of Culture, until in 1981 he became the

President of the Tunisian National Assembly.[10] Another epithet, that has long been attached to him, is that he is or was the only representative of an Arab Islamic existentialism, which however, as K. Skarzynska rightly pointed out, is to be understood rather in literary than strictly philosophical terms.[11] His three major works are the drama *The Dam*, written between September 1939 and June 1940, published in 1957,[12] and the two tales or novellas *Thus Spake Abū Hurayrah*[13] and *Birth of Oblivion*,[14] both written between 1939 and 1944, but published only in 1974. Two short sketches, entitled *The Traveller* and *Sinbad and Purity*[15] and a volume of critical essays[16] round off al-Mas^cadī's literary output in Arabic. I shall first tackle the drama, starting with a summary of its contents, and then discussing its interpretation and the problems involved. The same scheme will then be followed for the other two works.

2.

The Dam: The plot of this play is simple. In an arid desert valley a people or tribe live an archaic way of life, not only submitting passively to the conditions of aridity, but making it the core of their cult. They venerate a Goddess called Ṣahabbāᵓ who is the Goddess of the sun, of heat and of drought. At the beginning of the play a young couple arrive on one of the slopes encircling the valley: the rebellious intellectual Ghaylān – in the list of dramatis personae he is qualified as "a man, a false being" (*rajulun kāᵓinun zāᵓif*)[17] – and his wife Maymūnah, who strike their tent in front of a cave. He dreams of turning the barren ground into a green garden by building a dam, which will retain the rain that falls in the mountains and the water of a spring, that oozes away in the sand above the valley. The region could thus be irrigated. Unperturbed by ever new difficulties, the resistance of the priests and their adherents, a strike of the workers, a flood that destroys part of the almost completed dam, Ghaylān continues his work, decided to overcome every obstacle. An in fact, for a certain while, he seems to succeed. Notwithstanding several setbacks, the dam gradually rises and nears completion, when all of a sudden a thunderstorm of apocalyptic force destroys it and devours the hero and Mayārā (see below).

The play is divided into eight scenes located partly in the valley, partly on the slope and limited to a small number of actors. Ghaylān represents will-power and rebellion against fate, Maymūnah stands for natural life and is the longer the less willing to support his struggle, which in her mind is pure hubris and destroys their mutual happiness. Maymūnah is therefore, in the sixth scene, superceded by a fairy-like beauty called Mayārā, who personifies Ghaylāns dream. On the other side of the spectrum, there is the anonymous mass of the inhabitants of the valley, the priests and the Goddess Ṣahabbāᵓ. The plot bears traits of a fairy-tale oscillating between reality and myth. These traits are enhanced by the author's inserting a number of supernatural elements, such as mysterious voices and apparitions, a talking ass which belongs to the couple and glosses their actions in a more or less enigmatic or comic way, and, scattered before the cave, a group of stones that, in the fourth scene, turn into young girls and conduct an ironic conversation about man. One of the stone girls recites the gospel of Ṣahabbāᵓ. In the second scene, the priests of Ṣahabbāᵓ appear and celebrate the ritual of their religion, a dancing ceremony accompanied by litanies in an archaic, almost incomprehensible idiom, a parody of the mumblings of ancient Arab soothsayers, and reaching its summit when the flame of the Goddess descends upon the water in a vessel.[18] The prayer for this fire includes invocations to Ṣahabbāᵓ to destroy the dam and curses uttered against Ghaylān. At the end of the play, the supernatural carries the day in the aforementioned tempest which, even though crushing the dam, does not annihilate the hero and his fairy Mayārā, but, as it were, transports them to a realm where there dreams have become reality. Even though vanquished on the plane of facts, subjectively they feel like victors. It may be useful to give a literal translation of this significant ending:

Ghaylān and Mayārā: We have created a remedy (*tiryāq*) against storm and lightning, we have built, we have erected a dam. The tempest is unable to destroy it, so is the thunderstorm.
Maymūnah (who has noticed something in the illumination of the lightning): Look, look: the mountain is rousing itself, it moves and advances! Look, thousands of birds are drawing it by its hair, its black trees. Don't you see how it proceeds and its mill crunches and grinds the dam and the plan?
Ghaylān (to Mayārā): Look, the dam is soaring, look, the dam is rising!
Maymūnah: The dam is rubble, the dam is ruins falling into the abyss.
Mayārā (to Ghaylān): Don't you see a lamp shining at the end of the forest? Look, it is calling us. Glass, purity, decision and desire! Look, how it rests in the middle of earthquakes! How many trees the forest has. How firmly it twigs intertwine, and how clear a path is our lamp!
Maymūnah (like one being rescued): Look! . . . Look down the mountain, under the clouds, through the window, look at the opening, look at the plain with nothing in it, there is quiet in the plain, and tranquility.

Ghaylān and **Mayārā**: (embracing each other): Let us soar up with our heads and open a door for them in the sky! (They soar up while the storm has already carried them away.)
Maymūnah (looking at them, while they disappear before her in the storm): Now they have reached their desire and found rest. (She then gives a shout like the tearing of a new gown and looks towards the plain and says) The earth. This is the earth, I have discovered it!
(And she is driven down towards the darkness of the plain: she thinks that she is reaching it, fleeing to it and taking refuge to it, but the plain is moving away to an ever farther distance, and the earth before her is being dug up to the infinite. The mule neighs and cries from fear and strikes with his hooves. Yet it is tied up, fettered to the rock (and exposed) to the wind and the storm and the earthquake and the lightning).

The plot thus combines features of the realistic and the supernatural, of myth and of history. We have already pointed to the religion with its archaic rites, which of course brings to mind certain aspects of Islam. However, also the construction and destruction of the dam, even though not linked up with any particular event, clearly evoked historical associations. Thus, the figure of Ghaylān reminds a reader familiar with early Islamic history of the Buwayhid emir ᶜAḍud al-Dawlah (r. 944–983) who built the famous dam called after him *Band-i-amīr* in the vicinity of Shiraz, and who labelled himself *ghallāb al-qadar*, conqueror of fate, thus pronouncing his opposition against the Ashᶜarite doctrine of predestination, then already on the point of gaining dominance.[19] After his death, his critics of the religious camp contended that his success had abandoned him because of the hubris expressed in this epithet.[20] As for the destruction of the dam, one is certainly not mistaken in thinking of the *sayl al-ᶜarim*, the flood that destroyed the dam of Maʾrib according to the Koran:

"For Sheba also there was a sign in their dwelling place – two gardens, one on the right and one on the left: 'Eat of your Lord's provision, and give thanks to Him; a good land, and a Lord All-forgiving.' But they turned away, so We loosed on them the Flood of Arim, and We gave them, in exchange for their two gardens, two gardens bearing bitter produce and tamarisk-bushes, and here and there a few lote-trees. Thus we recompensed them for their unbelief."[21] Still another case al-Masᶜadī may have had in mind are the ruins of the Roman aqueduct which brought water from the mountains to Carthage, an impressive example in his immediate surroundings of high-flown human endeavour and its transience.

I cannot, of course, prove that the author had in mind these historical analogues, when he wrote *The Dam*, but at any rate they exist. In the light of Koranic ethics Ghaylān's enterprise of replacing God-ordained barrenness by man-created fertility amounts in fact to hubris and is thus pre-ordained to fail: it can only end in a new catastrophe. Incidentally, the term *ᶜutiy* "presumption" used in the warnings of Maymūnah is a Koranic expression.[22]

Al-Sudd is certainly a symbolic drama[23] with a transparent basic meaning: the antagonism of two irreconcilable attitudes, on the one hand an unshakable belief in a God-given existence with its inescapable hardships, that have to be suffered patiently, which means submission to God, to fate, to predestination; on the other hand rebellion, autonomy, the resolution to shape one's own fate, nature, the world, according to one's own will, and thus the contrary of passive acceptance. Yet, if the basic setting is clear, al-Masᶜadī has nevertheless shrewdly concealed his intrinsic intention as to which of these attitudes he approves of or prefers. The image of the rebel hero is ambivalent. On the one hand, he seems to be right in his intention to change things for the better. On the other, his attitude is shown to be one of hubris, or, as mentioned above, of *ᶜutiy* = presumption. Yet, the author spared him the expected humiliation at the end of the play. Even though the dam is crushed and thus Ghaylān's work is, at least for the moment, ruined, he himself seems untouched, his confidence unbroken.

This is why this play has been interpreted in various, even mutually contradicting ways. Whereas a Western reader would normally be inclined to understand it as an allegory of the antagonism between a backward religion and the impetus of modern progress,[24] Muslim interpreters such as Ṭāhā Ḥusayn preferred to see in it an allegory of Tunisia under French rule and "a mirror of the Tunisian heroism in its resistance against colonialism".[25] However, this interpretation sounds rather artificial, given the fact that in Tunisia at the time France was the representative of progress in a country dominated by stagnation and retrospection. Al-Masᶜadī himself refused this analysis. In his answer to Ḥusayn he wrote that what he had intended was to show the particular problems of the Muslim's attitude towards active life, for, while steadily conscious of the transitoriness of all human achievements in the face of God, the Muslim should still feel impelled to perform courageous deeds. According to al-Masᶜadī there are only two choices, represented in the play by either Ghaylān or Maymūnah: One, the attitude of Maymūnah, is to perceive in the rising sun already its setting and to be driven into despair. The other one is the decision to act aware of but undeterred by the transitoriness of things.[26] This interpretation is, however, hardly more convincing than Ḥusayn's. It is, at any rate, not very much in concordance with the figures themselves. For Maymūnah's despair has other roots: she is not an ascetic. On the contrary, she wants to enjoy life, and she despairs because her husband is constantly torn away from her by his high-flown and, as she sees it, unrealistic dreams. Nor does Ghaylān realize at any moment of the play the transience of human endeavour in the face of God. His activity is incited by the overwhelming discovery that, in the apparent barrenness of the wadi, a potential fertility lies hidden which needs human action. Even less convincing is a further interpretation of al-Masᶜadī, according to which Ghaylān typifies the Islamic mystic's craving for union with the absolute Being. On the one hand al-Masᶜadī here describes man's position in the universe in a strange mixture of Islamic and western philosophical terms:

> "When God blew into man (part) of His spirit, He created in him the substantial individual peculiarity which constitutes his divine nature and made him a small-scale image of his majestic absolute essence and thereby wanted him to become a personal cause (*ᶜillah*) capable of work and creation and purposeful action by dint of the free will He laid in him. This is man's position within Existence (*wujūd*) as a creator of his fate by his hand in free creation, and this is his position in Being (*kawn*), by which he is the *khalīfah* of God on earth, which he achieved by accepting the "deposit" (*amānah*) which God had offered to the Heavens and the Earth."[27]

On the other hand al-Masᶜadī describes Ghaylān as opposed to "*islām*" by his craving for mystical union in a particular sense:

> "How often Maymūnah and the voices and Ṣahabbāᵓ and the people of Ṣahabbāᵓ and the stones and the voice of the prophet call him to *islām* and *idhᶜān* (submission) and warn him by what is ordained for him in his life, and point to his limitations. Yet, he does not listen to them and denies being anything but an ideal (*mithāl*) of bold human behaviour, surpassing its limits, rising to "fusion and union" and keeping to that kind of sufism which does not cut the roots of life nor consider annihilation (*fanāᵓ*), but which means communion with the gods (!) (*al-āliha*) and fusion with them in the pure power of existence and the majesty of created force and the unshakability of productive life."[28]

This dynamic concept of sufism is, of course, totally different from the traditional one as held by the broad stream of Islamic mysticism, and in fact rather reminiscent of the ideas of Muḥammad Iqbāl who also refused the concept of annihilation and propagated the development of a Muslim Self, powerful and active through the submission under the will of God.[29] The apparent inconsistency of al-Masᶜadī's various interpretations is probably less due to a wavering attitude on the part of al-Masᶜadī as to the meaning of his work than to his intention to prolong the mystification already undertaken in the drama itself. Both religiously motivated inertia and rebellious hubris are being criticized in the play. But as far as the drama may be read as criticism of an Islamic attitude, the author has perhaps, particularly later on, preferred to leave this somewhat in the dark.[30] Nevertheless, the word *islām* is mentioned several times, always in a negative sense as viewed from the stand point of the hero. The voices of the Prophet of Ṣahabbāᵓ demand *islām*,[31], Ghaylān rejects it, e.g. in a conversation with Maymūnah where he underscores the importance of negating laws, borders, obstacles, of not admitting weakness and *islām*.[32]

In an oral comment during a public symposium organized in honour of al-Masᶜadī by the Tunisian ministry of culture and broadcast by Tunisian television in 1985, the author completely startled his audience when he point-blank explained that by *islām* he meant an attitude "far-spread in our countries" of passive inertia and fatalism. In the above-mentioned lecture, al-Masᶜadī thanks God "that we do not imitate our fathers", who would take refuge in God from Satan when their imam mentioned the name of the West or "the Franks"[33] and he states that the religion of Ṣahabbāᵓ will remind "some of you of what existed in our land in not very remote times, the songs and the ecstatic exclamations (*shaṭaḥāt*) which were executed by deformed "religious orders" such as the ᶜĪsāwiyya, the Tījāniyya, the Qādiriyya and others, which we inherited from the centuries of intellectual and religious decay, and which are a symbol of mental backwardness and stagnation that oppose on the intellectual level everything to do with progress, upward mobility and revolutionary innovation."[34]

Coming now to the question of how tradition and modernity are fused in this work, we may first recall the praise of von Grunebaum, who counted the work of al-Masᶜadī, and in particular *The Dam*, among the rare examples of a successful acculturation in modern Arabic literature. But in what way are the two elements used in this drama? First of all, the language of al-Masᶜadī, often praised as unsurpassed in its perfection, has to be mentioned as the omnipresent element of tradition, even though here too a modern element comes in with the use of often surprisingly courageous metaphors and similes. Furthermore, we have already noticed a number of features evoking various cultural and religious traditions such as the ceremony of the priests, the gospel of the Goddess etc. However, all of these elements appear in a more or less alienated perspective. The whole plot, even though in its basic structure imaginable in some mediaeval narrator's work e.g. at-Tanūkhī's *Nishwār al-muḥāḍarah*[35], or at-Tawḥīdī's *al-Imtā*[36] or, with a more mystical drift, in one of al-ᶜAṭṭār's epics,[37] is told in a modern way, with alienation effects, irony[38] and modern psychological implications. The question of influence thus arises, and this was, of course, vividly discussed in the fifties.

Ṭāhā Ḥusayn, the most outstanding of those Arabic critics who analyzed *as-Sudd*, saw in it, apart from an allegory of Tunisia under the French occupation, the result of French literary influence. He was sure that al-Masᶜadī had read some writings of Camus, such as *Le mythe de Sisyphe* or *Le malentendu*. Ghaylān's ever new and ever failing effort to build the dam must be influenced, Ṭāhā Ḥusayn insisted, by the myth of Sysiphus.[39] Al-Masᶜadī denied this: not only had he not read any works by Camus at the time when he wrote *The Dam*,[40] but – still more important – Ghaylān is not a Sisyphus, for what he does is, even if it is doomed to fail, meaningful, whereas Sisyphus' work is absurd.[41] Nevertheless, al-Masᶜadī admitted having read works by writers who on their part had perhaps influenced by Camus, such as Baudelaire, Valéry, Gide, Malraux, Saint Exupéry, Sartre, Giraudoux. Masᶜadī mentions also Shakespeare, Dostoyevski, Ibsen and Unamuno, and, among mediaeval Islamic authors, Abū l-ᶜAlāᵓ al-Maᶜarrī, Abū Ḥayyān al-Tawḥīdi, Abū Ḥāmid al-Ghazzālī and ᶜUmar Khayyām as having influenced him.[42] Other parallels were envisaged, such as the one existing between Ghaylān and Goethe's Faust or between the drama as a whole and Ibsen's drama *Bygmester Solness* known in English as *The Master Builder*[43] and again, Ghaylān was seen as a modern Oriental personification of the Nietzschean man of action.[44]

The Dam is thus in fact a work which combines, in a most ingenious way, old and new elements both in its structure and motifs as well as in its main concern, the antagonisms of fate and free will, tradition and innovation, society and individual, submission and rebellion.

3.

Coming now to the two other major works, it has at first to be stated that, though less well known and much less discussed, and even though they do perhaps not quite reach the convincing, powerful stamp of the drama, they are hardly less fascinating than the former.

The *Birth of Oblivion* tells the story of a doctor called Madyan and his wife Laylā, who work in the vicinity of a jungle fighting an epidemic that rages among the inhabitants of that region. When they began, they looked on this illness as a result of weak and cowardly submission (*islām*).[45] However, the doctor is torn between his present and his past which haunts him with the memory of a lost beloved, who, during his feverish dreams – for he has himself fallen ill with the disease – appears to him and talks to him. I quote part of this conversation because it shows the strange mixture of philosophy and phantasy that is so typical of Mas^cadī's works:

> Will you not come close, so that I can tell you of our past future.
> She said:
> Talk to me of that hope that has died with the death of matter and left behind the idleness of mind.
> He said:
> That was in fact the source of our fear and these difficulties were our illness. Our joys broke between matter and form like a nut in the nutcracker. And we would joke and say: Joy is like a mouse and we searched for the mouse of joy between the bottom and the bale, but the bale had crushed it on the bottom. Yet, today, Asmā^o, we are safe and tranquil. The difficulties have gone and the fear. I killed the matter and you killed the form and the mind.[46]

Overcome with a double despair – disease around him and despondency within himself – he craves for oblivion. Now *islām* is for him identical with the motionlessness of the highest being.[47] The warnings of his wife, a type reminiscent of Maymūnah in her sense of reality, do not reach him, even though long discussions take place between them, in which he describes his goal in various terms such as rest, immobility (*jumūd*), non-being (*^cadam*): "May the secret of persistent immobility and of eternal rest fall to my share, may I obliterate death, may I obliterate life, and may this be my last decision and my last effort!"[48]

One day, Madyan is lured by the voice of Asmā^o deep into the jungle until, all of a sudden, Ranjihād appears before him, a sorceress and priest of Salhawā, who promises him liberation from his senses, his pains and his joys: in short, oblivion, attainable by a draught from a spring in the jungle. This time, she only takes him to the Cave of the Sleeping, i.e. the Dead,[49] but at their next meeting, they proceed further into the jungle and Ranjihād explains him that this is the realm of the absolute time (*^cālam az-zamān al-muṭlaq*) where birth, life and death of every created being are gathered in one moment.[50] She also tells him that death is a vengeance upon man because of what he claims for himself in the way of power, beauty and purity, and recites for him the myth of creation, which reminds one of a similar myth in *The Dam*. The passage is about Salhawā and how he created the world, but it is also a parody of the biblical and the Koranic reports.

When he returns to his wife Laylā and tells her of his encounters and of his inclination to accept the offer of Ranjihād, she is upset and tries to dissuade him. He openly speaks of his idea of ridding himself of reason: "If man departed from the prisons of reason he would reach the truth and the untruth would fall off him, he would be cured and released."[51] Laylā warns him that this is nothing but illusion leading into error: "This is why fate has imprisoned us in reason, Madyan, and tied us to it, so that we do not lose our way!"

But he insists: "We have neither been bound nor emprisoned, Laylā. We only forgot the way of the absolute, (which is) madness,[52] and we fear the vertigo that is brought about when we transcend reason and human nature. We have locked our horizons and limited our range . . . Reason means only fetters!"[53]

Madyan can not be saved, he has already crossed the threshold. So he finally yields to the temptation. He believes that by giving up science, religion, one's self – those "dams erected on the basis of wisdom and reason to protect the wadi from the force of the torrent and life from madness"[54] – and by letting himself be conquered by madness, he will reach happiness, tranquility, eternity. And indeed, after having gulped the draught he has a short experience of ecstasy, and even Laylā beholds in his eyes a light like that of revelation. He himself describes his situation:

> "I am finding myself lucid, I am finding light in myself. Heaven has wetted me with the rain of purity and purified me. I am clean like clean linen. My power, my purity and my beauty have returned to me."

A few minutes later, he still believes that "this is tranquility and felicity and eternity". And he cries: "My heart is calm, calmness has conquered time. I do not pass nor change. I am existence, I am eternity, I have not changed since primordial times . . . I have drunk the Heavens and the Universe has taken abode in me!"[55] But then his agony sets in. He walks in the direction of the jungle, and there Ranjihād stands waiting for him. On beholding her, Laylā implores her for help, but she remains unmoved. In his last moments, Madyan realizes his error and confesses to Laylā:

> "This is the end, Laylā. My body has betrayed me, and my mind has betrayed me as well, it was not capable of eternity."[56]

As soon as he has died, Ranjihād gives her unsympathetic comment: "A moment of oblivion in a life as the life of his fathers. And he has left behind Laylā, dead among the living. Verily, existence is the eternal curse. Oblivion will never be born, annihilation (*fanā^ᵓ*) will never be born, time will never be conquered, heaven will never be reached. I am Confusion (*buhtān*)!"[57]

There are thus again certain parallels to *The Master Builder* and perhaps also other plays by Ibsen. At any rate, the central motif of a person overpowered by his past and losing his self-confidence is modern: a topic of Freudian psychopathology. Except for the language which is handled in the usual classical manner of al-Masᶜadī, and the fairy-tale motif, no traditional elements of any importance can be perceived. Even though at the outset, the situation in both *The Dam* and *Oblivion* is comparable – drought and an epidemic functioning as challenge for the respective heroes – the development in both works is different. For, whereas Ghaylān puts all his energy into his struggle for the common well-being, Madyan is gradually overwhelmed by his personal problems.

The last of the three major works, *Thus Spake Abū Hurayrah*, is again of a different vein. Its structure is a loose sequence of scenes about an ancient Arab hero who, however, has nothing to do with the famous traditionist of the same name. Al-Masᶜadī's hero is an uprooted man living in a remote past, who is wavering between debauchery, scepticism and the search of God or for any true and trustworthy values; a personality combining traits of Imruᵓ al-Qays, the wandering king-poet of pre-Islamic Arabia, and Abū Zayd, the roguish and roaming hero of the *Maqāmāt* of al-Ḥarīirī. Al-Masᶜadī here makes use of the well-known narrative device of traditional Arabic literature called *ḥadīth*, thereby evoking an ancient Arabic atmosphere. After an opening chapter called *fātiḥa*, the book comprises 22 chapters, each bearing in its heading the word *ḥadīth*, e.g. *Ḥadīth al-baᶜth al-awwal* ("Report of the first resurrection"), *Ḥadīth al-mazḥ wal-jadd* ("Report of merriment and seriousness") etc., and every chapter starts with the words *ḥaddatha* followed by the name of Abū Hurayrah or another witness. In this manner, the development of the hero from youth to death appears fragmentized in a prismatic perspective, the old device serving an unexpected modern function. Yet, this structure also corresponds with the hero's "broken" character. Abū Hurayrah starts as a boon companion and womanizer, but he is soon haunted by inner unrest[58] and starts his quest for that which is new, unheard of, no-existent; in other words the search of the absolute.[59] But regularly the ways he thinks untrodden, turn out to be used up, like the girl whom he had hoped to be a virgin and who turned out to be an old crone.[60]

Abū Hurayrah displays a tendency towards agnosticism. Thus, in one of his retrospections, he remembers his reaction when, while still a child, he lost his little sister "and I moaned, and my wailing lasted long and I thought it was Satan. But they told me it was God."[61] The question "God or Satan?" is taken up several times in this work, and the agnostic attitude is uttered more than once very clearly.[62] Thus, for instance, shortly after he has told the story about his sister, his companions remind him that it is time for prayer. But his answer is: "Whether we pray or do not pray, whether we are happy or suffer injury, do you think this makes any difference?" Then he adds: "The worst thing on this earth is that life is absurd (*al-ḥayāh ᶜabath*), or I don't know perhaps this is the best (thing) on it!"[63] Again a little later he sets free all his slaves, one after the other, then comments on this act by remarking: "By God, I wish I had so much strength of heart that I could smash life and see it in pieces, or so much of wisdom that I were able to play like children until my days fade away, or so much force that I could set free my life as I set free my slaves and it would go away!"[64] The topic of childhood is again taken up in the next *Ḥadīth*, and here Abū Hurayrah makes it clear that for him childhood is the time when the soul is not yet in the prison of adulthood: "We were kings like the kings of Byzantium, we were birds and wild animals and stormy winds, and we exhausted all the resources of God's creation."[65]

The topic of hubris is varied in a dream in which Abū Hurayrah sees workmen building lofty palaces and singing a song which could stem partly from *Mawlid an-nisyān* and partly from *al-Sudd*:

> Reason means ruin and thought means disease
> and the spirit is the echo of the spirit of non-being.
> Action means endurance and effort salvation.
> So let us build a building that denies non-being![66]

This vision is followed by the reciting of the Koranic passage on Pharaoh.

One of the hero's major experiences is told in the *Ḥadīth al-kalb* ("Report of the dog") following the afore-mentioned dream. Here, Abū Hurayrah acts for a while as prophet in an Arab tribe. He tries to teach them humanistic ideas, among other things he reproaches their indulgence in Holy War (*jihād*). I quote this passage not only because of its poignancy, but as an example of how the author adorns his texts with daring metaphors imbuing his classical diction with a modern tinge:

"The Holy War erects the sword amongst you so that it roars like thirsty rocks and kindles inexorable turmoils, and these are black upon you like pieces of the night or a stubborn flood. Do you call this the attitude of contented Muslims?[67] By God, this is truly one of the miracles! The wolves have clothed themselves in your blood, while lending you their wilderness, their thirst and their hunger. They have let grow their iron teeth in your mouths, so you started eating and killing each other. But neither will killing quench your thirst, nor pillaging still your hunger. By God, this is truly one of the miracles! You corrupt and destroy and turn what God created into ruins. And you don't know what you need. You are axes of destruction! Are you not ashamed, will you not repent?!"[68]

After a frustrating experience in a Christian monastery which leaves him disillusioned as to the possibility of transcending one's corporeal exigencies, he loses all confidence and doubts the existence of metaphysical realities. A witness describes this as follows: "And he became like one who hates man. And after that we did not notice in him any emotion. It was as if, in his interior, something of that by which man becomes man had died, or an insight had been blinded. This was the beginning of his descent towards his downfall."[69]

So there remains nothing other than "the absolute search for my essence."[70] Later on, he states that he has lost his belief in mankind and the possibility of living together with them, and that he longs for the unity, meaning the unity of all opposites, and that action is fine only if it is absolute and pure.[71] And again later on he formulates his goal with the words "nothing remained for me other than to search for the end![72]

Ultimately Abū Hurayrah, fed up with his frustrating adventures, loses his mind. Together with a friend, he mounts his horse and climbs the peak of a rocky mountain. After sunset, and after Abū Hurayrah has told a funny story of his past, they hear a beautiful voice singing a few short strophes of mystical content:

I am the Truth that calls you
I am Love that whispers to you
I am Longing that prevailed in you:
Come, over the time
ascend to my charm
and disclose from under my cover
light as the light of dawn
that instills you with my secret!
I am the Truth that prevailed in you

I am Love that whispers to you
I am longing that calls you:
My friend, friend of the Eternal,
Release yourself and come, let's hunt
the knowledge of the hidden world
the secrets of the Lord!
Rise like lances
when they are held upright
like the blowing of the winds
when they soar up to the peak of the mountain
and fly, o wing,
for there appear
the shores of eternity!

Abū Hurayra answers singing "as if fire was burning or as if he was God announcing the resurrection in the universe":

O Truth! Here I am at your service (*labbayka*)!
Blessings upon you, I am at your service!
My friend, your majesty!
I am now coming to you.
Come, o my heart!
This is the sky
in the zenith of height,
calling my spirit.
And this is my friend
whose lustre enlightens
the lights of Heaven,
illuminating my path.

Then he remained silent until I heard him saying: "This is what I had been seeking.'"

Shortly after, Abū Hurayra disappears in the darkness. The friend, the only witness, describes the noises that he has heard: "rolling stones and a neighing of pain and a cry of joy that filled the wadi and my flesh crept: it was like the feast of devils." The end of this report which is also the end of the book runs as follows:

"Then everything became silent and I called out, but nobody answered. So I stuck to my place until the morning. When the morning came, I looked around and lo, I was on the top of a mountain almost touching the sky, and lo, there was the blood on the rocks and lo, under me was an abyss, deeper than the eye's reach.

May God have mercy on Abū Hurayrah. He was greater than life itself."

This ending is strange and unexpected. Its clearly mystical overtones would seem to comply with what the author maintained was his intention in *The Dam*. Taken as a whole, however, the tale about Abū Hurayrah has as little mystical implications as does *The Dam*. The spiritual elevation is all the less convincing, since, shortly before, Abū Hurayrah had confessed to his friend that he had killed a beautiful girl whom both had known in their youth: "I killed her and I killed many others in addition to her in order not to kill myself."[73] The ending is thus again intentionally ambiguous.[74]

4.

Finally, a few remarks have to be added concerning the two short sketches *al-Musāfir* (The Traveller) and *as-Sindibād wa l-ṭahārah* (Sinbad and Purity). Both texts are contained in the volume *Mawlid al-nisyān wa-ta^ɔammulāt ukhrā*. The label *ta^ɔammulāt* ("considerations" or "reflections") indicates that al-Mas^cadī himself was aware of the reflective element in these two tales being stronger than the narrative one. While reading them, one gets in fact the impression that al-Mas^cadī wrote them in order to formulate a number of ideas already touched on in his longer texts.

In *al-Musāfir*[75] a traveller appears who has behind him long journeys in the East driven by the desire to discover "the secret of tranquility and of dream".[76] In a monologue he explains to himself the particular features of this oriental tranquility. Unlike the tranquility of Apollo, which is only a mask covering his inner strife, the tranquility of the man of the Orient means total unshakability, it is like marble, "the security and the wisdom of marble." (123) "The Oriental is unlimited, transcending the boundaries between man and God; in Him he lives and through God the depths of the absolute open before him." (126). There are only two possibilities: either he will be killed by the feeling of his weakness or the spirit of being, the spirit of Islam, the spirit of God will penetrate his spirit, as was the case of al-Ḥallāj, al-Ghazzālī and others who denied humanity and related to the world of the absolute being, the world of God (126/7). Yet, in the midst of such elevations, the traveller realizes that so far he has acquired nothing of that eastern tranquility. He recalls the two last stations of his travel; "the Town of Crumbs" (*qaryat Kisra*) where he saw a mountain consisting of skulls (a similar vision occurred also in *The Dam*) and "The Town of Abundance" (*qaryat Makthar*), where he beheld a Roman triumphal arch, which appeared to him – strange error! – as the symbol of the Orient! And he remembers how he ascended to heaven upon that arch. He now realizes that the eastern tranquility can neither be grasped by reason nor reached by effort. One must be clean from coertion, as is nature itself. Effort is neither wanted nor does it lead to any results: "That much effort imposes Being on the living, the effort of the tranquil universe which is 'well-pleased and well-pleasing'.[77] Not the effort of fighting and battle, nor the effort of the miner who cuts into the entrails of the earth and pillages it, nor the effort of Prometheus trying to get rid of his fetters, nor the effort of the steam-tug dragging the large ship into the harbour, nor the effort of the greedy voracious creature who precipitates himself upon the table of the world and devours it. Nothing but that the soul opens to Being, attentive and wakeful towards it and content with it and confident with it and submissive (*muslima*) to it. Man gives himself to Life and the Absolute Being gives man tranquility, space and satisfaction" (132/33)."

After two years of unrest, the traveller has come to rest and "he does not cease (to remain) in tranquility and dream."

Sinbad and Purity is very close to this sketch both in structure and content. Again the hero, either the well-known Sinbad of the *Nights* or a name-sake and companion in adventures of the latter, finds himself between two journeys and visits a tavern in the harbour. His justification is, that one needs purity either after or before a journey and that the tavern plays a similar role to the purification fountain before a mosque. The inspector of such an installation, who supervises those praying in their acts of cleansing and evacuation of the bowels, is in fact similar to an inn-keeper. (143) So Sinbad enters a tavern and meets a woman he has met before. But this time she is different. All of a sudden her face starts to change, taking on the form of all the women Sinbad has known before. "And how it is that she exhales the stink of every bloody butcher of a sultan and every beardy bribable *qāḍī*, and every teacher of boys involved in pederasty, and every thievish, rapacious landed proprietor, and every deceitful, hypocritical servant of God, and every high-placed villain whose roots are in mud and ignominy while his head is among the heads?" (149)

She sits down at his side and he remembers how often he has slept with her. But soon he rouses himself and leaves her, boarding the first ship he can reach and sending it to sea and into the storm. "This was his last journey, the purity of the depths embraced him."

These two sketches, not free of inner contradictions, hardly add clarity to our knowledge of the author's views and objectives. On the contrary, they pose new problems, which, however cannot be solved in this article. A few remarks must suffice. There are again elements of irony. Even though the end of *al-Musāfir* sounds quite earnest, one wonders how much of the preceding text can be taken at face value. Or has al-Mas^cadī really turned from the ideal of dynamism so vividly upheld in *The Dam* to almost its contrary in *al-Musāfir*? And how could it escape him that a Roman triumphal arch can symbolize anything but the ideal of oriental tranquility? Is he mocking at oriental self-delusion or has he himself fallen victim to it? And how have we to take the parallel between Islamic ritual purification and the cleansing function of a harbour tavern?

However that may be, a hidden network of structural and motif relations exists in al-Mas^cadī's five texts. If one tries to find a common denominator bridging the apparent differences between them, one might think of the search for the absolute. The three major male heroes Ghaylān, Madyan and Abū Hurayrah all set out, either from the very beginning or from a given moment of the development of the narrative, to pursue their particular aim to the exclusion of any other considerations: Ghaylān the completion of the dam, Madyan oblivion, Abū Hurayrah self-realization. And even the two minor heroes, the Traveller and Sinbad behave similarly. The Traveller seeks fusion with The Absolute Being, Sinbad seeks absolute purity. All of them follow their inner voices, they act as existentialists are expected to act. Mas^cadī's work – and this is a further fascinating aspect of it – is deeply involved in Islamic issues. It may even be read as an attempt towards a new interpretation of Islamic essentials. This is why he has rightly been called not just a representative of Arabic, but of Islamic existentialism – and the only one to have appeared so far. Ṭāhā Ḥusayn, who rightly points out that existentialism is of pagan origin and even to-day normally means heresy (*ilḥād*), rebellion against God or belief in oneself, labels al-Mas^cadī's existentialism as Islamic because he, like Gabriel Marcel in his Christian existentialism, "set limits to man's trust in himself, the most important of which is the religious one, which prevents man from pride and rebellion and reminds him in his heart that he is responsible before . . . God". Yet Ṭāhā Ḥusayn continues by saying that he is afraid that Islamic existentialism will probably not outlive al-Mas^cadī, just as Christian existentialism has hardly outlived Marcel.[78]

Tradition and modernity have been interwoven with remarkable skill by al-Mas^cadī in his three noteworthy literary productions as well as in his two short sketches. Not by the often all-too mechanical-device of collage techniques – inserting excerpts from mediaeval texts into modern fictional writing – but, by a careful choice of motifs, allusions, linguistic means and structural patterns, al-Masᶜadī has created texts that open vistas and perspectives from present to past and vice versa, texts that exemplify how a fusion between the French (and Western) mind and the Arabic literary tradition could be achieved – and that paved the way for later writers. But al-Masᶜadī also foresaw developments of which in his time only the germs existed.

Notes

1. I adopt this spelling of the name as against al-Misᶜadī suggested by the French spelling Messadi, which I have used in some former publications, since the form al-Masᶜadī has by now been standardized by writers like Ostle, Skarzynska etc.
2. M. Férid-Ghazi, "La littérature tunisienne contemporaine", *Orient* 12/1959 xx–xx.
3. G.E. von Grunebaum, *Studien zum Kultur- und Selbstverständnis des Islam*, (Artemis, Zürich & Stuttgart 1969), 269f.
4. R.C. Ostle, 'Maḥmūd al-Masᶜadī and Tunisia's "Lost Generation"' in *JAL* 8 (1977), 153–166.
5. S. Balas, 'Masraḥiyyat as-Sudd li-Maḥmūd al-Masᶜadī wa-abᶜāduhu al-wujūdiyya' in *al-Karmil* 2 (1981), 1–30.
6. 'Der Damm (*as-Sudd*). Ein modernes arabisches Drama von Maḥmūd al-Masᶜadī, ins Deutsche übertragen' in *Die Welt des Islams* 21 (1983), 30–79. A French translation had appeared two years earlier: Mahmoud Messadi, *Le barrage – drame en huit tableaux. Traduction et Introduction d'A. Guellouz* (Éditions Naaman Sherbrooke, Québec, Canada 1981).
7. 'Die Auflehnung gegen das Schicksal als religiöses und existentielles Problem in Masᶜadī's Drama der Damm' in J.C. Bürgel and H. Fähndrich (eds), *Die Vorstellung von Schicksal und die Darstellung der Wirklichkeit in der zeitgenössischen Literatur islamischer Länder* (Schweizer Asiatische Studien, Studienheft 7), (P. Lang, Bern 1983), 101–116.
8. "Poszukiwanie absolutu w dziele al-Masᶜadiego", in print.
9. Férid-Ghazi, *Le roman et la nouvelle en Tunisie*, (Tunis 1970); J. Bielawski et al., *Nowa i Współczesna Literatura Arabska* 19 i 20 w. Literatura arabskiego Maghrebu (Panstwowe Wydanictwo Naukowe, Warszawa 1989), 388–400; 545–46; S. Pantueek, *Tunesische Literaturgeschichte*, Wiesbaden 1974, 74–80; unfortunately, this chapter is not free from errors, thus, instead of Abū Huraira, we read throughout Adū Duraira!
10. Biographical information is to be found in the journal published by the Institut des Belles-Lettres Arabes (*IBLA* 1969, p.1), and in Bielawski's above-mentioned volume on Maghribī literature, 388f. (the chapter on al-Masᶜadī is by K. Skarzynska).
11. Bielawski, 389. Al-Masᶜadī himself stresses the necessity to understand literary existentialism in a broader than just philosophical sense and he believes that there is ultimately no difference between existentialist literature and *littérature engagée*, 'Taᶜlīq al-muᵓallif ᶜalā maqāl al-duktūr Ṭāhā Ḥusayn', reprinted in *al-Sudd* (247–272), p. 261.

12. *Al-Sudd. Riwāya fi thamāniya manāẓir.* (al-Dār al-Tūnisiyya li l-nashr, al-Ṭab^c^a al-thāniya 1974). The unusual vocalization – *sudd* instead of *sadd* – is marked on the cover, but is perhaps a misprint for *al-Saddu*, for on the title page, the *tashdīd* + *ḍamma* are over the *dāl*, not the *sīn*. This edition contains comments by Ben Milad (al-Ustādh Maḥjūb ibn Mīlād) Shadli Klibi (al-Ustādh al-Shādhilī al-Qalībī), two articles by Ṭāhā Ḥusayn and al-Mas^c^adī's answer to the first of these two articles.
13. *Ḥaddatha Abū Hurayrah qāl* . . . ^c^Uyūn al-mu^c^āṣara. Dār al-janūb li l-nashr. Tunis 1979.
14. *Mawlid an-nisyān* (al-Dār at-Tūnisiyya li l-nashr 1974).
15. *al-Musāfir* and *al-Sindibādu wa l-ṭahārah*, both contained in the volume *Mawlid al-nisyān wa-ta^ɔ^ammulāt ukhrā*, as mentioned in note 14.
16. *Ta^ɔ^ṣīlan li-kiyān*, Nashr wa-tawzī^c^ Mu^ɔ^assasat ^c^Abdalkarīm ibn ^c^Abdallāh. Tunis 1979.
17. According to the Tunisian literary critic Ben Milad, this strange epithet can only be explained by understanding it as referring not to the individual hero but to mankind in general, cf. Maḥjūb ibn Milād, 'al-Muqaddima al-ūlā li l-ṭab^c^a al-ūlā', reprinted in the above-mentioned edition of *al-Sudd* (151–83), p. 168f.
18. Cf. al-Mas^c^adī's own statement "the priests of Ṣahabbā^ɔ^ with their prayer and their litany and their dances and their dark, obscure language which, by intention (of the author) does not convey any meaning . . . represent the blind force of mankind who stumble in a world of irrationalism and ignorance", *Ta^ɔ^ṣīlan li-kiyān* 81.
19. Cf. H. Bowen, article '^c^Aḍud ad-Dawla' in *EI*².
20. Cf. my *Die Hofkorrespondenz ^c^Aḍud ad-Daulas und ihr Verhältnis zu andern historischen Quellen der frühen Buyiden* (Harassowitz, Wiesbaden 1965), 158f.
21. *Sūrah* 34, 14 trans Arberry.
22. Cf. e.g. *Sūrah* 25, 21.
23. Cf. Ṭāhā Ḥusayn, *laysat illā ramziyya, al-Sudd* 220. However, al-Mas^c^adī understood by *ramzī* mainly laconism and ambiguity, including a certain degree of obscureness (*ghumūḍ*), *Ta^ɔ^ṣīlan li-kiyān*, 40f.
24. Férid-Ghazi and Balas very clearly understood the religion of Ṣahabb ā^ɔ^ to be an allegory of (a distorted form of) Islam.
25. Ṭāhā Ḥusayn, 'al-Sudd – taḥlīl wa-naqd', in *al-Sudd* 215; 'Aṣdā^ɔ^ Tūnisiyya', ibid. 239/240.
26. *al-Sudd* 266.
27. *al-Sudd* 268; for the "deposit" cf. *Sūrah* 33,72.
28. *al-Sudd* 269.
29. Cf. A. Schimmel, *Gabriel's Wing*. A Study into the religious ideas of Sir Muhammad Iqbal. Studies in the History of Religions VI, Leiden 1963.
30. On the other hand, his position is very clearly expressed in a public lecture printed in his volume of essays. There he stresses that Ghaylān is conscious of his "existentialist responsibility", even though Maymūnah thinks Ghaylān's intention to "create" (*khlq*) is heresy (*kufr*). *Ta^ɔ^ṣīlan li-kiyān*, 76.
31. *al-Sudd* 116.
32. *al-Sudd* 23.
33. *Ta^ɔ^ṣīlan li-kiyān* 78.

34. ibid. 80.
35. On *Nishwār al-muḥāḍarah*, cf. Brockelmann *GAL* Suppl. I, 253.
36. On *al-Imtāᶜ wal-muʾānasah* cf. Brockelmann *GAL* Suppl. I, 436.
37. On ᶜAṭṭār cf. H. Ritter, *Das Meer der Seele*. Mensch, Welt und Gott in den Geschichten des Fariduddin ᶜAṭṭār. Leiden 1978.
38. Cf. Ostle's statements: "It becomes increasingly obvious that linguistic parody is an important part of the creative irony which exists at various levels throughout this work" (l.c. 157) and "One should emphasize that the linguistic parody to which al-Masᶜadī resorts so frequently in *al-Sudd* has as its aim not so much ridicule as serious irony and satire." (159)
39. *al-Sudd* 215; 233.
40. *al-Sudd* 255f.
41. *al-Sudd* 264.
42. *al-Sudd* 257.
43. J. Berque in his introduction to the French translation calls *The Dam "un drame symboliste, apparenté à Solness et à Tète d'or" Le Barrage* 9. *Tète d'or* is a play by the young Paul Claudel. Unfortunately, Berque does not expatiate upon these alleged parallels.
44. Shādhilī writes: "So it becomes clear that Ghaylān and Maymūnah represent two opposite visions of life: Maymūnah is Oriental submitting to the rules of being, whereas Ghaylān is related to Nietzsche, a destroyer and demolisher ascending towards creation." *al-Sudd* 196/7.
45. *Islāmukum lil-ᶜillati ḍuᶜfun yā jubanāʾ, Mawlid* 35.
46. *Mawlid* 22/23.
47. *Mawlid* 64/5.
48. *Mawlid* 66.
49. *Mawlid* 77f.
50. *Mawlid* 84.
51. *Mawlid* 100.
52. *nasīna sabīla l-iṭlāq al-junūna, Mawlid* 101.
53. *innamā l-ᶜaqlu ᶜiqāl, Mawlid* 101.
54. *Mawlid* 99/100.
55. *Mawlid* 110/11.
56. *Mawlid* 113.
57. *Mawlid* 114.
58. *qad ᶜāwadahu l-jaws, Abū Hurayrah* 104.
59. *laqad kāna dāʾima t-tawqi ilā sh-shams dāʾima l-khawfi min ṭulūᶜihā, Abū Hurayrah* 105.
60. *kuntu urīduhā ᶜadhrāʾ lam yaṭaʾhā wāṭiʾ fa-ʾidhā hiya ᶜajūzun fājirah, Abū Hurayrah* 131.
61. *Abū Hurayrah* 119.
62. Perhaps an influence of Sartre's *Le diable et le bon Dieu*?
63. *Abū Hurayrah* 120.
64. *Abū Hurayrah* 121.
65. *nastawfī jamīᶜa mā khalaqa Llāh, Abū Hurayrah* 126.
66. *Abū Hurayrah* 133.
67. *hal antum muslimūna rāḍūna*, could also be translated: "are you willing to submit, (are you) content?
68. *Abū Hurayrah* 143/4.

69. *Abū Hurayrah* 162/63.
70. *lam yabqa illā an aṭluba dhātī muṭlaqan, Abū Hurayrah* 202.
71. *la yaḥsunu l-fi[c]lu illā muṭlaqan mahḍan, Abū Hurayrah* 209.
72. *lam yabqa illā an aṭluba al-nihāyah, Abū Hurayrah* 214.
73. *Abū Hurayrah* 225.
74. In the above mentioned lecture, al-Mas[c]adī gives a brief summary of *Thus spake Abū Hurayra* and discusses the following stages of his "existentialist journey": Sensuality (*al-ḥiss*), love (*al-ḥubb*), bewilderment with man (*al-ḥīra fi al-nās*) bewilderment with God (*al-ḥīra fi Allāh*), passion and annihilation (*al-[c]ishq wa l-fanā*ʾ), *Taʾṣīlan li-kiyān* 69–75.
75. *Mawlid* 119–133.
76. *al-ṭamaʾ nīnah wa l-ḥulm, Mawlid* 120.
77. *rāḍiatan marḍiyyatan*, reminiscent of *Sūrah* 89.27f., God's invitation to the "tranquil or "confident" soul (*al-nafs al-muṭmaʾinnah*) to enter Paradise "Well-pleased and well-pleasing".
78. *al-Sudd* 244. According to Ḥusayn, existentialism was first Greek and Roman, then Christian, and finally Islamic. "And God bestowed existentialism on Islam through al-Mas[c]adī in our days," *al-Sudd* 236. I need hardly emphasize that Ghaylān in his limitless hubris is the contrary of what Ḥusayn here and al-Mas[c]adī in some of his comments make of him.

13

The Organizational Principles in Ibn Sallām's *Ṭabaqāt Fuḥūl al-Shuᶜarā*ᵓ

A Reconsideration

Adel S. Gamal
University of Arizona

Because *Ṭabaqāt Fuḥūl al-Shuᶜarā*ᵓ is the first book that has come down to us on Arabic literary criticism,[1] it has received much attention from modern scholars in the East and the West alike. This attention is primarily focused on the views of Ibn Sallām (231/846) on literary criticism, and to a lesser extent on the criteria upon which he classified the 134 poets whom he selected for inclusion in his book.

Ibn Sallām divided the poets whom he chose into two highly schematized groups, *jāhilī* and *islamī*. Each group consists of forty poets, distributed into ten classes, each class comprising four poets. After the *islamī* group, he placed a class of four *marāthī* poets, a class of 22 poets from Medina, Mecca, Ṭāᵓif, and Bahrain whom he named 'town poets', and finally a class of eight Jewish poets. A fair amount of research has been done on Ibn Sallām's criteria of classification. However, this research either ruminates on previous studies, especially that of Ṭāhā Ibrāhīm published in 1937; or offers partial solutions that, when tested against Ibn Sallām's work as a whole, fail to give a cogent interpretation of what it sets out to do. I propose 1) to examine the studies done hitherto on the intriguing issue of classification in Ibn Sallām's work, showing that they do not provide a satisfactory answer to this question, and 2) to suggest a new interpretation which might provide more coherent views.

As far as early Western scholarship is concerned, Kilpatrick remarks that Brockelmann was off the mark in linking the idea of Ibn Sallām's method of classifying poets, according to whether they were pre-Islamic or Islamic, with the requirements of the philologists. The latter needed to know to which epoch a poet belonged in order to be able to assess the linguistic evidence found in their poetry. Kilpatrick implies that Brockelmann's incorrect statement might be justified, since he was not working from the Ṭabaqāt itself but only from a fragment of it contained mainly in al-Suyūṭī's *Muzhir*. However, she observes that the first editor of *Ṭabaqāt*, Joseph Hell, and some other scholars who had this edition at their disposal did not modify Brockelmann's view or dissociate themselves from it.[2] To Kilpatrick's critique of Brocklmann I would like to add that there is no statement in Ibn Sallām's book to suggest that it was written in response to the philologists' needs.

As far as I am aware, the first fully-fledged study in Arabic scholarship on Arabic literary criticism was done by Ṭāhā Ibrāhīm in 1937.[3] The thesis which he presented regarding Ibn Sallām's criteria of classification has dominated the field for more than a half century, and subsequent writers were to add very little to it or hardly modified it at all.

Based on several remarks made by Ibn Sallām, Ṭāhā Ibrāhīm believed that the criteria upon which Ibn Sallām classified the poets in his book were:

Quality: this criterion is very obvious if Imruᵓ al-Qays, al-Nābigha, Zuhayr, and al-Aᶜshā are included in *jāhilī* class I. However Ṭāhā Ibrāhīm seems to suggest that Ibn Sallām sometimes combines quality with quantity, as can be seen from the example cited in the 'quantity' criterion below.

Quantity: the more prolific the poet is, the more advanced the class he is assigned. In support of this argument, Ṭāhā Ibrāhīm states that Ibn Sallām placed al-Aswad b. Yaᶜfur in *jāhilī* class V because, in ibn Sallām's own words: 'He has an outstanding long poem which rivals any great poem. Had he composed another one like it, we would have put him ahead of his peers.'[4]

Variety: poets whose poetry is restricted to one or two topics are not as gifted as those who tackle, and excel in, several topics such as ghazal, fakhr, *madḥ*, *hijāᵓ*, etc. Therefore, Ibn Sallām, maintains Ṭāhā Ibrāhīm, preferred Kuthayyir over Jamīl because 'his poetry deals with more topics than Jamīl's',[5] thus placing Kuthayyir in class II while placing Jamīl in class VI of *islāmī* poets.

The first two of these three criteria, holds Ṭāhā Ibrāhīm, are not Ibn Sallām's own; they were in circulation a long time before he wrote his book. In literary circles, the four poets included in *jāhilī* class I had already been acclaimed as the best poets of their time. Similarly, the first three poets in *islāmī* class I were already accorded such a place.

Now that Ṭāhā Ibrāhīm has established what he believes to be the three criteria upon which Ibn Sallām classified the *jāhilī* and *islāmī* poets, he contends that Ibn Sallām did not adhere to his own principles. It will suffice here to give just one example which Ṭāhā Ibrāhīm provides for each criterion. As far as quality is concerned, *jāhilī* class VI includes ᶜAmr b. Kulthūm, al-Ḥārith b. Ḥilliza, ᶜAntara al-ᶜAbsī, and Suwayd b. Abī Kāhil. These poets are far more accomplished and famous than those whom he placed one class ahead of them, class V. As regards quantity, Ṭāhā Ibrāhīm does not understand why a poet like Kaᶜb b. Zuhayr is placed in *islāmī* class II, while more prolific poets are in much later classes. Lastly, if the variety of topics in one's poetry is a measurement of his greatness and versatility, then how can it be justified that *islāmī* class VI (Ibn Qays al-Ruqayyāt, al-Aḥwaṣ, Jamīl, and Nuṣayb) lags behind class IV whose poets are not as versatile?

Furthermore, Ṭāhā Ibrāhīm believes that the idea of making each class of four poets was accidental, rather than a carefully considered method. The Arabic literary tradition had, as mentioned earlier, already established that four specific *jāhilī* poets are the most outstanding poets of that era. Therefore, Ibn Sallām was forced to include only four poets in each class. In support of this view, Ṭāhā Ibrāhīm contends that al-Rāᶜī was added to *islāmī* class I simply to meet the quota, or as Kilpatrick puts it 'something of a makeweight beside the giants al-Akhṭal, Jarīr and al-Farazdaq.' She further elaborates by stating that this order of precedence is less fixed among the lower classes of poets, and Ibn Sallām does not feel obliged to admit elsewhere that his system has forced an arbitrary classification on him.[6] Unable to understand the logic behind such a plan of work, Blachère asserts that the composition of the Ṭabaqāt is very artificial.[7] Furthermore, why did Ibn Sallām, wonders Ṭāhā Ibrāhīm, limit the classes to only ten? And why did he exclude the *muḥdathūn* poets, some of whom were his contemporaries, such as Marwān b. Abī Ḥafṣa, Abū Nuwās, and Abū Tammām?

A few years later (1945), Muḥammad Mandūr's celebrated book, *al-Naqd al-Manhajī ᶜinda al-ᶜArab*[8] came out. He endorses Ṭāhā Ibrāhīm's views with respect to the three criteria of classification in Ibn Sallām's work. However, Mandūr picks up a tiny thread in Ṭāhā Ibrāhīm's discussion of Ibn Sallām's concept about the interplay between the poet and his environment.[9] Poetry, like other forms of artistic expressions, is not created in a vacuum. It is the product of a person who lives at a certain time and in a specific place. Whether he is conscious of it or not, these two factors shape his literary production. Mandūr expands the concept of time and environment in further explaining the reasons behind Ibn Sallām's division of poets the way he did. It was inevitable, Mandūr maintains, that the poets be divided into *jāhilī* and *islāmī*. Islam brought about immense developments and changes which affected the Arabs in every aspect of their life – religious, moral, social, political, economic, and cultural. After making his divisions, Ibn Sallām found out that there were poets who did not rise in the realm of poetry to universality, but remained 'local poets', so he grouped them under the name of 'town poets.' Realizing that the concept of time and environment cannot be used as a basis to explain the inclusion of the class of four *marāthī* poets, Mandūr offers a new interpretation. He holds that these poets were 'compelled' to confine their poetry to one genre only, namely elegy. The immeasurable loss of their loved ones was so severe that they had to find relief, and their poetic expression provided that relief.[10]

With the exception of Ṭabāna and Kilpatrick, virtually all subsequent writers add nothing of substance to what Ṭāhā Ibrāhīm and Mandūr advance, whether regarding the issue of identifying the criteria of Ibn Sallām's classification system or in pointing out what is taken to be the shortcomings of that system. For the former either reiterate the same criteria verbatim as if the ideas were their own,[11] or in rare cases acknowledge the two scholars' contributions.[12]

Ṭabāna attempts to answer the last question which Ṭāhā Ibrāhīm poses regarding the absence of the *muḥdathūn* poets from the *Ṭabaqāt*. He offers a two-fold answer[13] which Kilpatrick cites in her article and then adds a third. She writes:

> *Muḥdathūn* poetry had not yet established itself in this period as worthy of equal consideration with *jāhilī* and *islāmī* poetry. Ibn Sallām knew some of the *muḥdathūn* poets, such as Bashshār, Marwān b. Abī Ḥafṣa, and respected their critical opinions enough to quote them. But the poetry he is concerned with in the Ṭabaqāt ends with the fall of the Umayyads.It has been suggested that he avoided classifying his contemporaries in the same way as bygone poets for fear of calling down the vituperation of those he displeased on his head, for men such as Bashshār and al-Farazdaq did not refrain from satirizing their critics among the philologists. Another hypothesis is that there was no critical agreement about the evaluation of living poets such as there was about those of earlier periods, and for Ibn Sallām, whose inclination was to rely on the opinions of earlier older scholars, this was a sufficient obstacle to prevent him from trying his hand at a pioneering evaluation. Yet another hypothesis may be advanced, namely that whereas it was no difficult task to find forty *jāhilī* and *islāmī* poets, Ibn Sallām would have been hard put to it to fill ten classes of *muḥdathūn*. Given his awareness of the formal structure of the Ṭabaqāt may have played quite an important role in his decision to end with the *islāmiyūn*.[14]

Kilpatrick suggests one more criterion of classification, namely, tribal adherence. This criterion very clearly lies behind the composition of *islāmī* class VIII, all of whom are members of Banū Murra clan, and to an extent behind the make-up of other classes.[15]

Against this background, I would like to re-examine the Ṭabaqāt and to take a closer look at other works by Ibn Sallām, fragments of which I have gleaned from different sources. As will be demonstrated, these materials will obviate many of the critics' remarks which they set against Ibn Sallām as blunders.

Ibn Sallām begins his book with these lines:

> We thought about the Arabs and their poetry – their renowned poets, knights, noblemen, and their feuds. It is all but impossible to exhaust the poets, knights, noblemen, and the feuds of even one single tribe. Therefore, we limited ourselves to that with which every scholar is familiar, and no Arabist can afford to dispense with, so we began by (writing about) poetry.[16]

It is quite clear that Ibn Sallām's intention was to write several books on the topics he enumerated. Unfortunately only one of them survived, namely, the *Ṭabaqāt*. Ibn al-Nadīm lists six books by Ibn Sallām: *al-Fāṣil fī Mulaḥ al-Akhbār wa al-Ashᶜār* (Maḥmud Shākir, the editor of the *Ṭabaqāt*, suggests "*al-Fāḍil*"), *Kitāb Buyūtāt al-ᶜArab* (which Ibn Sallām referred to, I believe, as "the noblemen"), *Ṭabaqāt al-Shuᶜarāᵓ al-Jāhiliyyīn*, *Ṭabaqāt al-Shuᶜarāᵓ al-Islāmiyyīn*, the *Ṭabaqāt Fuḥūl al-Shuᶜarāᵓ* (Maḥmūd Shākir suggests that these last two are in fact but one book), *Kitāb al-Ḥilāb wa Ajr al-Khayl* (Shākir suggests "*Ijrāᵓ*"),[17] and *Kitāb Gharīb al-Qurᵓān*.[18] The book about the knights (*al-fursān*) is mentioned by other writers, as will be discussed below. I would like to suggest the possibility that Ibn Sallām had two more books, one on singers and the other on the Umayyad-ᶜAbbasid poets whom he left out of the *Ṭabaqāt*. Although these two books are not mentioned in any source, the ample citations from them make it very difficult to disprove that they did exist at one point of time, as I will detail shortly.

With the exception of *Kitāb Gharīb al-Qurᵓān,* several sources have preserved quotations from these lost books. Since *Buyūtāt al-ᶜArab* and *al-Ḥilāb* have no bearing on the issue of the criteria of classification, it will suffice to give one example quoted from each book and indicate where more quotations can be found. With respect to *Buyūtāt al-ᶜArab*, Thaᶜlab (290/904) cites a long piece about the *siqāyat al-ḥājj* which was assumed by the Banū Hāshim. It tells us that when Abū Ṭālib b. ᶜAbd al-Muṭṭalib became destitute, several members of the Banū Hāshim assumed the responsibility of taking care of his sons. To continue his obligation towards the *Ḥājj*, Abū Ṭālib had to borrow 10,000 dirhams from his brother al-ᶜAbbās. The following year his financial situation did not improve, and he had to borrow 14,000 dirhams from his brother. For the third year in a row he asked his brother for money to meet his obligations. Al-ᶜAbbās advised his brother to pass on this honour to him since Abū Ṭālib was no longer able to afford the financial responsibilities it entailed, so he did. Till today the *siqāya* has remained within the Banū Hāshim.[19] I believe that the *akhbār* which Abū al-Faraj mentions about ᶜĀᵓisha bint Ṭalḥa are from *Buyūtāt al-ᶜArab* too.[20] Similarly are the *akhbār* about Khālid b. al-Walīd.[21] As for the book on horses, *al-Ḥilāb*, Ibn Qutayba has this *khabar*: Muslim b. ᶜAmr wanted to send a cousin of his to Syria and Egypt to buy horses for him. His cousin said: 'I have no knowledge about horses'. Muslim exclaimed: 'Aren't you an experienced hunter?' 'Yes,' he replied. Then Muslim said: 'Look then in a horse for the same quality you look for in a dog.' So, the cousin returned with horses, the like of which had never been seen in Arabia.[22]

As mentioned above, Ibn Sallām stated when he intended to write a series of books, that he 'began by writing about poetry.' After the *Ṭabaqāt* was completed, he wrote several books on poetry. One of these books is on the poetry of the knights, *Shuᶜarāᵓ al-Fursān*. Ibn al-Jarrāḥ (296/909) and Abū al-Faraj have preserved valuable quotations from this book. It seems that Ibn Sallām followed, more or less, in this book the same system he adopted in the *Ṭabaqāt*. Here are the references to some of these poets whom Ibn Sallām included in his book:

1. **Durayd b. al-Ṣimma**. Abū al-Faraj gives Durayd's genealogies then writes: Durayd b. al-Ṣimma is a brave knight and an eminent (*faḥl*) poet. Ibn Sallām placed him at the very top of the *shuᶜarāᵓ al-fursān*.[23] Abū al-Faraj also quotes Durayd's encounter with the famous poetess al-Khansāᵓ.[24]

2. **ᶜAmr b. Maᶜdīkarib**. Ibn al-Jarrāḥ writes in ᶜAmr's biography: ᶜAmr b. Maᶜdīkarib, the famous knight, Muḥammad b. Sallām ranked him fourth among the renowned Arab knights.[25] Ibn al-Jarrāḥ provides another three pieces of *akhbār* about ᶜAmr.[26] Abū al-Faraj quotes: 'ᶜAmr b. Maᶜdīkarib used to say: I fear not encountering the knights of the Arabs except their two free-born men and their two slaves. By the free-born, he means ᶜĀmir b. al-Ṭufayl and ᶜUtayba b. al-Ḥārith, and by the two slaves he means ᶜAntara and al-Sulayk b. al-Sulaka.'[27]

3. **Khufāf b. Nudba**. In Khufāf's biography, Abū al-Faraj writes: Ibn Sallām placed him in class V of the knights along with Mālik b. Nuwayra and his (Khufāf's) two cousins, Ṣakhr and Muᶜāwiya the two sons of

al-Sharīd, and Mālik b. Ḥimār al-Shamkhī.[28] Abū al-Faraj then relates Khufāf and Muᶜāwiya's raid on the Banū Dhubyān which resulted in the killing of Muᶜāwiya. To avenge Muᶜāwiya, Khufāf slew Mālik b. Ḥimār al-Shamkhī, who was then the knight and the lord of the Banū Fazāra.[29]

4. **Zayd al-Khayl**. In the biography of Zayd al-Khayl Abū al-Faraj writes: Abū Khalīfa (Ibn Sallām's nephew) wrote me on the authority of Ibn Sallām that Bujayr b. Zuhayr, al-Ḥuṭayᵓa, and a man from Fazāra went out for an animal hunt. Zayd al-Khayl came upon them and took them captives. Bujayr gave Zayd a mare and Zayd set him free. Al-Ḥuṭayᵓa apologized for having nothing to give, so Zayd set him free.[30]

5. **Rabīᶜa b. Mukaddam**. After quoting a b-poem, Abū al-Faraj cites: 'It is said that this poem is by Ḥassān b. Thābit, and it is said it is by Ḍirār b. al-Khaṭṭāb al-Fihrī. Abū Khalīfa wrote me on the authority of Ibn Sallām that these lines are by ᶜAmr b. Shaqīq of banū Fihr b. Mālik.'[31]

Unlike the previous poets, there is no reference to Zayd al-Khayl or Rabīᶜa's rank among the *fursān*, but I would argue strongly that these two *akhbār* are from Ibn Sallām's *Shuᶜarāᵓ al-Fursān*, given the nature of their *isnād*. In addition to these four poets, we see that four more poets are mentioned in item no. 3, and another four in item no. 2. The fact that these last four are described as being not only *fursān*, but also that ᶜAmr feared them the most, makes it almost impossible to dismiss the idea that they were not included in the *Fursān al-Shuᶜarāᵓ*. It is very likely that this book must have included many other poets who were also known as brave warriors such as al-ᶜArjī, Bakr b. al-Naṭṭāḥ, and Umayya b. al-Ḥārith, among many others.

These few quotations are not sufficient to provide us with a clear picture about *Fursān al-Shuᶜarāᵓ*. The citations in items nos. 1 and 2 seem to suggest that Ibn Sallām ranked the poets numerically, but the one in item no. 3 suggests that they were classified into classes, just like the *Ṭabaqāt*. However, that same quotation indicates that the class is made up of five poets, not four as in the *Ṭabaqāt*.

Although no mention is made of *al-Fāḍil fī Mulaḥ al-Akhbār wa al-Ashᶜār* in any source beside Ibn al-Nadīm's Fihrist, as far as I am aware, I would argue that the numerous excerpts found in some sources on the authority of Ibn Sallām strongly indicate that these excerpts must have been extracted from that book. These facetious stories or anecdotes and poems are about and by men and women who lived in the Umayyad and Abbasid eras. The few following examples should support this postulation.

1. In the biography of ᶜAmr b. Shaᵓs, Abū al-Faraj relates that when

Muḥammad b. al-Ashᶜath was killed, al-Ḥajjāj sent his head with ᶜIrār b. ᶜAmr b. Shaʾs to ᶜAbd al-Malik b. Marwān. The latter was impressed by ᶜIrār's eloquence and pure speech despite the fact that ᶜIrār was very dark, so ᶜAbd al-Malik recited:

Although ᶜIrār is not white
I like the dark-complexioned, broad-shouldered one.

Upon hearing the poem, ᶜIrār laughed in such a way that annoyed ᶜAbd al-Malik. The latter asked him angrily why he was laughing? ᶜIrār responded: 'Commander of the Faithful, do you know the person meant by that poem?' ᶜAbd al-Malik answered negatively. ᶜIrār then said: 'I am that person.' Amazed by this coincidence, ᶜAbd al-Malik laughed and gave him a handsome reward.[32] Similar anecdotes are told in the biographies of Abū al-Aswad al-Duʾalī[33], Sukayna bint al-Ḥusayn,[34] al-Dalāl,[35] Masᶜada al-Bakhtarī,[36] Abū Ḥayya al-Numayrī, who is an Umayyad-Abbasid poet.[37]

2. In the biography of Ḥammād al-Rāwiya Abū al-Faraj tells us that a man came to Ḥammād and recited some of his poetry. Impressed by the quality of the composition, Ḥammād did not believe that the man could compose such a poem. Ḥammād told the man if he really was the authour of this poem, he should not have any problem composing a satire about him. The man then left and came back after a while and began to recite a poem in which he satirized Ḥammād. After listening to five lines, Ḥammād begged the man to stop saying that he believed that the man was a good poet indeed. He implored the man not to recite that poem again. Ḥammād then remarked about how foolish he was to bring that upon himself.[39] Similar anecdotes are told about the Abbasid poet Abū Dulāma[39] and Ibn Abī al-Zawāʾid from whom Ibn Sallām relates the anecdote directly.[40] Several other anecdotes are also told by Abū al-Faraj.[41] A few other anecdotes are to be found in *al-Ḥayawān*,[42] *ᶜUyūn al-Akhbār*,[43] *Majālis Thaᶜlab*,[44] *Ṭabaqāt al-Naḥwiyyīn*.[45]

Abū al-Faraj included in his book 27 quotations about famous singers on the authority of Ibn Sallām. This suggests that Ibn Sallām very likely wrote a book on *Akhbār al-Mughannīn*. The nature of these materials does not indicate that they could have been parts of *al-Fāḍil fī Mulaḥ al-Akhbār wa al-Ashᶜār*, for they do not have anecdotal characteristics. Furthermore, some reference to genealogies can be found (which is indicative of a biographical work), such as in the biography of Ibn ᶜĀʾisha, where Ibn Sallām says that the mother of 'Ibn ᶜĀʾisha is a client of the family of al-Muṭṭalib b. Wadāᶜa al-Sahmī.'[46] The following two brief citations typify these kinds of *akhbār*:

1. No one doubts Jamīla's singing superiority. No one has ever claimed to be her equal. Every Medinan and every Meccan acknowledges her superiority.[47]
2. Muḥammad b. Sallām said: 'I asked Jarīr al-Madīnī about Ibn Surayj.' He answered: 'Woe to you! You mention his name without saying that he is the master of all singers and the unique peerless one among them!'[48]

More detailed *akhbār* about several of these famous singers are scattered in *al-Aghānī* such as al-Burdān,[49] Jamīla,[50] Ibn Surayj,[51] the two sisters – Sallāma and Rayya,[52] Sallāma al-Zarqāᵓ,[53] Ṭuways,[54] Ibn ᶜĀᵓisha,[55] ᶜAzza al-Mayalāᵓ,[56] Abū Kāmil,[57] and Ibn Misjaḥ.[58]

In *al-Aghānī* alone at least 41 *akhbār* are found about poets of whom no mention is made in the *Ṭabaqāt* and whose absence from this source has exposed Ibn Sallām to severe criticism. These poets are Umayyad, Umayyad-Abbasid, and Abbasid whom Ibn Sallām met and quoted directly. This seems even further to suggest that Ibn Sallām had yet another book which included some of the *islāmī* poets whom he had left out of the *Ṭabaqāt*, such as ᶜUmar b. Abī Rabīᶜa; *mukhaḍramū al-dawlatayn* poets, such as Bashshār; and Abbasid poets, such as Abū al-ᶜAtāhiya. It will suffice here to give one example of each time period.

1. **The Umayyad**: After Abū al-Faraj mentioned on the authority of Ibn Sallām that ᶜUmar's mother was from Ḥimyar, and that that was where his excellent *ghazal* came from,[59] he related that Ibn ᶜAbbās was in the mosque surrounded by a group of Khārijites, among them Nāfiᶜ b. al-Azraq. While they were asking him all kinds of questions and debating with him, ᶜUmar came in and sat close to Ibn ᶜAbbās. To the dismay of the Khārijites, Ibn ᶜAbbās turned away from them and paid ᶜUmar welcome and asked him to recite his long poem which opens with:

> Should you depart from Nuᶜm's encampment at the first hint of the morrow's dawn,
> or set off with the lengthening shadow, press forward into the next day's heat?[60]

Other Umayyad poets mentioned in *al-Aghānī* are al-Ḥārith b. Khālid al-Makhzūmī,[61] al-Majnūn,[62] Mūsā Shahawāt,[63] al-Ubayrid al-Riyāḥī,[64] al-Sarī b. ᶜAbd al-Raḥmān,[65] Miskīn al-Dārimī,[66] and al-Uqayshir.[67]

2. **The Umayyad-Abbasid**: Bashshār b. Burd's biography has several *akhbār* on the authority of Ibn Sallām. In one of them Abū al-Faraj mentions that Khalaf told Ibn Sallām that he heard about Bashshār, his

wit, and the excellence of his poetry. One day Khalaf listened to a poem by Bashshār which he did not particularly like, for it did not live up to what Khalaf had heard about Bashshār's reputation. Therefore he decided to pay him a visit. Upon seeing Bashshār, Khalaf was even more disappointed, for he saw a huge, blind, ugly-looking man. Bashshār, angered by some news which a person had just brought, composed on the spur of the moment a poem that impressed Khalaf.[68] Other poets from the same period are Ibn Mayyāda,[69] Ṭurayḥ al-Thaqafī,[70] and Ibn Abī al-Zawāᵓid, whom Ibn Sallām met.[71]

3. **The Abbasid**: A number of *akhbār* on the authority of Ibn Sallām are included in the biographies of several Abbasid poets in *al-Aghānī*. By way of example, in the biography of Abū al-ᶜAtāhiya Abū al-Faraj writes: Muḥammad b. Sallām said that Muḥammad b. Abī al-ᶜAtāhiya used to say that his family was from the tribe of ᶜAnaza and that their great grandfather Kaysān was from ᶜAyn al-Tamr. When Khālid b. al-Walīd conquered it, young Kaysān and other children were taken captives and sent to Abū Bakr. When ᶜAbbād b. Rifāᶜa al-ᶜAnazī knew that Kaysān was from ᶜAnaza, he beseeched Abū Bakr to set him free.[72] Other poets mentioned are Marwān b. Abī Ḥafṣa,[73] al-ᶜAbbās b. al-Aḥnaf[74] al-Taymī,[75] Ibn Munādhir,[76] and Ibn Qunbur. Ibn Sallām met with both Ibn Munādhir and Ibn Qunbur[77] and recorded some of their poetry. Furthermore, Ibn al-Jarrāḥ quotes some *akhbār* on the authority of Ibn Sallām in the biographies of the following poets: Abū al-Janūb and his brother Abū al-Ṣimt, the two sons of Marwān b. Abī Ḥafṣa,[78] Abū al-Baydāᵓ al-Riyāḥī,[79] and Muḥammad b. Umayya.[80]

These *akhbār* could be, of course, part of the book on the singers, just like Abū al-Faraj's is. However, the fact remains that Ibn Sallām wrote books on poetry other than the *Ṭabaqāt*. As mentioned above, after expressing his intention in the introduction to write on several subjects, Ibn Sallām said: 'We began by writing about poetry.' This is a general statement which is not qualified, at that particular place in the introduction, by any type of poetry or any period of time. I would argue that after he wrote the *Ṭabaqāt*, he wrote three or more books on poetry dealing with the poets whom he had left out of the *Ṭabaqāt*. Two of these books, *Shuᶜarāᵓ al-Fursān* and *al-Fāḍil fī Mulaḥ al-Akhbār wa al-Ashᶜār*, are mentioned by Abū al-Faraj and Ibn al-Nadīm respectively. I have attempted to establish, through examples and ample footnotes that Ibn Sallām wrote another book or two. Therefore, the criticism levelled against him in this regard by Ṭāhā Ibrāhīm, Ṭabāna, and Kilpatrick (see above), is obviated. So are the reasons these critics believe to be behind Ibn Sallām's blunders.[81] I propose to look anew at the method which Ibn

Sallām outlined in the introduction in an attempt to draw different conclusions from those presented thus far, and to correct some of the prevalent misconceptions. In addition to the paragraph quoted above, Ibn Sallām added:

We mentioned in detail the *jāhilī*, *islāmī*, and *mukhaḍram* poets who lived in the pre-Islamic and Islamic periods. We placed them in their respective places and cited whatever arguments we found regarding them as well as the scholars' remarks regarding their poetry.

From the well-known eminent (*fuḥūl*) poets, we selected forty poets. We grouped together the poets whose poetic characteristics are similar. In so doing we found that they represent ten poetic trends (*ṭabaqāt*). Each *trend* (*ṭabaqa*) comprises four poets of equal merit (pp. 23–24).

After careful examination and taking in consideration the remarks of scholars, we came to the conclusion that (each) four are acknowledged to be the best poets in a particular trend (*ṭabaqa*). However, there is disagreement among scholars (as to who is the best among these poets). We shall mention their disagreement and their agreement, name (each of) the four, and provide the arguments regarding each one of them. Starting with a certain poet does not mean that we prefer him (over the others), for we have to start with someone (p. 50).

All scholars, except the editor of the *Ṭabaqāt Fuḥūl al-Shuʿarāʾ*, understood the word *ṭabaqa* to mean "class." Consequently, they assumed that Ibn Sallām was attempting to rank the poets he had selected. Naturally they began to look for the criteria upon which he classified and ranked those poets. These criteria, as we have seen earlier, are: quantity, quality, variety, and tribal adherence. But then they were puzzled by some inconsistencies found in each criterion. The frontal attack on the first three criteria was launched by Ṭāhā Ibrāhīm and pounded in by all later critics. The fourth criterion, which Kilpatrick has suggested, i.e., the tribal adherence, has not yet been examined. She states that Ibn Sallām, especially in the case of the poets placed in *islāmī* class VIII (all are members of the clan of Banū Murra), may well have been drawing on a tribal *dīwān*. This hypothesis could be supported, she maintains, by the fact that a *Kitāb banī Murra b. ʿAwf* did exist, as attested by al-Āmidī.[82] This hypothesis too is open to criticism on conceptual grounds. It leaves unanswered the important question why, if this was one of Ibn Sallām's criteria, he did not follow it throughout all classes. Not only the *Kitāb banī Murra* was available to Ibn Sallām to consult, but also hundreds of other tribal *dīwāns*. The titles of sixty tribal *dīwāns* are scattered throughout al-Āmidī's *al-Muʾtalif wa al-Mukhtalif*, while Ibn al-Nadīm lists twenty-nine tribal *dīwāns*,[83] among them sixteen mentioned already by al-Āmidī. Although Ibn al-Nadīm does not list the tribal *dīwāns* compiled by Abū ᶜAmr al-Shaybānī (206/821), he states that they are some eighty *dīwāns*.[84] Two of these *dīwāns*: Banū Taghlib, and Banū Muḥārib are mentioned by al-Baghdādī.[85]

A new reading of Ibn Sallām's method of classification, which I have just quoted, and a new rendering, hence the understanding of the word ṭabaqa, will show that none of these four criteria had consciously and programatically crossed Ibn Sallām's mind. A new reading will also help solve what scholars consider to be problematic issues, such as why the *mukhaḍramūn* were not placed in a separate class as outlined in the introduction, why there were only ten classes in each division, and only four in each class, which did not work out at least in two cases, in *jāhilī* class I and in *islāmī* class II.

A long held view asserts that *muḥaddithūn* and *fuqahāᵓ* scholars arrived at the idea of *ṭabaqāt* before any others in Arab intellectual history.[86] Although Ibn Saᶜd's *Kitāb al-Ṭabaqāt al-Kabīr* (230/845) is the first and most important book of this genre which has come down to us, two of his predecessors, one of whom was his teacher, al-Wāqidī (207/823), wrote on the *ṭabaqāt*.[87] The other one was al-Haytham b. ᶜAdī (207/823) who, according to Ibn al-Nadīm, wrote *Ṭabaqāt al-Fuqahāᵓ wa al-Muḥaddithīn* and *Ṭabaqāt man rawā ᶜan al-Nabī wa Aṣḥābih*.[88] I would like to argue, however, that the Muᶜtazila preceded the former in that regard. Ibn Khallikān mentions a book by Wāṣil b. ᶜAṭāᵓ (131/748) entitled *Ṭabaqāt Ahl al-ᶜIlm wa al-Jahl*.[89] Be that as it may, literary writers like Ibn Sallām were inspired by these types of compositions. It follows then that, in writing his *Ṭabaqāt*, Ibn Sallām, some scholars contend, adopted their system of classification and ranking, especially that of Ibn Saᶜd.[90] This contention helps strengthen the central thrust of the previous hypotheses, i.e., a conscious attempt is made by Ibn Sallām to rank the poets he selected. I would argue that if Ibn Sallām was influenced at all in the composition of his book, then *Kitāb Fuḥūlat al-Shuᶜarāᵓ* by al-Aṣmaᶜī (215/831) would likely be the source of influence. Al-Aṣmaᶜī's book does not constitute anything like systematic compilation. It is, as Torrey remarks, scattered sayings, of very uneven value, made on many different occasions, and thrown together without any plan of arrangement. Some of the judgments were given in answer to questions, while others were the merest obiter dicta.[91] Nevertheless, several points, of cardinal importance are noteworthy:

1. The judgment expressed on the vast majority of poets is confined to one specific issue, whether the poet is *faḥl* or not.

2. The word *ṭabaqa* comes up in the following context: Abū Ḥātim (al-Sijistānī) said: I asked al-Aṣmaᶜī: 'Who is a better poet – al-Raᶜī or Ibn Muqbil?' He answered: 'They are very close.' I said: 'I am not satisfied with this answer.' So, he commented: 'Al-Raᶜī's poetry is more similar to early poetry' (i.e., *jāhilī*). I said: 'What about Ibn Aḥmar al-Bāhilī?' He replied: 'He is not a *faḥl*, and he is a lesser poet than them, but he is better than the poets of his *ṭabaqa*.'[92]
3. The epithet *fursān* is used three times to describe some poets who are either *fuḥūl* or not: a) Abū Ḥātim al-Sijistānī asked al-Aṣmaᶜī about Khufāf b. Nudba, ᶜAntara, and al-Zibriqān b. Badr. Al-Aṣmaᶜī replied: 'These are the best poets among the *fursān*, so is al-ᶜAbbās b. Mirdās. But he did not say that they are among the *fuḥūl*'[93] b) Abū Ḥātim asked him about Zayd al-Khayl. Al-Aṣmaᶜī answered: 'He is among the *fursān*'[94], and c) Abū Ḥātim asked him about Durayd b. al-Ṣimma. His answer was: 'Durayd b. al-Simma is among *fuḥūl al-fursān*.'[95]

It is more likely, then, to assume that Ibn Sallām made use of the two major concepts in al-Aṣmaᶜī's thesis – the *faḥl* and the *ṭabaqa*. Since al-Aṣmaᶜī did not attempt to 'rank' or 'classify' the poets, the word *ṭabaqa* in his book is more likely to mean 'a literary trend' than a 'class'. In all probability too Ibn Sallām's *Fursān al-Shuᶜarā᾽* was inspired by al-Aṣmaᶜī's book. Not only the same names of the *fursān* appear in Ibn Sallām's book, but also the same preference is made for Durayd b. al-Ṣimma.[96]

In the paragraph quoted above from Ibn Sallām's introduction, I have suggested that the word *ṭabaqa* means "a poetic trend."[97] It is worth repeating part of it here: 'We came to the conclusion that each four are acknowledged to be the best poets in a particular trend.' The word *ṭabaqa* in this context – *ᶜalā annahum ashᶜaru al-ᶜArab ṭabaqatan* – can hardly mean 'class' with any ranking implied. It can only mean *madhhaban*. In fact the proper sequence of the entire paragraph has been completely misunderstood. As a result, a number of questions were raised such as: Why ten classes, and why four in every class? A proper reading of that paragraph will show that Ibn Sallām: First, surveyed the well-known *jāhilī*, *mukhaḍram*, and *islāmī* poets. Second, he then selected the *fuḥūl* from among those well-known poets. Third, from those *fuḥūl* he chose forty *jāhilī* poets and forty *islāmī* poets. Fourth, after examining the poetry of these *fuḥūl* poets, he concluded that they represented ten distinct literary trends, which he called *ṭabaqāt*. Fifth, he further concluded that each four of them represented one of those trends, for they shared the same poetic characteristics, although each one of them was unique in his *madhhab*. Because he was not aiming at any categorical ranking, he stressed, by using two synonymous adjectives *mutakāfiᵓīn muᶜtadilīn*, that the poets were equally gifted. Then he cautioned the reader that, by starting each group with a certain poet, he was not giving him any preference over the others, for the author had to start with someone.

The semantic range of meaning for the root *ṭabaqa* further strengthens the argument put forth here. The basic meaning of this root suggests putting a thing upon, or above another thing commensurate therewith. One says (form II) *ṭabbaqa al-saḥābu al-jawwa*, the clouds covered the mid-air between the heaven and the earth; (form III) *ṭābaqtu al-naᶜla*, I sewed another sole upon the sole or the sandal; (form IV) *aṭbaqtu al-raḥā*, I put the upper mill-stone upon the lower; (form VI) *taṭābaqa al-shayᵓān*, the two things are like each other, or equal to each other, also *taṭābaqū ᶜalā al-amr*, they unanimously agreed to do something. Obviously, they can not agree unanimously unless they share a common or similar opinion. Hence, *ṭabaqu al-shayᵓi*, *ṭibquhu*, *ṭabīquhu*, *muṭbaquhu*, *muṭābiquhu*, and *ṭibāquhu* mean this thing is the match of this; or what suits, matches, tallies, conforms, corresponds, or agrees in measure, size, quantity, or the like.

Because the *ṭabaq* 'cover', is on top, the classes of people or things which are on top of each other are called *ṭabaqāt*. Since the classes of people are different and distinct, the circumstances characterizing these classes are also called *ṭabaqāt*, as in the saying "*fulān min al-dunyā ᶜalā ṭabaqātin shattā*", so and so passes from one earthly state to another.

This usage of the word *ṭabaqa* appears in the writings of Ibn Sallām's contemporaries and of the following century. Al-Jāḥiẓ (255/869) explains the differences between some words which seem like synonyms, but in reality are not. Then he makes the following comment '*wa hādhā al-maᵓkhadh yajrī fī al-ṭabaqāt kullihā min jūdin wa bukhlin wa ṣalāḥin wa fasādin*.' Obviously, the word *ṭabaqāt* does not mean 'classes' in this context, but the characteristics that distinguish generosity and avarice, righteousness and corruption.[98] Abū Ghassān Damādh, a contemporary of Ibn Sallām, makes the following comment on the love poetry of Bashshār: 'I do not believe that his poetry has the depth of the meanings (expressed) in the poetry of Kuthayyir, Jamīl, ᶜUrwa b. Ḥizām, Qays b. Dharīḥ and *tilka al-ṭabaqa*.'[99] Clearly all of them share the same poetic trend – platonic love poetry (*ᶜudhrī*), which is completely different from that of Bashshār. In the course of his discussion of the poetry of Abū Tammām and al-Buḥturī, al-Āmidī remarks: 'Many people placed them in the same *ṭabaqa* . . . but they are so different, for al-Buḥturī is a bedouin who did not deviate from the traditional canons of (Arabic) poetry.'[100] As is known, the quality and quantity of both poets are not disputable. However, their poetical trends or characteristics are markedly different. This is the reason why al-Āmidī denied that they could be in the same *ṭabaqa*.

In the light of this interpretation, the issue of classification, the questions raised about the criteria upon which the classification is based, and the lack of conformity with what they are set for are resolved. For this interpretation suggests that Ibn Sallām did not intend to rank the poets. But then the anticipated question arises: how do the statements, which critics take to suggest some measures of quality, quantity, versatility, and tribal adherence, fit in this interpretation? I hope that the following lines will answer this question.

Quality: there is no direct reference in Ibn Sallām's book to such a measure. It is inferred by critics from Ibn Sallām's placing specific poets in *jāhilī* class I and in *islāmī* class I. These poets were already accorded such a status in the Arabic literary tradition before the composition of Ibn Sallām's book. But this view, which is based on the premise of ranking, set a trap for critics because it does not hold true for the remaining nine classes in both divisions, as explained above.

Quantity: several comments are made by Ibn Sallām with respect to quantity. These comments are: 1) Before introducing *jāhilī* class IV (Ṭarafa, ᶜAbīd, ᶜAlqama, and ᶜAdī b. Zayd) he says: 'They are four eminent *(fuḥūl)* poets. Their place should be with the most prominent poets *(al-awāʾil)*, but the paucity of their poetry in the hands of the transmitters has caused them harm.' Critics believe that quantity was a decisive factor in placing these poets in class IV. I would ask, if that was true, why were they not placed in class nine or ten for example? Some of the poets of later classes (Ibn Muqbil in class V, ᶜAntara and Ibn Abī Kāhil in class VI, and Ibn Shaʾs in class X) are more prolific poets. In addition, taking the word *al-awāʾil* to mean poets placed in class I or II, would be reading too much into that word. For, if that is what Ibn Sallām meant, he would have simply said so. 2) *Jāhilī* class V consists of Khidāsh, al-Aswad b. Yaᶜfur, al-Mukhabbal, and Ibn Muqbil. Of al-Aswad, Ibn Sallām says: 'He has a single excellent poem. Had he composed another one like it, we would have preferred him over the poets of martabatihi.' It would be very difficult to say that two poems can really constitute a 'quantity'. If quantity was a criterion, then one would not understand why al-Aswad was placed in the same class with al-Mukhabbal and Ibn Muqbil. Both of them have many more poems to their names than al-Aswad. In Ibn Sallām's own words: 'Al-Mukhabbal has many (*kathīr*) excellent poems.'[101] 3) Ibn Sallām introduces *jāhilī* class VII with this comment: 'Four skilled poets who produced little (*muḥkimūn muqillūn*). This is what lowered them (*akhkharahum*).' I would make the same argument here which I made above for class VI. I think he means by the word "*akhkharahum*" their status in the eyes of the literary circles, but not their placement in the *Ṭabaqāt*. A similar statement is made about al-Rāʿī in *islāmī* class I: *ka'annahu ākhiruhum ʿinda al-ʿāmma*.

Versatility: the only example given by critics for this criterion is in the case of Kuthayyir. They argue that despite the fact that both Kuthayyir and Jamīl are *ghazalī* poets, Kuthayyir is placed in the *islāmī* class II while Jamīl is included in class VI because Kuthayyir is a more versatile poet than Jamīl. But a casual look at the other three poets in that class (Ibn Qays al-Ruqayyāt, al-Aḥwaṣ, Nuṣayb) will show that they were just as versatile as Kuthayyir was.

Tribal adherence: the inconsistency of this hypothesis has been pointed out earlier. Although Kilpatrick presented it intelligently and diligently, she cautioned that:

> . . . but this does not exclude the possibility that he (Ibn Sallām) was less concerned with the genealogical relationship between the poets than with certain poetic traits, perhaps common to them all, which may have represented in the case of Banū Murra a distinctive style as marked as the Hudhalī style whose existence Bräunlich has posited.[102]

This is a sound statement which is at the heart of my central hypothesis. All four poets were grouped together because they share some common literary traits, or their poetry is markedly distinct from the poetry of others by a special characteristic that set them apart from the latter. *Jāhilī* class VI (ʿAmr b. Kulthūm, al-Ḥārith b. Ḥilliza, ʿAntara, and Suwayd b. Abī Kāhil) is another good example of this distinguished characteristic. It is made up of poets known for one outstanding poem, the first three are *muʿallaqa* poets. The issue of "one poem" has been taken by critics as evidence of the criterion of quantity. Hence, this class was not put ahead of the preceding ones. Nothing could be farther from the truth, for Ibn Sallām describes two of the poets of this very class as being prolific. He says about ʿAntara: 'He has many poems (*shiʿr kathīr*), but this one is outstanding. Therefore, it was placed with (similar) outstanding poems whose composers have many other poems, but one single poem stood out (in their literary output)'. Ibn Sallām makes a similar statement about Suwayd. He writes: 'He has many poems (*shiᶜrun kathīr*), but this one is outstanding among his poems.'[103]

The hypothesis I am advancing here will also help solve another problematic issue, namely the absence of the *mukhaḍramūn* from the *Ṭabaqāt*. In the introduction, Ibn Sallām mentions that he will be dealing with *jāhilī*, *islāmī*, and *mukhaḍram* poets. However, this last group does not appear in the text. Instead, the *mukhaḍram* poets are distributed among the other two sections, the *jāhilī* and the *islāmī*. Ṭarāblusī suggests that the *jāhilī* section covers the pre-Islamic and the *mukhaḍramūn*, while the *islāmī* section includes the first two centuries of Islam.[104] But then he remarks that there are several anachronisms in these classes. One example of this is the placement of Bashāma b. al-Ghadīr and Qurād b. Ḥanash in *islāmī* class VIII, despite the fact that both of them are definitely pre-Islamic. Kilpatrick concurs and cites more examples.[105]

As in the critics' inferred hypotheses mentioned above with respect to the different criteria, Ṭarāblusī assumes that this is Ibn Sallām's plan regarding the *mukhaḍramūn*, then Ṭarāblusī faults him for not following this plan (of which Ibn Sallām really does not make any mention). In fact, a proper reading of this small phrase will reveal that Ibn Sallām is not suggesting any chronological order. If he were, the phrase would have read: *jāhilī*, *mukhaḍram*, and *islāmī*. For, to state the obvious, those poets who lived only in the Islamic era come after the *mukhaḍramūn*. Neither does the phrase suggest any kind of 'division.' He simply states: 'we mentioned in detail the *jāhilī*, *islāmī*, and *mukhaḍramūn* poets.' I would argue that Ibn Sallām had no intention of making the *mukhaḍramūn* a separate division. Rather, he placed some of them in the *jāhilī* section and some in the *islāmī* section, pursuing certain stylistic or poetic traits which they share either with the *jāhilī* or *islāmī* poets in each particular class. As for placing Bashāma b. al-Ghadīr and Qurād b. Ḥanash in *islāmī* class VIII, I am inclined, like Ṭarābulsī, to see this blunder as carelessness on Ibn Sallām's part. This is not the only mistake one finds in the book.[106] The editor of the *Ṭabaqāt* suggests that perhaps Ibn Sallām read or was informed that Bashāma and Qurād lived till the beginning of the Islamic era but did not convert to Islam,[107] as in the case of al-Aᶜshā, for example, I might add.

In this study I have tried to show that Ibn Sallām wrote several books on poetry other than the *Ṭabaqāt Fuḥūl al-Shuᶜarāʾ*. Establishing this fact has helped to clarify the mystery behind the absence of some poets of note and the *muḥdathūn*, as an independent class, from the *Ṭabaqāt*. I have attempted also to demonstrate that Ibn Sallām did not intend to rank the poets he selected, but rather to group them according to specific literary traits common to them all. The proper understanding of his plan, which is clearly stated in his introduction, and the grasping of the real meaning of this 'operative' word *ṭabaqa* to mean 'literary trend or trait', rather than 'class' with implication of 'ranking', is very crucial to the entire issue of classification. This interpretation will help us understand the reason behind excluding prominent poets such as ᶜUmar b. Abī Rabīᶜa from the *Ṭabaqāt*, especially from *islāmī* class VI (Ibn Qays al-Ruqayyāt, al-Aḥwaṣ, Jamīl, and Nuṣayb), all of them like ᶜUmar, are *ghazalī* poets from Ḥijāz. The answer is very simple. The love poetry (ghazal) of ᶜUmar is unique. It is different in style, poetic traits, and language from the ghazal of any other poet in the entire history of Arabic literature. If this was not the case, then it would be difficult to understand why Ibn Sallām would say that ᶜUmar's love poetry is far superior to that of Ibn Qays al-Ruqayyāt,[108] and yet he does not include ᶜUmar in that class with Ibn Qays or in any other class. I have expounded above the five stages of Ibn Sallām's selection process, and hopefully have answered such questions as: Why forty poets were selected? Why four poets only are included in each class? In this connection, the criticism directed at Ibn Sallām regarding this rigid mathematical system which forced him either to remove an equally gifted poet from a class because it already has four, or to fill in a class with a less gifted poet to meet the quota needs to be addressed.

At the beginning of *jāhilī* class II Ibn Sallām acknowledged that one of its members, Aws b. Ḥajar, deserves to be in class I, but was kept out of it because it already had four. As mentioned above, Ibn Sallām, after selecting forty *Fuḥūl* poets perceived that they represented ten distinct poetic traits. He further concluded that each trend was represented by four poets except, one would assume, class I, where five poets shared the same stylistic traits. He had no choice but to place Aws in class II. If we take a closer look at class II we will see that the literary characteristics of their poetry are in many ways similar to that of Aws. As is well known, Aws was Zuhayr's step father (Zuhayr is placed in class I), Kaᶜb is of course Zuhayr's son, and al-Ḥuṭayᵓa was the transmitter (*rāwī*) of Kaᶜb (both are included in class II). In other words, we have a poetic school whose members had acquired their craft by apprenticeship.[109] Placing Aws with two members of this school in class II does not seem to be too much off the mark. As for including al-Rāᶜī in *islāmī* class I with Jarīr, al-Farzdaq, and al-Akhṭal, I am not inclined to consider that this was done simply to meet the quota of four, or that he was something of a makeweight beside the other three giants. According to Ibn Sallām's method, which I have tried to establish, he must have seen that all four poets shared, to a varying degree of course, similar poetic traits. He states that there is intense disagreement among scholars as to who is the best poet among the first three. There is not, however, much disagreement about al-Rāᶜī, ' As if he, in their view, seems to be the last one (after those three.)'[110] That is the scholars' view of al-Rāᶜī, but not Ibn Sallām's. I would argue that it would have been very difficult to include in that class a fourth poet other than al-Rāᶜī, if the criteria of similar poetic traits is in play.

Although Ibn Sallām has indicated in the introduction his method of classification, unfortunately he did not explain the poetic traits of every class which prompted him to group them together. Some are relatively easy to infer, but a thorough study is still needed to explore the artistic similarity which makes every group of four poets a distinct class. Future studies should give more thought to the *ṭabaqāt* which come between the *jāhilī* and the *islāmi* sections.

Notes

1. Ibn Sallām's book, in all probability, is the first book on classical Arabic literary criticism. In his article '*Ṭabaqāt*' published in the *Supplément* to the first edition of the *Encyclopaedia of Islam* (1938, p. 151), Heffening states that, according to Ibn al-Nadīm, Yaḥyā b. al-Mubārak al-Yāzidī (202/818) wrote a book entitled *Ṭabaqāt al-Shuᶜarāᵓ*. This was an oversight on Heffening's part. Ibn al-Nadīm (p. 51) mentions in the biography of Yaḥyā several of his sons and grandsons who were also famous writers. His grandson, Ismāᶜīl b. Abī Muḥammad al-Yāzidī, was the one who authoured *Ṭabaqāt al-Shuᶜarāᵓ*.
2. Kilpatrick, Hillary, 'Criteria of Classification in the *Ṭabaqāt Fuḥūl al-Shuᶜarāᵓ* of Muḥammad b. Sallām al-Jumaḥī' in *Proceedings of the Ninth Congress of the Union Européene des Arabisants et Islamisants*, ed. Rudolph Peters (Brill: Leiden, 1980), p. 141.
3. Ibrāhīm, Ṭāhā, *Tārīkh al-Naqd ᶜinda al-ᶜArab min al-ᶜAṣr al-Jāhilī ilā al-Qarn al-Rābiᶜ al-Hijrī*. The first edition appeared in 1937. The edition used here is published by Dār al-Ḥikma, Damascus, 1974. For the following discussion of his views see pp. 112–16.
4. I have elected to use the word 'peers', which is the translation of Ibn Sallām's '*martaba*'. This word has been taken by virtually every scholar to mean '*ṭabaqa*', and consequently led to erroneous judgment. See the text in Ibn Sallām's *Ṭabaqāt Fuḥūl al-Shuᶜarāᵓ*, ed. Maḥmūd Muḥammad Shākir (Cairo: al-Madanī Press, 1974), 1: 147.
5. Ibn Sallām, op. cit., 1: 545.
6. Kilpatrick, op. cit. p. 143.
7. Blachère, Régis, *Histoire de la littérature Arabe des Origines à la Fin du XV Siècle J. – C.*, (Paris: A. Maisonneuve, 1952), 1: 139.

8. The edition used here is that of Dār Nahḍat Miṣr li al-Ṭabᶜ wa al-Nashr, Cairo, n.d. Pages 12–14 and 18–22 are devoted to Ibn Sallām and his book.
9. Ibrāhīm, op. cit. p. 112.
10. Mandūr, op. cit. p. 13.
11. Sallām, Muḥammad Zaghlūl, *Tārīkh al-Naqd al-ᶜArabī ilā al-qarn al-rābiᶜ al-Hijrī* (Cairo: Dār al-Maᶜārif, n.d.), pp. 102–107. Zaghlūl adds one more criterion, namely a religious one, in order to justify the inclusion of a class of eight Jewish poets. He also believes that the Jewish poets must have been a part of a separate book, and so is the case with the town poets too!; Badawī Ṭabāna, *Dirāsāt fi al-Naqd al-ᶜArabī min al-Jāhiliyya ilā Nihāyat al-Qarn al-Thālith* (Cairo: Maktabat al-Anglo, 1969), pp. 160–162; Daᵓūd Sallūm, *al-Naqd al-ᶜArabī al-Qadīm* (Baghdad: Maktabat al-Andalus, 1970), pp. 202–205. Sallūm claims that the pre-Islamic poets are arranged in a chronological order, each according to the date of his death!; Iḥsān ᶜAbbās, *Tārīkh al-Naqd al-Adabī ᶜinda al-ᶜArab*. The first edition was published in 1971, the one used here is the second edition (Beirut: Dār al-Thaqāfa, 1978), pp. 78–82; Muṣṭafā al-Shakᶜa, *Manāhij al-Taᵓlīf ᶜinda ᶜUlamāᵓ al-ᶜArab: Qism al-Adab* (Beirut: Dār al-ᶜIlm li al-Malāyīn, 1973), pp. 401–408; ᶜIzz al-Dīn Ismāᶜīl, *al-Maṣādir al-Adabiyya wa al-Lughawiyya fi al-Turāth al-ᶜArabī* (Cairo: Maktabat Gharīb, n.d.), pp. 232–235.
12. Sharaf, Ḥifnī, *al-Naqd al-Adabī ᶜinda al-ᶜArab* (Cairo: Maktabat al-Shabāb, 1970), pp. 266–268; Muḥammad Ṭāhir Darwīsh, *Fī al-Naqd al-Adabī ᶜinda al-ᶜArab* (Cairo: Maktabat al-Shabāb, 1976), pp. 347–351.
13. Ṭabāna, Badawī, op. cit. pp. 173–174. Also see Ḥifnī Sharaf, op. cit. p. 268. Sharaf believes also that Ibn Sallām, like many philologists of his time, was biased against the *muḥdathūn* poets because their poetry could never attain the magnificence of that of the *jāhilī* poets.
14. Kilpatrick, op. cit. pp. 148–149.
15. Ibid. pp. 144–145.
16. Ibn Sallām, op. cit. p. 3.
17. Ibn al-Nadīm, *al-Fihrist*, ed. Gustav Flügel (Beirut: Maktabat Khayyāṭ, n.d.), p. 113.
18. Ibid. p. 35.
19. Thaᶜlab, Aḥmad b. Yaḥyā, *Majālis Thaᶜlab*, ed. ᶜAbd al-Salām Hārūn (Cairo: Dār al-Maᶜārif, 1960). 1: 29–30. See other citations, 1: 31, 2: 443–444.
20. Abū al-Faraj al-Iṣfahānī, *al-Aghānī* (Cairo: Dār al-Kutub), 11: 180, 185, 188–189, 191. ᶜĀᵓisha's mother was Umm Kulthūm, the daughter of Abū Bakr, the first orthodox caliph. It is said that Muṣᶜab b. al-Zubayr offered her 500,000 dirhams dowry.
21. *al-Aghānī*, 16: 196. See also Ibn Rashīq, *al-ᶜUmda*, ed. Muḥyi al-Dīn ᶜAbd al-Ḥamīd (Cairo: Maṭbaᶜat al-Saᶜāda, 1955), 2: 192. This quotation in *al-ᶜUmda* is from a chapter entitled '*Uṣūl al-Nasab wa Buyūtāt al-ᶜArab*.' The latter part of the title is exactly like that of Ibn Sallām's book.
22. Ibn Qutayba, *ᶜUyūn al-Akhbār* (Cairo: Dār al-Kutub), 1:154–155. This quotation is also found in al-Jāḥiẓ, *al-Ḥayawān*, ed. ᶜAbd al-Salām Hārūn (Beirut: al-Majmaᶜ al-ᶜIlmī al-ᶜArabī al-Islāmī, 1969), 2:363.
23. *al-Aghānī*, op. cit. 10: 3.
24. Ibid. 10: 21–22.

25. Ibn al-Jarrāḥ, Muḥammad b. Da'ūd, *Man Ismuhu ᶜAmr min al-Shuᶜarā'*, ed. ᶜAbd al-ᶜAzīz al-Mānīᶜ (Cairo: Maktabat al-Khānjī, 1991), p. 140.
26. Ibid. p. 141, p. 143. (two of which are also cited by Abū al-Faraj in al-*Aghānī* 15: 222–3).
27. *Al-Aghānī*, op. cit. 8: 246.
28. Ibid. 18: 74.
29. Ibid. 18: 74–75.
30. Ibid. 17: 266.
31. Ibid. 16: 55.
32. Ibid. 11: 199.
33. Ibid. 12: 307–8.
34. Ibid. 16: 144, 150, 151, 161–3.
35. Ibid. 4: 274, 282, 285.
36. Ibid. 13: 270–1, 273.
37. Ibid. 16: 307–8.
38. Ibid. 6: 85.
39. Ibid. 10: 239.
40. Ibid. 14: 122.
41. Ibid. 2: 35 (in the biography of al-Majnūn), 7: 26 (in the biography of al-Walīd b. Yazīd), 23: 466 (in the biography of Ḥāritha b. Badr).
42. Al-Jāḥiẓ, *al-Ḥayawān*, op. cit. 3: 11.
43. Ibn Qutayba, *ᶜUyūn al-Akhbār*, op. cit. 2: 171.
44. Thaᶜlab, *Majālis Thaᶜlab*, 1: 8, 26, 36–37, 2: 451.
45. Al-Zabīdī, Muḥammad b. al-Ḥasan, *Ṭabaqāt al-Naḥwiyyīn*, ed. Muḥammad Abū al-Faḍl Ibrāhīm (Cairo: Dār al-Maᶜārif, 1973), pp. 44, 157, 164,179.
46. *al-Aghānī*, op. cit. 2: 3.
47. Ibid. 8: 188.
48. Ibid. 1: 314.
49. Ibid. 8: 277.
50. Ibid. 8: 188, 204.
51. Ibid. 1: 265, 294, 314, 9: 240, 241.
52. Ibid. 8: 337, 437, 438.
53. Ibid. 15: 67.
54. Ibid. 3: 27, 18: 63.
55. Ibid. 2: 203, 217–18, 235.
56. Ibid. 17: 163, 167–77.
57. Ibid. 7: 110.
58. Ibid. 3: 278.
59. Ibid. 1: 66.
60. Ibid. 1: 71–72. For more *akhbār* about ᶜUmar see: 1: 82, 2: 357–58, 17: 157–59; also see *Majālis Thaᶜlab*, 2: 444.
61. Ibid. 3: 313–314, 320, 325–326.
62. Ibid. 2: 38–39.
63. Ibid. 3: 352, 353–355, 356–357.
64. Ibid. 12: 126–27, 23: 492.
65. Ibid. 20: 200.
66. Ibid. 20: 206–07.
67. Ibid. 11: 253, 256.
68. Ibid. 3: 191. See other *akhbār* in the same volume pp. 140, 153, 176–178,

168, 203, 211.
69. Ibid. 2: 331.
70. Ibid. 4: 302.
71. Ibid. 14: 122.
72. Ibid. 4: 3.
73. Ibid. 10: 82.
74. Ibid. 17: 70–71.
75. Ibid. 20: 53.
76. Ibid. 18: 199–200.
77. Ibid. 14: 164, 165, 168.
78. Ibn al-Jarrāḥ, Muḥammad b. Daᵓūd, *al-Waraqa*, ed. ᶜAbd al-Wahhāb ᶜAzzām (Cairo: Dār al-Maᶜārif, 2nd, n.d.), pp. 48, 49.
79. Ibid. p. 69.
80. Ibid. p. 51.
81. The two-fold answer, which Ṭabāna provided (see above) lacks validity. *Al-Shi*ᶜ*r wa al-Shu*ᶜ*arā*ᵓ by Ibn Qutayba, who was contemporary with Ibn *Sallām* and died just thirty-six years after him, contains biographies of *muḥdathūn* poets. As for Kilpatrick's claim that 'Ibn Sallām would have been hard put to it to fill ten classes of *muḥdathūn*,' I am not sure on what basis this has been made. In Ibn al-Muᶜtazz's *Ṭabaqāt al-Shu*ᶜ*arā*ᵓ there are at least eighty biographies of poets who died before Ibn Sallām or a decade or two after him, which means that they were in the middle or the peak of their career during his life time. Moreover, Ibn al-Muᶜtazz did not include in his *Ṭabaqāt* all the *muḥdathūn* poets. He left out at least twenty poets among them very prominent ones like Ibn al-Rūmī and Dīk al-Jinn, whom Ibn al-Jarrāḥ mentioned in *al-Waraqa*. In the first few volumes of *al-Aghānī*, I have counted at least twenty poets from the Umayyad-Abbasid and the early Abbasid ages who are neither included in Ibn al-Muᶜtazz's *Ṭabaqāt* or *al-Waraqa*, such as Ibn al-Mawlā, Ḥakam al-Wādī, and al-Sayyid al-Ḥimyarī. I think it would be very difficult then to say that Ibn Sallām would have been hard put to it to fill ten classes of *muḥdathūn* Poets. This is of course assuming that he did not write about the *muḥdathūn*. I have tried to establish that he did.
82. Kilpatrick, op. cit. p. 144.
83. Nāṣir al-Dīn al-Asad arranged these *dīwāns* in alphabetical order in his *Maṣādir al-Shi*ᶜ*r al-Jāhilī* (Cairo: Dār al-Maᶜārif, 6th edition, 1982). pp. 543–44, 546–47.
84. Ibn al-Nadīm, op. cit. P. 68; see also al-Qifṭī, *Inbāh al-Ruwāh*, ed. Muḥammad Abū al-Faḍl Ibrāhīm (Cairo: Dār al-Kutub, 1950), 1: 221.
85. Al-Baghdādī, ᶜAbd al-Qādir, *Khizānat al-Adab*, ed. ᶜAbd al-Salām Hārūn (Cairo: Maktabat al-Khānjī), 1:21, 22, 7:28, 8:558–60, 11:142.
86. See a good summary of the controversy surrounding this issue and its sources in George Makdisi's '*Ṭabaqāt*-Biography: Law and Orthodoxy in Classical Islam,' *Islamic Studies*, vol. 32, no. 4, (Islamabad, Pakistan: Islamic Research Institute, International Islamic University, 1993), pp. 371–73.
87. Ibn al-Nadīm, op. cit. p. 89. Ibn al-Nadīm makes the following interesting comment about Ibn Saᶜd's books: 'the materials of his books are taken from al-Wāqidī's works.'
88. Ibid. p. 101.

89. Ibn Khallikān, *Wafayāt al-Aᶜyān*, ed. Iḥsān ᶜAbbās (Beirut: Dār al-Thaqāfa, n.d.), 6: 11.
90. Ḥafṣī, Ibrāhīm, 'Rechèrches sur le Genre *Ṭabaqāt* dans la Littérature Arabe', *Arabica* XXIII (1976), pp. 239, 245–46, and see also XXIV (1977). p. 151; Munīr Sulṭān, *Ibn Sallām wa Ṭabaqāt al-Shuᶜarāᵓ*, (Alexandria: Manshaᵓat al-Maᶜārif, 1977), pp. 138–41; ᶜAbd al-Wāḥid al-Shaykh, *Qaḍāyā al-Naqd al-Adabī wa al-Balāgha* (Alexandria: al-Hayᵓa al-Miṣriyya al-ᶜĀmma li al-Kitāb, 1980) p. 177; Jihād al-Majālī, *Ṭabaqāt al-Shuᶜarāᵓ fī al-Naqd al-Adabī ᶜinda al-ᶜArab* (Beirut: Dār al-Jīl, 1992), pp. 30–34.
91. Torrey, Charles, ed. *Kitāb Fuḥūlat al-Shuᶜarāᵓ* (Beirut: Dār al-Kitāb al-Jadīd, 1971), p. 40.
92. Ibid. p. 12. See also p. 16 in connection with al-Aṣmaᶜī's comment about Ibn Harma.
93. Ibid. p. 14.
94. Ibid. P. 15.
95. Ibid. P. 15. See also p. 18.
96. It is worthy to note here that Abū ᶜUbayda Maᶜmar b. al-Muthannā (209/824) had a book entitled *Ṭabaqāt al-Fursān*. There is no indication whether the book dealt strictly with warriors, or warriors who were also poets. See Yāqūt, *Muᶜjam al-Udabāᵓ*, (Beirut: Dār Iḥyāᵓ al-Turāth al-ᶜArabī, n.d.), 19: 162.
97. So does the editor of the *Ṭabaqāt*, Maḥmūd Shākir, in the introduction to the second edition.
98. *al-Ḥayawān*, op. cit. 1: 250.
99. *al-Aghānī*, op. cit. 3: 182–83.
100. Al-Āmidī, al-Ḥasan b. Bishr, *al-Muwāzana*, ed. Sayyid Ṣaqr (Cairo: Dār al-Maᶜārif, 1961), 1: 6.
101. Ibn Sallām uses here the word *martaba*, not *ṭabaqa*. The preference he is referring to is, I believe, his own personal preference, which has no bearing on the placement of the poet within the class. In the *marāthī* class, Ibn Sallām says about Mutammim: 'He is the one whom we prefer.' Correct reading of the context in which the statement is made will make it clear that Ibn Sallām preferred Mutammim over his brother Mālik. Therefore, he selected him in the *Ṭabaqāt*, while he included Mālik in *Shuᶜarāᵓ al-Fursān*.
102. Kilpatrick, op. cit. pp. 144–45.
103. Ibn Sallām, op. cit. 1: 152–53.
104. Al-Ṭarāblusī, Amjad, *La Critique Poétique des Arabes jusqu' au V Siècle de l'Hegire* (Damascus: Institut Francais de Damas, 1956), p. 36.
105. Kilpatrick, op. cit. P. 144. While Ṭarāblusī is inclined to set this mistake and other ones down as carelessness on Ibn Sallām's part, or his nephew, Abū Khalīfa, who transmitted the *Ṭabaqāt*; Kilpatrick does not consider them as mistakes. She explains them in the light of the tribal adherence criterion.
106. In talking about Kaᶜb al-Ashqarī, Ibn Sallām called him Kaᶜb al-Shaqarī, from the Shaqara of Banū Tamīm. As is well known, Kaᶜb is from the Yemeni tribe, al-Ashāqir, see *Ṭabaqāt Fuḥūl al-Shuᶜarāᵓ*, 2: 693.
107. Ibid. 1: 65.

108. Ibid. 2: 648.
109. Ḍayf, Shawqī, *al-Fann wa Madhāhibuhu fī al-Shiʿr al-ʿArabī* (Cairo: Dār al-Maʿārif, 1969), p. 25.
110. Ibn Sallām, op. cit. 1: 129.

14

On Rhyming Endings and Symmetric Phrases in Al-hamadhānī's *Maqāmāt*

Tamás Iványi
Eötvös Loránd University, Budapest

0. In the following paper we would like to present some statistical data, accompanied by examples and conclusions based on the analysis of the formal aspects of Badī^{c} al-Zamān al-Hamadhānī's *Maqāmāt*. The text used was basically that of the edition of Shaykh Muḥammad ^{c}Abduh, the more complete Istanbul edition having been relied on in three passages which were left out by ^{c}Abduh for moral reasons.[1]

"These 'sketches'" – says Régis Blachère about the *maqāmāt* " . . . are made up according to a strict balance; they are of rhymed and rhythmic prose, mixed with verse; the learned, sometimes precious, style constitutes the principal but not the sole concern of the author".[2] The aim of the present study has only been to provide a starting point for a later analysis of how this 'principal' – formal – concern correlates with the author's interest in shaping the contents of the *Maqāmāt* and how the semantic and thematic material is organized in them.[3] Since, to the best of our knowledge, there is no comprehensive linguistic and stylistic analysis and evaluation of al-Hamadhānī's *Maqāmāt*, this paper can represent only a first step towards this end in the form of an attempt to portray some of the most striking formal features of the *Maqāmāt* backed by figures.[4]

In the terminology the use of the word *saj^{c}* has been avoided.[5] Instead of rhymes or *rawī*[6] the expression 'rhyming ending' is used, while instead of parallel members the term 'symmetric phrases' seemed preferable.[7] The style of the *maqāmāt* is considered 'balanced' or 'proportional text', where the means of proportioning embrace rhyming endings as well as a kind of pulsing rhythm. This rhythm or harmony is, however, frequently interrupted by 'dissonant' parts, not because the author could not have continued the pulsation as long as he wanted but *first* because he complied with the semantic requirements of his text as a whole, or in other words, the contents of his story, and *second* because a monotonous pulsing would not suit human perception and would give a dull sense.[8]

1. Rhyming endings

The whole text under investigation comprises 20,245 words from the Beirut edition and 696 more taken from the Istanbul edition, giving all together 20,941 words. By word, the written form is meant here. The number of words would be 5,600 more if one-letter words (prepositions and conjunctions) had been counted independently.[9] This, however, did not seem necessary, because words are used here exclusively as quantitative units for measuring the length of the text or some of its parts and are not to be regarded as qualitative factors.

It is not always possible to define unambiguously and with absolute certainty which endings are to be classified as rhyming, or which phrases are to be counted as symmetric or parallel and which are not. For this reason the numbers of occurrences are always rounded so as not to give a false impression.

The whole text under examination contains 351 lines of verse with all together 2,790 words (=13.3 %). The remainder, here called 'prose-text' may be segmented into about 4,900 phrases, of which a little less than two thirds, about 2,860, are defined by their being rhymed in one way or another, and the rest (about 5,800 words in about 1,680 phrases) do not rhyme. This also means that, while the average number of words in a phrase with rhyming ending is 3.5, this number is greater (3.75) in the case of the non-rhyming phrases. The breaking of the non-rhyming parts into phrases can, of course, only be made on a subjective basis. Here we have considered a phrase as an utterance (or sentence) which can be independently understood. Thus a subordinate clause has not been regarded as such a phrase. Among the non-rhyming phrases, however, there are many stereotype expressions, among other things 524 occurrences of the verb *qāla* and its inflected forms.

The length of non-rhyming (and so, in general, asymmetric) phrases can vary from one word (usually قال) to two-three word phrases forming a whole narrative passage:[10]

فليس يبيع إلا الأعلاق / ثم قرع الباب / ودخلنا الدهليز

But it may be as long as 13 words:[11]

وهذه الحلقة تراها اشتريتها في سوق الطرائف من عمران
الطرائفي بثلاثة دنانير معزية

The *Ghīlānī maqāma* as a whole provides good examples of rhymeless phrases, since less than one fifth of the text has rhyming endings while three fifths are rhymeless (the remaining one fifth being poetry).

1.1 The number of rhyming phrases may extend from two to three or rarely to five. The rhyming endings are in 88% of cases couplets, in about 11% triplets and only one percent are real quadruplets or quintuplets. The triplets are of two types: real triplets, and what may be called semi-triplets. The latter type means that most commonly the first of the three phrases is a preparatory phrase (in both its form and its contents), reflecting only partially the characteristics of the given rhyme. If the second and third members are symmetric (balanced) phrases as well, this first phrase is not, but in that case the rhyming is usually perfect. Accordingly, we suppose here the conscious use of formal devices by the author. In the following we would like to present some examples of what has been described above.

Couplet:[12]

شهدت حتى مصارع العشاقِ

ومرضت حتى لمرض الأحداقِ

Ordinary triplet:[13]

عليه باب غير أنه من خليطي ساجٍ

وعاجٍ

مزدوجين أحسن ازدواجٍ

Or:

وهي تدور في الدورِ

من التنور إلى القدورِ

ومن القدور إلى التنورِ

Asymmetric triplet (2+1):[14]

كيف حصلتُها

وكم من حيلة احتلتُها

حتى عقدتُها

After the first two parts, there is not only a linguistic and semantic boundary beside the essential coherence of the whole tripartite sentence, but also an alteration of rhyming pattern which preserves only the final element -*hā* in the 3rd part.

Asymmetric triplet with the form 1+2:[15]

وقد أخرج من دور آل الفراتِ

وقت المصادراتِ

وزمن الغاراتِ

The rhyming is complete, but only the second and third phrases are symmetric.

Asymmetric triplet with the form 1+2:[16]

فما استأذن على سمعي

مسافة مقامي

أفصح من كلامي

There is no complete rhyme in the first, only the pronoun ending being identical, while the second and third form a complete rhyming couplet.

Quadruplet (sometimes plus one, forming a quasi-quintuplet):[17]

سلوا / الملوك وخزائنَها

والأغلاق ومعادنَها

والامور وبواطنَها

والعلوم ومواطنَها

والخطوب ومغالقَها

Quadruplet consisting in reality of two couplets, one with perfect, the other with imperfect rhyming:[18]

من الذي / ملك أسوارَها

وعرف أسرارَها

ونهج سمتَها

وولج حرتَها

Real quintuplet (plus perfect parallelism):[19]

سلوا عني / البلاد وحصونَها

والجبال وحزونَها

والأودية وبطونَها

والبحار وعيونَها

والخيل ومتونَها

The rhyme consonant, the *rawī* is a sonorant (liquid or nasal) sound in about 42% of cases; also, the labial /*b*/ and the dental /*d*/ occur more times than the average and their statistical probability would allow. The total number of occurrences of all sonorant sounds in the text is 5,955 (about 30% of all sounds), and, if we extract from this the occurrences of the particles and the inflected forms of the verb *qāla* which cannot in principle occur at the end of a rhyming phrase, we get an even smaller rate (around 20%). That is the probability of their occurring in a rhyme.

The 42% rate of occurrence in a rhyming ending position shows a very ancient trait in the rhyming of the *maqāmāt*, the relic of an age when the most important ending in an (artistic) prose text was a sonorant. It also supports a phonologic theory according to which the sonorants form an independent class within the Arabic sound system (together with the real consonants, real vowels and the glides).[20]

1.2 The rhymes in al-Hamadhānī's *maqāmāt* have, in a high percentage, very complicated forms, not differing much in this respect from those of the poetic rhyme (*qāfiya*). It is only rarely true that these rhyming endings are nothing more than *rawīs*. In about 35% of the rhymes there is a common long vowel before the *rawī*[21]; in a very large number of cases (in all together 55% of all the rhymes), in addition to the rhyming letter, the whole morphologic pattern is prescribed by the rhyme (this latter, however, partially overlaps with the former category). This trait binds the *maqāma* rhyme with earlier prose where this pattern generally represents the sole connection between the parallel members.[22] The most frequent morphologic pattern used is *fa*ᶜ*l* (22%). Here it may be interesting to note that the *fā*ᶜ*ila(tun)* form, once the most frequently used ending form (e.g. in the Koran[23]) has lost its special significance in the *maqāmāt* (occurring only in 6% of cases). It is also to be noted that identity in grammatical category of the forms is not always required (e.g. a broken plural may harmonize with a *maṣdar*: *ru'ūs* – *julūs*; or an *i*ᶜ*rāb* ending with a *binā'* vowel: *qaṣdaka* – *laka*). A detailed list of statistical data will be omitted here.[24]

1.3 The so called prose rhymes show two other important similarities to the poetic rhyme. First, unlike the early *saj*ᶜ, the *i*ᶜ*rāb* endings are always identical in the rhyming pairs.[25] This being such an unequivocal feature of these rhymes (as well as of the *qawāfī shi*ᶜ*riyya*), it can be relied on in deciding, for example, whether four phrases having the same consonantal endings are really a quadruplet or form only two (very similar but essentially different) couplets, because the *i*ᶜ*rāb* endings differ. Hence the correctness of our division may be supported by other, mainly semantic, means. The highly classical nature of these rhyming endings demonstrates the learned and basically written character of the *Maqāmāt*, since it is hardly possible to imagine that these endings would have been pronounced in live recitation.[26]

Second, in many cases there is what is called in poetry *khurūj*, i.e. a final third person suffixed pronoun (*-hu* or – *hā*) after the rhyme letter, its occurrence rate being 18% in the whole text, though in some (longer) *maqāmāt* it may reach even the 30% mark. Contrary to this, the rate of rhymes consisting only of either a pronoun, a verbal inflection, a nominal case ending or a *tā' marbūṭa* is very low, no more than 7%.[27] It occurs also very rarely that the rhyme conists only of a *rawī*. On the other hand it happens very often with the forms *faᶜl*, *faᶜīl*, *afᶜāl* and *faᶜāl* that not only the *lām*, but also the *ᶜayn* may be identical (or a related sound). Otherwise there is at least a *tā' marbūṭa* or a pronoun after the *rawī*.

The following are some examples of the use of related sounds in the rhyming endings:

(i) the *rawī* is *mīm*, while the previous consonant is either *lām* or *mīm*.[28]

عليما / رميما

(ii) the *rawī* is *bā'*, and the previous consonant is either *nūn* or *rā'*.[29]

أعنابا / أترابا

(iii) the *rawī* is *mīm*, and the previous consonant is either *nūn* or *mīm*.[30]

المنام / الغمام

1.4 The rhyming in the *Maqāmāt* sometimes allows quite complicated structures not possible in Classical Arabic poetry because of the latter's obligatory monorhymes. For instance, there is a special technique by the help of which parallelism (i.e. symmetry in syntactic form) and rhyming partly run together and partly separate: at the beginning of the twenty-first *maqāma* four phrases are symmetric, but rhyme separately in two pairs.[31]

وسخن ماؤه ليغسلَ

وهيئ تاباته ليحملَ

وخيطت أثوابه ليكفنَ

وحفرت حفرته ليدفنَ

All the above phrases contain a passive verb at the beginning and a subjunctive verb at the end. The rhyming endings are similar but not identical (*lām* and *nūn*). All of this is supported with a small shift in the middle of the phrases, from a masculine to a feminine subject.

In a similar pattern in the same *maqāma* even the rhyme is partly identical having the same pronoun after different *rawī*s.[32]

A ونساءٍ / قد نشرن شعورَهنّ

B يضربن صدورَهنّ

C وجددن عقودَهنّ

D يلطمن خدودَهنّ

The rhymes are similar in A & B and C & D, while A is parallel to C and B to D. In other words the whole A plus B couplet is symmetrical in its structure with C plus D, with B and D being *ḥāl* sentences relating to A and C respectively. The overall unity of the four phrases, i.e. two couplets, is secured by the formula of the rhyming endings of the pattern *fuᶜūlahunna*.

1.5 The exact repetition of the rhyming ending is not allowable in the *maqāma* genre. There is a quadruplet of the two-plus-two type, for instance, in the *Maqāma maḍīriyya* where there seemingly are complete repetitions of the rhyming words.[33]

لا يصلح هذا الإبريق إلا لهذا الطستِ

ولا يصلح هذا الطستُ إلا مع هذا الدستِ

ولا يحسن هذا الدستُ إلا في هذا البيتِ

ولا يجمل هذا البيتُ إلا مع هذا الضيفِ

Here there are complete repetitions inside the lines. Whether these are to be counted as rhymes or not can be decided not only by knowing that repetition is not used, as a rule, in rhyming endings, but also by the difference in the *iᶜrāb* endings which is also not permissible in al-Hamadhānī's *Maqāmāt*. Thus the first *al-ṭasti* does not rhyme with the second *al-ṭastu* but it certainly forms a kind of inner rhyme, or better to say 'echo' together with *al-dastu* and *al-baytu* in the third and fourth phrases. This cannot be called a proper *abab* type of rhyming because it does not occur with enough frequency in the text, but it is rather an auxiliary or supporting rhyme for which there are some other parallel places.

2. Symmetric phrases

2.1 The usual concept of parallel members (called symmetric phrases here) must be supplemented with two important remarks. First, while all the symmetric phrases in the *maqāmāt* possess rhyming endings, there are many phrases supplied with rhymes which are not parallel or symmetric at all. Second, contrary to the usual concept, we restrict here the notion of parallelism to structural or syntactic parallelism. Semantic parallelism is either so vague an idea that it cannot be used for practical (and statistical) purposes, or it always goes along with syntactic balance. It may be noted here that the difference between symmetric and asymmetric structures is very characteristic and easy to detect. Semi- or quasi-parallelism occurs only if the rhyming is also imperfect. Such is the case with the 2+1 and 1+2 triplets mentioned above, where the first or third member may only be regarded as supplementary.[34]

1.	دعوه
2.	ولا تردعوه
0.	وإن سمعتم له أنيبا
3.	لا تجيبوه

Here there is a contrastive parallelism between an imperative and a prohibition in the first two phrases. The structural symmetry is perfect between the second and the third phrases of the triplet, but the placement of an imperfect rhyming is meant to point to some defect in the triplet. There is an introductory part inside the triplet, between the second and the third members, which is unusual and destroys the perfect harmony. The plural ending and the pronoun, however, are there to call attention to the formal symmetry and semantic connection between the phrases *lā tardaʿūhu* and *lā tujībūhu*.

One could easily say that this analysis seems arbitrary and what we really have here is a randomly imperfect rhyming which the writer put there because he could not find a better one. Thus the length of the third part has nothing to do with the imperfection of rhyming, but, since throughout the whole text such imperfection of the first or third member of a triplet always occurs together with a correspondent imperfection of the rhyming ending, one feels that this co-occurrence cannot just be an accident.

2.2 On the length of symmetric phrases

According to a widely held view, symmetric (or parallel) phrases may have varying, and even greatly different lengths.[35] This view cannot be justified without strong reservations since symmetric phrases are almost always segments of equal or similar length. This is self-evident, since they mostly have a similar syntactic structure and also similar morphological patterns (which means in Arabic identical or nearly identical length). The image of unequal duration may be the consequence of a mental illusion. We all listen to or read a text linearly, and parallelism generally appears to consist of a longer first and a shorter second member, divided by the rhyming ending of the first member. It may come to our mind only later that what seemed to be the first member in reality consists of two parts; an introductory (or transitory) non-rhyming, non-parallel part and a symmetric, rhyming segment. In al-Hamadhānī's *Maqāmāt*, a rhyming or symmetric couplet is more frequently interrupted by non-rhyming or at least asymmetric parts than later in al-Ḥarīrī's *Maqāmāt*.[36] These initial portions form part of these interruptions and ensure a kind of rhythm which is strongly connected to the contents of the *maqāma*:[37]

(حدثنا عيسى بن هشام قال)

كنت وأنا فتي السن // أشد رحلي لكل عماية

وأركض طرفي إلى كل غواية

Here the first phrase seems twice as long as the second. The symmetric couplet, however, begins within the whole verbal phrase *kāna yafʿalu*, with only the *yafʿalu* part, the whole previous *jumla ḥāliyya* being only an introduction to the symmetric couplet. If, however, the second member is longer than the first it really means that we have to do with an unproportionate (but rhyming) couplet. (For this latter see the previous example with *lā tujībūhu*.)

The examples of asymmetric phrases are abundant. Of course their not being parallel syntactically does not exclude the existence of some other type of rhetorical links between the members, e.g. *jinās*:[38]

الأمر على ما ذُكِرَ / فافعل كما أُمِرَ

Here there is no semantic parallelism and no complete syntactic parallelism either, although we can find a partial balance between the two subordinate sentences:

ما ذكر ... ما أمر

This is strengthened by the *jinās* between *al-amru* at the beginning of the first phrase and *amara* at the end of the second, marking a kind of coherence between the two phrases.

So, we can say that there are symmetric, partially symmetric and quite asymmetric rhyming phrases:[39]

A.) Symmetric phrases:[40]

انظر إلى /

الأمم الخاليةِ

والملوك الفانيةِ

انمحت آثارهم

وبقيت أخبارهم

B.) Partially symmetric phrases:[41]

كيف /

انتسفتهم الأيامُ

وأفناهم الحمامُ

C.) Asymmetric phrases:[42]

كم اختلست أيدي المنونِ

من قرونٍ

بعد قرونٍ

Besides these linear types there are multi-level symmetric structures where a symmetric rhyming couplet (or triplet) grows inside a symmetric construction of a larger scale, not supplied with rhyming endings:[43]

(فقلنا

من القارع

فقال ...)

وحرٌّ //

قاده الضرُّ

والزمن المرُّ

وضيفٌ //

وطؤه خفيفٌ

وضالته رغيفٌ

وجارٌ //

يستدعي على /

الجوعِ

الجيب المرقوعِ

وغريبٌ //

أوقدت النار على سفرِهِ

ونبح العواء على أثرِهِ

The four introductory one-word phrases preceding four symmetric couplets here make us feel that there is symmetry and balance of a higher order between different text units.

As has been mentioned before, about two thirds of the prose text features rhyming phrases: 62% of these rhyming phrases (equal to 42% of the whole prose text) constitute strictly parallel phrases. We may extract from the sum of words of the prose text the large number of the occurrences of the quotation word *qāla* – it occurs, as has been stated, 524 times – and also the names of the two protagonists (ᶜĪsā b. Hishām and Abū al-Fatḥ al-Iskandarī) – all together 205 occurrences. The above rate then becomes a little higher, by 3%, to be precise.

To simplify the picture, only three categories have been chosen from among the many different types of full symmetric phrases.

First type: When both members of the parallel couplets (since parallelism is restricted in 90% of cases to couplets) are full sentences, structurally independent from each other. These constitute 28% of all symmetric phrases:[44]

(كنت في بعض بلاد فزارة ... وأنا أهم بالوطن)

فلا الليل يثنيني بوعيدِهِ

ولا البعد يلويني ببيدِهِ

Even these seemingly complete sentences show, however, that it is quite impossible to excerpt any part of a text without feeling the need to explain things (e.g., word order, use of the *yafᶜalu* form, etc.) in it by referring to the antecedent parts.

Second type: When the only structural difference between the members is a particle or grammatical word at the beginning of the first phrase, which, however, relates to the second or third phrase as well. Their ratio is 14%. For example:[45]

فإنكم //

إذا استشعرتموه لم تجمعوا

ومتى ذكرتموه لم تمرحوا

وإن نسيتموه فهو ذاكرُكم

وإن نمتم عنه فهو ثائرُكم

وإن كرهتموه فهو زائرُكم

Third type: The remaining 58%, that is the largest part of all structurally parallel phrases, are such that the symmetric phrases start after a shorter or longer introductory part. This makes the reader think that the members are of different length.[46]

وليكن //

ليلي الأمرِ

يومي النشرِ

رقير القشرِ

(كثيف الحشوِ)

لؤلئي الدهنِ

كوكبي اللونِ

One last thing that should be noted here is that the proportion of symmetric structures, the members of which consist only of one word, is very low (2.6%), as compared to al-Ḥarīrī's *Maqāmāt*, where it is a much more frequent phenomenon.[47]

3. Summary

3.1 The form of al-Hamadhānī's *Maqāmāt* shows a more complicated and, at the same time, more diversified picture than one would think in reading certain simplified definitions given not only by various European and Arab handbooks and encyclopaedias, but also by monographs written by modern Arab authors on al-Hamadhānī.[48]

This complexity means two basic things: First, there are manifold and not at all monotonous patterns of connections between the different types of formal elements (rhyming, parallelism, length of the symmetric phrases, the frequency of their occurrence, and so on) forming a rhythm in the text which underlies the artistic effects of the *Maqāmāt*. Second, the choice and the rhythm of formal elements do not stand on their own, but are strongly linked with the semantic content of the clauses and with the course of the narrative in general.[49]

3.2 As final conclusions, the following main distinctive characteristics seem to merit consideration:

1. On the one hand, the use of a rhyming technique very similar in its complexity to that of the poetic *qāfiya*, and especially its rigid compliance with the rules of *iʕrāb* after the *rawī* points to a form of highly artificial written prose. Therefore one cannot accept the usual European presentation of the parts and phrases of a *maqāma* without vowel endings. On the other hand, some atavistic traits can be detected, as well as reminiscences of an oral literature. The most astonishing of all of these is perhaps the high frequency of the occurrence of liquid and nasal sounds (classified here as members of a so-called sonorant class) as rhyme letters, *rawī*s.
2. The rhyming endings are similar to those of many earlier and later products of the so-called rhyming prose in the extensive use of pronouns and inflectional endings in the rhyming words (not only *-hu* and *-hā*, but also *-ka, -kum, -ī, -nī, -an, -ūna*, etc.). However, these weak rhyming elements usually do not stand alone, but almost always follow a proper rhyme or at least a *rawī*.

3. As for the use of symmetric phrases the following can be stated:
   a) At least one third of all the rhyming phrases do not take part in symmetric phrases (i.e., parallelism) in a strict sense.
   b) It makes no sense to speak about parallel elements of differing length, but only about symmetric couplets or triplets of different length. This means that the members of one balanced pair should be of identical or nearly identical extent, but – contrary to the situation in poetry – there is no special limit set for the length of all such pairs.
   c) Strictly speaking, parallelism in al-Hamadhānī's *Maqāmāt* means almost exclusively a symmetric arrangement of syntactic devices and structures, even if there may exist traits of parallelism on other linguistic (phonological or semantic) levels too, at one and the same time. That is, if we cannot find a quite complete syntactic parallelism among phrases of the same rhyming endings, we cannot, as a rule, discover there semantic parallelism either. In other words, we may say that parallelism in the *Maqāmāt* means first of all repetition of structure and only then repetition of meanings.

Notes

1. The omitted passages are: the complete 26th *Maqāma Shāmiyya* (333 words); one anecdote from the end of the 31th *Maqāma Ruṣāfiyya* (328 words); and verses 8–13 from the first poem in the 19th *Maqāma Sāsāniyya* (35 words).
2. Blachère 1972:106. Cf. Horst, 1987:221.
3. For a first step towards fulfilling this aim, see Iványi 1993.
4. Even a monograph on al-Hamadhānī's literary activity written in Arabic and published recently, Muṣṭafā al-Shak^{c}a's work deals little with the formal aspects of the *maqāmāt*, devoting only seven of 468 pages to their style. I am grateful to Hilary Kilpatrick for calling to my attention Mahmoud Messadi's *Essai sur le rythme dans la prose rimée en arabe* (Tunis, 1981). Unfortunately it was too late to take Messadi's analysis into consideration in the present article.
5. In this we accept the views of A. F. L. Beeston, who emphasises the difference between the soothsayers' *saj^{c}* and that of the later prose writers. See Beeston 1971, 1983 and 1990. On *saj^{c}* see also Krenkow 1972.
6. As modern Arab writers do when speaking of the *maqāma* rhymes. See, for example, ^{c}Ukkāzī 1992: *'al-tasjī^{c} al-mutawāzī'*.
7. Considering the fact, pointed out later in this paper, that parallelism usually means here symmetric syntactic structures.
8. It can even be said that the aforementioned rhythm of the *maqāma* is ensured by this alternation of what may be called 'well-formed' and 'formless' parts.

9. An even greater number, around 38,800, would derive from counting separately everything that ancient Arab grammarians considered independent words (or rather morphemes).
10. The 22nd *al-Maqāma al-Maḍīriyya*, p.109 (ed. Beirut).
11. *Ibid*, p.108.
12. The 4th *al-Maqāma al-Sijistāniyya*, p. 21.
13. The 22nd *al-Maqāma al-Maḍīriyya*, p. 117.
14. *Ibid*, p. 109.
15. *Ibid*, p. 111.
16. The 3rd *al-Maqāma al-Balkhiyya*, p. 14.
17. The 4th *al-Maqāma as-Sijistāniyya*, p. 20.
18. *Ibid*, pp. 20–21.
19. *Ibid*, p. 20.
20. This theory has been presented in Iványi 1977 and 1978.
21. It would be a *qāfiya mutarādifa* in poetry.
22. See, for example, the works of al-Tanūkhī or al-Tawḥīdī, or even the *ḥikāyāt* of al-Azdī.
23. For the different patterns in the Koran and the special place occupied by the *fāᶜila(tun)* form, see Müller 1969, esp. pp. 13ff.
24. The whole list of figures, including those relating to other, mainly rhetorical features, and the results of comparative research done between al-Hamadhānī's *Maqāmāt* and other products of Arabic prose will be published later.
25. Interestingly enough, it occurs occasionally that, as is allowed in poetry, an indefinite nominal case ending may rhyme with a definite one (e.g., *-i/-in*).
26. The *maqāma* being prose not poetry; in *waqf* it would, of course, lose its endings if read aloud.
27. All very common types of rhyming in the prose literature of previous centuries or even in the 1–12th, see e.g. al-Azdī's *ḥikāyāt*.
28. The 26th (or 27th in the Istanbul edition) *al-Maqāma al-Waᶜẓiyya*, p. 131.
29. The 18th *al-Maqāma al-Qazwīniyya*, p. 89.
30. The 10th *al-Maqāma al-Iṣfahāniyya*, p. 54.
31. The 21st *al-Maqāma al-Mawṣiliyya*, p. 99
32. The 21st *al-Maqāma al-Mawṣiliyya*, p. 98.
33. The 22nd *al-Maqāma al-Maḍīriyya*, p. 113.
34. The 21st *al-Maqāma al-Mawṣiliyya*, p. 100.
35. Horst (1987:226) cites the following example of what he regards as rhyming and parallelism in al-Hamadhānī's *Maqāmāt*. The quotation is published with this segmentation and without *iᶜrāb* at the end of the parallel members:

    Fa-la-qad kunnā wa-llāhi min ahli thamm
    wa-ramm
    nurghī ladā ṣ-ṣabāḥ
    wa-nuthghī ᶜinda r-rawāḥ

36. Therefore, as Beeston (1990:132) has already emphasized, 'it is the Ḥarīrian *maqāmāt* that have come to be considered as the typical examples of the genre; it is indeed not unknown for literary historians to describe Ḥarīrī's work as if such description were applicable to all *maqāmāt* including those of Hamadhānī, notwithstanding the differences.' See, for

example, Brockelmann & Pellat 1991:109 where it is stated that 'In summary, the original *maqāma* appears to be characterised fundamentally by the almost exclusive use of rhymed prose'. This may be right in connection with al-Ḥarīrī, but certainly not if stated about al-Hamadhānī as we have tried to point out. For a really inadequate characterisation of the form of al-Ḥarīrī's *Maqāmāt*, see Margoliouth & Pellat 1972, where the most important note is that 'verbal exuberance leads to acrobatics' in his *Maqāmāt*.

37. The 5th *al-Maqāma al-Kūfiyya*, p. 24.
38. The 21st *al-Maqāma al-Mawṣiliyya*, p. 99.
39. More specific definitions will be given in the aforementioned forthcoming publication.
40. The 26th (or 27th) *al-Maqāma al-Waᶜẓiyya*, p. 133.
41. *Ibid.*
42. *Ibid*, p. 132.
43. The 5th *al-Maqāma al-Kūfiyya*, pp. 25–26.
44. The conjunctions *thumma/fa-/wa* – have not been taken into consideration. The example is from the 14th *al-Maqāma al-Fazāriyya*, p. 68.
45. The 11th *al-Maqāma al-Ahwāziyya*, p. 57.
46. The 12th *al-Maqāma al-Baghdādiyya*, p. 61.
47. It must be mentioned, however, that al-Ḥarīrī made his phrases rhyme more continuously, with less interrupting non rhyming, non parallel segments, so he needed more of this type of simpler material than al-Hamadhānī did.
48. Cf., for example, al-Shakᶜa 1983.
49. This statement would perhaps be regarded as commonplace speaking about any piece of European literature, but it is not a generally accepted idea in connection with Arabic belle-lettristic prose. Although it is this crucial point which we are most interested in exploring, investigation in this paper has been confined to the first point.

References

Primary sources

al-Azdī, *Ḥikāyāt* = al-Azdī, *Ḥikāyāt Abī l-Qāsim al-Baghdādī*, ed. Adam Mez, Heidelberg 1902.

al-Hamadhānī, *Maqāmāt* = Abū al-Faḍl Badīᶜ al-Zamān al-Hamadhānī, *Maqāmāt*, Istanbul: Maṭbaᶜat al-Jawā'ib, 1298/1880. Also: ed. Muḥammad ᶜAbduh, Beirut (Dār al-Mashriq), 1968.

al-Ḥarīrī, *Maqāmāt* = Abū Muḥammad al-Qāsim b. ᶜAlī b. Muḥammad b. ᶜUthmān al-Ḥarīrī, *al-Maqāmāt al-Ḥarīriyya.*, Cairo (ᶜĪsā al-Bābī al-Ḥalabī), 1938.

Secondary sources

Beeston, A. F. L., 1971. 'The Genesis of the *Maqāmāt* genre', *JAL* 2, pp. –12.

—— 1983. 'The Role of Parallelism in Arabic Prose', *Cambridge History of Arabic Literature: Arabic Literature to the End of the Umayyad period*, Cambridge University Press, pp.180–185.

—— 1990. "Al-Hamadhānī, al-Ḥarīrī and the *maqāmāt* genre', *Cambridge History of Arabic Literature: ᶜAbbasid Belles-Lettres*, Cambridge University Press, pp. 125–135.
Blachère, Regis, 1972. 'al-Hamadhānī'. *EI* 2 III, pp. 106–107.
Brockelmann, Carl & Pellat, Charles, 1991, '*Maqāma*'. *EI* 2 VI, pp. 107–115.
Horst, H., 1987. 'Besondere Formen der Kunstprosa', in Helmut Gätje (ed.), *Grundriss der arabischen Philologie,* II. *Literaturwissenschaft*, Wiesbaden (Ludwig Reichert), pp. 22–227.
Iványi, Tamás, 1977. 'Preliminary Distinctive Feature Analysis of Classical Arabic Consonants', *Acta Orientalia Hung.* 31, pp. 217–236.
—— 1978. '"Continuance" and "Stridency" in Semitic', *Acta Orientalia Hung.* 32, pp. 207–229.
—— 1993. 'Dynamic vs. Static – a Kind of Parallelism in al-Hamadhānī's *Maqāmāt*', in K. Dévényi, T. Iványi & A. Shivtiel (eds.), *Proceedings of the Colloquium on Arabic Lexicology and Lexicography (C.A.L.L.), Budapest, –7 September 1993. The Arabist* (*Budapest Studies in Arabic*) 6–7, pp. 49–58.
Krenkow, F., 1972. 'Sadjᶜ'. *EI* 1 III, pp. 43–44.
Margoliouth, D. S. & Pellat, Charles, 1972. 'al-Ḥarīrī'. *EI* 2 III, pp. 22–222.
Müller, Friedrun R., 1969. *Untersuchungen zur Reimprosa im Koran*, Bonn.
al-Shakᶜa, Muṣṭafā, 1983. *Badīᶜ al-Zamān al-Hamadhānī: rā'iᶜ al-qiṣṣa al-ᶜarabiyya wal-maqāla al-ṣaḥafiyya*. Beirut, (ᶜĀlam al-Kutub).
ᶜUkkāzī, Inᶜām Fawwāl, (ed.), 1992. *al-Muᶜjam al-mufaṣṣal fī ᶜulūm al-balāgha*, Beirut (Dār al-Kutub al-ᶜIlmiyya).

15

The Prose Literature of Pre-Islamic Arabia

Alan Jones
University of Oxford

In a recent article (The Language of the Qurʾān, hereafter abbreviated to LQ)[1] I argued that the traditional pious equation that (a) the language of the Qurʾān is identical with (b) the *ʿarabiyya* of early poetry on the one hand and with (c) the dialect of Quraysh, the spoken language of Muḥammad, on the other, is both late – it appears to have become prevalent no earlier than the third/ninth century – and mistaken. Evidence that the equation with (b) cannot be correct was first assembled by Vollers (though his conclusions about it were mistaken);[2] but even if we stop with the cautious view of Rabin 'that [the] literary diction [of the Qurʾān] contains some elements of [the] spoken idiom of the milieu',[3] we are at one remove from the language of poetry. The absence of rhyme and metre also have a considerable effect. On the other hand, the way that the *mufassirūn* specifically comment on the rare Meccan forms in the Quranic text is enough to invalidate the equation with (c). However, it is clear from the strong reaction of the Meccans that they understood the Qurʾān even if they rejected its message, and I suggested that this was because there were other registers that were in common use and to which the language of the Qurʾān has much greater natural affinities. These were the registers of the soothsayer (*kāhin*), the orator (*khaṭīb*) and story-teller (*qāṣṣ*) and also, in Medinan material, that of the written documentary style. Incidentally, in this article I shall talk about both styles and registers, whereas in LQ, in which I was focusing on variations in linguistic levels, I referred largely to registers. This is really a question of emphasis: there is a considerable overlap between style, the way in which material is couched, and register, the level of language at which it is pitched.

The existence of soothsayers, orators and story-tellers is well enough attested; but severe difficulties are caused by the paucity of of extant pieces that we may reaonably term *kāhin*- or *khaṭīb*-material, while the recasting of *qāṣṣ*-material during oral transmission means that it is only by back projection that we can say that it was essentially simple and direct in style. Equally, we have only a few clauses of what we may call documentary material. Most problematical of all is the dialectal material. The medieval sources regard the existence of dialects as axiomatic – and they are right to do so – but not one of them has preserved a single complete sentence from any early dialect.

Despite these difficulties, one can state with reasonable confidence that the pattern of the main registers of pre-Islamic Arabic was:

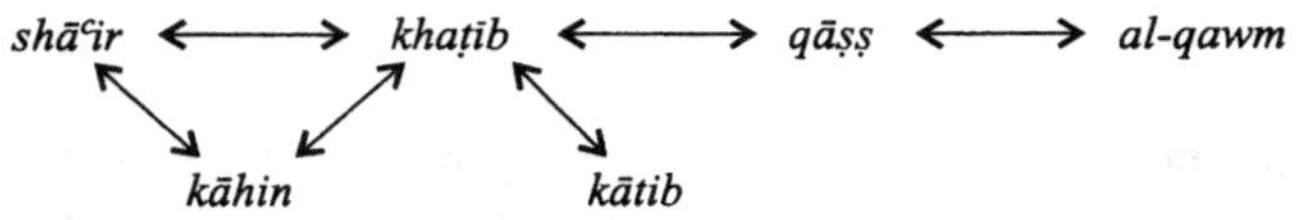

The *kāhin* and the *kātib* were, by and large, denizens of the settlements. The *shāᶜir*, the *khaṭīb* and the *qāṣṣ* were found among both the nomadic tribes and the people of the settlements, though it seems clear that their role was more important and had greater status among the *bedu*. One must assume that the principal register was the one with least status: the language of the people – dialect.

Another question that must be raised but which cannot be answered definitively is the relationship of the registers to each other. If we ignore the stylistic elements (rhyme and metre in poetry; assonance in *kāhin* utterances; and parallelism in the formal *khuṭba*), the range of registers is not great. Nor does the documentary style appear to be far removed from these, being very similar to unadorned *khuṭba* style. That leaves the registers about which we can only guess: those of the *qāṣṣ* and of ordinary tribal discourse. It seems to me to be fair to posit that the *qāṣṣ* would act in the way that we can observe with story-tellers in general: he would use a number of overlapping registers, ranging from something close to the ornate expression of the *khaṭīb* to the language of the ordinary people, but having as his mean a clear narrative style.

The most likely hypothesis about early dialects is that they were in the process of discarding *iᶜrāb*, and that this disappearance of *iᶜrāb* was occurring at quite different rates. As I said in LQ, I doubt whether anyone would now wish to subscribe to the view that there was any dialect that was more or less identical with the poetic *ᶜarabiyya* (or any other register for that matter).

Nevertheless, it is important to appreciate that the distance between the poetic register and that of dialect, the widest gap, was less than one might at first be inclined to think. Everything we know indicates that the passive knowledge of higher registers and complex styles was standard – otherwise these registers would lose most of their point. Moreover, passive knowledge could from time to time be turned to active use. The composition of laments in full poetic form by women who were not normally poets is well-attested; and we can hardly believe that their compositions were not extempore. The fact that some of them got into grammatical difficulties in composing their laments (see my *Shawāᶜir al-Jāhiliyya*,[4] passim) shows the change to active use was not straight-forward, but it could be managed.

What I want to do here is to suggest that when we think about literature and society in pre-Islamic Arabia we should give much more weight than has hitherto been the case to the role of the *khaṭīb* and the *qāṣṣ*. This is in no way an attempt to argue against the primacy of the poetic register; but it is salutary to remember that in general when the poet, the orator and the story-teller function together, experience is that the amount of material that each produces is in inverse proportion to his prestige.

The *khaṭīb*

What appears to have singled out the *khaṭīb* from among the large number of people who made speeches was his eloquence and his ability in the use of the high *khuṭba* style. This does not mean, of course, that others making formal speeches did not or could not use the style. The examples I quoted in LQ, by Abū Bakr and ᶜUthmān respectively, and those I cite below, show that this was not so. The title of *khaṭīb* is an indication of excellence, based on experience.

To repeat some of what I said in LQ, there appear to have been two types of *khaṭīb* in pre-Islamic Arabia. Much the more important was the tribal *khaṭīb*, who, together with the *sayyid* and the *shāᶜir*, was one of the leading members of the tribe, a person who had come to prominence because of his ability as a spokesman. His role was similar in some respects to that of the poet, though the medium of the *khaṭīb* was eloquent prose and not verse. It was his duty to praise his tribe and denigrate its enemies and to take part in any negotiations concerning the tribe. Usually this was his sole responsibility, though there are reports of the occasional *khaṭīb* who doubled as *qāṣṣ* or as *shāᶜir* or even as *sayyid*. Our prime source of information for this type of *khaṭīb* is the not totally reliable al-Jāḥiẓ (*Kitāb al-bayān*, passim[5]) but there is some con-firmatory evidence in poetry, both pre-Islamic and later (e.g. Labīd, al-Quṭāmī, the *Mufaḍḍaliyyāt* and the *Ḥamāsa*).

We have less information about the second type, the peripatetic *khaṭīb*. One has to presume that his role was essentially like that of the peripatetic poet, i.e. his services could be bought. However, it may well be that some of the itinerant *khaṭībs* preached ethical messages, urging, for example, that one should do what is right and avoid what is wrong; and in a few cases the message is likely to have been overtly religious. This would certainly appear to have been the case with Quss b. Sāᶜida, 'eloquent as the Bishop of Najrān', about whom there is a story that when a delegation from Bakr b. Wāᵓil met the Prophet he recited to them a piece of a speech by Quss that he had heard at one of the fairs at ᶜUkāẓ. The clear acceptance that Bishops of Najrān were eloquent is interesting in itself.

The use of parallelism as a central feature of the high *khuṭba* style seems to me to have important literary, and perhaps general cultural, implications. It is a feature that appears to be part of a continuum in high-register Semitic that we find also in Akkadian, Hebrew, Aramaic, Syriac and Ethiopic. Given the continuum one may conclude that the style of the *khuṭba* expresses the central high-level register, from which Arabic poetry is a further complex development.

Two examples will have to suffice here (for others see LQ). The first is to be found in the accounts of the battle of Ḥunayn in 630 AD. It is attributed to the poet Durayd b. al-Ṣimma, who had been brought, a blind and helpless centenarian, in a litter to the site of the battle. When told where the site was, he is alleged to have said:[6]

Niᶜma majālu l-khayl
Lā ḥaznun ḍirs
Wa-lā sahlun dahs
Mā lī asmaᶜu rughāᵓa l-baᶜīr
wa-nuhāqa l-ḥamīr
wa-bukāᵓā l-ṣaghīr
wa-yuᶜāra l-shāᵓ?

What a good place for the cavalry to operate.
[It is] not rugged ground that bites into the feet,
nor a plain so full of dust that one loses direction.
[But] why do I hear the groaning of camels,
and the braying of donkeys
and the weeping of children
and the bleating of sheep?

There is of course a risk that the whole passage is apocryphal, but stories about the death of so famous a poet as Durayd would have spread quickly, and it seems fair to assume that it is an early piece, and for those interested in the development of *saj*ᶜ it is an important fragment. One could argue that it is very little different in style from *kāhin*-material. However, that is not true of the content, which is concrete and not gnomic. Here part of the parallelistic effect is due to the brevity of the clauses which bind the assonance tightly into the structure. However, looser structures are more common, as can be seen in my second example. This is part of the dying address of one of the Prophet's ancestors, Quṣayy b. Kilāb, to his eldest son ᶜAbdu l-Dār. Again there is a problem about the apocryphal nature of the story, and I suspect that the surviving text has suffered some alteration in transmission. But even with these caveats the piece looks archaic:[7]

Lā yadkulu rajulun min-humu l-Kaᶜbata ḥattā takūna anta taftaḥu-hā
Wa-lā yaᶜqidu li-Qurayshin liwāᵓan li-ḥarbi-hā illā anta bi-yadi-ka
Wa-lā yashrabu aḥadun bi-Makkata illā min siqāyati-ka
Wa-lā yaᵓkulu aḥadun min ahli l-mawsimi ṭaᶜāman illā min ṭaᶜāmi-ka
Wa-lā taqtaᶜu Qurayshun amran min umūri-hā illā fī dāri-ka

None of them shall enter the Kaᶜba until you open it for them;
None shall give the Quraysh a banner for their war but you with your own hand;
None shall drink in Mecca unless you provide the drink;
None of the people who come for the pilgrim season shall eat food unless you provide it;
Quraysh shall not decide any matter concerning them except in your house.

The *qāṣṣ*

The existence of story-tellers in pre-Islamic times is well-attested; and even if it were not, the use of the root *qṣṣ* in the Qurᵓān would go most of the way to establishing it.

However, one of our great problems is how we are to relate the *qāṣṣ* of pre-Islamic Arabia to the corpus of stories that has survived in works of the ᶜAbbāsid period. This raises not only the question of the amount of material that has survived but also that of its basic reliability.

The first problem, how much activity there was, cannot now be answered with any degree of precision. But all that has been learned about the rate at which material disappears in the course of lengthy oral transmission indicates heavy loss; and as a sizeable corpus has survived we may assume that there was very considerable original activity. When we turn to the problem of reliability, the natural course of oral transmission, as well as plain commonsense, leads us to the somewhat trite view that some is true, some is false, and some is a mixture of the two. That in turn leads us to the much more central, and much more difficult, question of how we are to assess which is true, which is false, and which is a mixture.

Such questioning is a central task for anyone who wishes to cull information about life and culture in pre-Islamic Arabia. How are we to justify such statements as "one can also be reasonably sure that a fair number of stories, e.g. about the war of al-Basūs, contain genuine information that has passed through generations of story-tellers"; or "the majority of stories about sixth-century poets are highly unreliable, but there is an improvement in the quality of information in the seventh century"?

I believe that reassessment is just as important here as it is with the corpus of pre-Islamic poetry (on the latter problem see my *Early Arabic Poetry* 1, 17–21); and here I should like to outline a framework in which it might be approached. I begin with spurious material, which is perhaps easiest to spot.

In many cases one can see how a line (or several lines) of poetry has been misunderstood and how this has given rise to a legend. Take, for example, the famous story that concerns not one but two notorious *ṣuᶜlūk* poets, al-Shanfarā and Taᵓabbaṭa Sharrā (see *EAP*, 1, 205–6):

Taᵓabbaṭa Sharrā, al-Shanfarā and ᶜAmr ibn Barrāq set out to raid the Bajīla tribe. However, they found that Bajīla, having had warning of their coming, had laid an ambush for them near the water where they would have to drink. When they approached it in the darkness of the night, Taᵓabbaṭa Sharrā said to his companions, 'There is an ambush by the water. I can hear the pounding of the men's hearts.' The other two answered, 'We cannot hear anything. It must be the pounding of your own heart that you hear.' Taᵓabbaṭa Sharrā laid his hand on his heart and said, 'It is not pounding, and it isn't accustomed to pound.' They said, 'Well, by God, we must get to the water, whatever happens.' Al-Shanfarā went down first; but when the men lying in ambush saw him, they recognized him, and let him drink without molesting him. So he drank, and returned to his companions and said, 'There is no one at the water. I have drunk my fill at the cistern.' Taᵓabbaṭa Sharrā answered, 'Yes, but they do not want to take you. It is me they desire to catch.' Then Ibn Barrāq went down, and drank and returned unmolested. He, too, said, 'There is no one at the spring.' Taᵓabbaṭa Sharrā answered, 'It is me they want, not you.' Then he said to al-Shanfarā, 'When I bend down to drink at the cistern, the men will spring upon me and bind me a prisoner. Then run as though you were fleeing, but double back and station yourself at the foot of that hill over there. When you hear me cry, "Catch him! Catch him!" run up to me and release me from my bonds.' Then he said to Ibn Barrāq, 'I shall tell you to give yourself up as a prisoner to the Bajīla. Don't go far from them, but do not put it in their power to catch you.' Then Ta'abbaṭa Sharrā went forward and down to the water; and when he bent down to drink, the men in ambush sprang upon him and took him prisoner, and tied his arms behind him with a bow-string. Then al-Shanfarā darted away to the place where Ta'abbaṭa Sharrāhad told him to go, and Ibn Barrāq withdrew just so far that they could see him. Then Ta'abbaṭa Sharrā said, 'O men of Bajīla, would you like to gain some advantage? Will you be easy with me as regards a ransom if I persuade Ibn Barrāq to give himself up as a prisoner?' 'Yes,' they said. Then he shouted, 'Woe to you, Ibn Barrāq! al-Shanfarā has fled, and is warming himself at the fire of the sons of so-and-so; and you know what a tie there is between us and your people. Will you not surrender yourself, so that they will be easy with us in respect of ransom?' ʿAmr answered, 'Not until I have tried my pace in a run or two.' Then he began to run briskly in the direction of the mountain and to return again in his tracks; until, when the men of Bajīla thought that he was getting tired and that they could take him, they set out to run after him. And Ta'abbaṭa Sharrā called out, 'Catch him! Catch him!' and they went off, running after him as hard as they could. Then he began to draw them on by pretending to slow down, and then to get still further off. Meanwhile al-Shanfarā had come up from behind to Ta'abbaṭa Sharrā, and cut his bonds. And when the Ibn Barrāq saw that his bonds had been cut, he made for him, and the two, ʿAmr and al-Shanfarā, joined Ta'abbaṭa Sharrā where he was standing. Then Ta'abbaṭa Sharrā said to the men, 'Did you admire the running of Ibn Barrāq, O tribe of Bajīla? Now, by God, I will run you a race that will make you forget it.' Then he and al-Shanfarā moved off, and all three outstripped their pursuers and reached home in safety.

The basis for the story lies in three lines of the *Qaṣīda Qāfiyya* of Ta'abbaṭa Sharrā (lines 4, 5 and 8 [*EAP* 1, 209–12]). These read:

4. I escape as I escaped from the Bajīla, when I ran at top speed on the night of the sandy tract at al-Raḥṭ –
5. The night at al-ʿAykatān, when they shouted and urged on their swiftest runners against me at the place where Ibn Barrāq ran;
8. And then I escaped, running alongside one possessed, a man swift in running, long-striding, and they did not seize my spoils.

[Verses 6 and 7 are a mixture of simile, *waṣf* and hyperbole that do not affect the story.]

The most obvious discrepancies are that in the poem (a) al-Shanfarā is not mentioned; (b) sandy low-lying ground (*khabt*) is involved and there is no mention of water; (c) Taᵓabbaṭa Sharrā carries off some booty. These are major points of difference, yet the commentary on the *Mufaḍḍaliyyāt*[8] gives the story as part of the explanation of verse 4, using al-Aṣmaᶜī (died c.820 AD) as its authority. However, I suspect that al-Aṣmaᶜī would have probably dealt with the story in the same way as Abū l-Faraj does in the Aghānī[9] and used it as prefatory background to the poem. The discrepancies are then less obvious – the introductory story fades rapidly into the background once the recitation of verses starts. The poem has suffered some accretion [see *EAP* 1, 206–7], but it gives the impression of being a genuinely archaic piece, not all that well understood in the ᶜAbbāsid period, if we are to judge by the commentaries. In contrast, the story is crisp and couched in prose that would have been clear enough in ᶜAbbāsid times.

A final comment about spurious legend: it is still possible for such material to be early, but there is no way of showing whether this is the case or not; but if a story is clearly not based on the poem it is alleged to illuminate, one can hardly be confident about it.

To illustrate three other types of material that we might link back to the early *qāṣṣ*, authentic stories, stories muddled in transmission, and stories existing in different forms, I should like to use a well-known story-tellers' device and digress to that slightly specialized form of story-telling known as *ḥadīth*. The *ḥadīth* corpus may be dangerous territory, though it is by no means as dangerous as neo-Schachtians would have us believe. Whatever has happened to the corpus in the course of time, it has undoubtedly preserved some material of real antiquity, including colloquial and dialectal features. Such material is often difficult to spot, but it does deserve sifting. (That, incidentally, is a view with which Schacht agreed on the last occasion that I was fortunate enough to talk to him.)

In the most controversial area, that of authentic material, I believe that there is a good example on the topic of 'the widow's year', i.e. year of isolation before remarriage, referred to in passing in the *Muᶜallaqa* of Labīd, line 88:

> They are givers of bounty to the stranger dwelling among them and to widows when their year [of mourning] has elapsed.

There is a reasonably clear description of this period of isolation and mourning in al-Bukhārī, *al-Ṣaḥīḥ, Kitāb al-Ṭalāq, bāb* 46, where we read:

'When a woman was bereaved of her husband, she would go and live [alone] in a small, miserable tent, wearing the poorest clothes and not using perfume until a year had passed. At that time an animal would be brought to her – a donkey, a sheep or a bird – and she would rub herself against it. The animal seldom survived this. Then she would come out and be given some dung which she would throw. Then she could resume using perfume etc. as she wished.'

I know of no attempt to link this to any point of Islamic law – though there is one;[10] and even though the story is used to back up another point, being a pendant to a *ḥadīth* in which the Prophet is depicted as saying that a woman suffering from ophthalmia should not use *kuḥl* to treat it during the period of her *ᶜidda*, I see no reason to consider the passage spurious. However, one has to say that the language does not strike one as particularly archaic but rather gives the impression of some modification with the passage of time.

One of the most interesting examples I know of a story muddled in transmission is to be found in al-Bukhārī (*al-Ṣaḥīḥ, Kitāb al-aṭᶜima, bāb* 1). Here it is essential to look at the Arabic text:

aṣāba-nī jahdun shadīdun, fa-laqītu ᶜUmara bna l-Khaṭṭābi, fa-staqraʾtu-hu āyatan min kitābi llāhi, fa-dakhala dāra-hu wa-fataḥa-hā ᶜalay-ya; fa-mashaytu ghayra baᶜīdin fa-kharartu l-wajh-ī mina l-jahdi wa-l-jūᶜi, fa-idhā rasūlu llāhi qāʾimun ᶜalā raʾs-ī, fa-qāla "yā Abā Hurayra" fa-qultu "labbay-ka yā rasūla llāh wa-saᶜday-ka"; fa-akhadha bi-yad-ī fa-aqāma-nī wa-ᶜarafa lladhī bī; fa-nṭalaqa bī ilā raḥli-hi, fa-amara lī bi-ᶜussin min labanin, fa-sharibtu min-hu, thumma qāla "ᶜud fa-shrab yā Abā Hirr"; fa-ᶜudtu fa-sharibtu ḥattā stawā baṭn-ī fa-ṣāra ka-l-qidḥi. qāla, fa-laqītu ᶜUmara, wa-dhakartu lahu lladhī kāna min amr-ī, wa-qultu lahu "tawallā dhālika man kāna aḥaqqu bi-hi min-ka yā ᶜUmar, wa-llāhi laqadi staqraʾtu-ka l-āyata, wa-la-ana aqraʾu min-ka". qāla ᶜUmaru "wa-llāhi la-an akūna adkhaltu-ka aḥabbu ilay-ya min an yakūna lī mithlu ḥumri l-naᶜami".

This is the accepted text of what appears to be a fairly inconsequential piece, hardly the sort of stuff to be slipped into the corpus to bolster some legal point. As it stands, perhaps the most interesting feature is the use of the so-called 'iterative dual' *labbay-ka wa-saᶜday-ka* (Wright 2, 74). Certainly, the story-line is not clear. The problem lies in the following two sentences, both of which have suffered (a) from the addition of *hamzas* that were not part of the original text, and (b) from the absorption of glosses based on *āyatan*/*al-āya*:

(i) *fa-staqra'tu-hu āyatan min kitābi llāhi, fa-dakhala dāra-hu wa-fataḥa-hā ʿalay-ya*;
(ii) *laqadi staqra'tu-ka l-āyata, wa-la-ana aqra'u min-ka*

Close examination shows that the story-line centres on the fact that *hamza* had largely disappeared from Ḥijāzī dialects, and thus the Ḥijāzīs used *istaqrā* for what in non-Ḥijāzī dialects would be two forms: *istaqrā* and *istaqra'a*.(Similarly the fourth form *aqrā* was used for both *aqrā* and *aqra'a*; and the elative *aqrā* was used for both *aqrā* and *aqra'u*.) It is also clear from the last sentence that Abū Hurayra did not enter ʿUmar's house. That appears to indicate that *fa-dakhala dāra-hu* has been misplaced. One may therefore reasonably reconstruct the first sentence as: *fa-staqraytu-hu* (or perhaps even *fa-qultu aqri-nī*) *wa-fataḥa ʿalay-ya fa-dakhala dāra-hu*; and the second as: *laqadi staqraytu-ka wa-la-ana aqrā min-ka*.

The tradition now has a point (and it is not a legal one): because of the Ḥijāzī homonyms ʿUmar misunderstands Abū Hurayra, taking his request for sustenance as one for exposition of the Qur'ān. According to the story the Prophet is not put to the same verbal test – he understands from looking at Abū Hurayra. With the loss of knowledge of the early Ḥijāzī dialects and with the spread of the use of *hamza* the point was lost. Further obscurity was added by the gloss, though this might in fact have preceded the addition of *hamza*. The reconstructed text is strongly in favour of the tradition being early.

Though there have been some modifications in the text of the story of Abū Hurayra, it has an archaic flavour which has entirely disappeared from the story of the three poets. This of course may be due to the story of the three poets actually being of later origin, even though in all probability it refers to events that preceded those in the story of Abū Hurayra by at least fifty years; but even if it were not, any archaic features have disappeared.

Incidentally, the story about Abū Hurayra is not the only one to revolve around the confusion caused by Ḥijāzī homonyms arising from the dropping of *hamza* (with similarly garbled results in the transmitted texts). The best attested story of the killing of Mālik b. Nuwayra, chief of the Banū Yarbūʿ, during the Ridda wars by a force led by Khālid b. al-Walīd centres on Khālid saying *adfū asrā-kum*. This was taken by the Tamīmī in charge of the prisoners to mean 'despatch [m.pl. imperative of *adfā* 'to despatch'] your prisoners', and the prisoners were put to death. However, Khālid asserted that he had meant 'keep your prisoners warm'.[11] That could be true in the Ḥijāzī dialects, as the eastern *adfi'ū* [m. pl. imperative of *adfaʾa* 'to keep warm'] had become *adfū* with the dropping of *hamza*. One may perhaps suspect that Khālid, who is generally agreed to have claimed Mālik's wife as spoils of war, was not unaware of the ambiguity.

It is unfortunate that one rarely finds an example like these where reconstruction is both possible and convincing. We must conclude that in the majority of cases accretion is undetectable.

Turning finally to the problem of multiplicity of form, let me quote a *ḥadīth* that is well-attested, as it has a bearing on three legal topics: buying food on deferred payments; fixed terms; and pledging something as security. Though some western scholars may consider it open to suspicion because it deals with these three points, the phrase *min yahūdiyyin* seems to be a counter-indication, as that phrase is not likely to feature in a way that is not remotely pejorative in a tradition that is not early. Here are half a dozen of the versions:[12]

[inna] l-nabiyya shtarā ṭaᶜāman min yahūdiyyin ilā ajalin wa-rahana-hu dirᶜan min ḥadīdin

[inna] l-nabiyya shtarā ṭaᶜāman min yahūdiyyin ilā ajalin wa-rahana-hu dirᶜa-hu

[inna] l-nabiyya shtarā min yahūdiyyin ṭaᶜāman ilā ajalin maᶜlūmin wa-rtahana min-hu dirᶜan min ḥadīdin

[inna] l-nabiyya shtarā min yahūdiyyin ṭaᶜāman ilā ajalin wa-rtahana min-hu dirᶜan min ḥadīdin

ishtarā rasūlu llāhi ṭaᶜāman min yahūdiyyin bi-nasīʾatin wa-rahana dirᶜan lahu min ḥadīdin

ishtarā rasūlu llāhi min yahūdiyyin ṭaᶜāman bi-nasīʾatin wa-rahana dirᶜa-hu

The point is clear. A frequently told story or tradition will almost inevitably give rise to variants, even with a relatively brief text. In these circumstances, transmission *bi-l-lafẓ* is a mirage, though equally transmission *bi-l-maᶜnā* is not.

These four categories or any similar criteria – and in my view markedly different criteria are not realistic – indicate the need for a cautious approach to individual stories. That will probably result in the recovery of little more than skeletal information. So be it. Occasionally, there will be some help from poetry – though the help may point in different directions. Take, for example, the story of the War of Dāḥis and al-Ghabrā°, to which quite a number of poems, including two of the *Mu^callaqāt*, are linkeḍ There is a mass of extant material on this war, with an account of the episode that finally brought peace taking over three pages in Lyall's translation (*Ancient Arabian Poetry*, pp. 107–110). A little of the story is confirmed by part of Zuhayr's *Mu^callaqa*; yet, as Lyall himself says, the episode describing the violent conduct of Ḥuṣayn ibn Ḍamḍam (verses 40–46) seem to tell of a graver dissension than is set out in the story. Lyall has another interesting note (op. cit. p.115) which seems to me to encapsulate the problems that face us:

> The traditions relating to the War of Dāḥis (as it was called after the famous horse the wager in regard to which was the cause of dispute) are very full, and abound in graphic incident throwing much light on the life of those days. To abridge them, or to summarize the many stories they contain (of which that given in the introduction is a fair specimen), would be to do them wrong; I hope to have some opportunity hereafter of setting them forth at length. The tribes which took part in the war were, on the one side, ^cAbs, and on the other that branch of Dhubyān called Fazāra: other branches of Dhubyān were afterwards drawn into it, but the main struggle was between these two. The combatants belonged to the great clan of Ghaṭafān, who dwelt in those days south of the western portion of the mountains of Ṭayyi° and of the oasis of Taimā°, between Yathrib on the west and the lands of the Banū Asad on the east . . . . The War of Dāḥis is said to have lasted forty years, like that of al-Basūs.

From the historical point of view Lyall is too trusting in his assessment of the value of the stories. This is because he wrote at a time when the problems of the authenticity of early poetry were recognized but those of the contamination of orally transmitted prose were not. In other respects he seems more justified. There is little evidence that details of ethos and attitudes have been changed, either intentionally or unintentionally, though they are of course open to story-tellers' licence.

From a literary point of view I would accept Lyall's stance. Even with the stories that are of dubious origin, it is the skill of the story-telling that matters; and I do not think it starry-eyed to believe that the standards were set in pre-Islamic times.Nor is it not too much to say that constant elements in the *qāṣṣ* style are discernible; nor is it unreasonable to project them backward on the one hand, to the time when the original material has disappeared or has been transmuted and even to link it with similar narrative styles in other Semitic languages; and to project them forward on the other hand to such oral classics as *Alf layla wa-layla* and *Sīrat ᶜAntar*. Yet it is a typical irony of fate that it was once stories of the *qāṣṣ* were committed to writing that their influence became much more pervasive and lasting.

A general reflection

It is quite clear that with a virtually non-existent corpus of *khaṭīb*-material and with a much modified corpus of *qāṣṣ*-material it is only general comments that might have some validity. More than anything else I would wish to stress the importance of the *khaṭīb* and the *qāṣṣ*. If the poet's prestige were ten times that of a story-teller, to use an arbitrary figure, one might also expect the story-teller to have a repertoire at least ten times that of a poet. On that basis his linguistic influence, as opposed to his prestige, would probably be greater than that of the poet. The same consideration applies, with different figures, to the *khaṭīb*.

The conclusion is simple. In dealing with the pre-Islamic period we cannot ignore the *khaṭīb* and *qāṣṣ* of those times. When it comes to later ages we must also give weight to their enormous influence. It is still with us.

Notes

1. 'The Language of the Qurᵓān', *Proceedings of the 1992 Colloquium on Arabic Lexicology and Lexicography*, Budapest, 1994
2. Karl Vollers, *Volkssprache und Schiftsprache im alten Arabien*, Strassbourg, 1906. It is a pity that Vollers' conclusions were so wrong-headed, as there is much of value in the book.
3. Rabin, *Ancient West-Arabian*, London, 1947, p.4.
4. 'Shawāᶜir al-Jāhiliyya', *Proceedings of the 1991 Colloquium on Arabic Grammar*, Budapest, 1991.
5. For a slightly more optimistic assessment of the value of the pieces in the *Kitāb al-bayān*, see Leder and Kilpatrick, 'Classical Arabic Prose Literature', *Journal of Arabic Literature* 22 [1992], p.2.
6. Ibn Hishām, *Sīra* (Cairo, 1955), 2, p.428.
7. Op. cit., 1, pp.129–130.
8. *al-Mufaḍḍaliyyāt*, (ed. Lyall), text, p.6–7.
9. Abū l-Faraj, *Kitāb al-Aghānī*, 21, 12–2.
10. The passage might to be thought to provide corroboration for Q 2:240, but this is not a view that has commended itself to Muslim authorities.
11. For the story see al-Ṭabarī, *History*, I, p.1925; also *Kitāb al-Aghānī*, 15, 201.
12. For the examples in Bukhārī and Muslim alone, see Bukhārī, *istiqrāḍ*, 1; *buyūᶜ*, 14,22,37,88; *salam*, 5,5; *rahn*, 1,2,5; *khums* 18; Muslim, *musāqāt*, 124,125,126; *jihād*, 42.

16

Modernity In A Classical Arabic *Adab* Work, The *Kitāb Al-aghānī*

Hilary Kilpatrick

The *Kitāb al-aghānī* is not now most people's idea of a modern book. But modernity, in this essay, I take to mean what was new in the 4th/10th century, when Abū al-Faraj al-Iṣbahānī was writing.[1] I would suggest that certain aspects of the *Aghānī* deserve the epithet "modern", either because they are characteristic of the general evolution of prose literature in Arabic in the late 3rd/9th and early 4th/10th century, or because they seem to be innovations of Abū al-Faraj's.

Such an approach to the *Aghānī* is inspired by the general theme of this conference. Moreover, it focuses attention on one of the important tasks facing researchers on classical Arabic prose literature, the study of *adab* compilations and their evolution. Very little systematic investigation has been undertaken into the history of 'Abbasid prose literature, particularly the widespread form of the compilation.[2] Yet to understand properly the varied and plentiful manifestations of this form, they need to be examined in the appropriate context, that is, against the background of other examples of it. And both synchronic and diachronic comparisons can be helpful.

To discuss the modernity of the *Kitāb al-aghānī* requires a mainly diachronic approach. But given the scarcity of research into compilations, affirmations about what was, or was not, new in 'Abbasid prose at a given moment can only be provisional at this stage. Intensive study of the *Aghānī* is time-consuming, and very hard to combine with equally systematic investigation of other major compilations. So I would like to offer the following observations as a contribution to a wider enquiry which must be undertaken by several scholars in cooperation.

The first reason for regarding the *Aghānī* as at least partly modern is that it contains modern material. Of course, it also contains many older *akhbār* too. Some of them, the *ayyām* accounts, go back in spirit if not in letter to the pre-Islamic period,[3] while other accounts present political events, scholarly exchanges, rhetorical jousts, squabbles at court and love affairs from the first three centuries of Islamic history, as well as legendary encounters and entertaining tales in popular circulation at the time. But among the great variety of material which Abū al-Faraj transmits, there are four categories which can be considered as new in his time, or at least of recent origin, first encountered in the compilations of the previous generation of writers. These are anecdotes alluding to the details of the *kātib*'s profession, anecdotes which betray insight into psychology, private letters which reveal something of their authors' inner life, and samples of elegant, sophisticated prose, such as Abū al-Faraj uses to defend certain controversial poets and singers.

Akhbār which depict the details of 'Abbasid administrative practice are already to be found in Muḥammad b. ᶜAbdūs al-Jahshiyārī's (d.331/942) *Kitāb al-wuzarā' wa-al-kuttāb*, and they form an important part of Abū ᶜAlī al-Tanūkhī's (d.384/995) *Al-faraj baᶜda al-shidda*.[4] In the *Aghānī* there is one good example of the genre, Abū al-Faraj's own account of the scene he witnessed where the head of the administration of the eastern provinces (*dīwān al-mashriq*), al-Bāqiṭānī, admonished a newly-appointed governor for making a disparaging remark and went on to recall the professionalism of al-Muhtadī's vizier, Sulaymān b.Wahb (d.272/885), and his assistant Abū al-ᶜAbbās b. Thawāba (d.277/890) in drawing up letters for the caliph. Al-Bāqiṭānī still regarded their competence and integrity as an ideal, even though his contemporaries were far from attaining it (*Aghānī*, XXIII, 146–8).[5] Apart from the fact that Abū al-Faraj is here recounting a scene in which he took part, the *khabar*, which illustrates the high point of 'Abbasid bureaucratic practice while indicating that it is a thing of the past, is scarcely conceivable in earlier *adab* collections.

More common in the *Aghānī* are *akhbār* which reflect an interest in psychology. Among them the most prominent group focusses on personalities suffering from a form of mental disturbance, the *muwaswisūn* Juᶜayfirān (*Agh.* XX, pp.188–96), Khālid *al-kātib* (XX, pp.274–87) and Mānī (XXIII, pp.18–7). Unlike Majnūn, the archetype of the *ᶜudhrī* poet driven to madness by an unhappy love affair and fleeing human contact, these poets belong to the urban society of Baghdad and remain at least on its fringes, even when unbalanced. Often, surrounded by friends or an appreciative, cultivated audience, they are capable of behaving normally; indeed it is the alternation between normality and unpredictable or unconventional behaviour which gives the articles on them much of their interest.[6]

As portrayed in the *Aghānī* they possess a certain individuality. What drove Ju^cayfirān to melancholy was his rivalry with his father over one of the latter's slave girls and subsequently his father's turning him out of the house and disinheriting him. After the old man's death, Juᶜayfirān engaged in a lawsuit to get back his inheritance but lost it, and it was then that he suffered a mental collapse. The clash between father and son offers a credible motive for Juᶜayfirān's subsequent behaviour, which expresses alienation and an acute sense of society's hypocrisy. Of the three characters, Juᶜayfirān comes closest to the type of the "wise fool".[7]

The second member of this group, Khālid *al-kātib*, loses his psychological equilibrium later in life; indeed the epithet "*muwaswis*" is not automatically attached to his name.[8] Several *akhbār* depict him quite normally producing occasional poems for patrons and engaging in *hijā'* with rivals, including Abū Tammām. But a possible clue to his breakdown is his reluctance to compose poetry except about his affairs of the heart, which suggests that his patrons' demands for other genres may have placed a strain on him. This, combined with the competitiveness of the literary salons and disappointments in love and friendship, could have led to his becoming emotionally unstable, if he was as highly strung as his poetry suggests.

The third figure, Mānī, is described as already unbalanced when he arrives in Iraq from Egypt. He, too, suffers from hypersensitivity, which manifests itself when he breaks off from reciting his poetry to berate and buffet an elderly muezzin with a quavering voice. But when invited to attend a drinking party at Muḥammad b. ᶜAbdallāh b. Ṭāhir's house, he shows himself entirely in possession of the required intellectual qualities and social graces. A trait in the *Aghānī* which underlines Khālid's and Mānī's mental confusion is that they each refer to themselves once in the third person (*Agh.* XX, p.285; XXIII, p.182).

In his presentation of these unbalanced, hypersensitive poets, Abū al-Faraj goes beyond his predecessors, as far as can be judged.[9] The *Aghānī* articles are fuller than the corresponding sections in Ibn al-Muᶜtazz's *Ṭabaqāt al-shuᶜarā' al-muḥdathīn*,[10] Ibn al-Jarrāḥ's *Kitāb al-waraqa*[11] or al-Marzubānī's *Muᶜjam al-shuᶜarā'*,[12] while their focus on individuals sets them apart from the treatment of *shuᶜarā' al-majānīn* in Ibn ᶜAbd Rabbih's *al-ᶜIqd al-farīd*[13] or *al-Nawkā wa-al-majānīn wa-al-muwaswisīn* in al-Jāḥiẓ's *Kitāb al-bayān wa-al-tabyīn*,[14] which seeks to define the traits of a group. Behind Abū al-Faraj's portrayal of the three poets can be sensed a desire to depict the phenomenon of mental illness in its complexity and variety, without forcing it into a formalised scheme of *ᶜuqalā' al-majānīn*.[15] If he is derivative, because he quotes already existing *akhbār*, he is also original because, with the material he has collected from his different sources, he constructs a more subtle picture than other authors.

Another type of material which reflects an interest in psychology, but here most often the psychology of the writer, are private letters, especially those in prose. The private letters quoted in the *Aghānī* are penned by *kuttāb*, eminent members of highly placed families, or their close associates. Some are in poetry, exchanges between lover and beloved, or between (prospective) owner and slave girl, which might come down to the same thing, or between close friends. Notes in verse are preserved from the early 'Abbasid period on,[16] but prose correspondence between lovers or friends is a later development,[17] if the evidence in the *Aghānī* is reliable. For the poetess Faḍl (d.257/871) and her lover Sa^{c}īd b. Ḥumayd (d. after 251/866) still exchange notes in poetry, and Sa^{c}īd's letters to his friends are also couched in verse (*Agh.* XVIII, pp.160–7). Although Faḍl's eloquence in prose composition is referred to, no examples of her art are quoted. By contrast, some of the letters which the singer ^{c}Arīb (d.277/891) wrote to one of her lovers, Ibrāhīm b. al-Mudabbir (d.279/893) are incorporated into the article on him. Here is one of them, quoted by Abū al-Faraj from Ibn al-Mu^{c}tazz's collection of ^{c}Arīb's correspondence:[18]

> "You are dearer to me than my hearing, my sight, my mother and father and those who have known and are known to me. How are you? May you be preserved from harm, and may God blind him who hates you and smite him at this prayer of mine, which I hope will be answered, God willing.[19] How are you finding the fast? May God acquaint you with its blessings and aid you to obey Him. I hope you will be spared all unpleasantness through God's power and might. Ah, how I long for you! Ah, how I miss you! May God restore you to the best state to which he has accustomed you, and not give cause to any enemy or envious person to gloat over me because of [what has befallen] you.
>
> I received your letter. May I not be without it except when your presence renders it superfluous. Then I remembered its bearer, and sent my messenger to invite him in so that I could ask him about you. But I found he had already left. Had I seen him, I would have laid my cheek on the ground [for him to walk on], for he deserved it." (*Agh.* XXII, pp.174–5)

Such a passage, with its balanced composition and its rhetorical figures, draws on motifs, for instance the *ḥāsid*, the envious one, found in poetry. But one also senses behind the exclamations and some of the hyperbole traces of colloquial speech. At all events, it reflects more directly the writer's individual personal experience than would a poem on the same theme; it can be regarded as an expression of a *ḥassāsiyya* which, if not *jadīda* in Abū al-Faraj's time, had emerged less than a century earlier.

The development of the possibilities of expression inherent in prose achieved by the end of the 3rd/9th century is well illustrated in a letter of thanks ᶜUbaydallāh b. ᶜAbdallāh b. Ṭāhir (d.300/913) sends the prince ᶜAbdallāh b. al-Muᶜtazz (d.296/908) for his treatise on the acceptability of altering older songs to suit a performer's range and taste (*Agh.* X, pp.276–7). ᶜUbaydallāh's prose is constructed out of balanced phrases, occasionally rhyming, with historical allusions and conceits and a penchant for paronomasia and antithesis. The advance in elegance and sophistication which has taken place becomes clear when this letter is compared with one written by Isḥāq al-Mawṣilī (d.235/850) to ᶜAlī b. Hishām (d.217/832) complaining about their separation and ᶜAlī's silence, and then describing a book the musician is preparing about songs and singing girls (*Agh.* XVII, p.122).[20] The personal part of the letter is half in verse, while the description of the book is factual and plain. Even allowing for the difference in aim of the two letters and in status of their writers and recipients, it is possible to measure the evolution of Arabic prose in the intervening years, an evolution which is linked to an increase in insight into mental and emotional processes as well as to greater familiarity with techniques of dialectic.

The best examples of this sophisticated prose style in the *Aghānī* are Abū al-Faraj's own extended interventions. Unlike the short comments he makes on his material, which do not differ greatly from the remarks earlier writers make in passing on the information they quote, these passages are apologetic in tone, serving to defend his evaluations of controversial poets and musicians,[21] or, in the case of the Preface, to justify his way of arranging the material in the book (*Agh.* I, pp.3–5). The tone in these interventions is committed, reminiscent of a *khuṭba* in its seeking to convince the reader, but the style is marked by the author's experience as a *kātib*, accustomed to drawing up and working with administrative documents. The parallelism is restrained, rhyme is virtually absent, but rhetorical figures – antithesis, paranomasia, apostrophe – and procedures – refutation, disposition – are regularly exploited. Abū al-Faraj stands here at the crossroads between *khuṭba, risāla* (in the sense of treatise) and restrained *inshā'*, and although he is almost certainly not alone in employing such a style, I suspect that it is characteristic of the age in which he lived, being later superseded by the much more ornate manner of al-Tawḥīdī, al-Ṣāḥib b. ᶜAbbād and their fellows.

As well as including some recent or contemporary material, the *Aghānī* can be designated as modern because of the way in which it is compiled. The earliest compilations are modest affairs, bringing together information on one clearly defined subject, such as Ibn al-Kalbī's (d.206/821) *Kitāb nasab al-khayl fī al-jāhiliyya wa-al-islām*, which lists the names and owners of famous horses among the pre-Islamic and early Islamic Arabs together with lines of poetry in which they are mentioned. The organisation of material around historical events, for example in Abū Mikhnaf's (d.157/774) *Maqtal al-Ḥusayn*, around people, as in Ibn Qutayba's (d.276/889) *Kitāb al-shiʿr wa-al-shuʿarā'*, or around abstract qualities and literary genres, both found in the same author's *ʿUyūn al-akhbār*, scarcely represents an advance in method, even if the scope of the books is more ambitious. By contrast, in his *Ṭabaqāt fuḥūl al-shuʿarā'*, Ibn Sallām al-Jumaḥī (d.231/845) goes further in ordering the "biographical" sections into groups based on stylistic criteria associated with pre-Islamic and Islamic manners of poetic composition.[22] Another case where the compiler can be seen to be working on two levels, that of the book as a whole and that of individual sections, is al-Jāḥiẓ's (d.255/869) *Kitāb al-bukhalā'*, in at least some parts of which the anecdotes need to be read not only separately but in the context of their sections for their full bearing on the book's theme to be understood.[23]

By Abū al-Faraj's time compilation had produced a monument, al-Ṭabarī's (d.310/923) *Tārīkh al-rusul wa-l-mulūk*. Not only is the scope of the book unequalled, its compiler has exploited the possibilities offered by the arrangement of material to express indirectly a personal comment on events and actors.[24] On a more modest level, al-Jahshiyārī's (d.331/943) *Kitāb al-wuzarā' wa-al-kuttāb* exemplifies the development of the compilation as a multi-purpose work; the procession of portraits of vizirs goes hand in hand with a history of the evolution of secretarial practice and a series of examples, all useful and some entertaining, of how an administrator can survive when his patron falls from favour or dies.

The *Aghānī* must be assessed as a compilation against the background of previous examples of the form. The first important point is that in integrating music into it, Abū al-Faraj has gone beyond his predecessors, who generally included both poetry and prose in their works but were not interested in singing. It is impossible for us now to appreciate the music of the *Aghānī*, but today's reader can still gauge from the frequency of the descriptions of melodies and the care taken to record variants how important that component of the work was. The earlier books of songs from which Abū al-Faraj quotes almost always consist, as far as can be judged, simply of the texts of songs with their melodic and rhythmic modes.[25] Isḥāq al-Mawṣilī's *Kitāb al-aghānī* might be thought to have provided a model for Abū al-Faraj's book of the same name, but the references to it in the *Aghānī* and the *Fihrist* indicate that it was organised on different lines. Ibn al-Nadīm describes it as being in ten parts, and lists the initial line of poetry in each one; this list bears no relation to the ordering of material in Abū al-Faraj's *Aghānī*. He also subscribes to Abū al-Faraj's verdict, which he reports, that the only genuine part of this *Aghānī* circulating under Isḥāq's name is the first one, on the legitimacy of listening to music (*al-rukhṣa*).[26] There is no such section in Abū al-Faraj's book, nor is there any place for it in the scheme he devised, although *akhbār* on the subject are scattered through various articles.[27] And he observes that the *Aghānī* ascribed to Isḥāq is no more than a compilation of the *dīwāns* of the Ancient poets which his son Ḥammād transmitted from him (*Agh*. XVII, p.112).

The book Isḥāq describes in his letter to ᶜAlī b. Hishām comes somewhat closer to Abū al-Faraj's *Aghānī*, at least as far as the content is concerned. Here is the passage:

> "And furthermore I am engaged in writing an entertaining, original book which includes the names, genealogies and countries of residence of eminent singers,[28] their economic situation and the period in which they lived, the differences between them in their manner of singing and composing,[29] some of the reports about them, and also the accounts of the well-known and memorable singing girls of the Ḥijāz, Kūfa and Baṣra, the poems which were composed about them, their owners, who bought them, and who their fans were. [I also mention] which legal experts and noble members of the community considered listening to music legitimate".(*Agh*. XVII, p.112)

Between this projected book and Abū al-Faraj's *Aghānī* there is considerable common ground, but there are also fundamental differences. Isḥāq is concerned exclusively with musicians and music, he does not mention ordering the material in any particular way (though it is possible that he did so), and because he was working about a century before Abū al-Faraj he had less material to draw on and fewer examples of types of compilation before him. I believe this description may have suggested to Abū al-Faraj the general idea of a Book of Songs, but that he then evolved a much more complicated scheme for it which integrated not only singers and music but also poetry, poets and important historical events into the general frame.[30]

Abū al-Faraj's attitude to compilation in the *Aghānī* is marked by a consistent search for diversity. The book falls into three parts. The first part is constructed round the list of the Top Hundred songs, each one of which introduces an article on its poet and composer (assuming they have not been treated before), the second round the names of royal composers, in chronological order, the articles on them being interspersed with those on the poets whose verse they set to music, and the third round songs chosen by Abū al-Faraj himself. The articles fall into four categories, according to subject: those on a historical event; those which treat a relationship (usually a love affair) between two people; those in which the introductory song forms the subject of all the *akhbār*, and those, by far the largest group, which are "biographical" in the broadest sense of the term, that is to say, focussed on a person. I am not taking into consideration here those articles, consisting of one or two *akhbār*, which are too fragmentary to fit into any classification, and those in the last volumes which are evidently unfinished.

As far as the composition of the individual articles is concerned, those which recount a historical event are easy to follow; its causes, development and aftermath are presented in chronological order, with few flashbacks. Digressions are rare and brief, unless they are already to be found in Abū al-Faraj's source. The articles on events quote at length from the *Ayyām al-ᶜarab*, the *Sīra* of Ibn Hishām, al-Ṭabarī and other early histories. Where Abū al-Faraj allows himself to rework his source, digress or add material from elsewhere, this may have the effect of an indirect commentary, as for instance in the article on al-Rabīᶜ b. Ziyād and the beginning of the war of Dāḥis and al-Ghabrā' (XVII, pp.179–208). In the version quoted in the *Aghānī*, the villain of the piece is Ḥudhayfa of the Banū Fazāra, who is killed in the end, but the article is rounded off with a line in which Ḥudhayfa is boasting of his exploits during another *yawm*, Dhū Ḥusā, of which he is the hero.[31] Abū al-Faraj's relativising the exploits and misdeeds of protagonists of the *ayyām* has the effect of creating a distance between them and the reader, and thus, so it seems to me, of throwing into relief the senselessness and cruelty of the conflicts.

The articles on relationships – of love or otherwise – are less obviously structured. Often they depict not a story which moves from the first meeting to the final break, but a series of specimens of behaviour: quarrels, reconciliations, moments of serene happiness, suspicions, exchanges of gifts. Since the *akhbār* depicting these incidents generally contain no indication as to when they occurred during the relationship, the compiler can be considered to have acted honestly in refusing to impose a chronological order on them. And these articles often end with poems devoid of a narrative frame. What is important is not the love story, or other relationship, in itself, but the patterns of behaviour and the models of literary expression which it offers. And their exemplary character is underlined by the absence of a narrative setting, which would inevitably confine them to a certain time and place.

The third category of articles are those organised around a song, that is to say that the song not only introduces the article but it reappears in each *khabar*. Thus the article can be read as the history of the song. This type of link has at times escaped the editors of the *Kitāb al-aghānī*, who have either tacked the *akhbār* on to the preceding article, or labelled them *akhbār mutafarriqa*, miscellaneous anecdotes.[32] In reality these articles trace the song's life from its composition on through the different occasions when it was performed, in a generally chronological order of *akhbār*, thus demonstrating the capacity of art to survive the vicissitudes of time, which is one of the recurrent motifs in the *Aghānī*.

The final category, by far the largest, is made up of "biographical" articles, in the loosest sense of the term. They vary from a couple of pages to a hundred or more in length, and they exemplify a number of methods of compilation. The difference in length is partly due to the amount of available material, but partly to the compiler's choices; Abū al-Faraj sometimes omits themes which he presumably judges inappropriate (for instance al-Ḥusayn b. ᶜAlī's murder in the article devoted to him) and he may emphasize others by including many similar *akhbār* to illustrate them. Space does not allow me to discuss the compilation of these articles in detail, but I will mention what I consider the main types as further proof of the diversity of methods Abū al-Faraj employs in the *Aghānī*.

(a) *Chronological organisation*. The article on Umm Ḥakīm, who was not averse to a drink, starts off with information about her grandmother and mother, their beauty and various marriages, before treating Umm Ḥakīm herself, her first marriage which ended in divorce, her second marriage to Hishām b. ᶜAbd al-Malik and her alcohol-friendly attitude. The last section treats what she left to posterity – her children and her cup, for long a valued item of the caliphal treasury (*Agh.* XVI, pp.274–81).

(b) *Organisation according to style.* In some cases *akhbār* which are evidently influenced by folk narrative traditions, or else have been reworked to enhance their literary qualities, are relegated to the end of an article. For instance, the section on Imru' ul-Qays consists chiefly of an account of his journey through the Arab tribes to seek support for his plan of vengeance, but closes with a story told during a *samar* organised by a governor about the poet's search for a bride, whom he tests by asking her riddles, and with an account of a dispute between the poet and a chieftain of Banū Asad anxious to protect the innocent members of his tribe from Imru' ul-Qays's vengeful wrath, where both parties express themselves in the balanced, rhythmic prose of Umayyad *khuṭbas* (IX, pp.77–101, 103–3, 103–5). Style is usually combined with other types of organisation, as in the article on Qays b. Dharīḥ, where the *akhbār* are also arranged along chronological and thematic lines (IX, pp.18–220).[33]

(c) *Organisation according to successive themes*. In Kuthayyir's article (IX, 3–39) an introduction on the poet's family is followed by a profile sketch of the subject himself, the critics' verdicts on his poetry, his slightly ridiculous appearance and behaviour, his Shīᶜī views, his panegyrics of the Umayyads, his love poems dedicated to ᶜAzza, his infidelities, death and burial. The article is rounded off with a *khabar* affirming the excellence of his poetry.

(d) *Alternation of themes*. Here sections on literary subjects (value of the poet's oeuvre, relation of the poems to the poet's actual experience) alternate with episodes of the subject's life, as in the treatments of Dhū al-Rumma (XVIII, pp.–52) and ᶜUmar b. Abī Rabīᶜa (I, pp.6–248). Such articles are reminiscent of those mediaeval paintings or icons in which the subject's portrait, his "essence", as it were, is surrounded by little scenes depicting characteristic incidents from his life. In the *Aghānī* articles, the poet's literary persona is at the centre.

(e) *Integral presentation*. In some articles on prominent poets and musicians of the ᶜAbbasid period there appears to be no organisation at all. Abū al-Faraj is here resorting to a technique which, for want of a better term, I designate "pointilliste". That is, each *khabar* he includes counts as a single brush-stroke, and together the *akhbār* constitute a picture of the subject in his entirety. Unlike a portrait, which the viewer can take in at one glance, a written text is read over time, and there is always a risk that what has been read will be forgotten. Hence, in these articles where Abū al-Faraj has chosen not to dissect the subject into themes or a series of chronological moments, the focus moves continuously from one aspect of his life and work to another. In such articles, however, analysis reveals a gradual change in the presentation of certain recurrent issues or characters; for instance, in Bashshār's article (III, pp.135–250) the caliph al-Mahdī is not mentioned until half way through, and the *akhbār* in which he appears trace the evolution of his attitude to the poet from friendship to suspicion and finally the decision to have him killed.

This list does not cover all the types of organisation found in *Aghānī* articles, nor the possibility of mixed forms. But it shows that Abū al-Faraj had a great variety of methods of compilation at his disposal, the fruit of experiments carried out by generations of compilers. It is worth noting, too, that a number of Abū l-Faraj's asides in the text refer to the decisions he took about arranging his material; they prove that on many occasions he was making conscious choices. The fullest of these asides introduces the article on Qays b. Dharīḥ, in vol. X, which has already been referred to, and it can be shown to correspond exactly to how the article turned out.

The last "modern" aspect of the *Aghānī* I will discuss concerns the *isnāds*. Abū al-Faraj is faithful to this technique of Muslim scholarship (unlike some of his contemporaries); he follows his teacher al-Ṭabarī in sometimes combining lists of authorities, but he does not leave them out – although later abridgements of the *Aghānī* usually do. But as some of his comments show, he considered that the *isnād* was not always a guarantee of the information contained in the *matn*. The most blatant example of an awareness of the *isnād's* limits comes in the first part of the article on Majnūn, ten pages (out of ninety odd) taken up with contradictory *akhbār* about the poet's historicity, name and mental state.[34] After this implicit demonstration of the technique's shortcomings Abū al-Faraj says, "I will now mention some admired sequences (*jumalan mustaḥsanatan*) of *akhbār* about him, without taking any responsibility for their authenticity (*mutabarriᵓan min al-ᶜuhdati fīhā*)", and continues for another 85 pages (II, pp.–95).

The *isnād* is also sometimes used to literary effect. The interruption of a *khabar* just after it has started in order to insert a new *isnād* heightens suspense. It can also permit a change of narrator from third to first person, as the following example shows:

> "I was told by Ibn ᶜAmmār and also by Wakīᶜ [. . .] on the authority of Saᶜīd b. Yaḥyā al-Umawī, who related the following information transmitted by al-Muḥabbar b. Qaḥdham via Hishām b. ᶜUrwa from ᶜUrwa's father: 'When al-Qāsim b. Muḥammad b. Abī Bakr and his sister arrived from Egypt',
>
> "And this information was also transmitted to me by Muḥammad b. Abī l-Azhar with a chain of authorities going back through Ḥammād b. Isḥāq, his father, al-Haytham b. ᶜAdī and

> ᶜAwāna to al-Qāsim b. Muḥammad b. Abī Bakr, who related: 'When Muᶜāwiya b. Ḥudayj al-Kindī and ᶜAmr b. al-ᶜĀṣ killed my father (i.e. Muḥammad b. Abī Bakr) in Egypt . . .'" (XX, p.316)

There are a number of such instances, although they do not always involve a change from third to first person narration, or *vice versa*.

And finally, I cannot escape the impression that Abū al-Faraj sometimes employs the precise, earnest scholarly technique of the *isnād* with his tongue in his cheek, when he combines it with anecdotes such as that of the poet al-ᶜUqayshir, who one day when visiting his usual tavern was cheated out of two dirhams by a woman pretending to be the tavern-keeper's wife. Later he learned that she was a well-known swindler called Umm Ḥunayn. The tavern-keeper agreed to give him some wine that day on credit, and he composed three lines on the incident, regretting his credulity and lamenting the loss of the money. The text continues: "ᶜAbdullāh b. Khalaf mentioned this anecdote on the authority of Abū ᶜAmr al-Shaybānī and expanded it as follows: 'The tavern-keeper was called Ḥunayn, and the woman swindler told al-ᶜUqayshir that she was Umm Ḥunayn, the mother of the tavern-keeper he dealt with, and so she was able to take two dirhams and make her escape'". ᶜAbdallāh then mentions the three lines already quoted, followed by eight, vividly describing Umm Ḥunayn committing adultery and being caught in the act by her husband. The anecdote continues with the tavern-keeper protesting at his mother being insulted, and the poet maintaining that he only meant the Umm Ḥunayn who cheated him, whoever she might be. Finally, the tavern-keeper buys his silence with two dirhams' worth of wine. (XI, pp.260–3)

On the one hand, then, Abū al-Faraj employs the *isnād* quite seriously as a technique of scholarship, like his teachers. And on the other, he sometimes takes a more detached attitude to it, implicitly calling its value into question, using it as a means to heighten suspense at the beginning of a *khabar*, or letting a discrepancy appear between the serious technique and the frivolous subject-matter it is applied to. This sophisticated attitude to the *isnād* is, I would argue, another indication of the "modernness" of the *Kitāb al-aghānī* – although it may well exist in other works of the 4th/10th century.

New kinds of material, new interests, the further development of techniques of compilation, a sophisticated attitude to the *isnād*, and of course a unique concern with music – these all make the *Kitāb al-aghānī* a modern book for its time, and help to explain its continuing popularity. And I do not doubt that other major works of the same period could also be shown to be modern for their time, if they were studied in detail. If this paper has aroused curiosity about the modernity of 4th/10th century Arabic prose literature, it will have served its purpose.

Notes

1. According to Ibn al-Nadīm, who knew him personally, Abū al-Faraj died in about 363/973 (Ibn al-Nadīm, *Al-fihrist*, ed. Riḍā Tajaddud, 3rd ed., Beirut, 1988, p.127). He completed his early book, the *Maqātil al-Ṭālibiyyīn*, in 313/925 and he may well have been working on the *Aghānī* from that time on. He did not finish it.
2. A preliminary attempt is Stefan Leder and Hilary Kilpatrick, "Classical Arabic prose literature: a researchers' sketch map", *JAL* XXIII (1992), pp.2–26, especially pp.16–23.
3. Cf. Alan Jones' discussion of pre-Islamic prose literature in the present volume.
4. Cf. Antonella Ghersetti, "Un tema sempre attuale: malgoverno e disonestà dei pubblici funzionari. Testimonianze nella letteratura d'*adab* del X secolo", *Oriente Moderno* N.s IX (1990), pp.10–114, which draws extensively on the *Faraj*.
5. Abū al-Faraj ᶜAlī b. al-Ḥusayn al-Iṣbahānī, *Kitāb al-aghānī*, 24 vols., Cairo 1927–1974. All references are to this edition. For al-Bāqiṭānī, see D. Sourdel, *Le Vizirat abbaside*, 2 vols, Damascus 1959–60, p. 302.
6. Cf. Albert Arazi, *Amour divin et amour profane dans l'Islam médiéval,à travers le diwan de Khālid al-kātib*, Paris 1990, pp.36–7. Ibrāhīm al-Najjār suggests that the mental instability of these poets was in part a consciously adopted pose; see Ibrāhīm al-Najjār, *Majmaᶜ al-dhākira aw shuᶜarā' ᶜabbāsiyyūn mansīyūn. Al-juz' al-thānī: masālik al-ghazal*, Tunis 1988, p.297 and op.cit. *Al-juz' al-thālith; bayna al-jidd wa-al-hazl*, Tunis 1989, p.415.
7. As depicted by Michael W. Dols, *Majnūn: the Madman in Medieval Islamic Society*, Oxford 1992, pp.362–3.
8. This is the conclusion the *Aghānī* article points to. Al-Najjār, op.cit., *Masālik al-ghazal*, pp.63–4, adds that his apparently poverty-stricken old age (he died aged over eighty) also affected his mental state. Cf. Arazi, op.cit., pp. 24–5.
9. Al-Najjār indicates Abū al-Faraj's role in rescuing Mānī and Juᶜayfirān from oblivion, op.cit., *Masālik al-ghazal*, p.293 and *Bayna l-jidd wa-l-hazl*, p.416.
10. Ibn al-Muᶜtazz, *Ṭabaqāt al-shuᶜarā'* ed. ᶜAbd al-Sattār Aḥmad Farrāj, 4th ed., Cairo 1981, pp.38–2 (Juᶜayfirān); 382–3 (Mānī *al-majnūn* [sic]); 404–6 (Khālid).
11. Muḥammad b. Dāwūd b. al-Jarrāḥ, *Al-waraqa*, ed. ᶜAbd al-Wahhāb ᶜAzzām and ᶜAbd al-Sattār Aḥmad Farrāj, Cairo 1953, does not include material on the three poets discussed here, but has sections on two other poets who are certainly eccentric, Abū l-Mukhaffif and al-Faḍl b. Hāshim b. Jadīr (pp.114–6 and 120–22). I thank Professor A.S. Gamal for drawing my attention to this source.

12. Muḥammad b. ᶜImrān b. Mūsā al-Marzubānī, *Muᶜjam al-shuᶜarāʾ*, ed. ᶜAbd al-Sattār Aḥmad Farrāj, Damascus, n.d., p.387 (Mānī). In this and the two preceding sources the compiler is essentially interested in the poetry, at least in these specific cases, and the prose information serves simply to create a context for the verses.
13. Aḥmad b. Muḥammad b. ᶜAbd Rabbih, *Al-ᶜIqd al-Farīd*, ed. Muḥammad Saᶜīd al-ᶜUryān, 8 vols., Cairo n.d., vol.VII, pp.142–166, especially pp.157–66.
14. ᶜAmr b. Baḥr al-Jāḥiẓ, *Al-bayān wa-al-tabyīn*, ed. ᶜAbd al-Salām Muḥammad Hārūn, 2nd ed., 4 vols., Cairo 1380/1960–138101961, vol.II, pp.225–77.
15. Arazi, op.cit., pp.266 ff. seems to imply that the *ᶜuqalāʾ al-majānīn* constituted a recognised category with mystical tendencies early on. Dols, op.cit., p.376, points out that the phenomenon is only supported by evidence from the 6th/12th century on.
16. A selection of such exchanges are preserved in Abū al-Faraj al-Iṣfahānī, *Al-imāʾ al-shawāᶜir*, ed. Jalīl ᶜAṭiya, Beirut 1404/1984.
17. The *Imāʾ al-shawāᶜir* includes one much earlier example of a prose exchange, between Danānīr and her master Muḥammad b. Kunāsa (p.55). But the notes quoted, which must date from before 207/823, the date of Ibn Kunāsa's death, are akin to *tawqīᶜāt* in their terse and pointed style.
18. For the existence of this book, see Manfred Fleischhammer, *Quellenuntersuchungen zum Kitāb al-Aġânî*, Habilitationsschrift, Halle (Saale), 1965, pp.110–1.
19. The vindictiveness of this passage may appear less gratuitous when it is recalled that Ibrāhīm b. al-Mudabbir was a prominent official and *nadīm* who spent some time in prison as a result of his rivals' intrigues.
20. For further discussion of this planned book, see below.
21. Abū Tammām (*Agh.* XVI, pp.383–4); Isḥāq al-Mawṣilī (V, pp.268–70); Ibrāhīm b. al-Mahdī (X, pp.95–7); ᶜArīb (XXI, pp.54, 56–7); Ibn al-Muᶜtazz (X, pp.274–7).
22. I adopt the interpretation of the term *ṭabaqa* put forward by A.S. Gamal in his paper in this volume.
23. Fedwa Malti-Douglas, *Structures of Avarice. The Bukhalāʾ in Medieval Arabic Literature*, Leiden, 1985, pp.46–55, and, for a discussion of the group of anecdotes told by the *masjidiyyūn*, Ibrāhīm Jiryis, "Qirāʾa fī qiṣṣat Muᶜādha al-ᶜAnbariyya", *Mawāqif*, (Al-Nāṣira), 3–4 (1993), pp.59–79.
24. See, for instance, the analysis of al-Ṭabarī's and al-Balādhurī's accounts of the murder of Khālid al-Qasrī in Stefan Leder, *Das Korpus al-Haiṯam ibn ᶜAdî (st.207/822). Herkunft, Überlieferung, Gestalt früher Texte der aḫbâr Literatur*, Frankfurt am Main 1991, pp.14–75; and of al-Ṭabarī's account of the fall of the Barmakids in Kees Versteegh, "De val van de Barmakiden volgens Ṭabarī", in Ed de Moor (ed.), *Elf wijzen van interpreteren. Essays over het lezen van teksten uit het islamitisch cultuurgebeid*, Nijmegen 1992, pp.117–26.
25. *Agh.* IX, pp.293–6, where Ḥammād b. Isḥāq al-Mawṣilī is the source for al-Wāthiq's songs; XIV, 190–1, where he is the source for Muḥammad al-Zaff's songs; XXIII, pp.79–80, where the songs of Abū Ḥashīsha which various caliphs liked best are quoted from a book by the composer/singer himself. Cf. Ighnāṭiyūs ᶜAbduh Khalīfa (ed.), *Mukhtār min Kitāb al-lahw wa-l-malāhī li-ibn Khurdādhbih*, (Nuṣūṣ wa-durūs 17), Beirut 1969, pp.25–6, 30–1, 33–5, 43–4.

26. Ibn al-Nadīm, op.cit., pp.158–9.
27. For further discussion of this point, see my *Abû l-Faraj al-Iṣbahânî as a sociologist and historian of literature*, Annual lecture of the Irene Halmos Chair of Arabic Literature, Tel Aviv University, 1994 (in the press).
28. This translation of "*al-qawm*" is dictated by the rest of the sentence.
29. As has been pointed out by J.E. Bencheikh, "Les musiciens et la poésie. Les écoles d'Isḥāq al-Mawṣilī (m.225 H.) et d'Ibrāhīm b. al-Mahdī (m.224 H.)", *Arabica* XXII (1975), p.114, the terms *mughannī* and *ghinā*ᵓ indicate not only singing but also composing and accompanying oneself on an instrument.
30. Ibn Khurdādhbih's opuscule mentioned above (n.25) comes quite close to Isḥāq's description, as far as it goes. Although Abū al-Faraj had a very low opinion of Ibn Khurdādhbih, he may also have taken this text into account when planning the *Aghānī*.
31. The *Aghānī* account of the war of Dāḥis and al-Ghabrā' follows very closely the text of the *Naqā'iḍ Jarīr wa-al-Farazdaq* (ed. A.A. Bevan, Leiden, 1905–12, vol.I, pp.83–98 = *Agh*, XVII, pp.187–208). The only significant divergence occurs right at the end. Whereas the *Naqā'iḍ* concludes with a poem by one of the victorious ᶜAbs, and then explains an allusion in its last line to Ḥudhayfa's underhand behaviour during Dhū Ḥusā, the *Aghānī* quotes all but the last line of the poem, mentions the occasion, Dhū Ḥusā, and then puts the final line in Ḥudhayfa's mouth, making him the boaster there instead of the ᶜAbsī. Given that the rest of the account is reproduced so accurately, it is unlikely that this is a copyist's error.
32. *Akhbār* attached to the preceding article: *Agh*, VI, pp.100–119, after ᶜAbādil's article, pp.96–100 (particularly carelessly, since the *ṣawt* introducing the independent section is one of the Top Hundred); XV, pp.104–110, which has nothing to do with al-Khansā' but treats al-Akhṭal's panegyric of Yazīd b. Muᶜāwiya when he protected him from the wrath of the Anṣār; XV, pp.254–262 and 262–265, which deal with an episode of the *ridda* wars in Bahrain and one of ᶜUmar b. Abī Rabīᶜa's adventures respectively, and have no connection with the early ᶜAbbasid singer Hāshim b. Sulaymān. *Akhbār mutafarriqa*: XII, 113–125, where more than one song forms the subject of the section; XV, pp.139–44, which focuses both on the *ṣawt* and on the historical occasion for its words. But some sections are appropriately entitled, e.g. IX, pp.6–76, "*Al-armāl al-thalātha al-mukhtāra*".
33. See my discussion of the composition of this article, "*Aḫbâr manẓûma*: the Romance of Qays and Lubnâ in the Aġânî" in Wolfhart Heinrichs and Gregor Schoeler (eds.), *Festschrift Ewald Wagner zum 65. Geburtstag. Band 2: Studien zur arabischen Dichtung*, Beirut/Stuttgart 1994, pp.350–361.
34. A. Khairallah, "Collective Composition and the Collector's Art. Observations on the Dîwân of Maǧnûn Lailâ", *La signification du Bas Moyen Age dans l'histoire et la culture du monde musulman*, Actes du 8me Congrès de l'Union Européenne des Arabisants et Islamisants (Aix-en-Provence 1976), Aix-en-Provence 1978, pp.12–2.

Part 3

Language

17

An Incomplete Egyptian Ballad on The 1956 War

Pierre Cachia
Columbia University

In the course of the field work which eventually led to the publication of my *Popular Narrative Ballads of Modern Egypt*[1], I made it a practice to ask as few leading questions as possible in order to let my informants reveal their own priorities. What emerged was that among the ballad-mongers who did not specialize in the epic cycle of the Hilālīs, by far the most popular themes were accounts of "honour crimes" in which fierce retribution is visited upon women who offend against the strict (if unequal) code of conduct still prevalent among the masses. Closely allied were other feats of bravery and violence, mainly motivated by revenge. Following at some distance were ballads of a religious character, either embroidering a Qur'anic story or recounting the deeds of a holy man.

Not once was I volunteered a song celebrating some national event and reflecting the kind of loyalty to the State which is very much in honour among the educated modernists – what Albert Hourani has defined[2] as "territorial nationalism" to distinguish it from pan-Arabism or pan-Islamism.

One of my informants was Muḥammad Ramaḍān Sayyid Aḥmad, known as Abū Drā^c -i.e., "the One-Armed." He was of peasant stock. His first home had been with his mother and stepfather, but when he was about five years old his father – whom he had not known before – claimed him and took him to Uṭūr in the district of Kafr ash-Shaykh near Ṭanṭā in the Delta. There he worked in the fields along with his father, and it was when trying to oil a water-wheel while it was turning that he lost his arm. At the age of nine, enamoured of song, he went – without his father's knowledge – to the greatest *mūlid* in Egypt, the one commemorating the birth of as-Sayyid al-Badawī in Ṭanṭā, and there he chanced to meet an uncle of his and persuaded him to take him to Cairo; but fearing that he would be returned to his father, he took to the streets where he made a living as a newspaper vendor. He then attached himself to a succession of folk singers and musicians until he could strike out as a performer on his own. Because the main outlet for folk literature is at the festivals of holy men whose burial places are scattered all over Egypt, most of his career involved travelling about the countryside, but in time he achieved such popularity that he transferred most of his activities to Cairo, where the pickings were greater.

It was there that I had several sessions with him. That was in 1972, during the month of Ramaḍān when Muslims who had fasted all day sought relief and entertainment well into the night. Abū Drā^c and his troupe, which included several musicians and at least one female singer, occupied the stage in a temporary pavillion erected just outside a coffee-shop in the vicinity of the mosque of al-Ḥusayn, the grandson of the Prophet. A modest entrance fee was charged, refreshments could be ordered from the café waiters, and patrons who wanted to honour a companion would send their request to the stage along with an appropriate sweetener, and the performer would oblige even at the cost of interrupting his song.

Abū Drā^c was proud of the fact that he had performed six times in the presence of President ^cAbd an-Nāṣir, who had made him a member of the "Military Theatre" (*al-Masraḥ al-^cAskarī*) – apparently a sinecure – at a salary of thirty Egyptian pounds a month. He therefore seemed to me the likeliest source for the kind of nationalistic ballad which might have rounded off my collection, and I asked him if he had any to offer. He was not clear what I meant, and asked, "Like what?" I specified: "Something about one of the recent wars against outsiders." "Ah, yes," he replied. "I myself have composed one about the Battle of Port-Said," which had been fought in 1956. He could not undertake to sing it there and then since he was about to take the stage, but at my request he began to recite it into my tape-recorder.

The form it took was that of the *mawwāl ṣa^cīdī*, which I have described at some length in my book and even more fully in an earlier article.[3] The metre is basically the *basīṭ*, but with the classical hemistich functioning as a complete line and with the *fā^cilun* foot sometimes shortened to *fa^clun* not only at the end of the line but also within it – i.e.

Not all lines scan perfectly, and in my transcription I faithfully reproduce Abū Drā^c's rendering even when a slight change in vocalization or an allowable alternative would bring it closer to metrical regularity – as, for example, in line 14 where *ᶜašra li-miyya* would scan better than his *u ᶜašara li-miyya*.

More stringently observed are the demands of the rhyme. When the *mawwāl ṣaᶜīdī* is used as a lyrical song, it usually consists of a thirteen-line fixed form poem with the rhyme scheme:

a a a b c b c b c z z z (z)a

i.e. having a last line that rhymes with the first, but often containing an internal 'z' rhyme as well. For narrative purposes, the entire thirteen-line unit may be used as a stanza, but more commonly (as in the present instance) it is stretched out by adding any number of alternately rhyming sestets before the final tercet, the final line still rhyming with the first even if hundreds of lines have intervened.

Moreover, it is a matter of pride for the poet to elaborate every rhyme into a polysyllabic and extremely complicated paronomasia, of a kind unrecorded in classical Arabic and known to the folk practicioners as *zahr*, i.e. "flower." This is achieved by deliberate distortion of the normal pronunciations: vowels may be altered, dropped, lengthened or shortened, gemination is treated cavalierly, and glottal stops are often elided. Even differences of dialect are pressed into service for this purpose. Thus in the two interlaced sets occurring between lines 56 and 61 of this text, the 'g' sound occurs in words belonging to different registers of Egyptian Arabic, as will be specified below. In the end, the only stable and readily recognizable element in the pun is the succession of consonants.

It has to be said that the artifice monopolizes a good deal of the artist's resources, that the wording of entire lines is often strained as a result, and that the puns themselves are so obscure that some researchers have worked on similar texts without realizing that they were faced with a demanding play on words and not with mere repetition.

In my transcription, I have added to each of these puns, between square brackets, the form in which the words would normally appear in prose, at least insofar as I have been able to make them out.

All these features necessitate a meticulous system of transcription. The Arabic script is ill-suited to the representation of a colloquial text, mainly because it veils or disguises variations in pronunciation and departures from classical norms. Besides, the colloquial has a number of phonemes that are not recognized by classical scholars, including more of what are termed "dark," "emphatic," or "pharyngalized" consonants than occur in the alphabet, such as the 'm' in *m̱ayya* (water), and even the 'r' in *gâr̲î* (my neighbour) as against the 'r' in *gârî* (current). After experimenting with several systems of transliteration, I opted – mainly because it avoids digraphs – for Brockelmann's, with some extensions which Arabists will readily recognize (such as the underlined 'm' in the example already given) and only two radical departures: to avoid too many variations of the 'h', I have borrowed from our Spanish colleagues the 'x' for Arabic *khāᵓ* and adopted 'ğ' for its voiced equivalent, the *ghayn*. In addition, two letters of the Arabic alphabet call for special treatment. They are *jīm* and *qāf*, which are pronounced differently in different parts of Egypt, but which – as has already been pointed out – may occur in the same text. In Cairo and broadly in the North or Lower Egypt, they become 'g' and a glottal stop respectively. In what is usually termed Upper Egyptian or Ṣaᶜīdī pronunciation but would be better described a "provincial" since it is heard also in the villages of the Delta, they become 'j' and 'g' respectively. To reduce confusion, I transliterate *jīm* as either 'g' or 'j' following the performer's usage, but represent the *qāf* by 'q' when it is reduced to a glottal stop, by 'ḡ' when it is used for punning with Cairene *jīm*, and also by 'ḳ' on the few occasions when the performer affects the classical pronunciation.[4]

Here, then, is what Abū Drāᶜ recited:

MAᶜRAKIT BUR SAᶜÎD
THE BATTLE OF PORT-SAID

qûlû li-ᵓingilṭira ᵓilli lina xadnâh [xaḍḍâna]
Tell England, which is acting scary towards us
bahṛıkum fi s-siyâsa kan ğawîṭ xadnâh [xuḍnâh]
Deep was your sea in politics, [but] we've waded through!
ma hu l-kanâl kamân kan min ḥaqqina xadnâh
Why! The Canal was ours by right, and we've seized it.
li l-ğarbı wayya ṣ-ṣahayna xiṭṭa dâbirha [dabbarha]
The West has a plot it has hatched with the Zionists
ᶜašân niḥârib maᶜâhum wi l-kanâl nisibûh [nisîbuh]
To make us engage in war with them, and abandon the Canal.
yîgu l-ingilîz ᶜa l-kanâl yiḥtallu ḡal dâbirha [da barrıha]
The English come to the Canal to occupy it – you'd think it was their land,
lâkin raᵓisna gamâl ṣâḥi li-hum nisibûh [naṣṣabûh]
But our President Gamal was awake to them. He was set high.
bi faḍl rabbi qaṭaᶜna l-kullı dâbirha
Thanks to my Lord, we have extirpated it all.

wi l-ʿarabi ʿand il-kifâḥ nâsil is-silâḥ nisibûh [nâsi ʾabûh]
For an Arab in battle, with weapon drawn, forgets his [own] father.
xaṭab raʾisna fi l-azhar sa nuḳâtilhum
In the Azhar mosque, our President proclaimed: We shall fight them
l-agl iš-šaraf wi l-karâma wi hiyya ḥurriyya [ḥariyya]
For the sake of honour and self-esteem, which are worth it.
wâḥid li ʿašara bi ʾizn a͟l͟lâh nuqâtilhum [niʾti lhum]
[Even] one against ten, by God's leave, we shall meet them.
ya mutna šuhda ya ʿišna ʿêša ḥurriyya
We shall either die as martyrs or live a life of freedom.
u ʿašara li miyya bi ʾizn a͟l͟lâh nuqâtilhum [niqtilhum]
[Even] ten to a hundred, by God's leave, we shall kill them.
wi f bur saʿîd fi l-ḳitâl ḥaribna biḥurriyya [? baḥriyya]
[In] Port Said, in battle, we fought a navy
wi bur saʿîd kânit bi d-dammı ḥurriyya [ḥarrîqa]
And Port-Said in battle was avid for blood.
il-gêš yimût ʿa l-kanâl bi ʾamrı m ilʾabṭâl [?il-qubṭân]
The soldiers die on the Canal by order of the (?) Captain.
wi sabaq il-ʾusṭûl li l-fidaʾiyyîn yaḥmîha
The fleet hastened to the commandos, to protect them –
ʿašara li miyya wi zâyda himmit ilʾabtâl [il-battâl]
Ten to a hundred, the efforts of the evil one increasing.
wi maṣrı fi ʾamân wi qâm mandûb yaḥmîha [yiḥammîha]
Cairo was safe, but a representative came forth to rouse it.
wi f bur saʿîd it-tarîx bi ymaggid il-ʾabṭâl
In Port-Said, history is glorifying the heroes.
min šaʿb wa bulîs wi gêš il-ʾumma yaḥmîha [yâ ḥimâha]
[Drawing on] people, police, and army – how inviolate is the nation!
fi bur fuʾâd il-maṭâr gabbâna wi ddâyir[5] [id-dêr]
In Port-Fuad, the aerodrome, the Gabbana, and the monastery
kullı firqa bi tinzil fi barašuṭṭât
Unit after unit comes down in parachutes.
fi bur fuʾâd il-maṭâr gabbâna wi ddâyir [id-dêr]
In Port-Fuad, the aerodrome, the Gabbana, and the monastery.
ṣâḥib id-dinya mîn ya mḥarrar min iššuṭṭât [iš-šaṭaṭ]
Who is it who controls the world [I ask you] who are free of excesses?
da fi l-qitâl fi l-kanâl kinnu gaḥîm narha [naqarha]
The fighting on the Canal was like an inferno belabouring it.
sâmiʿ ʾazîz ir-ruṣâṣ kan raʿdı ṭalqitna
One could hear the whizzing of bullets – our volley was thunder.
il-mitrayûz wi l-banâdiq bi l-ʾulûf narha [narâha]

Machineguns and rifles one could see by the thousands.
ḥarb il-fanâˀ ˀaw bak̤âˀ bi n-naṣr ṭalqitna [ṭallı ˀatâna]
A war of extinction, or survival with a victory that loomed and came to us.
muk̤âwmit iš-šaᶜbı ṣabbat ᶜa l-ᶜadu narha
The people's resistance poured its fire on the enemy.
tiqûl sibûᶜa maḥbusîn wi s-sawra ṭalqitna [ˀaṭlaqitna]
You might say they were caged lions that the Revolution released.
min dâr ˀilâ dâr u min ḥayy il-qitâl ilâ ḥayy
From house to house, and from one embattled quarter to another
yâ mâ staǧâsu l-ᶜida min hôlı ḍarbitna
How the enemy sought succour from the terror of our blows!
talat firaq li l-ingilîz ma faḍalš minhum ḥayy
Of three English units not one man was left alive.
baᶜatulna ᶜašara firaq ḥakkimit ḍarbitna [dâyir betna]
They sent us ten units that took firm positions round our home.
kan id-difâᶜ mustamît wi n-nabî ˀallâh ḥayy [ḥayya]
Desperate was the defence – and God honoured the Prophet!
d aḥna ᶜarab li l-qitâl wi l-ḥarbı ḍarbitna [durbitna]
For we are Arabs – fighting and warfare our wont.
fôq il-manâzil ḥarîm fôq il-midân ᶜalmâˀ [ᶜulamâˀ]
On top of the houses were women, [towering] over the battlefield were the ulema,
wi fi š-šawâriᶜ biḥêra min dammı ᶜaddîna [ˀaᶜâdîna]
And in the streets a pool of our enemies' blood.
bi nḥibbı ḥarb iš-šaraf ḥubb il-ᶜaṭaš ᶜa l-mâˀ
We love an honourable war as keenly as thirst loves water.
fôq ḍaḥâya l-ᶜadu bi r-rigl ᶜaddîna [ᶜaddêna]
Over the enemy victims, on foot we crossed.
tinḥiris il-manzala[6] fi qaṭᶜ il-ᶜida ᶜalmâˀ [ᶜallâma]
May Lake Manzala be guarded, so expert in cutting down the foe,
wi bur saᶜîd tinšakar ṣaddat ᶜaddîna [ᶜudwânna]
And may Port-Said be thanked that turned back aggression.
wi galâl disûqi nasaf gêš il-ᶜida filmayy [fi l-mayya]
Galal Disuqi blew up the enemy force in the water,
u bi l-madâfiᶜ yidâfiᶜ kull sanya ˀiddini [tdinn]
Defending with cannon which every moment reverberated.
bi tnen mudammarât ᶜand it-tarîx filmayy [fallı miyya]
With two destroyers, in a historic moment, he downed a hundred.
gat bawârig li birṭanya ma gûš ˀiddini [qaddna]
British battleships came, but did not measure up to us.

infarag iṣ-ṣabâḥ li l-ʿurûba min ʿama ʾiddini [ʾîdin]
The morning brought relief to Arabs from Eden's blindness.
50   iskindiriyya ma fî-š ṭayyâra bi t-ʿaddî
In Alexandria, not one plane got past.
       fi l-mîna nâṣir wi ẓâfir fâtiḥ il-mirṣâd
In the harbour, Nasir and Zafir had open gunsights.
       qâyid ʿalêh il-gunûd fi n-nâr bitʿaddi [bi tuʿadd]
[There was] a leader who, under fire, was responsible for the soldiers,
       ǧêr iṭ-ṭawâbi ʾalât il-ḥarbi bilmirṣâd [bi l-murrı ṣâdda]
As well as fortresses and instruments of war in bitter defence.
       yom ṭallat minnu ʾisraʾîl wi faransa bitʿaddi [bi t-taʿaddi]
On the day when Israel and France looked on aggressively,
55   illi tiqarrab bi-tiǧraq w iḥna bi l-mirṣâd
Any that came forward was sunk, for we were on the alert.
       aṣl iṭ-ṭayyarât ʿandîna wi slaḥna min gawwi [guwwa]
For we had planes, and our weaponry was stored inland
       niʿuzha baʿdên ʾiza ʿtada l-ʿadu nigi lîh
For we might want them later, and if the enemy attacked we would step forward to him
       min ṭayyarât mîg sarîʿa w naffasât gawwi
Including fast Mig planes and aerial rockets.
       li l-xâyin illi ʿtadaʾ bn il-waṭan nigilîh [niglîh]
As for the treacherous national who attacks us, we polish him off.
60   wi mugrim il-ḥarbi fi l-gamʿiyya kan marîḍ ǧawwi [qawi]
In the [United Nations] Assembly the war criminal was as if seriously ill.
       raḥ maglis il-ʾamn yixraṣ bi l-lisân iǧilîh [yiqûl êh]
He went to the Security Council but his tongue was silenced – what could he say?
       amar iš-šiblı ṭalab igtimâʿ gamʿiyya dawliyya
The lion gave orders, demanded an international meeting
       wi kullı mandûb yimassil dawlitu fîha [yifîh]
Where each delegate would represent his country and speak out.
       ana ʿarabi aṣîl wi yôm in-naṣrı dawliyya [dawa liyya]
I am a true Arab, and the day of victory to me was a healing draught.
65   ʿala ʾisraʾîl il-karîha l-môt ḥalâl fîha [fahqa]
As for hateful Israel, a gasping death is licit for it.
       illi malak ingilṭirra muš râgil dawliyya [di wiliyya]
The one ruling England is not a man, it's a she!
       wi faransa balad il-ʿagab šuft il-ʿagab fîha
And of France, the land of wonders, I indeed saw a wonder!

waqfa šu^{c}ûb il-^{c}âlam yiwaggihu l-^{ɔ}inzâr
The peoples of the world took a stance, addressing a warning.
ṭalabu min ingilṭira waqf il-qitâl ma rḍûš
They demanded of England a cease fire – they refused.
di šu^{c}ûb il-^{c}âlam il-ḥurrı t^{ɔ}ayyidna
The peoples of the free world are backing us
w iṭṭallaqu fi l-ḳitâl fi ṣ-ṣaffı wayyâna [wayy ^{ɔ}annu]
They set forth to the struggle, standing in ranks – Ah, they lamented.
taḥya l-^{c}urûba da n-naṣrı ^{ɔ}itḥakkamit ^{c}alêh ^{ɔ}idna
Long live Arabism! The grasp of our hand is firm on victory
fi l-ḳurâ wi tara maramîh wayyâna
Throughout the villages, and its extent is visible with us.

The recitation was not without a few hiccoughs. Abū Drā^{c} hesitated a little at line 15, where the rhyme word is either a repetition of the one in line 13 or is a particularly awkward paronomasia, and line 16 may be presumed to be a correction or an alternative, since rhyming lines ought not to follow each other at this point. There was another lapse at line 25, which is a repetition of line 23, and the sestet to which they both belong is left unfinished. There should also be a line rhyming with *fil̠mayy* between lines 48 and 49. But it is at line 68 that the pattern began seriously to break apart. Both it and the next line are left without rhyming partners. Abū Drā^{c} halted briefly in the middle of line 71, and soon after he had to stop altogether. He called on members of his troupe to help, but none could remember how the ballad ended, and he had to give up.

Now in previous sessions with me, and earlier in the same session, Abū Drā^{c} had recorded without faltering dozens of short folk songs and two full-length narrative ballads, one his own version of "Šafîqa w Mitwalli"[8] – a notorious "honour crime" based on an event that had taken place in 1925 – and a composition which he attributed to one of his early teachers and which tells the story of a holy man.[9] Yet in this instance, only sixteen years after the event that the ballad was intended to celebrate, his memory had failed him. Surely this indicates that, unlike those other songs, it had dropped out of his repertoire. Coupled with the fact that no other performer had offered me anything comparable, this invites the inference that the patriotic themes which inform so much of the elitist writings of the educated modern Arabs have little currency with the public that is served by the folk literature.

No less weighty and heavy with implications is the evidence here provided of the major role played by memory in the transmission of Arab folk texts. Humans are indeed capable of much greater retentiveness than literate people are inclined to believe. Reliance on memory is very much a part of traditional Islamic education, and among the unlettered it is both necessary and generally expected. Great feats of memorization are attributed alike to great scholars and to the early *rāwis*[10] whose oral transmission of pre-Islamic poetry was deemed by such as Ibn Qutayba[11] to be more reliable than the written record.

Some of these feats may well have been exaggerated, but so is Western scepticism concerning them. I owe to Professor L. P. Harvey the information that in sixteenth century Spain a Morisco narrator of prose romances named Ramón Ramírez, who along with many others had had to profess Christianity but who admitted to having at times observed some Islamic rites, fell into the clutches of the Inquisition in 1595, died while imprisoned four years later, was subsequently convicted of heresy and had his bones dug up and burned. What is significant here is that one of the causes of his downfall was precisely his memory, for his tormentors presumed that it must have been diabolical assistance that "enabled him to recite long passages from novels of chivalry (and other books) when he did not have the actual text before him."[12]

To such long-rooted incredulity among Westerners, modern scholarship has added a new dimension. The study of Western folk literature has been much illumined by the Parry-Lord theory of oral-formulaic composition, and scholars are keen to assert its validity and universality. Some, such as Michael Zwettler and James Monroe, have made brave attempts at detecting traces of the technique in early Arabic poetry, and not in the pre-Islamic period alone. The temptation is strong to assume that it is the mainstay of Arabic folk literature also. I have in fact received an invitation to contribute to a special number of the *Journal of Mediterranean Studies* which sets out not as a proposition to be investigated but as a "given" from which to start that "the Mediterranean is a region where folk-poetry, singing, and extemporizing in music and words/texts, has both a long tradition and a living presence . . . . Folk-poetry has also been associated with the growth of nationalism and 'national identity.'" Do the facts bear this out?

Improvization is of course by definition oral composition, although not necessarily formulaic, and there are indeed indications that some Egyptian performers do improvize. It is consistent with the Parry-Lord theory that these are mostly specialists of the Hilālī epic cycle, and at least one of them is reported to have memorized formulaic phrases he did not understand[13]; but the phenomenon is rarer among the balladmongers who were the objects of my immediate interest. Even this generalization, however, is too sweeping, for one finds within the same tradition artists who have different priorities and different skills. Some performers go for musical and metrical regularity, others for the dramatic potential of the story they have to tell. Some are more responsive than others to the mood of their public. The end-products, therefore, can scarcely be expected to conform to one pattern, and I have noted elsewhere[14] some of the variations. But the kind of *mawwāl* presented here, with its demanding puns and complicated rhyme scheme, I have never known to be the result of anything but careful composition and memorization.

I have in fact heard Abū Drā^{c} sing unrehearsed compliments to members of his audience, but these invariably consisted of punning tercets. And when I did question him about more extensive improvization, his response – perhaps making a virtue of necessity – was supercilious: "Those are games that peasants play. *I* am an artist!"

Of course oral composition and improvization are linked but not necessarily co-extensive terms. The fact that an illiterate poet may compose a ballad orally and then commit it to memory has long been recognized, and scholars have sought the hallmark of oral composition – the formula – in poetry that has come down to us in written form, and even in compositions produced long after writing had come into wide use. But the most extensive cases have been made only by stretching the "formula" almost to include regular grammatical constructions. Of the more stringent kind of formula that could convincingly form a building brick for a sung narrative, I find little evidence, at least in this kind of *mawwāl*. The verifiable fact is that several of the performers I was able to question had a repertoire of hundreds of songs which they acknowledged they had learned by rote, some picked out of a book, even the illiterate among them calling on the services of literate acquaintances to help them in the process of memorization.[15] Furthermore, if the mainstay of the oral composer is the possession of a stock of set formulae and if, as is evident, the overwhelming interest of the *mawwāl*-poet is the *zahr*, then it is not irrelevant to stress that I have hardly ever come across the same pun in different compositions.

On these puns I have another observation to offer, not immediately related to orality but relevant to Western assumptions. Western writers on the subject make much of the power of a paronomasia to bring to mind a multiplicity of notions or images that may have a bearing on the context. Such indeed may be the effect on the listeners of a *mawwāl* as they strain to make out the intricacies of the wordplay, but what they rack their brain for is to pick out the form that best fits the slot, and whenever one discusses the matter with the practicioners of the art, they invariably assign a precise meaning to the homonyms at each of their separate appearances. In the present instance, I noticed that Sir Anthony Eden's name in the distorted form in which it occurs at the end of line 49 could also – appropriately in that context – be taken to be *id-dani* (the vile one). When I raised this point with Abū Drā^c^, he conceded that that was also possible, but in such a dismissive way that I was left with the distinct impression that the *double entendre* had not been in his own mind.

To conclude: I was at the time greatly disappointed not to have a sample of a patriotic ballad to include in my survey of the genre. Yet it is the fact that this particular text had slipped out of its author's memory that I now want to use as a peg for making two far-reaching observations, which are also two earnest appeals to the community of Arabists and Arab scholars.

The first arises from the manifest unpopularity of the theme. Almost inevitably, it is the written literature of the modern Arab élite that reaches out beyond the borders of the Arab world and that penetrates both the ivy-covered walls of Western universities and the ivory towers of even Arab academia. It is easy then to assume that the picture it draws of Arab modernist concerns is also an index of the forces at work in the entire society. A look at contemporary folk literature is a useful, indeed a necessary, corrective to this assumption, and I contend that a study of it *and* of the colloquial forms of the language in which it occurs ought to be an integral part of any programme of modern Arabic studies. There must be an end to "surveys of modern Arabic literature" that make not even a tangential reference to this other vast field of Arab creativity.

This in turn stresses the need to encourage field research in Arab folk literature, and extensive recording of it. The material may not be to everyone's taste, but it has much light to throw on Middle Eastern culture, and possibly on folk arts in general. There is an opportunity here to observe a live phenomenon that has died elsewhere, and the urgency lies precisely in the fact that it too is changing rapidly under changing conditions, and may well be approaching the end of its span.

My second *cri de coeur* is this: Even as I welcome all who are willing to labour in this vineyard, I must urge them not to rush into theory, especially not ready-made theories, and least of all theories that assume the universality of whatever conforms with European or Western reality, for the temptation is then strong to bend the evidence to one's pet notions. The subject is immense, the work done in it as yet minimal. A strong foundation of fact is yet to be laid, and generalizations ought to be guarded and confined to the area that has been thoroughly investigated. My own research, specifically in the field of the narrative ballad, has so far uncovered more diversity than uniformity alike in methods of composition and transmission as in the formation and status of the balladmongers and the character of their performances.

The academic mind is enamoured of consistency and seeks regular patterns everywhere, but perhaps it needs to be reminded that reality is not always as neat as we should like it. It ought not to surprise even the most cloistered of us to discover that artists are often strongly individualistic and that tradition is seldom monolithic, so that in matters of art even more than in other pursuits, conformity is not necessarily the supreme rule, and the researcher's richest rewards are not always the well-tried recipes.

Notes

1. Oxford, Clarendon Press, 1989, hereafter *Ballads.*
2. In *Arabic Thought in the Liberal Age*, Oxford University Press, 1962.
3. *Ballads*, pp. 3–34, and "The Egyptian Mawwāl – its Ancestry, its Development, and its Present Forms", *Journal of Arabic Literature*, 8 (1977), pp. 77–103.
4. The modifications are:

   - the underlining of a number of consonants, such as *m* and *r* not recognised as "dark" or velarized in classical Arabic.
   - additional vowels ê and ô, long, replacing the diphthongs *ay* and *aw* of classical Arabic.
   - the use of an undotted *i* (ı) for the neutral vowel used to break a consonantal cluster or to regularize the metre.
   - the distinction between the various ways in which *qāf* is pronounced, as mentioned in the main text.
   - the distinction between the two ways in which *jīm* is pronounced: g (without the diacritical in Brockelmann) for Cairene, j for "Upper Egyptian" pronunciation.
   - mainly to avoid having too many variations of the same Latin letter, Brockelmann's symbol for *khā*ᵓ is replaced by x.
   - for typographical reasons, *dhāl* and *thā*ᵓ are represented by ḏ and ṯ, but only when the performer pronounces them in classical fashion.

   The text is transcribed exactly as pronounced, without any attempt to make it fit either a classical or a supposed colloquial norm. A complete table of the symbols used follows, with their equivalents in Arabic script.

'	ء	ḇ	ب
'	ع	d	د or ذ
a	َ	ḏ	ذ
â	ا	ḍ	ض
b	ب	ê	يَ

f	ف	š	ش
g	ج (Cairene) *or* ق (provincial)	t	ت or ث
h	ه	t̲	ث
ḥ	ح	ṭ	ط
i	ِ	u	وُ
î	يِ	û	وُ
ı *or* (i)	schwa	w	و
j	ج	x	خ
k	ك	ğ	غ
ḳ	ق	y	ي
l	ل	z	ز
l̲	ل	ẓ	ظ or ض
m	م		
m̲	م		
n	ن		
ô	وْ		
q	ق		
r	ر		
r̲	ر		
s	س or ث		
ṣ	ص		

5. Newspaper reports mention only three areas in the vicinity of Port-Said where parachutists were dropped: Port-Fuad, the aerodrome of al-Jamīl, and the Jabbana. This last word means "cemetery".
6. Some parachutists were reported to have fallen into the lake.
7. Possibly a reference to a report that "an Israeli" named Leonardo Alfred was arrested for signalling with an electric torch during an air-raid.
8. Two other versions of the story are in *Ballads*, pp. 268–322.
9. "ğarîb" in *Ballads*, pp. 268–322.
10. See George Makdisi, *The Rise of Humanism in Classical Islam and the Christian West*, Edinburgh University Press, 1990, p. 202.
11. *Kitāb al-Shiᶜr wa al-Shuᶜarā'*, Beirut, Dār al-Thaqāfa, 1964, introduction, p. 26; also *Introduction au Livre de la Poésie et des Poètes*, introduction, traduction et commentaire par Gaudefroy-Demombynes, Paris, Société d'Édition "Les Belles Lettres", 1947, p. 20.
12. L.P. Harvey, "Oral Composition and the Performance of Novels of Chivalry in Spain", *Forum for Modern Language Studies*, X, 3 (July 1974), pp. 270–286, especially pp. 272 and 278.

13. Susan Slyomovics, *The Merchant of Art*, Berkeley, University of California Press, 1987, p. 29.
14. *Ballads*, pp. 36–48.
15. *Ballads*, pp. 50–51, 167.

18

Mysticism in Arabic Writing

Kinga Dévényi
Budapest

0. "One should not think that one can get at the secret of letters with the help of logical reasoning. One gets to it with the help of vision and divine aid".[1]

Where there are secrets, efforts are always made to reveal them. This is what is meant by the title 'Mysticism in Arabic writing'. In want of divine aid I cannot aim at disclosing the secret of letters in the following paper. I shall, however, endeavour to present an outline of the different mystical activities concerned with Arabic writing, analyzing the different features of this writing and trying to connect them to the emergence of these different activities.

There are several branches of mysticism that can be mentioned in connection with writing and likewise they can have a great number of possible and probable sources. Without aiming at an exhaustive list of these branches, we shall try to mention a few important ones.

1. Branches of mysticism connected to writing

1.1 Separate letters

1.1.1 The alphabet

One large territory of mysticism present in all the major Semitic writing systems is related to the alphabet, the order of the letters in it, the magical power of the letters, which is often related to their different numerical values, and the meaning of the names of the letters.[2] These alleged meanings can range from the mystical to the erotic, with a wide variety of shades within them, one saying for example that these are the names of the devils and another stating for example that these are the names and attributes of God, hence we have for *bāʾ* the meaning "*bahjat Allāh*" (the splendour of God).[3] In an erotic explanation the same *bāʾ* means "a man who very frequently has intercourse."[4]

1.1.2 Initials

Mention must be made here of the *psychological* reality of initials as well in writing and in speech, too, but perhaps in this respect writing enjoys primacy. In mystical literature certain letters as initials of a word or a whole phrase are used by metonymy in place of the whole word or phrase, so *nūn* stands for *naṣr* "victory", and *ṭāʾ* for *ṭalab al-ḥaqq wa-l-ḥaqīqa* "the search for truth and reality".[5]

One of the most famous mystical letter interpretations is associated with the letter *qāf*, meaning the "Mount *Qāf*", the mythical mountain that surrounds the world. Without dwelling any further on its implications in mystical literature, suffice it to mention here, that in the popular belief it was the letter *qāf* itself which gave its name to the mountain.[6]

1.1.3 Letter symbolism in poetry

Still staying within the framework of individual letters, we must mention letter symbolism in poetry in general, and in Sufi poetry in particular.

Let me quote only two of the many examples. The first is a line from Bakr ibn an-Naṭṭāḥ, using *lāmalif* as a simile:

innī raᶜaytuka fī nawmī tuᶜāniqunī
kamā yuᶜāniqu lām al-kātibi l-alifā[7]

The second is from the *tāʾiyya* of the great mystical poet Ibn al-Fāriḍ where he speaks about the letter *bāʾ* and its point, a question to which we shall return later. It runs as follows:

wa-law kunta bī min nuqṭati l-bāʾi khafḍatan
rufiᶜta ilā mā lam tanalhu bi-ḥīlatī[8]

1.2 Numerical value

Another enormous branch of mystical activity is linked to the numerical value of the characters. It appears in innumerable varieties in the Arab world throughout the ages.

1.2.1 *ᶜilm al-abjad*

One type of speculations is called *ᶜilm al-abjad*, gematria, and is linked to the great Greek mathematician Pythagoras, as well as to Jewish kabbala[9] and ancient Mesopotamia.[10] But since it was practised by Muslims, it is linked to the Qurᵓān as well. According to these mystics, the secrets of the world are hidden in the numerical value of the letters.

Jus to given an example,[11] there is a special relationship between the numerical values of the letters in the word *rakiba* (*r-k-b* : 200-20-2), and this special relation in a given text, which is usually a page of the Qurᵓān, gives a magical light and a magic dimension to this word.

These mystics, practising the "science of the alphabet" are among those who prepared magic squares with numerals or letters or both.[12]

1.2.2 *ᶜilm al-jafr*

Another field where the numerical value of letters receives great emphasis is the *ᶜilm al-jafr*, which, deviating from its original form of esoteric knowledge of an apocalyptic nature, reserved to the *imāms* who were the heirs and successors of ᶜAlī, became assimilated to a divinatory technique accessible to the wise, whatever their origin, particularly to the mystics.[13] In the writings belonging to this genre, and among them in the first place al-Būnī's (d. 1225) *Shams al-maᶜārif*, one finds the occult properties of (*ᶜilm al-abjad*) and isopsephy (*ḥisāb al-jummal*), the indication of the numerical value of a name which one wishes to keep secret, the transposition of letters in a single word, for the purpose of forming another word, the combination of letters composing a divine name with those of the name of the object desired . . . the formation of a word by putting together the first letters of the words of a phrase.

1.2.3 *al-ḥurūfiyyūn*

The speculations on the numerical value of the letters have played a considerable part in other tendencies of Muslim mysticism as well. Here we have to mention the gnostic-cabbalistic set known as *al-ḥurūfiyyūn*, founded around 1387 by the Persian Faḍlallāh Astarābādhī (d. 1394). In his attempt to explain the real, inner meaning of the Qurᵓān and Islam, he based his explanation (*taᵓwīl*) on the disclosure of the connection between the mystical meanings of numerals, letters and parts of the body. He also maintained that the letters have cosmic significance and influence. In this practice one Qurᵓanic phrase is changed into another which has the same numerical value in order to get its "true" meaning.[16]

1.2.4 The Bektashi-order

The teachings of the ḥurūfiyyūn were carried further by the Bektashi-order, who taught that the human face, like a piece of calligraphy, can be read as a mute Qurʾān. Sufis in India even held the view that e.g. ᶜAlī is written twice upon the face, hence we have wonderful calligraphies of the names of *imāms*, etc. in the form of the human face.[17]

1.2.5 Temperament

Other mystics divided the letters into four groups according to their temperament and the elements they are supposedly linked with, like *fire – air – water – earth.*[18]

1.2.6 Practical magic

A similar and yet different intrusion of mysticism into Arabic writing is the case of practical, everyday magic, divination, in which again the qualities attributed to the individual letters and their numerical values may play a decisive role. In the different magical tables that have been and still are in use to establish friendship or enmity, to cure illnesses or to determine the chances of a marriage, we can find that the letters are not only coupled with numerical values and elements, as we have seen before, but there are qualities (richness, enmity, intimacy), scents (rose, musk) corresponding to them. They all have a special sign among the signs of the Zodiac, and also have a special planet, a *jinn* and even a guardian angel. Going into the description of the particularities of how a divination based upon one of these tablets proceeds would be far beyond our present topic. Still, mention must be made of another element of these tables, and these are the names of God, that is to say His 99 epithets, because each letter is considered to correspond to one of these names, starting with that letter.[19]

Next to the practical divination from letters we must not forget the importance of writing – or more precisely of scribbling – in the course of making amulets and charms, where the illegibility of the writing seems to add to the supernatural force and mystical value of the object.[20]

1.3 Larger units: ᶜilm al-ḥurūf

Last but not least in our enumeration of the different ways of the "intrusion" of mysticism into the field of Arabic letters and writing in general, we have to mention those activities the centre of which is the Qurʾān or God.

1.3.1 God's names (*asmāʾ Allāh al-ḥusnā*)

The principle of what is known as the science of letters (*ʿilm al-ḥurūf*) is the idea that the nature and secret of letters exist since the letters turned into one another before the creation of the world in order to form words. These words live inside the created things, and before the creation they were identical with the ideas of things.[21] So the secret of every creature resides in the written form of the word which is its name. Hence the letters have a supernatural power from which the universe could be created, in other words, they are the pillars of the universe. So if the letters indicate a deeper reality beyond that of the surface meaning of words (that can be understood by anybody), this knowledge of theirs could have been gained by them only from God in the course of creation. What else can be then the aim of the mystic (*ʿārif*) than to acquire this veritable knowledge in order to get closer to God? I do not wish to treat at this point the mystical legends about the creation of the letters,[22] but would like only to mention briefly how the letters in God's names and the Qurʾān gained significance for the mystics. Ultimately it was the Creator who stood in the centre of the "science of letters". So the main aim was the analysis of the 99 names of God, to reveal as they said "their beauties", and to establish what the secret "most sublime name" (*al-ism al-aʿẓam*) of God was. It was of utmost importance for them, since, in their belief, whoever acquired the knowledge of this name, which is revealed only to prophets and other saints, would have power above the other believers.[23]

According to the mystics, all the letters glorify God in some way or another. And it is so, because there exists nothing but God, His names, His deeds and His attributes, everything is He, or through Him or towards Him. So finally every creature, be it an ant or a gnat, is nothing but a way of appearance of God's name. Nevertheless, even the mystics chose from among the infinite numbers of God's names the 99 accepted by Muslims in general. From these 99 names there are some which deserve special attention. I would like to mention only one, the name *Wāḥid*. This is regarded not only by mystics but also by other muslims theologians as the most important attribute of God, since it emphasizes and expresses one of the basic – if not the most important – dogma of muslim faith, the *tawḥīd*, the belief in and the profession of the unity of God.[24]

1.3.2 Important phrases

The importance of the name *Wāḥid* is once again further enlarged by the numerical value of its characters (19 = 6 + 1 + 8 + 4), this number (19) being the key number of *taʾwīl*, the mystical interpretation of the Qurʾān, and of the mystical sciences in general. We find the number 19 emerging in another very important phrase: *bism-illāh ar-raḥmān ar-raḥīm*, which is composed of 19 (3 + 4 + 6 + 6) letters.[25]

Other phrases that are examined by mystics include the *shahāda*. It is divided into two parts *lā ilāha illā Allāh* and *Muḥammad rasūl Allāh*, each one being formed by 12 letters, showing – according to the mystics – that the Prophet had 12 ancestors in his tribe, the Quraysh, and that he had also 12 descendants, the Shīʿī *imāms*.[26]

1.3.3. The Qurʾān and its letters

The Qurʾān and its letters are naturally also venerated in some special ways. Even those seven letters that are not contained in the opening chapter of the Qurʾān, the *Fātiḥa*, i.e. *th, j, kh, z, sh, ẓ, f*, are regarded as having a special sanctity. They are connected to the most important names of God, the names of the guardian angels, the seven kings of the *jinn*, the days of the week and the stars.[27]

Those letters which stand at the beginning of 29 chapters of the Qurʾān lent themselves very easily to varied mystical and non-mystical explanations.[28] According to a tradition, for example, Ibn ʿAbbās thought that they were from the epithets of God.[29]

2. The possible sources of mysticism connected to writing

Having reviewed the main branches of mystical activities and territories in Arabic writing, let us try to find out now what the possible sources are of this mysticism, or, to put it differently, in what did this mysticism originate?, since sources and origins cannot always be separated in our topic.

2.1 History

The mystical approaches that are manifested in relation to Arabic writing are quite deeply rooted in history. It is well known, and has already been mentioned here as well, that the calculation of the numerical value of words and phrases existed on the one hand in the Ancient East, which means here the ancient cultures of Mesopotamia and Egypt, and on the other hand it was present in Classical Antiquity as well as in the Jewish heritage.

Concerning the alphabet itself, we know of the view in Babylon, according to which the stars form a celestial alphabet, a celestial writing. Later, in Isaiah 34:4 we read that "the heavens shall be rolled up like a scroll", so once again we get an image of the sky as a papyrus full of mysterious writing. The same simile is found in the Qur᾽ān 21:104: "On *that* day we will roll up the heavens as a written scroll is rolled up" (*ṭayy as-sijill*). In Late Antiquity we also encounter the view according to which the letters have a special relationship with the stars, with the sky, and that their forms have astronomical significance.[30]

Concerning the stories about the shape of the letters, the meaning of the names of the letters, the creation of the alphabet and similar topics, Muslim traditions most often reflect the equivalent places in the rabbinic Haggada.[31]

It is well known that Islamic culture took over and absorbed quite readily the heritage of earlier cultures. But in this more than astonishing similarity between the different traditions the take-over could have been helped by two factors, namely the gradual development of Arabic writing and the long use of the original Semitic alphabet-order, the *abjad* (which is even used today in pagination and indention), in which alphabet the letters were arranged according to their ascending numerical value, or, to put it the other way round, numerical values were assigned to the letters according to their alphabetical order. These two factors could have helped the development of mysticism, even if in these particular points its main source can be found in history.

2.2 The Qur᾽ān

Secondly, beside the historical factor, we must not neglect the central role of the special character of the Qur᾽ān as a possible source of mysticism. The Qur᾽ān is regarded by Muslims as the word of Allah (*kalimat Allāh*). It was revealed in the Arabic language and written down in the Arabic script, which is of divine origin. The Qur᾽anic *rasm*, the text without diacritical and vowel marks, is regarded sacred on the one hand as the written form of the word of Allah. On the other hand, speculations about the nature of the well-preserved table (*al-lawḥ al-maḥfūẓ*) – mentioned in the Qur᾽ān, (85:22): *bal huwa Qur᾽ān majīd fī lawḥ maḥfūẓ* – also emphasize the sanctity of Arabic writing, since the Qur᾽ān is considered to be forming only a part of this table allegedly kept since the creation of God. What we may call mystical speculations and explanations entered here also the different commentaries of the Qurʾān and the large volumes of Muslim traditions.[32]

2.3 The character of Arabic writing

Finally I have found a third possible source for the entrance of mysticism into Arabic writing in the characer of the Arabic and, generally speaking, of Semitic scripts themselves. This is the point which I would like to investigate further, since it seems to me quite convincing that the consonantal (and as such, defective) character of these scripts together with their gradual and quite long and slow development greatly facilitated the introduction of mystical thoughts into this field. So, even if we cannot disregard or discard the two points mentioned above, we may perhaps find, in my opinion, the most important source of this mysticism in the history and development of the Arabic script itself. So in the following, I should like to present an outline of the development of Arabic writing as far as it can be significant from the point of view of our present topic.

2.3.1 Adoption

The first phase is that of the adoption. Whether we accept the Nabatean origin or the Syro-Palmyran one,[33] there is one thing that seems to be certain, namely that the take-over cannot be linked to a certain point of time nor to a certain person: it was rather the result of a long process. We cannot even discard the possibility of a development under multiple influences, i.e. one leaving space for the Nabatean and the Palmyran influences alike. But what is more important from our point of view is that this was not an ad hoc take-over of an outside system, but a take-over after a long symbiosis, and this is what most probably made possible the preservation of all the characteristics of the original system, including the preservation of the ancient order of the alphabet, reflected in mediaeval stories about the origin of the alphabet[34] and continued use alike, together with the numerical value of the letters.

2.3.2 Systematization

While in the first phase (3–6th centuries) there were only minor alterations made on the forms of individual letters, and so the texts/inscriptions must have been relatively well readable, the second phase (6–7th centuries) is certainly marked by a relative deterioration in the usability of the writing. By this time several characters which had previously been different fell together, and points were not yet systematically introduced to differentiate between them. This development was a logical outcome of the adoption of another writing system and the extensive use of writing. Nevertheless, for an outsider, a person uninitiated into the contents of a written document, this unification of letters – whereby the 28 sounds were represented by only 17 letters, and among them those that could hardly have been differentiated, as *dāl/dhāl* from *rāʾ/zāy* that differed slightly and only in their size – made it completely impossible to grasp the meaning or to have the faintest idea what the writing was about.

So by this time (6/7c.) the independent and primary connotative meaning of writing had considerably decreased. At least two things compensated for the loss of the independent illegibility of writing. In the case of commercial documents the content must have been evident, and in case of the Qurʾān, people memorised it, so they knew by heart what was written down.

How early and how far writing was general is a controversial issue. Today more and more evidence (archaeological findings among it) seem to point to the fact that, even in the pre-Islamic age, writing had much greater significance than we used to admit. But writing is not equal automatically to reading, as we all know, i.e. it does not automatically involve total legibility or the possibility of perfect reading of an unknown written text fluently without any external help. And in my view, the defectiveness of this early writing must have played a great role in keeping the Qurʾān and a great many other texts so long as texts which had to be memorised.

Let us suppose that a person was reading a text he was familiar with. Besides the difficulties of reading the characters themselves, there were two other factors (still present today!) that made his task more difficult. Firstly, that Arabic is a consonantal script, so, after differentiating between the consonants that looked much the same, he had to supply the vowels, and secondly, that the text was most probably written in the *ᶜarabiyya*, the literary language, which by that time was surely not his mother tongue. So our reader had to master the grammatical rules of this language, often far removed from those governing his mother tongue, to be able to read the selected text properly.[35]

All this, of course, did not prevent the written text from being understood and interpreted by experts – i.e. the fulfilment of the primary function of writing – but they *alienated* the reader from the text to a degree that surpassed the average level of alienation (because writing *does* alienate people from its linguistic/cognitive contents in greater or lesser degree in any case).

To sum up our second point we can say that we have seen the difficulties which this writing presented even for the initiated. We must also bear in mind that by this time it was also, if not first and foremost the sacred writing of the Qurʾān. These factors must have facilitated the emergence and formation of mystical views at this point in the development of Arabic writing.

The mystical views that surround for example the opening letters of 29 of the Qurʾānic chapters might have originated at this period, since these letters are those which were, according to a later tradition, those without points (*ʾ, ḥ, r, s, ṣ, ṭ, ʿ, q, k, l, m, n, h, y*).

2.3.3 Dots

The third phase in the development of writing is marked by the introduction of diacritical points (*naqṭ/iʿjām*) to differentiate between the letters. This was necessitated by the increasing number of official documents written in Arabic during the reign of the Caliph ʿAbdalmalik. The introduction of points[36] (linked by tradition to al-Ḥajjāj ibn Yūsuf, governor of Iraq) did not change for a long time the uncertainty that surrounded writing. Although in the case of the Qurʾān the use of diacritical points and later of other signs (vowels, etc) became, we might say, general from roughly the second half of the 8th century, the Qurʾān-philologists (*qurrāʾ*) and the jurisprudents (*fuqahāʾ*) conducted very heated debates about the permissibility of their introduction into the sacred, revealed *rasm* of the Qurʾānic text.[37]

In other, more secular territories, different views preoccupied the users or non-users of these devices. According to one group of views, the excessive use of points in writing was a sign of the author's not having a high opinion of the reader.[38] Other anecdotes tell us about the misfortunes and calamities caused by the incorrect use of points. According to one, a great number of people were castrated in a province instead of being simply counted: *akhṣi* versus *aḥṣi*.[39] In any case, the use of points in everyday texts was not adopted very quickly, and we have texts even from the 13–14th centuries which scarcely contain diacritical points, a fact which naturally does not facilitate their reading.[40]

Turning back to what the introduction of points might have meant from the mystical point of view, we can see that it had a far-reaching and definite effect. To illustrate this, let us start by having a look at a passage about the creation of the alphabet: "God created the pen from green light, then made it speak in the form of 28 letters, these became the basis of speech. Then He provided them with sounds, so that they could be heard and pronounced. Then the pen uttered these letters (i.e. the sounds). The first among them was *a point* . . . it prostrated itself in front of God, adoring Him – so it became the *hamza*. And when God almighty saw its humbleness, He stretched it and elongated it, so it became the *alif*, and it was used in speech".[41] Whether we can find a direct correspondence between this mythical point and the point as one of the three essential elements (beside the *alif* and the circle) of calligraphy would perhaps be worth-while investigating.

But let us turn now to another manifestation of the importance of the point in mystical speculations. One of the most wide-spread mystical legends concerns the point under the letter *bāᵓ*. Before relating this legend in the words of the famous mystic, the Andalusian Ibn ᶜArabī (1165–1240), attention should be paid to the fact that the alienation of the point from the letter, which is quite clear from this legend, well reflects its special function, and in our case, certainly points to the later introduction of the point to the writing system. It points to a development which is independent from that of the letter itself. In other writing systems nobody thinks of according special attention or importance to the points above the letters. This is the case in English, for example, where letters form a unit together with their points if they have one. This special development of the points in Arabic is what might have given birth to this legend as well, which, in different forms, is alive in the Sunnite and the Shiᶜite mystical traditions alike.

"The Prophet said the following: God sent down from heaven 104 books as revelations. He put he knowledge available in the first hundred into the remaining four: the Torah, the Gospel, the Psalms and the Qurᵓān. Then He put the contents of the first three into the Qurᵓān. At the same time the Qurᵓānic knowledge is included in its first chapter, the *Fātiḥa*. The knowledge contained therein is included in its opening phrase (*bism-illāh ar-raḥmān ar-raḥīm*). But the knowledge in the *basmala* is also contained in its first letter, the *bāᵓ*, and finally in the point which is under this letter. In such a way, the point of the letter *bāᵓ* became the container of the universe, that is of everything which can be bound in the Qurᵓān and in the other heavenly books."[42] In Shīᶜī circles we find the same legend in the form of a saying attributed to ᶜAlī, "I am the point under the *bāᵓ*", which apparently means tat he is in possession of universal knowledge.[43]

2.4.3 Vowels

The development which happened in what we may call the fourth stage of Arabic writing did not leave such a dramatic impact as did the introduction of diacritical points. This era (roughly the second half of the 8th c.), after previous attempts, witnessed the final development and introduction of *ashkāl*, that is the signs of short vowels and other secondary signs connected with the pronunciation of vowels and consonants. The lesser impact of these signs upon the imagination of the people can be connected with the rare use of these signs, which were and are confined almost exclusively to the Qur'ān, dictionaries and textbooks, but hardly ever appeared or appear in everyday writing.[44]

2.3.5 Calligraphy

From the end of the 8th c. on we can speak of the fifth stage in the development of Arabic writing, the history of which stage continued up to the introduction of printing in the 19th c., but which has never died out for a moment, and the revival of which we can experience today. I am speaking about the development of what we – outsiders – call calligraphy. Though using this term myself, I would like to emphasize that although the Arabs differentiate between the calligrapher (*khaṭṭāṭ*), the simply copyist (*nassākh*) and the scribe (*kātib*), they do not differentiate between what we call ordinary writing and calligraphy, both being designated by the word *khaṭṭ*.

Arab authors define *khaṭṭ* by quoting a saying attributed to Euclid according to which "writing is the geometry of the soul, even if rendered into visible form by corporal means [i.e., the hand]"[45] For a muslim, calligraphy was the fulfilment of writing, its most perfect function. He could express through it his admiration of that instrument that 'God bestowed upon mankind'. If a Qur'anic passage was to be written somewhere, it had to be dressed in a proper form, since this form was the contribution of man to what was created by God. So it is not surprising that even in a work that has nothing to do with mysticism, and which contains practical information about what a scribe should know, the author said the following, among other things, when asked to describe the characteristics of *khaṭṭ*: "Writing is a work of the soul, and there is no difference between its types; it catches the eye and captures the heart . . . the whole seems to move though it is motionless."[46] We can find similar descriptions in other works as well. All point to the opinion of muslim men of letters that calligraphy cannot be solely regarded as an artistic product, it is more than that, since it always reflects the spiritual aims of the calligrapher as well.

To illustrate this point I should like to quote a few lines from an early 17th century treatise on calligraphers and painters:

"The aim of Murtaḍā-ᶜAlī in writing
Was not merely characters and dots,
But fundamentals, purity and virtue;
And he pointed to this by the beauty of his writing.
He who said: 'Writing is one-half of knowledge'
Is the leader of prophets in knowledge and mildness.
It was with reference to the writing of Murtaḍā-ᶜAlī
That the Prophet said 'one-half of knowledge.'
Such writing (in comparison) with the limitations of mankind!
That was another pen and another hand!
The pure *qalam* of the Exalted Majesty
Drank water from the spring of Paradise."[47]

There are two closely linked factors which we must bear in mind when thinking about calligraphy. The first one is that calligraphy is most often exercised upon Qurᵓanic passages, or some other sacred names or expressions. Thus the reader is presented with a text, the content of which is familiar to him. So he does not have to decipher it but can concentrate his attention on the form, the rhythm etc of the rendering. Secondly, the calligrapher, as has been emphasized by Muslim authors throughout the ages, always wants to convey a message which is beyond the actual text. In achieving his task he is helped by the first point, namely that the text is well known to the readers. The interpretation of the secondary task of the calligrapher is very fertile soil for the imagination of mystics.

Conclusion

Writing plays a significant role within mystical thinking because, according to the mystical teachings, the letters contain the ultimate knowledge from the time of the creation of the universe. As can be read in a tradition according to which Jaᶜfar al-Ṣādiq (d. 765), the 6th Shiᶜi *imām* would have said: "In the first place a thought surged in God, an intention, a will. The object of this thought, this intention, and this will were the letters from which God made the principle of all things, the signs of everything perceptible, the criteria of everything difficult. It is from these letters that everything is known".[48]

Though the different mystical activities in this field are connected in some way or another with the content of written words, at the same time they have an independent function, detached from and irrespective of that content.

In the above paper an attempt has been made to approach the different mystical activities connected with Arabic writing from the point of view of the analysis of the writing. In this approach I have tried to find those historical and structural characteristics of the Arabic scrip which could have helped the development of mysticism in it and its spread in the Muslim world.

Since mystical thoughts and speculations have always been connected to one or another distinctive feature of the writing (see Table 1), it seems that the chosen method of investigation might be fruitful in helping to acquire a knowledge of the sources of mystical teachings and a better understanding of their sometimes intriguing text. For example, the origin of the legend quoted above according to which the letters turned into one another to form words can most probably be connected – at least in its present form – to the stage after the take-over, i.e. that of systematization (see Table 2), when the cursive character of Arabic writing was firmly established. Ibn ᶜArabī's explanation of the six non-joinable letters can probably be connected to the same period.[49]

From the point of view of research on Arabic writing, the significance of the study of mysticism seems to be that it may contribute to the *complex* analysis of writing, and support facts known from other sources, like, e.g., the question of the points of the letters: When were they introduced? How were they received? How was their significance appreciated? And so on.

So it seems certain that what I have termed mysticism in Arabic writing is an important aspect of a comprehensive analysis of writing, an aspect which would merit support from facts known from other sources, like, e.g., the question of the points of the letters: When were they introduced? How were they received? How was their significance appreciated? And so on.

So it seems certain that what I have termed mysticism in Arabic writing is an important aspect of a comprehensive analysis of writing, an aspect which would merit further research.

Table 1: The static features on the synchronic level

distinctive features	shape	phonetic value	name	numerical value	place in the *abjad*	place in the *alifbāʾ*
straight stroke above line/2 units does not connect	ا	/ʾ/	*alif*	1	1.	1.
straight stroke above line/1 unit connects one dot below final form: forward up	ب	/b/	*bāʾ*	2	2.	2.
straight stroke above line/1 unit connects two dots above final form: forward up	ت	/t/	*tāʾ*	400	22.	3.
oblique stroke above line/1 unit connects one dot below final form: backward down	ج	/j/	*jīm*	3	3.	5.

Table 2: The diachronic level

0. origin	→	Semitic writing system
↓		
I. takeover	→	numeric value, original order, the name of the letters
↓		
II. systematization	→	the shape of the letter
↓		
III. dots	→	today's alphabetical order
↓		
IV. vowels		
↓		
V. calligraphy (and the final development of writing)	→	secondary and dynamic features

Notes

1. The saying is attributed to al-Būnī, *Laṭāʾif* (Ibn Khaldūn, *Muqaddima* III, 1161; Rosenthal 1958: III. 140.) Cf. the closing chapter of Būnī's *Shams* corroborating it.

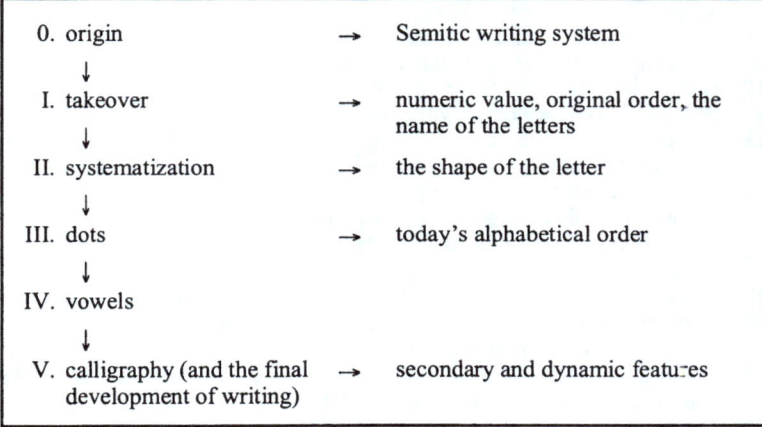

2. See e.g., Dornseiff 1925: 133ff; Goldziher 1872: 768ff [= 1967–73 I, 169ff].
3. Goldziher 1872: 784.
4. As we can read it in the *Kitāb al-Ḥurūf* attributed to al-Khalīl ibn Aḥmad, p. 34.
5. Cf. Schimmel 1975: 422.
6. See e.g., al-Qazwīnī, *Āthār* 224. Cf. Lane, 1883: 104–106; Schimmel 1975: 260, 421.
7. aṣ-Ṣūlī, *Adab al-Kuttāb* 62: "I saw you in my dream embracing me as the writer's *lām* embraces the *alif*". For the different versions of this line see Rosenthal 1961: 19.
8. Ibn al-Fāriḍ, *Dīwān* 31. In Nicholson's translation (1921: 209): "But hadst thou been with me as the *kasra* below the *dot* of the letter *b*, thou wouldst have been raised to a rank that thine own effort did not gain for thee".
9. On the question of Jewish influence upon Arabic letter mysticism and numerology, especially felt in al-Būnī's *Shams*, see Vajda 1948.
10. See Dornseiff 1925: 35ff, 52ff.
11. Ibn Khaldūn, *Muqaddima* III, 1160.
12. For the origin and evolution of magic squares see al-Ghazāli, *Munqidh* 46, 50. For a more modern usage consult Lane 1890: Ch. XII. For some present-day examples see Fodor 1990: 43, 52, 54, 62, 76, 80, 82, 83, 87, 88, 90, 136, 138–140, 162, 167, 181.
13. For this branch of mystical writings see Goldziher 1981: 180–181, 189ff (and esp. 190 fn72); Hartmann 1924: 108ff; Fahd 1987: 221–224. al-Būnī treats *ᶜilm al-jafr* and the role of the *Imām* Jaᶜfar aṣ-Ṣādiq in detail, *see Shams*, 335ff.
14. al-Būnī, *Shams* Chapters 31 and 38.
15. al-Būnī, *Shams*, Chapters 21–30.
16. About the *ḥurūfiyyūn* see Goldziher 1981: 224; Ritter 1954.
17. Goldziher 1981: 147, 224; Schimmel 1975: 413. For general information on the Bektashis see recently Birge 1994.
18. See e.g., in many places in al-Būnī, *Shams* and Ibn ᶜArabī, *Futūḥāt* vols. I–11. For a modern summary of the theme see Bakhtiar 1976: 114–115. The importance of this theme may be seen from the fact that Ibn Khaldūn devoted a whole chapter in his *Muqaddima* (V1/30, III, 1159–1195) to a detailed description of the different branches of the science of [the secrets] of letters.
19. al-Būnī's *Shams* can be regarded as a handbook of practical magic and has been relied upon as such by later writers ever since its compilation. There is a great number of later, mostly anonymous booklets on this topic, too. See, e.g., *al-Luᵓluᵓ*. For an excellent European overview of the whole question, see Doutter 1909, esp. pp. 171ff.
20. The largest number of amulets is contained in Fodor 1990. See, e.g., pp. 88–89, 137 148–151, 193–194, etc.
21. See al-Būnī, *Laṭāᵓif*, Ibn ᶜArabī, *Futūḥāt*, vols. I–II. Cf. Chittick 1989: 127–130.
22. For legends about the creation of the letters see, e.g., Haydar Āmulī, *Sharḥ* 289; ar-Rāzī, *Ḥurūf* 133. See also Goldziher 1872: 783 [= 1967–731, 184].
23. See al-Būnī, *Shams* Chapter 16 (Parts 1–99).

24. The importance of the initial *Wāḥid*, the letter *wāw*, is well shown by the following anecdote: "The earthquake of 1776/7 (1190 H.), one of the most terrible of the many that have afflicted Tabriz, is still spoken of as 'the Great Earthquake'. The calamity fell in the middle of the night. At dawn survivors were running hither and thither hoping to find those buried in the debris who might still be alive. One search party discovered a spark of light from deep down in the basement of a ruined house. They set to work frantically, hoping to effect a rescue. When they finally dug their way through, they discovered a man sitting on the floor bent over a small piece of paper, working by the light of a candle, intensely absorbed in writing. They called to him to hurry out, more shocks were coming, and the ruins were still dangerous; but there was no response. He bent over his work, still absorbed. Several times they shouted to him, till finally he looked up, asking why they were disturbing him. When informed that the town had been almost demolished by an earthquake, that thousands had been killed, and there was hardly time left for him to escape, he repled: 'What is all that to me?' and proudly exhibited his paper on which was a perfect *wāw* . . . 'After many thousands of trials I have at last achieved one that is absolutely perfect', he said, 'and such a perfect letter is worth more than the whole city'." (Pope & Ackerman, 1939: II, 1726.)
25. See, e.g., Haydar Āmulī, *Sharḥ 310; al-Qushayrī, Laṭāʾif* I, 44. al-Būnī, *Shams* 33ff.
26. See al-Būnī, *Shams*, esp. 131ff.
27. al-Būnī consecrated a whole book on the sanctity of these letters: *Kitāb sharḥ sawāqiṭ al-fātiḥa ash-sharifa* (enumerated by Fahd 1987: 232).
28. For an account of the different views, cf., e.g., Jones 1962.
29. al-Būnī, *Shams* 62–63.
30. See, e.g., in Dornseiff 1925–81ff.
31. See Goldziher 1872: 769, 783 [= 1967–73: 170, 184].
32. See al-Qushayrī, *Laṭāʾif* III, 313; al-Qalqashandī, *Ṣubḥ* II, 472–474.
33. For a recent survey, see Naveh 1982: 153–162.
34. See, e.g., al-Balādhurī, *Futūḥ* 476–477 and al-Qalqashandī, *Ṣubḥ* III, 14–15.
35. Again we must mention here that there is some debate going on about the earliest appearance of diglossia, but by he time of Muḥammad it is generally accepted to have existed in Arabia.
36. For a possible Syriac influence see Goldziher 1994: 6ff.
37. Cf. aṣ-Ṣūlī, *Adab* 57ff.
38. aṣ-Ṣūlī, *Adab* 57.
39. See aṣ-Ṣūlī, *Adab* 59.
40. E.g., the memoirs of the Syrian prince Usāma ibn Munqidh – *Iʿtibār* – has been edited twice with 30–40% differences in the choice of the dots (and consequently the letters) between the editions.
41. ar-Rāzī, *Ḥurūf* 133.
42. Haydar Āmūlī, *Sharḥ* 310.
43. About the point under the *bāʾ* cf. Nicholson 1921: 209, fn.
44. There is, however, at least one work of utmost significance, Ibn ʿArabī's *al-Futūḥāt al-makkiyya*, where the author pays great attention to the role the vocalic signs play in 'the spiritual reality of the world', making them in this way an integral part of his ontology and cosmology. See *Futūḥāt* II,

sections 1–37. About the place of letters in his ontology, cf. Chittick 1989: 128–130.

45. See aṣ-Ṣūlī, *Adab* 41.
46. aṣ-Ṣūlī, *Adab* 50.
47. Minorsky 1959: 108.
48. Vajda 1961: 119.
49. Ibn ᶜArabī, *Futūḥāt* I, section 686: "The sacred letters (*al-ḥurūf al-muqaddasa*). As for the word 'sacred', that is, the dependency from others, it means that [this type of letter] is not connected in writing to other letters but [other] letters are connected to it, [since] it is self-contained. [The sacred letters] are steered by six planets of the apogee. From them take the directions their origin. The knowledge of these six letters is a vast sea of unknown depth. Their true nature is known only to God. They are the keys of the unknown, and we get to know their effects by way of exploration. They are as follows: *alif, wāw, dāl, dhāl, rāᵓ, zāy.*"

References

Primary Sources

ᶜAbdattawwāb, Ramaḍān, ed. 1982. *Thalātha kutub fī l-ḥurūf li-l-Khalīl b. Aḥmad wa-Ibn as-Sikkīt wa-r-Rāzī*. Cairo: Maktabat al-Khānji & Riyad: Dār ar-Rifāᶜī.

a-Balādhurī, *Futūḥ* = Abū l-ᶜAbbās Aḥmad al-Balādhurī, *Futūḥ al-buldān*. Ed. by M. J. de Goeje. Leiden: E. J. Brill, 1870.

al-Būnī, *Laṭāᵓif* = Abū l-ᶜAbbās Aḥmad b. ᶜAlī al-Būnī, *Kitāb laṭāᵓif al-ishārāt fī asrār al-ḥurūf al-ᶜulwiyyāt*. Lithograph, Cairo, 1899/1900.

al-Būnī, *Shams* = Abū l-ᶜAbbās Aḥmad b. ᶜAlī al-Būnī, *Shams al-maᶜārif al-kubrā*. Beirut: al-Maktaba ash-Shaᶜbiyya, 1985.

al-Ghazālī, *Munqidh* = Abū Ḥāmid Muḥammad b. Muḥammad al-Ghazālī, *al-Munqidh min aḍ-ḍalāl wa-l-mawṣil ilā dhī l-ᶜizza wa-l-ghalāl*. Ed. by Jamīl Ṣalībā & Kāmil ᶜIyād. Beirut: Dār al-Andalus, 1983.

Khalīl, *Ḥurūf* = al-Khalīl b. Aḥmad al-Farāhīdī, *Kitāb al-Ḥurūf*. In: ᶜAbdattawwāb 1982: 9–48.

Haydar Āmūlī, *Sharḥ* = Sayyid Haydar Āmūlī, *al-Muqaddimāt min Kitāb naṣṣ an-nuṣūṣ fī sharḥ Fuṣūṣ al-ḥikam li-Muḥyī d-Dīn Ibn al-ᶜArabī*. Ed by Henri Courbin & ᶜUthmān Ismāᶜīl Yaḥyā. Tehran, 1975.

Ibn ᶜArabī, *Futūḥāt* = Muḥyī d-Din Ibn ᶜArabī, *al-Futūḥāt al-makkiyya*. Ed. by ᶜUthmān Yaḥyā & Ibrāhīm Madkūr. 14 vols. Cairo: al-Hayᵓa al-Miṣriyya al-ᶜĀmma li-l-Kitāb, 1972–90.

Ibn al-Fāriḍ, *Dīwān* = Sharaf ad-Din ᶜUmar Ibn al-Fāriḍ, *Dīwān*. Ed. by Ibrāhīm as-Sāmarrāᵓī. Amman: Dār al-Fikr li-n-Nashr wa-t-Tawzīᶜ. 1985.

Ibn Khaldūn, *Muqaddima* = Abū Zayd ᶜAbdarraḥmān b. Muḥammad Ibn Khaldūn, *al-Muqaddima*. Edited and ann. by ᶜAlī ᶜAbdalwāḥid Wāfī, 3 vols., Cairo: Lajnat al-Bayān al-ᶜArabī, 1957–58; Cairo: Dār Nahḍat Miṣr, 1977. [English transl. = Rosenthal 1958].

al-Luᵓluᵓ = al-Luᵓluᵓ wa-l-murjān fī taskhīr mulūk al-jānn. Cairo, n.d.

al-Qalqashandī, *Ṣubḥ* = Abū l-ᶜAbbās Aḥmad al-Qalqashandī, *Ṣubḥ al-aᶜshā*. 14 vols. Cairo: al-Maṭbaᶜa al-Amīriyya, 1913–1919.

al-Qazwīnī, *Āthār* = Zakariyā Muḥammad b. Maḥmūd al-Qazwīnī, *Āthār al-bilād wa-akhbār al-ᶜibād*. Ed. by F. Wüstenfeld. Göttingen 1849.

al-Qushayrī, *Laṭāᵓif* = Abū l-Qāsim ᶜAbdalkarīm b. Hawāzin al-Qushayrī, *Laṭāᵓif al-ishārāt*. Ed. by Ibrāhīm Basyūnī. Cairo: al-Hayᵓa al-Miṣriyya al-ᶜĀmma li-l-Kitāb, 1981.

ar-Rāzī, *Ḥurūf* = Aḥmad b. Muḥammad b. al-Muẓaffar b. al-Mukhtār ar-Rāzī, *Kitāb al-Ḥurūf*. In: ᶜAbdattawwāb 1982: 115–161.

aṣ-Ṣūlī, *Adab al-kuttāb* = Abū Bakr Muḥammad b. Yaḥyā aṣ-Ṣūlī, *Adab al-kuttāb*. Edited by Muḥammad Bahjat al-Atharī & as-Sayyid Muḥammad Shukrī al-Ālūsī. Beirut: Dār al-Kutub al-ᶜIlmiyya, n.d.

Usāma ibn Munqidh, *Iᶜtibār* = Abū Muẓaffar Usāma b. Murshid ibn Munqidh ash-Shaydhari, *Kitāb al-iᶜtibār*. Ed. by H. Derenbourg. Paris, 1880. Also ed. by Ph. K. Hitti. Princeton: Princeton University Press, 1930.

Secondary Sources

Birge, John Kingsley. 1994. *The Bektashi Order of Derwishes*. London: Luzac Oriental.

Bakhtiar, Laleh. 1976. *Sufi Expressions of the Mystic Quest*. London: Thames and Hudson.

Chittick, William C. 1989. *The Sufi Path of Knowledge. Ibn al-ᶜArabi's Metaphysics of Imagination*. Albany: State University of New York Press.

Dornseiff, Franz. 1925. *Das Alphabet in Mystik und Magie*. Leipzig & Berlin: B. G. Teubner.

Doutté, Edmond. 1909. *Magie et religion dans l'Afrique du Nord*. Alger: Typographie Adolphe Jourdan.

Fahd, Toufic. 1987. *La divination arabe*. Paris: Sindbad.

Fodor, Alexander. 1990. *Amulets from the Islamic World. Catalogue of the Exibition held in Budapest, in 1988. The Arabist. Budapest Studies in Arabic* 2. Budapest: Eötvös Loránd University & Csoma de Körös Society.

Goldziher, Ignaz. 1872. 'Linguistisches aus der Literatur der muhammedanischen Mystik'. *ZDMG* 26.764–785. [= Goldziher, Ignaz. 1967–73. *Gesammelte Schriften* (= *Collectanea*, II/1–6.). Ed. by Joseph De Somogyi, 6 vols., Hildesheim: Georg Olms. I, 165–186.]

Goldziher, Ignaz. 1981. *Introduction to Islamic Theology and Law*. Trans. by Andras and Ruth Hamori. Princeton, New Jersey: Princeton University Press.

Goldziher, Ignaz. 1994. *On the History of Grammar Among the Arabs. An Essay in Literary History*. Trans. and ed. by Kinga Dévényi & Tamás Iványi. (= *Amsterdam Studies in the Theory and History of Linguistic Science*, 73.) Amsterdam/Philadelphia: John Benjamins.

Hartmann, R. 1924. 'Eine arabische Apokalypse aus der Kreuzzugszeit. Ein Beitrag zur Ǧafr-Literatur', *Schriften d. Königsberger Gelehrten Gesellschaft, Geisteswiss. Kl.* 89-116. Berlin.

Jones, Alan. 1962. 'The mystical letters of the Qurᵓān'. *Studia Islamica* 16.5–11.

Lane, Edward William. 1883. *Arabian Society in the Middle Ages*. Ed. by Stanley Lane-Pool. London.

Lane, Edward William. 1890. *An Account of the Manners and Customs of the*

Modern Egyptians. Written in Egypt during the Years 1833–1835. Repr. of the 3rd ed. London, New York & Melbourne: Ward, Lock and Co.
Minorsky, V. (transl.) 1959. *Calligraphers and painters. A Treatise by Qāḍī Aḥmad, son of Mīr-Munshī*. (= *Smithsonian Institution. Freer Gallery of Art Occasional Papers*, 3/2.) Washington.
Naveh, Joseph. 1982. *Early History of the Alphabet. An Introduction to West Semitic Epigraphy and Palaeography*. Jerusalem: The Magnes Press and The Hebrew Univ.; Leiden: E. J. Brill.
Nicholson, Reynold A. 1921. *Studies in Islamic Mysticism*. Cambridge: Cambridge University Press.
Pope, Arthur Upham and Phyllis Ackerman, eds. 1939. *A Survey of Persian Art from Prehistoric Times to the Present*. 6 vols. London & New York: Oxford University Press.
Ritter, H. 1954. 'Die Anfänge der Ḥurūfī sekte'. *Oriens* 7.1–54.
Rosenthal, Franz. 1958. *Ibn Khaldūn, The Muqaddimah: An introduction to history*. 3 vols., London: Routledge & Kegan Paul. 2nd ed. with corrections and augmented bibl. (= *Bollingen Series*, 43.). Princeton, N.J.: Princeton Univ. Press. 1967.
Rosenthal, Franz. 1961. "Significant Uses of Arabic Writing". *Ars Orientalis* 4.15-23.
Schimmel, Annemarie. 1975. *Mystical Dimensions of Islam*. Chapel Hill: The University of North Carolina Press.
Vajda, G. 1948. 'Sur quelques éléments juifs et pseudo-juifs dans l'encyclopédie magique du Būnī'. *Ignace Goldziher Memorial Volume*, Part I., ed. by Samuel Löwinger & Joseph [de] Somogyi, 1.387–392. Budapest: no publisher.
Vajda, G. 1961. 'Les lettres et les sons de la langue arabe d'après Abū Ḥātim al-Rāzī'. *Arabica* 8.113–130.

19

Rescuing Arabic Rhetoric from Neglect

A Text-linguistic Approach

Basil Hatim
Heriot-Watt University

1 Overview

At the outset, a terminological clarification is perhaps in order. Although fully aware of the semantic gap, I use 'rhetoric' as a convenient cover term for *al-balāgha* which subsumes the three Arabic rhetorical 'sciences' *ᶜilm al-maᶜāni*, *ᶜilm al-bayān* and *ᶜilm al-badīᶜ*. The term 'text linguistics' is used here to refer to the inter-disciplinary study of 'text' in 'context', and the manner in which these intimately relate to each other in highly systematic and diverse ways. A 'text' is a sequence of sentences (or any alternatively conceived language elements) which relays a set of mutually relevant communicative intentions, and which ultimately serves an overall rhetorical purpose such as 'describing' or 'counter-arguing'. Finally, 'context' includes aspects of message construction such as 'intentionality' or the purpose for which utterances are used, 'intertextuality' or the way texts constantly refer to other texts, and 'register' membership or the assignment of a text to a particular 'field' of discourse (subject matter), 'tenor' (level of formality) and 'mode' (written vs. spoken, etc.).

The primary aim of the present study is pedagogical. While it is conceded that the rhetorical tradition of Arabic is extremely rich, and has over the centuries been developed in an extremely elegant and elaborate fashion, one of the problems faced by the present-day student of Arabic remains to be one of 'accessibility'. The rich rhetorical heritage is in my view often impenetrable, buried as it were in specialized books and often not helpfully communicated by the specialists. I say this as a native speaker of Arabic who was introduced to rhetoric through formal education in Arabic, and I am sure that the situation is even more drastic for those who approach rhetoric through Arabic as a foreign language.

Another, perhaps thornier, problem confronting present-day students of rhetoric is the undifferentiated mass of information that is scattered rather unsystematically in books that are heavy both in style and in content. Leaving aside these matters of presentation which are perhaps not insurmountable, a more serious problem encountered by the average user of this kind of rhetorical material is the bias in the choice of data which tend to exhibit a one-sided predominance of certain sources almost to the total exclusion of others. Arab rhetoricians habitually exemplify from the Qurᵓanic text and the classics of Arabic poetry, two of the more widely-used points of reference to which conclusions are invariably related. That this should be a problem does not so much emanate from any intrinsic reason why this sort of data should or should not be heavily drawn upon, as it does from the potentially misleading nature of the findings. This is particularly the case when replication of such findings is sought while analysing texts belonging to, say, a different variety of Arabic to the classical or a different genre to the Qurᵓān or poetry.

In an attempt to make available material within the Arabic rhetorical enquiry both less daunting and more relevant, I propose two basic methodological procedures, both of which I have recently tried out to best effect in my own work with students of Arabic as a foreign language and, at a more advanced level, in the training of translators and interpreters (Hatim, forthcoming). One, is to subject rhetorical insights handed down to us by the classical Arab rhetoricians to a comprehensive re-appraisal, using the principles and methods of modern linguistics, with the proviso that the kind of linguistics used is one that is particularly sensitive to text in context (e.g. Halliday 1985). The second procedure to make more amenable the undifferentiated mass of rhetorical material is to relate the various rhetorical insights systematically to both the rhetorical predilections of the modern user of Arabic and to his or her concerns in actually using the language.

2 A Brief Example

Ample exemplification of the way in which rhetorical insights are made to relate to modern language use will be provided in the course of the following discussion. However, an immediate demonstration of what I mean by rhetorical conventions, predilections and concerns with modern language use may perhaps be helpful at this juncture. Under the label *iltifāt*, Arab rhetoricans have identified an interesting phenomenon which involves a 'sudden' pronominal shift from, say, the third person to the first person in a sequence of two or more adjacent sentences. In the grammar of Arabic usage, reference-switching of this kind is deemed to be rule-defying which the Arab rhetorician allows only under certain strict conditions of use. These include restrictions such as the need to motivate such a shift by, for example, having a 'noteworthy' rhetorical purpose to attend to (see, e.g. Lāshīn 1983; Abū ᶜAlīl 1984)). To exemplify from a widely-discussed domain of discourse, the Qurᵓanic text admits the use of *iltifāt* in the service of a variety of implicit rhetorical aims. Consider, for instance, *sūrat al-Fātiḥa* where, to distinguish 'mere praise' (*al-ḥamd*) from 'genuine worship of God only' (*al-ᶜibāda*), an interesting shift from third person to second person is opted for:

> *al-ḥamd^{u} lillāh^{i} rabb^{i} al-ᶜālamīn al-raḥmān^{i} al-raḥīm, mālik^{i} yawm^{i} al-dīn iyyāk^{a} naᶜbud^{u} wa iyyāk^{a} nastaᶜīn*

Against the background of such rhetorical conventions and flouting of conventions subscribed to consciously or unconsciously by all literate users of Arabic, we as consumers of this rich rhetorical heritage, have a host of practical concerns that such rhetorical insights can help with. For example, in translating direct (quoted) speech from English into Arabic within a genre such as the 'news report', very few people stop and ponder the oddness of uncritically rendering the reference-switching involved in English direct speech into the same reporting mode in Arabic, a language whose punctuation system can hardly be said to be functional. Consider, for example:

> "My advice to the Scots medics is for as many as possible simply to refuse to go", he said.

To render this into Arabic as something like "*wa qāl^{a} inna naṣīḥatī*" is at best stylistically ungainly. The question is now: why should this be odd in a news report and yet perfectly acceptable in the Qurᵓanic text, for example? Arabic rhetoric has provided us with a plausible answer, but only indirectly, this indirection being a problem that will be unravelled shortly as part of our re-appraisal. But before the illustration above could invite the unwarranted conclusion that only rare genres such as the Qurᵓān admits *iltifāt*, an example of this phenomenon put to best effect in a contemporary genre other than the news report may be instructive. The genre in question is 'political speech' and the variety of Arabic used is the Modern Standard. Consider the following quote from a speech by President Ḥāfiẓ al-Asad of Syria, who, directing his reference specifically at the PLO leadership, first uses the third person then suddenly switches to the first person:

> *wa hāʾulāʾᵃ al-munāḍilūnᵃ hum alladhīn akkadat ḥaqāʾiqᵘ al-ḥayāt annahum yumāthilūnᵃ shuᶜūbahum fī kullⁱ ᶜaṣrⁱⁿ wa fī kullⁱ makān fa lakum ayyuhā al-munāḍilūnᵃ aynamā kuntum mā lanā wa ᶜalaykum mā ᶜalaynā fī al-sarrāʾ wa al-ḍarrāʾ.*

Here, reference-switching is optimally effective, and the reason for this is simply the availability of a 'noteworthy' rhetorical purpose to serve. At a phase of acute tension in Syrian-Palestinian relations, al-Asad needed to underline and thus make more prominent the juxtaposition of "you" and "us", pointing an accusing finger and saying that 'we are in it together', that 'no dissension is to be tolerated' and that 'we each must fulfil our part of the bargain'.

3 A Text-linguistic Model of Arabic Rhetoricity

Briefly, the most important result of my search for a set of linguistic-stylistic principles that can capture the essence of rhetorical thinking has been to see 'rhetoricity' in Arabic as enshrining the valuable linguistic insight regarding the 'paradigmatics' of the communicative act: what could have been said but was not, presumably for a 'good reason' (Lyons 1970). This is on the one hand; on the other, Arabic rhetorical thinking seems to revolve around an important stylistic notion which recasts paradigmatics in terms of the idea of a 'norm' (what could, indeed what was expected to, have been said, but was not) and the twin-notion of the 'motivation' behind the departure from such a norm (i.e. the good reason principle) (Fowler 1986). That is, a preoccupation for Arabic rhetoricans of all persuasions has been to figure out the rhetorical purpose behind *al-ᶜudūl ᶜan aṣl al-kalām* ("deviation from norms"), a field of inquiry that found its fullest expression in examining *iᶜjāz al-qurʾān* (Qurʾanic inimitability).

Building on both core-linguistic notions such as 'paradigmatics' and stylistic parameters such as 'norm and deviation', modern text linguistics has postulated 'stylistic informativity' as one of a number of standards of textuality that have to be met for text coherence to be upheld. These standards include situationality, intentionality, intertextuality, cohesion and coherence. Of more immediate relevance for our purpose here, however, is 'informativity', a standard of textuality which Beaugrande & Dressler (1980:7–8) define in the following terms:

> [Informativity] concerns the extent to which the occurrences of the presented text are expected vs. unexpected or known vs. unknown ...... The processing of highly informative occurrences is more

demanding than otherwise, but correspondingly more interesting as well.

It is with this capacity of text utterances to defy our expectations and thereby enhance text 'interestingness' that we shall be concerned in the remainder of this paper.

4 Stylistic Informativity in Arabic Rhetorical Thinking

Departing from set textual and/or contextual norms is one basic source of the interestingness (unexpectedness, unknownness) of a given text element. Defying expectation was thus central in the work of the Arab rhetorican who wanted to begin precisely where the grammarian had left off. In the speech of the Arabs, there were numerous intriguing examples of what on the face of it appeared to be cases of 'abusage', aberrations that had to be accounted for within what came to be recognized as independent fields of inquiry in their own right. For example, *Majāz al-Qurʾān* (where the word *majāz* only meant "the permissible") was Abū ʿUbayda al-Muthannā's contribution to what we shall here refer to as stylistic informativity or rhetorically-motivated deviations from expected norms. A number of devices were studied, including *iltifāt*, *al-taqdīm wa al-taʾkhīr* (word order), *al-tikrār al-muʾakkad* (emphatic repetition), and so on. These were analyzed in terms of the way departures occur from some postulated norm to serve a variety of rhetorical purposes in the Qurʾanic text.

To illustrate this kind of linguistic/exegetical work, I have selected one particular area of language use studied by rhetoricians under alternative labels such as *ḍamīr al-shaʾn* (pronoun of prominence) or *ḍamīr al-qiṣṣa* (pronoun of narrativity). Whatever the rubric, what is involved is a case of departing from some expected norm in order to perform any one of a number of rhetorical purposes. Within the particular rhetorical phenomenon under discussion, the expected norm prescribes that a pronoun must be made to refer backward (anaphorically) and not forward (cataphorically) to a nominal element (Ḥusayn 1973). To achieve this, the nominal element must always occur first, an expectation defied by the sentence-initial use of the pronominal element instead, and the forward directionality of the reference entailed by having a pronoun first. This does not only take the text receiver by surprise, but actually offends grammatical correctness. A commonly-cited example of this is the Qurʾanic verse:

fa innahā lā taᶜmā al-abṣār[u] wa lākin taᶜmā al-qulūb[u] allatī fī al-ṣudūr
(*al-Ḥajj* 46)

Truly it is not their eyes that are blind, but their hearts which are in their breasts.

According to the grammar rules of Arabic usage, a pronominal element (*hā*), must always be anaphoric, referring to some antecedent element. Here, however, the pronoun is used to refer forward (i.e. cataphorically) and the sense is recoverable only when the reference to some subsequent nominal is invoked. In attempting to account for this peculiar directionality of reference, rhetoricans came up with the following rationale: the 'focus' of narration is *lā taᶜmā al-abṣār*, with *innahā* virtually performing the function of a rhetorical deictic, something like "what the narration will focus on is that it is not . . ." Now, if the element said to be focal had nothing to justify such focus, cataphora would be shunned by both grammarian and rhetorician.

It is this kind of abusing cataphora (when no rhetorical purpose is in evidence to sanction its use) that we would do well to consider here, as our Arabic newspapers are literally riddled with such totally uncalled-for aberration. I bring in journalese and illustrate this particular phenomenon from modern standard Arabic to preclude once again unwarranted conclusions that rhetorically-motivated cataphora is a Qurᵓanic rhetorical device or one that is only found in similarly lofty speech. I also want to show how modern text linguistics can help us systematize classical rhetorical thinking and, perhaps more significantly, to demonstrate how such a re-appraisal can shed light on present day concerns which we all share as language users.

I reiterate my claim that to use cataphora for 'no good reason' in Arabic news reporting is at best sloppy. An example of such an aberration is:

fī kalimatih[i] allati alqāhā . . ., qāl[a] Mubārak

In a news report, this is both textually incorrect and contextually inappropriate. This verdict has nothing to do with whether journalistic norms allow or disallow such a style; it is specifically to do with the 'news report' as a genre. Consider the following example from an Arabic editorial where the use of cataphora is optimally effective, efficient and appropriate:

fī kull^{i} kalām^{in} qālah^{u} wa fī kull^{i} ^{c}amal^{in} qām^{a} bih^{i} mundh^{u} ḥarb^{i} al-khalīj aṣarr^{a} al-malik Fahd ^{c}alā an yakūn^{a} sabbaq^{an} fī fi^{c}l^{i} al-khayr

The question raised in the discussion of reference switching above may be raised once again here: What makes both the Qurʾanic and the editorial use of cataphora appropriate, and denies news reporting this facility? As we have pointed out above, Arabic rhetoric has provided a plausible answer, but only indirectly. In a sense this indirection is a basic weakness of the kind of rhetorical material we have to work with. Assuming that the problem of accessibility and presentation could somehow be overcome, the difficulty of working with a mass of undifferentiated rhetorical insights remains to be a particularly difficult problem for the student of Arabic rhetoric: rhetorical insights tend to be heavily illustrated from the Qurʾanic text and the classical Arabic poetical heritage. To reiterate my initial argument, there is of course nothing unsound about this particular bias towards a certain kind of data. But, for the modern Arabist, such a bias does raise the important issue of the need to make the necessary adjustments. A framework is therefore needed within which text in context could be looked at more comprehensively.

5 Genre, Text and Discourse

Modern text linguistics steps in here and provides us with a useful way of approaching rhetorical material and making it more amenable to systematic observation. This would be to view language use within three basic categories to which text users constantly refer: genre, discourse and text. Within such a framework, genre is taken to refer to a social occasion and to the way this is conventionally associated with set forms of linguistic expression (e.g. the editorial or the news report). Text refers to the specific rhetorical purpose conventionally realised through language (e.g. to counterargue). Finally, discourse conventionally represents in language the value and belief systems of a societal institution (e.g. racism).

To recast this in more concrete terms and view it from the perspective of analyzing actual language use, genre structures may be as broad as 'the sermon' or as narrowly defined as the actioneer's 'falling gavel' with the words "going, going . . . . gone", with genres such as the 'Letter to the Editor' or the news report falling somewhere in between. Text has a similar transactional function but with the basic difference that textual conventions relate, through the concatenation of mutually relevant communicative intentions, to the expression of a rhetorical purpose (such as narrating, arguing, instructing). Discourse, finally, relates to "systematically-organized sets of statements which give expression to the meanings and values of an institution" (Kress 1985:7).

The Qurʾān, for example, would thus be classified as a unique genre, Qurʾanic discourse as the mouthpiece of an institution of which the Qurʾān would be the ultimate constitution, and Qurʾanic texts would be treated as tokens of the kind of output typically associated with the institution in question. The three categories are not unrelated, however. The unique genre of the Qurʾān tends to attract the kind of discourse typically associated with both commitment to a cause and didacticism (i.e. educative discourse). The type of texts considered ideal for the fulfilment of such discoursal goals would obviously be a mixture of exposition (narration etc.) and argumentation (rebuttal etc.), with the latter being by far the more predominant function.

Now, these distinctions are extremely important from the perspective of utilizing rhetorical insights. The modern user goes invariably wrong when rhetorical routines prescribed for a given context are uncritically applied in a different context. The oddness of reference switching or cataphora in news reporting, for example, may be accounted for in terms of the fact that news reporting is simply too ephemeral a genre to entertain noteworthy rhetorical purposes, the discourse is too uncontentious to contain and ultimately uphold the necessary argumentative thrust, and the kind of texts yielded by news reporting usually tend towards the narrative/informative end of the continuum where the need to persuade is not often an issue. The genres 'political speech' or 'editorial' within modern standard Arabic, on the other hand, have totally different rhetorical goals to serve. In these kinds of text, the discourse is usually highly contentious, and the texts encountered are often argumentative in tone, two basic preconditions for the need on the part of the text producer to try to enhance persuasive appeal.

The basic thesis underlying this kind of analysis could thus be summed up by saying that 'passive' genres such as that of reporting hardly if ever justifies the deployment of language in an optimally 'dynamic' manner. Bearing in mind that the passive-dynamic distinction may best be seen as a continuum, it is safe to conclude that the performance of rhetorical 'ploys' in a genre such as the news report would be very low on the list of priorities to which text users attend. Maximally operative genres such as the editorial or the political speech, on the other hand, almost by definition invite the kind of intensive deployment of attention-getting rhetorical devices, simply because persuasiveness is the *raison d'ètre* of this kind of writing.

References

Abū ᶜAlī, Muḥammad Barakāt (1984), *Dirāsāt fī al-Balāgha*, Amman: Dār al-Fikr.

Abū ᶜUbayda al-Muthannā (d. 210 A.H.), *al-Majāz fī al-Qurʾān*.

Beaugrande, R. & de Dressler, W. (1980), *Introduction to Textlinguistics*, London: Longman.

Fowler, R.= (1986), *Linguistic Criticism*, Oxford: OUP.

Halliday, M. A. K. (1985), *A Functional Grammar of English*, London: Arnold.

Hatim, B. (forthcoming), *Arabic Rhetoric: the Art of Motivating Deviation from the Norm* (to be published by Benjamin).

Ḥusayn, ᶜAbd al-Qādir (1973), *Fann al-Balāgha*, Cairo: Maktabat Nahḍat Miṣr.

Kress, G. (1985), *Linguistic Processes in Sociocultural Practice*, Victoria: Deakin University Press.

Lāshīn, ᶜAbd al-Fattāḥ (1983), *al-Maᶜānī fī Ḍawʾ Asālīb al-Qurʾān*, Cairo: al-Maktaba al-Umawiyya.

Lyons, J. (1970), *New Horizons in Linguistics*, Harmondsworth: Penguin.

20

The Dispute of Coffee and Tea

A Debate-poem from The Gulf

Clive Holes
University of Cambridge

1 Bedouin and sedentary poetry in Arabia

In the past few years, no less than three book-length studies of contemporary Bedouin vernacular poetry have appeared: one each by Sowayan[1] and Kurpershoek[2] on the poetry of central Arabia, and one by Bailey[3] on that of Sinai and the Negev. These writers have pointed to the similarities of this so-called *nabaṭī* poetry in theme, structure, and even poetic idiom to the pre-and early Islamic *qaṣāʾid*, echoing the opinion of the pioneering German orientalist Albert Socin[4] that there is a lineal link between the two. But the Bedouin tradition is not the only vernacular poetic tradition which thrives in contemporary Arabia. In the settled communities around the coasts of the peninsula, as well as in neighbouring Mesopotamia, there exist *ḥaḍarī* poetic traditions which, circumstantial evidence suggests, may in some cases be as old or even older than those of the Bedouin, harking back to cultures which predate Islam. The origin of this poetry is not tribal, its themes are not lyrical or encomiastic, and its language is not high-flown: all of which negatives perhaps help explain why it has been neglected by Arabs and traditional Arabists alike. This *ḥaḍarī* poetry often deals with the banal: the pains and pleasures of the Arab equivalents of the butcher, the baker and the candle-stick maker, treating them in a satirical, often comical fashion, and employing an idiom which, though by no means the plain vernacular of everyday speech, is nonetheless nearer to it in vocabulary and syntax than the stylised diction of the contemporary Bedouin bard. Part of the reason for its neglect also lies in the fact that, even more than the Bedouin poetry, it remains an oral tradition: when collections of poems are printed, the run is small and quickly exhausted, and they rarely circulate beyond the confines of the poets' own communities.

2 The debate- or dispute-poem

In this paper I shall present an example of a particularly interesting poetic genre, the so-called *munāẓara* or 'debate-poem', from the *ḥaḍarī* poetic tradition of Bahrain, together with some brief comment on its contemporary social, and literary-historical significance. In the Bahraini debate-poem, two (sometimes more) non-human combatants – animals, seasons of the year, inanimate related objects, occupations, etc – engage in a verbal duel in which each tries to demonstrate superiority over the other through a combination of argument and abuse. The poet himself participates in the poem, typically setting the scene at the beginning and resolving it at the end, if the ending is not self-evident, by issuing a judgement in favour of one of the participants and/or reconciling them. The debate which forms the meat in this poetic sandwich may be in the form of one long speech by each combatant, or, more often, the two take it in turns, appealing to the poet for the right to speak. In a recently published collection, for example,[5] there are lengthy debates between oil-wells and pearling, summer and winter, coffee and tobacco, four different colours of silk cloth, as well as the poem presented here, between coffee and tea. In the same collection, there is a group of poems called *muḥāwarāt* which differ slightly from the *munāẓarāt* in that here there is not so much a debate as an altercation about a specific grievance, e.g. between the captain of a pearling dhow and a rat which had been eating the ship's provisions,[6] between the poet and a troublesome mosquito, and between the poet and a worn-out overcoat which he was wondering whether to replace.

Students of comparative literature will know that similar dispute poems between non-human combatants are found in many literatures of the ancient world: Ancient Egyptian, Old Norse, Provençal, mediaeval Latin, Persian, and, most intriguingly in this context, all the literary cultures of Mesopotamia which preceded the Arab conquest – from Sumerian to Akkadian to Aramaic and its Christian variety, Syriac.[7] The Sumerian and Akkadian debates in particular, between combatants such as the hoe and the plough, the tree and the reed, the heron and the turtle, summer and winter, bear a remarkably close formal resemblance to the Bahraini Arabic debate poems described here. The first examples we have in Aramaic/Syriac, the languages which co-existed with Arabic for many centuries in the Fertile crescent, date from the 4th century AD. The genre was still popular enough in Iraq for examples to be composed in Syriac as late as the 9th century, two centuries after the Arab conquest: we have one of this date between the vine and the cedar by a certain

David bar Paulos.[8] In Classical Syriac, the debates are mostly between biblical figures (eg Joseph and Potiphar's wife, Christ and the Pharisees[9]); but in the post-Classical period, in debates between, e.g. gold and wheat, cup and wine, the same type of personification occurs as in the earlier Sumerian and Akkadian debates to which Brock[10] claims the Syriac tradition was heir. Debate-poems form part of the Syriac Christian liturgy in Iraq up to the present time.[11] Moreover, in the secular sphere, the tradition continues up to almost the present day: an anonymous example from Urmia, a Christian Neo-Aramiac-speaking area of Kurdistan, was published in an American *emigré* newspaper in 1909: 'the tea-kettle and the boys'.[12]

In Arabic, the poetic debate in the sense meant here makes its first appearance in proto-type form, in – significantly – 9th century Baghdad. This is a short work written in *saj^c* entitled *salwat al-ḥarīf bi munāẓarat al-rabī^c wa l-xarīf* ('The artisan's diversion by the debate between spring and autumn) attributed, probably erroneously, to al-Jāḥiẓ. From then on, it gradually becomes a distinct, if marginal sub-genre of the Classical poetry of the 12th, 13th and 14th centuries,[13] and a somewhat more substantial genre in Middle Arabic and the modern vernaculars: examples survive in dialects as disparate as Cairene, Yemenite, Algerian and Morrocan.[14] The key point is that, as can be appreciated from an examination of the titles of the poems, the Arabic debate has been, from the earliest times, an entirely *ḥaḍarī* phenomenon which has focused on *ḥaḍarī* concerns. In the Fertile Crescent, the function of the genre may have fluctuated from one culture, and one period to another – sometimes as a vehicle for popular wisdom, sometimes, as in Syriac, as a species of Christian religious dialectic, sometimes as a didactic instrument, sometimes as an oblique means of social satire – but this merely illustrates its flexible, protean nature within the *ḥaḍarī* social milieu. In literary-historical terms, there are no credible Arabic antecedents for the genre in pre-Abbasid times, and the evidence suggests a literary transfer from Syriac/Aramaic to Arabic in Iraq during the Abbasid period, and possibly thence to other settled areas of the Arab world.[15]

3 Bahrain and southern Mesopotamia as a religio-cultural entity

Before we turn to the literary aspects of the Gulf debate-poem, however, it is worth considering another possible, and admittedly more speculative explanation for why the genre turns up in Bahrain (and indeed, coastal Oman[16]). Ancient Bahrain, which as well as the eponymous islands of today included the whole of the coastal region of north-eastern Arabia, was a predominantly Christian area for several centuries before Islam, as was coastal Oman. In the Syriac sources, Bahrain is part of the Nestorian diocese of Beth Qaṭrāye, and Oman is known as Beth Mazūnāye. Bahrain was important enough for synods of Christian bishops to be held in Masmāhīj, or as it is known today, the village of Samāhīj, on the Bahraini island of Muḥarraq in 410 and 576 AD.[17] Aramaic/Syriac toponyms in Bahrain such as *māḥūz* 'area of land' and *dēr* 'monastery', as well as much recently discovered archaeological evidence, and abundant Syriac ecclesiastical records and correspondence,[18] all point to a stable Nestorian Christian, pastoral economy in Bahrain and north-eastern Arabia for at least two centuries before Islam,[19] as well as in southern Iran. As far as can be ascertained, the languages spoken by this settled Bahraini population were Aramaic and to some degree Persian, with Syriac functioning as a liturgical language.[20] The religious and cultural contacts with Mesopotamia and south-western Iran were close.

My speculation is that the contemporary Bahraini debate poetry may hark back to this pre-Islamic period of cultural unity between southern Mesopotamia, south-western Iran and north-eastern Arabia. There is no direct literary evidence for this supposition, but it is interesting to note, that in Bahrain, the debate poetry is an entirely Shīᶜī phenomenon, or, to be more precise, a *Baḥrānī* phenomenon. *Baḥrānī* (pl. *Baḥārna*) is a term which refers to the indigenous Arabic-speaking Shīᶜite population of Bahrain and the Gulf coast. The *Baḥārna* themselves claim that they are the 'original' population of these coastal areas. The reality is certainly more complex than this, but there is good reason to think that the *Baḥārna* do represent an ancient layer of population, part of which, according to local tradition has ancient links with Yemen, but an element of which may well be, as Serjeant claimed 25 years ago,[21] the arabised descendants of the Christian and Jewish population of north-eastern Arabia referred to earlier, who were among the earliest converts to Islam and Shīᶜism. For one thing, the village *Baḥārna* dialects, like those of the *ḥaḍar* of Oman, are quite different from those of the Najdi-descended populations which began arriving in the islands from central Arabia 250 years ago. These *Baḥārna* dialects contain a fascinating mix of phonological and morphological features which seem to connect them both with Yemen and southern Arabia on the one hand, and the sedentary populations of southern Iraq on the other. Indeed, some of the *Baḥrānī* features have echoes in the Aramaic dialects spoken in Mesopotamia during the first millennium.[22] It is worth noting that there is a strong Iraqi dialectal influence on the poetic koine in which the contemporary *Baḥrānī* debate poems are written which is absent from the everyday non-poetic speech of the *Baḥārna*.[23] This is a consequence of the fact that for the *Baḥārna*, as for other Gulf Shīᶜa, southern Iraq is the local cultural capital of Shīᶜism. But this fact does not preclude the possibility that the debate-poem may have been part of an ancient *ḥaḍarī* cultural heritage, shared by the populations of southern Mesopotamia and north-eastern Arabia, which were unified in the pre-Islamic era by Nestorian Christianity just as they are today by Jaᶜfari Shīᶜism. If this suggestion sounds far-fetched, it is worth reminding ourselves that the more fully documented topic of Bedouin poetry shows that an oral poetic tradition can indeed survive intact in its essentials for more than a millennium; why should we think such a thing less likely for the *ḥaḍarī* communities which over the same period have maintained their own quite distinct social coherence?

4 The Dispute between Coffee and Tea

The poem is attributed to ᶜAbdallāh Ḥusayn al-Qārī of Manama, Bahrain, and is undated, although the collection in which it appears was first published in 1955. The other *munāẓarāt* in the collection, some by the same poet, are dated between the mid-1930's and 1950, and some refer to specific historical events. The Dispute between Oil-wells and Pearl-diving, for instance, was clearly written at the time of economic transition in the mid-30's, while the Dispute of Summer and Winter was triggered off, the poet tells us in a preamble, by the unusually hot summer of 1950 and the fact that poor Bahrainis had not the money to afford air-conditioning or escape to the cooler climate of Lebanon.

The 'plot' of the Dispute between Coffee and Tea is as follows. The first few lines set the scene: it is *lēlat il-jumᶜa*, Thursday evening, traditionally a time of relaxation and fun, and the poet is lying awake in bed with the coffee-pot and tea-kettle bubbling away in front of him. Suddenly the two come to life, greet him politely and one of them, coffee, asks him to act as judge in a dispute between them. The debate proper then begins. Coffee speaks first (l.4–13), accusing tea of being a Persian, an unwelcome guest and an overweening tyrant, constantly vaunting his polished spoons, kettles and Japanese crockery. While coffee claims she is the symbol of male sociability, tea is depicted as being clandestinely sipped by women hidden away in private houses. Having first asked permission of the poet, tea then replies, contrasting coffee's dark colour, typical of slaves and Indians, and bitter taste with his own ruddy colour, ambergris fragrance and sugar-sweetness. Tea lists his qualities, claiming he is all things to all men: a soother of pain, a relaxation from work and stress, and a drink that can both put drinkers to sleep and wake them up. Whereas the servant coffee is roasted and pounded, and, according to tea, his drinkers are wild and uncivilised, tea struts like a mighty panjandrum among his more civilised urban bibbers (l.16–30). There is then a rejoinder from coffee (l.3–43), in which she repeats many of the same accusations, and adds another, that tea-drinking corrupts youth and leads to alcohol-drinking. The argument degenerates into a slanging match as coffee mobilises her army of cups, coffee pots, roasting pans and stirring rods to attack tea (l.44–54). Tea flees, seeking the poet's protection, which is granted (l.45–58). In the final seven lines, the poet effects a reconciliation and marriage between the two, who kiss, make up and pledge their loyalty to him.

While, at a literal level, the poem is basically an opportunity for the poet to put on an amusing display of verbal ingenuity, there is a good deal of oblique allusion to the local social and cultural milieu. The vituperative element, for example, plays on the negative associations which each of the combatants potentially carries for the local listener. So tea, because of its non-Arabian origin, is depicted variously as an *ibn il-ᵓaᶜājim, hallī lifā min īrān* 'son of the Persians, an intruder from Iran', a *Hōlī*[24] 'a Persian impostor', and *ibn il-ḥumrān* 'a son of the Reds' (=Russians). Tea is dispensed from a Russian samovar into Russian *istikānāt* or Japanese crockery, having been boiled in a *ġūrī* 'kettle' and stirred with *xawāšig* 'spoons' (both Persian words). In lines 14–15, the poet even addresses tea partly in Persian. The point is that tea is an outsider, an alien, who uses foreign words and foreign artefacts. The context for these jibes is that there had never been much love lost between Bahrain and Iran, which maintained a territorial claim on the islands until 1971; and the village *Baḥārna* communities in which these poems were recited have a history of regarding the Iranian migrants to Bahrain, whether Sunni *Hwala* or Shīᶜī *ᶜAjam*, with suspicion. Nor were Japan and Russia in particularly good odour at the time this poem was written: the discovering in Japan during the 1930's of a method for culturing pearls artificially effectively put paid to the Bahraini pearling industry, and the Russians had been perceived as a threat in the Gulf region ever since the Bolshevik Revolution. The jibes against coffee, on the other hand, as *umm il-bidwān* 'mother of the Bedouin', *ᶜabdah minti maᶜtūga* 'an unfreed black slave', and a *bānyān* 'Indian' play on the common perception of the Bedouin as unruly and wild, and on the fact that the dark colour of coffee is similar to the skin of slaves or Indians, both of which groups had a low place in the social order. There is little that could be termed logical argument in the debate; apart from the swapping of colourful insults, there are unsubstantiated accusations that consuming one or other of the drinks leads to moral turpitude and the corruption of youth (tea), to unsociability (tea), or to lack of worldly success (coffee). But there is little or no evidence adduced. The concluding section seems to emphasise the pointlessness of conflict, expressed via the ingenious metaphor of the marriage of opposites symbolised in the common Gulf practice of alternately drinking small cups of bitter cardamom-favoured coffee and glasses of super-sweet tea (1.64–6)

If there is anything 'deep' to be said about the Gulf *munāẓara*, it is probably that it plays out in a humorous, and defusing poetic form the cultural contact and change which have always been a feature of Gulf communities. The Dispute of Coffee and Tea, like that between Oil-Wells and Pearling, in which the modern marvels of motor-cars, record-players, and wage-earning do verbal battle with the heroism, fellowship and romanticism of a dying age, is a rehearsal of one aspect of this cultural clash, and, ultimately, of the necessity to keep the old and the new in balance and harmony. So, even where the poet pronounces at the end of his poem in favour of one of the disputants, as he does in the case of oil-wells, this judgement is mitigated by an *envoi* in which the necessity of valuing the qualities of the loser, and of reconciling conflicts is emphasised:

gūmū tṣālaḥū, yiṣlaḥkum il-maᶜbūd
allah yirabḥich wi l-ġōṣ lēnā yiᶜūd
tistaġnī l-xalg u yṣīr dahr isᶜūd
wi l-līlū tfūz ib ribḥ tijjārah
il-kull minhum samiḥ wi z-zaᶜal ᶜanhum rāḥ
u itbaddal shatamhum yā xalīlī imzāḥ

'Come and make peace now, for God reconciles,
May pearling return! Be oil's profits in piles!
Let people get richer, and happier too,
And pearl-merchants profit from pearls from the blue.
Each was content, and all anger was gone,
Instead of their insults, friend, the disputants joked on'.

Notes

1. Sowayan, S. *Nabaṭī Poetry* Berkeley, Los Angeles and London, University of California Press, 1985.
2. Kurpershoek, P. M. *Oral Poetry and Narrative from Central Arabia, I: the*

Poetry of ad-Dindān, a Bedouin Bard in Southern Najd, Leiden, Brill, 1994.

3. Bailey, C. *Bedouin Poetry from Sinai and the Negev*, Oxford, Clarendon Press.
4. See Socin, A. *Diwan aus Centralarabien*, Leipzig, Teubner, 1900–1, especially Teil III, section 22, pp 46ff on the 'form and content' of Bedouin poetry, which he begins with the comment: 'Die in dem Diwan zusammengestellten . . . Gedichte erwiesen sich in vieler Beziehung, nach Inhalt, Form und Sprache als directe Fortsetzung der altarabischen Dichtkunst'.
5. Al-Nāṣirī, Sheikh, M.A. *Tanfīh al-Khāṭir wa Salwat al-Qāṭin wa l-Musāfir*, Bahrain, Maktabat al-Māḥūza, 2nd edition, 1972.
6. See Holes, C. D. 'The Rat and the Ship's Captain: a dialogue-poem (*muḥāwara*) from the Gulf, with some comments on the social and literary-historical background of the genre' in *Dialectologia arabica – A Collection of Articles in Honour of the Sixtieth Birthday of Professor Heikki Palva*, Helsinki, *Studia Orientalia* 75(1995) pp 10–120.
7. See the extensive bibliography in Reininck, G. J. and Vanstiphout, H. L. J. *Dispute Poems and Dialogues in the Ancient and Mediaeval Near East*, Louvain, Peeters, 1991.
8. Brock, S. 'The Dispute Poem: from Sumer to Syriac' *Bayn al-Nahrayn* 7 No 28 (1979), p 418 (Arabic pagination).
9. Brock, S. 'Syriac dispute poems: the various types' in Reinink and Vanstiphout (n.7), pp 109–119.
10. Brock (n.8) pp 425–6, Brock (n.9), p 109.
11. Brock (personal communication) notes that Pennacchietti's three neo-Aramaic versions of 'the thief and the cherub' (Pennacchietti, F. A. *il ladrone e il cherubino*, Torino, Silvio Zamorani editore, 1993) are translations of a Classical Syriac dialogue poem still used liturgically in Iraq.
12. Yaure, L. 'A poem in the Neo-Aramaic dialect of Urmia', *Journal of Near-Eastern Studies* 26 (1957), pp 73–87.
13. For some examples, see Wagner, E. 'Die arabische Rangstreitdichtung und ihre Einordnung in die allgemeine Literaturgeschichte' in *Akademie der Wissenschaften und der Litteratur in Mainz. Abhandlungen der geistes- und sozialwissenschaftlichen Klasse*, Jahrgang 1962, Nr 8, Wiesbaden 1963, pp 437–476, esp. pp 449, 455; Heinrichs, W. 'Rose versus narcissus: observations on an Arabic literary debate' in Reinink and Vanstiphout (n.7) pp 179–198, Van Gelder, G. 'Arabic debates of Jest and Earnest' in the same volume pp 199–211, and Van Gelder, G. 'The conceit of the pen and the sword: on an Arabic literary debate', *Journal of Semitic Studies* 32/2 (1987) pp 329–60.
14. In Cairene we have cat v. mouse (Littmann, E. 'Der Katzenmäusekrieg' in *Zentralblatt für Bibliothekswesen, Beiheft 75* (1950), Leipzig, pp 24–259); cobbler v. Koran-teacher, railway-engine v. telegraph, telephone v. telegraph (all in Littmann, E. 'Neuarabische Streitgedichte' in *Festschrift zur Feier des zweihunderjährigen Bestehens der Akademie der Wissenschaften in Gottingen*, II, 1951, pp 26–66); water-melon v. date, cream v. honey (in Bouriant, U. *Chansons populaires arabes en dialecte du Caire*, Paris, Leroux, 1893, pp 20–25, 159–60 (reproduced in al-Bāqlī, M.Q. *ʾAdab*

al-Darāwish, Cairo, 1970 pp 200–207)). In Serjeant's *Prose and Poetry from the Ḥaḍramawt*, London, Taylor's Foreign Press, 1951, there are four examples: grains v. fruits, tea v. coffee, women's skin colours (green v. white v. yellow), and stove v. mosque-lamp; excerpts from a number of debates in Judaeo-Arabic by the 17th century Yemeni Jew Shalom Shibzi (tobacco v. coffee, the bachelor v. the husband, coffee v. qat, San[c]aa v. Ta[c]izz, Aden v. Mocca) are in Bacher W., 'Zur Rangstreit-Litteratur: aus der arabischen Poesie der Juden Jemens' in *Mélanges Hartwig Derenbourg*, Paris, 1909, pp 13–47. Finally two examples, the dark girl v. the pale girl, the townsman v. the bedouin, respectively from Médéa, Algeria and the Moroccan Tafilalt are in Sonneck, C. *Chants Arabes du Maghreb*, Paris Librairie Orientale et Americaine, 1904, pp 115–123 (Arabic pagination) with translations on pp 196–205.

15. Modern (southern) Iraqī examples of debate poems may be found in [c]Alī al-Khāqānī *Funūn al-Adab al-Sha[c]bī*, part IV, Baghdad, 1962, pp 73–82: summer v. winter, the road v. the cigarette, rest v. effort, by poets from the towns of Baṣra, [c]Amāra and Ḥilla.
16. In Ghaylānī, S.M., *al-Adab fī Balad al-Shirā[c]: Dīwān al-Shā[c]ir Sa[c]īd [c]Abdallāh Walad Wazīr* there are three examples of *munāẓarāt/muḥāwarāt*. This Omani poet was born in the port of Ṣūr in 1905.
17. Potts, D. *The Arabian Gulf in Antiquity. Vol II: From Alexander the Great to the Coming of Islam*, Oxford, Clarendon Press, 1990, pp. 124–5.
18. Beaucamp, J. and Robin, C. *L'évêché nestorien de Masmāhīj dans l'Archipel d'al-Baḥrain'* in Potts, D. (ed) *Dilmun: New Studies in the Archaeology and Early History of Bahrain*, Berlin, Dietrich Heiner Verlag, 1983, pp 17–196.
19. Potts, D. (n.17) pp 353–4.
20. Potts, D. (n.17) pp 221, 223–4.
21. Serjeant R. B. 'Fisher-folk and fish-traps in al-Baḥrain', *BSOAS* 31 (1968), p 488.
22. The following points are of particular interest: (1) the *Baḥārna* (B) dialects, like Aramaic/Syriac, but unlike all the surrounding Arabic dialects, have lost the interdental series /th/, /dh/, /ẓ/: they have /f/, /d/, /ḍ/; (2) again, quite unlike other Arabic dialects of N.Arabia, the 2 f.s. and 2 com.pl. pronouns are *intīn(a)* and *intūn(a)*, with corresponding perfect verb forms *katabtīn(a)* and *katabtūn(a)*. All of these forms are attested in the Aramaic/Syriac of the first millenium (cf the Aramaic data in Brockelmann, C. *Grundriss der vergleichenden Grammatik der semitischen Sprachen*, Berlin 1908, Vol I pp 302, 572, 576); (3) the B Dialects obligatorily insert an *-n(n)-* between an active participle and a suffixed object pronoun, e.g. *kātlinnah* 'he has killed him', and also, in the dialect poetry, between an imperfect and an object suffix, e.g. *azawwijannik* 'I marry you'. Both types of form are also found in Oman, and the imperfect verb form is typical of southern Mesopotamian *ḥaḍarī* dialects (Ingham, B. 'Urban and Rural Arabic in Khuzistan', *BSOAS* 36 (1973) p 548). Brockelmann reports the imperfect verb form with *-n(n)-* for several varieties of Aramaic, and considers it a decayed form of the energetic (op. cit. pp 64–2). Both Greenman (Greenman, J. 'A sketch of the Arabic dialect of the central Yemeni Tihama', *ZAL* 3, 1979, pp 47–61) and Maṭar (Maṭar, A.A. *Ẓawāhir Nādira fī*

Lahajāt al-Khalīj al-ᶜArabi, Qaṭar, Dār Qaṭrī bin al-Fajāᵓa, 1983 pp. 73–76) report that the unusual combination of features in (1) and (2) above also occurs as a bundle in the Yemeni Tihama, the area which Arab sources, and the *Baḥārna* themselves, claim was the origin of the most ancient layer of the Arab population of Bahrain (Al-Tājir, M. A., *Language and Linguistic Origins in Bahrain*, London, KPI, pp 16–21). Maṭar goes further and claims that this distribution of language features is explained by the fact that both Bahrain and the Tihama were anciently affected by Aramaic influences.

23. For a detailed discussion of this influence, and of the stigmatised *Baḥrānī* features which are avoided in the poetic language of the *munāẓarāt* poety, see Holes (n.6).
24. At the time this poem was written, *Hōlī* (pl. *Hwala*) was a pejorative term used to refer to a distinct section of the Sunni population of Bahrain (and Qatar). The *Hwala* are Shāfiᶜī Sunnis who claim they were orginally Arabs who migrated to the coast of southern Iran. They were expelled by Reza Shah in the 19th century and returned to the Arab side of the Gulf, where they integrated fully with the *ᶜArab* (=descendants of the Najdī Sunnis who arrived in Bahrain in the18th century), today being indistinguishable from them in dress and speech. Today, the *Hwala* are heavily represented in Bahraini business and government (e.g. the Al-Muᵓayyad, Fakhroo, Kanoo families). See Khuri, F. I. *Tribe and State in Bahrain*, Chicago, 1980, pp. 2–4.

Munāẓarat al-gahwa wa sh-shāy
The dispute between coffee and tea

balwat il-ᶜarab
bane of the Arabs

1	*lēlat il-jumᶜa ya xwān*	*	Last Thursday, my friends, late at night,
	muḍṭajiᶜ u anā sahrān		I lay wide-awake, my eyes bright.
2	*sahrān anā bi manāmī*	*	Wide-awake in my bed I was lying,
	lēn il-gahwa jiddāmī	*	The coffee-pot softly was sighing,
	wi l-c̲h̲āy yiġlī ḥāmī		The tea on the hearth gently bubbled,
3	*wi yfūr minhum duxān*	*	And steam from the two rose untroubled.
	iwgafū mā bēn īdayya	*	When, bingo! The pot stood before me!
	u abdu līya t-taḥīya		The kettle too, greeting me warmly!
4	*u gālat lī n-nibārīya*	*	The Malabar lass got in quickly,
	u tiḥkī ḥakī z-zaᶜlān	*	And sounding a tiny bit prickly,
	nrīdik tiḥkum yā ḥākim		Said 'Sir, would you please judge between us,
5	*bēnī u bēn iẓ-ẓālim*	*	Between me and this tyrant so heinous?
	aᶜnī bn il-ᵓaᶜājim	*	I mean this offspring of the Persian,
	hallī lifā min īrān		A guest for whom all feel aversion.
6	*jā yiftixir ᶜalayya*	*	His vaunts and his boasts sting like nettles,
	bi xawās̲h̲igah u ġūrīyah	*	His bright polished spoons and hot kettles,
	u ṣḥūnah l-jābānīya		His saucers and Japanese crockery,
7	*u smāwarah ibn il-ḥumrān*	*	And his Red samovar – it's a mockery!
	mā yidrī anā s̲h̲lōnī	*	He doesn't know me or my colour,

	bi l-muglā lō ḥimsūnī		How, burnt in the pan, I turn duller,
8	*u bi l-hāwin lō daggūnī*	*	Or when in the mortar they pound me,
	tihra^{c} *lī kill il-*^{c}*irbān*	*	The Bedu rush in to surround me.
	tbassaṭ bi z-zall il-majlis		My sitting-room's furnished with carpets,
9	*u il-kil jālis yiḥris*	*	Where, patiently, each on the floor sits,
	u bi rayḥatī mitwannis	*	They sniff me – their senses I've captured!
	u yiṭrab min yishrab finjān		They drink just one cup – they're enraptured!
10	*u hū bi d-dūr imxashshash*	*	But tea, into houses they slip him,
	wiyyā l-ḥarīm im^{c}*ash*^{c}*asha*	*	So hidden veiled ladies can sip him.
	li-ġrīb lō marr mā ydishsh	*	Unauthorised men are forbidden,
11	*bētah illā b istī*^{ɔ}*dhān*	*	(Lest they espy what must stay hidden!)
	u anā muḍyafī maftūḥ	*	With me, though, there's always a welcome,
	li l yishtihi u rād iyrūḥ		For all, come they oft, come they seldom
12	*u li l-ġurbatīya masmūḥ*	*	If strangers drop in, they're permitted,
	tudxul u tiḥṣal iḥsān	*	Nay, honoured! – by all, that's admitted!'
	lamman sima^{c} *ṣadd lēhā*		Tea listened, then turned to address her,
13	*u ẓall yitḥammas a*^{c}*lēhā*	*	He'd fired himself up to full pressure,
	u gallī smi^{c}*t laġīhā*	*	"D'you hear all her nonsense?" he spluttered,
	min ruxṣatik aḥchī al-ān		"Let me speak, that'll all be rebutted!"
			the poet
14	*goftam balī takallam*	*	I said "Go ahead then, speak freely,
	ay dust-e-man lā tahtamm		Don't be anxious, my friend, 'cos I really
15	*ve man* ^{c}*alēkum aḥlam*	*	To you will be kind, sensitivities mind,
	wa l-ġaḍab ^{ɔ}*aṣlah shayṭān*		For anger is Satan's work, merely!"
			ash-shāy
			tea
16	*gāl ilhā yā maḥrūga*	*	Said tea to coffee,: "Oh you burnt one,
	yā sōdā yā madgūga	*	All blackened and crushed, your good looks gone,
	^{c}*abdah u minti ma*^{c}*tūga*		You're a slave-girl who hasn't been freed yet,
17	*xaddāmah* ^{c}*ind il-ka*^{c}*bān*	*	A skivvy the Bedu still need, yet
	sh il kabrich sh il xallāch	*	How come you're so proud and so haughty?
	laġwiya . . . zāyid laġwāch!		Loquacity's truly your forte!
18	*tridī a*^{c}*addid balwāch*	*	Yellow one, shall I list your disasters,
	yā ṣafrā yā umm il-bidwān	*	One by one to your Bedouin masters?
	ismich yā ġabra gahwa		You dullard! Your real name is coffee,
19	*il kull il-xalāyij balwa*	*	To all who imbibe, catastrophe!
	lā mēwa inti u lā shahwa	*	A fruit you are not, nor a savour,
	u lā rāḥa inti li t-ta^{c}*bān*	*	Nor relief for the tired from their labour.
20	*u anā li l-awādim rāḥa*	*	But me, I give all relaxation,
	u marham il kill ijrāḥah	*	I'm a balm, soothing wounds and vexation,
	u muḍrib ib kill sāḥa		I entertain in every forum,
21	*u sharrābī dāyim farḥān*	*	They drink me with cheer and decorum,
	waj^{c}*ān aṭayyib rāsah*	*	For pain I'm a cure you can measure,
	ḍajrān ilah anāsa		When fed up, I offer you pleasure.
22	*na*^{c}*sān udhhib in*^{c}*āsah*	*	I banish the sleepy-head's sleep,

sahrān anim is-sahrān	*	The sleepless, I make him count sheep,
u mā tin^{c}idd kil balāwich		Your miseries cannot be numbered,
23 *u yiblash kilmin wiṣal lich*	*	Who drinks you by ill-luck's encumbered.
ribḥ u maṣāliḥ mā bich	*	In you there's no profit or use,
sharrābich dāyim xasrān		Who drinks your drink, you cook his goose!
24 *u anā l-awānī ṣīnī*	*	But my crocks are fine, oriental,
u inti ba^{c}ad shiftīnī	*	You've seen that – and this point's essential –
kil il-mala iyḥibbūnnī		All love me, and love with abandon,
25 *u atbaxtar mithl is-sulṭān*	*	I strut like a mighty panjandrum.
u lō rādū yi^{c}milūnich	*	To make you, though, what a performance!
bi l-muglā u yḥimsūnich	*	The roasting pan first: prime importance!
26 *u bi l-hāwin ydiggūnich*	*	You're pounded to bits in a mortar,
maḥrūga chinnich bānyān	*	Burnt brown like an Indian's daughter.
lōnich sawād il-mamgūt		Your darkness disgusts, there's no question,
27 *lōnī shabīh il-yāqūt*	*	But rubicund, that's my complexion.
shīrīn dhōgī u man^{c}ūt	*	My sweet taste, all praise and all hallow,
ṭa^{c}mich talx u ^{c}alqam kān	*	You're acrid, and bitter as aloe,
28 *dhayigtī mithil is-sukkar*	*	I'm sweet, oh, so sweet! sugar candy!
rayiḥtī shibh il-^{c}anbar	*	My ambergris fragrance is dandy,
lōnī jamīl u aḥmar	*	My red hue quite wins beauty's laurel,
29 *shikl il-^{c}aqīq u marjān*	*	I shine like agate, or sea-coral.
rab^{c}ī kilhum mitmadnīn	*	My folk are well-mannered and civil,
u rab^{c}ich l-akthar mitwaḥshīn	*	But yours mostly wild like the devil.
30 *balwat il-^{c}arab lā tifxarīn*	*	Oh bane of the Arabs, no vainglory!
yā umm il-ḥathal mā lich shān		You're the dregs in your cup! End of story!
		il-gahwa
		coffee
31 *gālat lih iskit yā ḍalīl*	*	She said "Just pipe down! You're misguided,
lā yā bōl il-^{c}ajājīl	*	You're calves' piss, by all men derided!
u yā ġasāl il-fanājīl		For washing up you're up to scratch,
32 *wēn inta u bint is-sūdān*	*	But the black girl and you? It's no match!
mā tigdar itṣaff ḥawlī	*	With me you in no way compare, but
lākin laġwī u fuḍūlī		You meddlesome fool still you tut-tut!
33 *yā l-farsī u yā l-hōlī*	*	You're a Persian dressed up, just a cheap fake,
aḥsan lik gaṣr il-lisān	*	Best keep that tongue still for your health's sake
it^{c}ayyirnī itgullī ^{c}abdah	*	You slander me, claim I'm a slave,
34 *u a^{c}lēk ānī sayyida*	*	When really it's you that's my knave,
mā tigdar faḍlī t^{c}iddah	*	My virtues? Too many to list!
shāyi^{c} ismī ib kill imkān		My name is on everyone's lips,
35 *ismik yā aġbar shāhī*	*	While your name, you bird-brain, is tea,
il kill il-xalāyij lāhī	*	Time-waster to all, unlike me!
mā rti^{c}ēt illā bjāhī		You're only raised up through my rank,
36 *bismī irtifi^{c}lik hash-shān*	*	For your fame it's me you should thank.
u aḍrub ba^{c}ad lik amthāl	*	I'll make my point clear as I can:
lō wāḥid ṣādaf rajjāl		When someone bumps into a man,
37 *ḥabb y^{c}izmah ib dāk il-ḥāl*	*	And wants to invite him straightway,
gūl, ēsh ygullih ib wijdān	*	What words, prithee tea, does he say?

ygullih itfaḍḍal wiyyāy		With feeling he says "Come with me,
38 *li l-bēt itgahwa yā hwāy*	*	Let's go home, dear friend, drink coffee!"
mā ygullih shrab kūbat shāy	*	He doesn't say "Fancy some tea?"
yā mxarrib kill is-shubbān		You wrecker of youth's probity!
39 *kam shabāb itxarrab*	*	Through you many a young man's gone bad,
min gabil kān imgarrab	*	Who once was a nice friendly lad,
ḥatta l-xamar ẓall yishrab		They even drink alcohol too,
40 *fiᶜlik afᶜāl shayṭān*	*	That's Satan's work – all 'cos of you!
imsawwa lik shāy xānah	*	They've even erected tea-houses,
bihā l-wilid sakrānah		In which our youth sits and carouses,
41 *u ib liᶜbatik ṭarbānah*	*	They tipsily drink in a haze –
u inta s-sabab li-l-ᶜiṣyān	*	Because of you, youth disobeys!
murr u shūf il-maʾātim		Now come and see our funeral houses,
42 *maᶜmūra bī yā gāshim*	*	That's where, bully, I wear the trousers!
kilmin lifā min il-awādim	*	Each man, wheree'er from, who drops in there,
lāzim yinṣabb lih finjān		To pour him a cup, we take great care,
43 *u ᶜāyin maḍāyif li-shyūx*	*	And look at our elders' posh guest-rooms,
mabsūṭa bi z-zall wa l-jūx	*	With rich rugs and drapes they're all festooned."
rād il-ḥachī u hū manfūx		All puffed up, tea made as to speak then,
44 *gālat lih inchabb yā xawwān*	*	Said coffee "Clear off, treach'rous heathen!
lā tiḥchī bas u lā ykūn	*	Be quiet! Don't brag and don't boast:
tifxar, tarā ythūr il-kawn		The world may rise up, one huge host!
45 *ᶜindī junūd u tidrī shlōn*	*	I've soldiers, of that you're aware,
u hassa aᶜammir il-maydān	*	Whom I'll deploy now on the square!"
gallihā ashū thadh"rinnī		Said tea "Hmm . . . That sounds like a warning,
46 *u bi ḥarbich txawfinnī*	*	Your threats don't scare me! (said he, yawning),
mā aẓunnich tᶜarfinnī	*	You don't know that I'm in fine fettle,
yā maḥrūga bi n-nīrān		Oh brown-skinned one, roast on hot metal!"
47 *ġiḍbat u ṣāḥat bi l-ḥāl*	*	At that coffee flared up and shouted,
u iṭṭashshar minhā l-ḥithāl	*	Her dregs all spilt out as she spouted,
yā fanājīlī yā d-dalāl		"Rally round all my cups, coffee pots!
48 *wēn il-gumgum ᶜālī sh-shān*	*	And the copper one, biggest I've got!
wēn il-muglā u l-miḥmās	*	The roasting pan too! Where's the ladle?
dhāk il ẓafar rāᶜī l-bās		He's won every fight since the cradle!
49 *arīd akshif il ḥārbat ir-rās*	*	I want to teach this headstrong fool,
haṭ-ṭāġī nasl iṭ-ṭuġyān	*	This despots' son, despot so cruel,
wēn il-hāwin wēn īdah		A lesson! Where's pestle, where's mortar?
50 *wēn il-bīz u ᶜaḍīdah*	*	Where's the muffler and his supporter?
il mixbāṭ il-ḥarb ᶜīdah	*	To stirring-rod war's like a sport,
xallhum yiḥḍurūn al-ān		Come gather round now, all report!"
51 *nādū ᶜalēhā labēch*	*	They shouted back "Ma'am! Present all!
kilnā xadam bēn īdēch	*	We're servants at your beck and call,
yāhū illadhī itjarrā ᶜalēch		Who was it who dared challenge you?
52 *iḥchī yā bībī in-niswān*	*	Oh grandest of dames, tell us do!"
gālat had-daᶜī l-agshar	*	She said: ᶜSee this wretch! See this rogue here?

	dāyim ᶜalayya yifxar		He claims that to me he's superior!
53	*lāzim yiṣīr imᶜaffar*	*	He needs to be brought down to earth,
	u abaddidah aᶜlā t-turbān	*	And have his nose rubbed in the dirt!
	u akassir kil awānīh		I'll smash all his cups and his crocks,
54	*u kill illadhī muxtaṣṣ bīh*	*	And all of his porcelain stocks,
	kill istikān u ġūrīh	*	Every samovar glass, and his kettle,
	u ṣḥūnah māl il-jābān		His Japanese plates, too, I'll settle!"
55	*min ᶜāyan kathrat li-jnūd*	*	When tea saw her army was huge,
	ẓall yixtifī u bīya ylūd	*	He hid, and from me begged refuge,
	yuqsim ᶜalayya bi l-maᶜbūd		And, swearing by God, he implored:
56	*riddha ṣ-ṣufur wa s-sūdān!*	*	"Send them back, pale or black, coffee's horde!
	il-hāwin, ᶜannah ḍammnī!	*	From mortar protect little tea!
	u ᶜan īdah lā yiḥtamnī!		The pestle's attack might smash me!
57	*wi l-muglā lā yiltamnī!*	*	And don't let pan strike as he could!
	u miḥmāsah shūf zaᶜlān!	*	If looks could kill, roasting pan's would!"
	nādaytah sh mālik lā txāf		I called out "Don't fear the ability,
58	*minhā yā xull il-ashrāf*	*	Of coffee, dear friend of nobility,
	ˀamn yā kāmil il-awṣāf	*	To harm you, majestic perfection:
	inta bi ḥimāyat sulṭān		You've got this king's royal protection!"

iṣ-ṣulḥ wa z-zawāj

peace and marriage

59	*u raddēt ilhā bistibshār*	*	I turned to her, joy on my face:
	haydī yā bint in-nībār	*	"Dusky maid, you of Malabar race,
	wēsh hal-fiᶜl hallī ṣār		What is it that's caused your reaction?
60	*ḥatta tᶜamrī l-maydān*	*	Why've you sent your troops into action?
	hādhā qabīḥ, hādhā ᶜēb	*	It's unpleasant, shame unprecedented!
	yā miskī u ᶜaṭrī u ṭ-ṭīb		Oh musky one, fragrant and scented,
61	*lā yiġīḍich hādhā ġrīb*	*	Don't let this strange man aggravate you!
	yitgashmar wiyyāch al-ān	*	He's teasing, just trying to bait you!
	u anā rīd azawjannich bīh		I'd like to wed you to this man, though!
62	*līch ahuwwa u ṣirī inti līh*	*	Make you his, him yours, that's my plan, so,
	lā yiġīḍich u lā tiġīḍah	*	Don't fight one another for ever!
	iṣtaliḥū u ṣīrū bi makān		Please come and make peace, be together!"
63	*gālat ya ġātī b amrik*	*	Said she, "Noble sir, I'll obey you,
	allah yiṭawwil ᶜumrik	*	God give you long life! And I pray too,
	dāyim saᶜīd ib dahrik		That you'll be content all your life,
64	*iḥna lik mithil il-ġilmān*	*	And we will serve you without strife!"
	u anā xadht li-wkāla	*	So, acting for their joint concern,
	nōba lēhā u nōba lah		And sipping them both, each in turn,
65	*u ᶜigidt u humma fwālah*	*	I wed them; with them for refreshment,
	u ṣtalaḥū u anā farḥān	*	They made peace, and I felt contentment.
	lākin hīch ġarāmī		For me, you see, love's a real must,
66	*gāmū yiḍḥakū ḥāmī*	*	The newly-weds laughed fit to bust!
	u tbāwasū jiddāmī	*	They kissed, on my lips the two mingled,
	u il-kull li th-thāni xadrān		At the touch of each other they tingled!

21

Some sociolinguistic concepts of style and stylistic variation in spoken Arabic

With reference to Nagīb Maḥfūẓ talking about his life

Gunvor Mejdell
University of Oslo

The wide range of variability in spoken Arabic across the diglossic High variety vs. Low variety dichotomy is a well attested phenomenon and has been the focus of several studies in Arabic linguistics. Suggestions have been made to define various numbers of intermediate levels or varieties between the two poles and basic codes of standard *fuṣḥā* and the local vernacular *ᶜāmmiyya*. My inclination is to regard the highly fluctuating and variable speech produced by different speakers in response to similar situational contexts as a matter of individual verbal strategies, as stylistic choices. This paper is an attempt to relate some analytical concepts from contributions to the study of style in the general sociolinguistic literature to a sample of what I conceive of as stylistic variation. The sample is a recording of Egyptian grand author Nagīb Maḥfūẓ talking about his life (published in the cassette series *Mishwār ḥayātī*, presentations of outstanding cultural figures intended for the broader public.) I have investigated 90 minutes of a total of approx. 200 minutes, and a few excerpts will be attached in transcription for illustration.[1]

The sociolinguistic study of style is part of the study of language variation and language choice. It is concerned with *intraspeaker* variation as opposed to *interspeaker* (social and regional dialects) variation, with categories of *uses* of language rather than the social categories of *users*. Its assumption is that speech is situated in context, in communicative situations, and will vary according to specific components of the situation, of the context, and/or serve various functions and purposes for the speaker in his/her communication and interactions. Style is the link between context and function, and linguistic form.[2]

The link between context and linguistic form is regulated by social evaluation, the norms and expectations of the speech community, the normal associations between code and situation. "It is not the event or state of affairs being talked about that determines the choice, but the convention that a certain kind of language is appropriate to a certain use" (Halliday 1968:150) There is a culturally shared evaluation in Arabic speech communities that *fuṣḥā* features are rated stylistically higher than *ᶜāmmiyya* features. The main device or strategy in responding to a more formal situation and produce a corresponding higher level of style is to introduce *fuṣḥā* features in speech. The process of this "classicization" and its linguistic results operate in a wide, flexible and tolerant frame – there exists to-day no single established norm for speech on intermediate levels of formality.

The linguistic dimension refers to and implies the analysis of linguistic items and features that may have value as stylistic markers.The linguistic features that are potentially stylistically (or socially) significant are features for which there exist alternatives in the linguistic repertoire. In Arabic, language variation related to the informal-formal dimension may be analysed with reference to the use of features from the two codes/varieties of *fuṣḥā* (standard Arabic – SA) and *ᶜāmmiyya* (vernacular or colloquial – Coll. or in the case of Egyptian coll., EC). Certain linguistic constraints, however, seem to operate on the kind of combination and mixing of features from SA and Coll. that may occur – to which I shall briefly return, though this does not constitue a major concern of this paper.

I do not pretend that variants of SA and Coll. constitute the only potential markers of style in Arabic. They presumably will be accompanied by universally observed and recognized potential stylistic clues or markers – like speed, syntactic complexity, repetitions, tags – and should be studied accordingly. Clues like interruption of speech, false starts and hesitations are strongly represented in formal speech – and may be interpreted as fillers while concentrating on producing elevated speech. The degree of complexity in sentence structure, generally regarded as a marker of formal style, in the spoken data I have investigated is quite low – even in speech approximating spoken SA. This could be attributed to the lack of fluency in spoken SA. In the present sample, speed of production is significantly lower in the passages approximating SA (1, 2 compared with 4 – 7).

When it comes to identifying the stylistic (and social) significant linguistic variables Labov 1970 provides a useful distinction: an *indicator* is " any variable which serves to mark varieties of language, but which is not perceived at a highly conscious level in the speech community". A *marker* is a variable "which has taken on social evaluation, and is perceived at a conscious level . . . such variables may be used for intentional metaphorical switching, while indicators may not". In other words: markers have stylistic value, while indicators tend not to.

The language form of our present recording is characterized by frequent shifting between and mixing of features from SA and EC, as should be illustrated by the excerpted passages. The proportion of SA features is higher in passage 1 than in 2 and even less in 3. Passages 4–7 are almost purely EC – apart from SA collocations that may be considered verbal routines or quasi-formulaic units, like 4,1: *lā yustaham(m) bih*; 4,4: *la tuṣaddaq al-ʾān*; 7,4–5: *la yansāhum abadan*. 8 is an example of a passsage where the style drops from a language form approaching *fuṣḥā* to a very colloquial form only to rise again in the last phrases.

Adapting the terminology of marker vs. indicator we may consider all features that contrast between SA and EC as indicators of the respective code. However, not all indicators seem to carry the same degree of social evaluation as being stylistically significant. In other words, not all features seem to function equally, have the same value, as markers of style. An obvious indicator of EC like preverbal *bi-* does not seem to a strong marker of casual style, but easily combines with SA verb forms in more formal styles (ex. 3,1: *wa-law annaha / bituḥaqqiq /nagāḥan*; 8,1: *khallīna natazakkar suʾāl biyuṭraḥ ʿādatan*). Certain potentially variable features do not vary in any significant way from one passage to the other, like fem. constr. *-it* and the system of pronoun suffixation – all but one instance following EC, even in 1 – which is the passage closest to SA. These, which we may label *indicators* of EC code, co-occur with other linguistic features that do vary: the phonetic realizations of /q/ and /aw/, the morphological shape of verbal stems and prefixes, demonstratives and relative pronouns, cases of negation. These features are to be considered *markers* of more or less casual /informal or careful/ formal, style. The co-occurrence of variants marked for informal style (EC variants) and of variants marked for formal style (SA variants) in the same passage do not by themselves signal change of style within the passage: "A style may be said to be characterized by a pattern of recurrent selections from the inventory of optional features of a language. Various types of selection can be found: complete exclusion of an optional element, obligatory inclusion of a feature optional elsewhere, *varying degrees of inclusion of a specific variant without complete elimination of competing features*" (Winter 1969:3, my italics). This is *pace* the analysis of Mitchell 1986, who assigns "style" to the single linguistic item, which is defined as +Formal or –Formal. Co-occurrence of items identified as +F and –F in the same sequence or even phrase constituent, leads Mitchell to conclude that style shifting incessantly occurs even in close sequences and constituents. Co-occurrence of such items rather contribute to define the stylistic level of the passage on the linguistic dimension. Compared with other passages, with a different ratio of the same variables, they contribute to situate mixed styles higher or lower on the continuum.

A style marker is a linguistic variable which is the subject of evaluation of the speech community. The salience of certain variable features in relation to others, could perhaps be attributed to their being focussed upon in formal language instruction: the /q/ as phonological marker, the demonstrative construction, the relative pronouns, negation – are all highly contrastive features emphasized in school. Of course, the *iᶜrāb*-system is also heavily focussed in formal education. The use of *iᶜrāb* is indeed a stylistic marker – a marker of high-flown style, considered by most speakers as too elaborate, too formal for most spoken purposes, and therefore[3] largely avoided or neglected in most positions. Instances of nominal *iᶜrāb* with nunation is in the present sample only found in the accusative case: 1,–2: *u kāna wālidi/ muwaẓẓafan*; 1,5–6: *aᶜtaqid / annahu laᶜiba / dawran*; and again the same idiom in 1,7: *kama annahu laᶜiba dawran / hāmman / ākhar*; and 3,1: *wa-law annaha / bituḥaqqiq / ragāḥan*; 3,4–5: *illi khalaqit al-insān al-miṣri fī zālik al-waqt / khalqan gadīdan*.[4]

The analysis on the linguistic dimension must further take into consideration linguistic constraints on mixing of features from SA and Coll, which have been suggested by several researchers in the field (Schmidt, Holes, Owens, Eid, and others). These include the principle of constraints on mixing of Coll. lexical stems with SA grammatical suffixes (f.i. *ᶜaynayn*, *ᶜinēn*, *ᶜaynēn* but **ᶜinayn* does not occur, is not accepted); the collocational constraint on mixing Coll. attributive demonstrative with the SA form of the lexical unit (*dh/zālika l-waqt, dh/zālika l-waᵓt, il-waᵓti da*, but **il-waqti da* does not occur); and the collocational constraint preventing the SA rel. pronoun being followed by a Coll. verbal form (*illi qaddamat, illi ᵓaddimit, allati qaddamat* but not **allati ᵓaddimit*). Even though single counter-examples may have been attested, these constraints seem to operate generally.

Situational/contextual and functional components serve the analytical purpose of explanation, or less ambitiously, interpretation, of the actual occurrences of variable linguistic forms in relation to style. The concept of context is elaborated variously by researchers with different analytic approaches. Discourse analysts tend to concentrate on the more immediate context of an utterance (like conversational turn-taking) – while researchers in the ethnography of communication-tradition have developed various "sprawling taxonomies – embracing every variable one could desire to explain style shift" (Allan Bell's critique of Dell Hymes, Bell 1984).

The ordering and internal ranking of contextual components vary and reflect the discussion in the field. There is general agreement however on the relevance of the following components: The *situation* is defined by *setting* and *activity type* as well as *topic* (some include *purpose*) and *participants* (speaker, addressee, audience and relationships among them). These components contribute to define the relative formality of the context or situation, the informal-formal dimension being the main dimension to which style is generally supposed to relate: "In most, perhaps all, cultures, scenes (setting and activity type) may be arranged along dimensions of public-private, sacred-secular, serious-trivial, impersonal-personal, polite-casual, high-culture-low-culture, open network – closed network and many other value-scales. In large part, these diverse scales seem to be subsumed – for participants as well as analysts – under one bipolar dimension of formal vs. informal" (Brown and Fraser 1979: 45). As Biber 1988 points out, these dimensions are continuous rather than absolute – more or less formal, more or less interactional, more or less public, more or less planned.

In our Nagīb Maḥfūẓ text, the situation is the formal interview, being recorded for public sale. It appears as sequences of monologue, interrupted by a (ghastly) musical theme every 10–15 minutes. The setting and participants are constant (the interviewer is not heard speaking, but it can be inferred that she is a woman, from the occasional acts of direct address to her from the author). It may be assumed that she poses general questions and asks for general comments. However, we lack information on the language form(s) used by the interviewer – which means the recording is seriously deficient as data for the analysis of the potential effect of interviewer's linguistic influence. (Normally, given the relationship between the participants, the authority of the distinguished author, the interviewer would start out in SA, and then accommodate to the language form of the author.)

The actual situation contains components that are ambiguous when it comes to ranking it on the formal – informal dimension. The interview situation typically combines features of public performance on the one hand and personal interaction on the other. The purpose of the communication is partly ideational (Biber 1988:42), partly interactional. Fluctuating style(s) in a given situation may be an indication that the situation or context itself is stylistically ambiguous. This mirrors the following observation by Enkvist 1964: "In many contexts, styles can be expected to overlap. If in a given context different speakers use different styles, which they elsewhere agree in associating with the same contextual ranges, this context is stylistically ambiguous", (pp 43–4).

As for *topic*, although the general topic is the speaker's life experience – it may be subdivided into topics of more or less direct personal involvement – family relations vs. professional career – reflections on love vs. literature and politics. There does not seem to be any obvious relation between the topic and the level of style in various passages: Personal experiences and family life are occasionally spoken about in a style approaching SA, while literature and politics frequently are treated in a style close to EC. It appears that purpose (mentioned above) is more important than topic for choice of language form.This confirms the observation by Kanakri 1988: "Participants and the social situation seem to play a more important role than topic and setting" (p 230).

Contextual or situational factors should not, however, be considered the sole extra-linguistic variables influencing style in speech. Speakers are not sociolinguistic automata reacting mechanically to a given context. They are able to manipulate the norms governing the use of styles. Studies of social and stylistic variation suggest that different varieties and styles may be used by speakers to influence and define, even change the situation – in our case affecting the degree of formality. Styles may reflect speakers' *responsive* as well as *initiative design* (in the terms of Allan Bell). The metaphorical and initiating uses of language are functional – linguistic features may be used to mark and express social, cultural and political attitudes, values and identities. They may also have special discourse or rhetorical functions, such as marking parts of speech for emphasis, or as side remarks – as when stepping out of a narrative to comment.

One problem, however, with establishing comprehensive sets of potential components and factors to explain or interpret stylistic variation, is that they may easily become the "sprawling taxonomies" that Bell 1984 criticizes – applied *ad hoc* to any speech phenomenon one would like to comment on. A reductionist alternative is Labov's Principle of Attention, which states that "styles can be ordered along a single dimension measured by the amount of attention paid to speech" (Labov 1972: 208). The principle intuitively seems to apply well to the Arabic situation, where speakers concentrate to produce SA features when elevating their styles. One could easily accept this general principle as making sense in Arabic – the more formal the situation, the more attention paid to speech. However, objections raised by Bell 1984, as to its lack of explanatory power, are convincing: "Attention is a mechanism, through which other factors can affect style. Certain topics or addressees or settings tend to evoke graded degrees of attention which may result in parallel graded styles . . . Attention is at most a mechanism of response intervening between a situation and a style . . . it could never be a satisfactory explanation of style . . . . we would still have to go behind the mechanistic attention variable to see what factors in the live situation are actually causing these differing amounts of attention." (p 150).

Bell proposes an alternative unified framework for and explanation of intraspeaker linguistic variation which he terms *audience design*. In short Bell argues that "speakers design their style for their audience", and that "nonpersonal contextual or situational variables, like topic and setting, can be shown to have less effect on style than the audience variables". These other variables and their effect on style are derived from audience-designed shift. ". . . the universality of a formal-informal continuum subsuming diverse factors derives from this common origin" (p.181). He states that "it seems that the sharper the differences in linguistic code, the less non-audience variables influence style shift" (p180). *Initiative design*, by which speakers use style to redefine the existing situation, is also seen as deriving from audience design, "trading on accepted norms for what is appropriate speech for certain audiences or topics". A third notion in Bell's framework is *referee design*: " the referees are a class of persons (ingroup or outgroup) with whom a speaker chooses to identify, not present at an interaction like the addressee is, but possessing such salience for a speaker that they influence speech even in their absence". Bell stresses the special relevance of the concept for mass communication: "a good case can be made for regarding all mass media language as referee designed" (p 147).

Applying the audience design approach to Nagīb Maḥfūẓ's *Mishwār ḥayātī*, the question is: who are the referees our distinguished author is designing his speech for, what is/are the target norm(s)? Having argued that the interview situation, the context of speaking in this case, was ambiguous as to formality vs. informality, I am inclined to claim a corresponding ambiguity in the nature of the referees. One group of referees is the broad audience, the ordinary people (in practice the middle classes who would buy this kind of cassette). Nagīb Maḥfūẓ has always identified with the ordinary middle class Cairene, speaks their language, and signalizes his loyalty to this audience (ingroup? referees) through his choice of EC. However, there exists another quasi-referee, with another target code – the cultural expectations (shared by ordinary people as well as the elite) that an intellectual and writer is able to express himself in elevated, cultured and literary style (some kind of SA). Admitting that I may be stretching Bell's argument too far, I am none the less tempted to give SA the status of "distant outgroup target code" and then quote Bell at length – suggesting its potential value for understanding the highly variable nature of the mixed styles we are concerned with:

"When the outgroup code is distant, attempted shift is partial and imperfect. It focusses on a few salient features in which the referee code differs from the speaker's.This is, however, usually all that the situation demands. The aim of referee design is for your speech to put the audience in mind of a particular reference code. A few token shifts should successfully convince the immediate audience" . . . "Referee design usually takes a feature which is (semi)categorical in the target code and tries to adopt it. Because that shift is rarely complete, the speaker turns a categorical rule of the target code into a variable one" (pp190–1).

In conclusion to this (somewhat simplistic) survey of concepts and approaches in the general sociolinguistic literature which I have found relevant and potentially useful applied to the study of stylistic variation in spoken Arabic, I should like to stress the complexity of the data in this field of research. The mixed styles of Nagīb Maḥfūẓ in our sample may be interpreted as a response to the ambiguous nature of the media situation – in terms of aspects of formality and informality – combining the "privacy" of the face-to-face conversation with the "officiality" of the public performance. It may be interpreted as intitiative and referee design in order to cope with conflicting demands of the referees. These interpretations are suggestions as to what kind of processes may motivate stylistic choice. It remains to be said that, in any case, Nagīb Maḥfūẓ creatively draws on the full range of linguistic resources available to him – moving up and down the Arabic stylistic continuum.

Samples from *Mishwār ḥayātī*: interview with Nagīb Maḥfūẓ

Samples 1 and 2 are from the beginning of the recording; 3 – 8 are from various sections of the 90 minute tape.

In cases of close transition between words, I have attempted to mark liaison by writing the connecting vowel affixed to the preceding word: *zālika l-waqt* (close transition) vs. *zālik al-waqt* (no liason), though I must admit that the distinction was not always clear, and might have been handled with more precision. I have aslo tried to render vowel quality and length as accurately as possible, as well as interdental vs. sibilant realization – but sometimes the distinctions were quite blurred on the tape.

1

wulidt / fi ḥidāshar / itnāshar sanat alf-u-tus^cumiyya wa-ḥidāshar //u kāna wālidi / muwaẓẓafan ḥatta stawfa / ḥayātu ka-muwaẓẓaf / summa / ᶜamala / fi / at-tigāra // wa kāna liyyi / mina l-akhawāt / arbaᶜ inās / wa zakarān / baqiya minhum ᶜala qayd il-ḥayā / akh / wa-ukht wa-ana // wa-qad wulidti fi ḥayyi l-gamaliyya / aw ḥayyi l-ḥusēn / wa-ᶜala waghit taḥdīd / fi midān bēt il-ʾāḍi // wa hāza l-midān / aᶜtaqid / annahu laᶜiba / dawran / fi tarīkh maṣr / al-qadīma / munzu l-faṭimiyyīn / fa-kāna fīh / bēt al-qāḍi / wa kāna fīh bayta l-māl // kama annahu laᶜiba dawran / hāmman / ākhar / fi aḥdās / sawrit alf u-tusᶜumiyya wa-tisaᶜṭāshar //

2

ᶜan al-ḥayā / as-siyasiyya / ᶜindama wulidt / ṭabᶜan / la ᶜārif ᶜanha shayʾan illa / min it-tarīkh / li-anni / wulidt / fi al-fatra / as-sābiqa / lil-ḥarb al-ᶜuẓma / il-ʾūla // innama . . . eh / lamma balaght / aẓunni inni ḥawāli s-sādisa / aw as-sābiᶜa / qāmit sawrit tisaᶜṭāshar / u-kān ḥadas infigāri ḍakhm // fa-shaddi ntibāhi / raghmi ṣighar sinni / ila s-siyāsa / bi-quwa /lam takun fil-ḥusbān // wa / min al-gāʾiz / giddan / anna hādhihi l-gazba l-ūla / hiya illi rabbaṭitni bil-ihtimām is-siyāsi / ṭīlat ḥayāti / ḥatta hāzihi l-laḥẓa //

3

u-natīgit it-tarbiya di / wa-law annaha / bituḥaqqiq / nagāḥan / wa-stiqāma / innama / bituṣīb ish-shakhṣiyya/ fi stiqlalha / az-zāti / wa fi / gurʾitha / li-daraga kbīra // yimkin / il-gīl / iza kān / il-asāra s-sayyiʾa lam tubdi fīh / bil-quwa fa-da baʾa / bi-faḍl / shēʾ / la yargaᶜ lil-usra u-l-madrasa / da faḍl as-sawra nafsaha / illi khalaqit al-insān al-miṣri fi zālik al-waqt / khalqan gadīdan / gaᶜalathu yastahīn / bi-gamīᶜ / at-taqalīd / as-sayyiʾa / as-sābiq(a)

4

il-ginēh kān fi zālika l-waqt /shēʾ / lā yustaham(m) bih / yaᶜni / yakfi aʾullik addīki fikra yaᶜni/ inn il-badle ṣūf inglīzi / bit-tafṣīl / kānit bi-ginēh u-nuṣṣ / āh / kānit bi-ginēh u-nuṣṣ / wa-kunna masalan nurūḥ nākhud ṭabaʾ kebāb / kān bi arbaʾ sēgh / ṭabaʾ kāmil [..] il-ḥagāt di / zayy il-khayāl baʾa / la tuṣaddaq al-ʾān

5

il-ḥaʾīʾa/ illi shaggaᶜni / ᶜala inni akūn muwaẓẓaf / u-inni adrus il-adab / wa-aḥāwil kitabtu / wa-inni astamirru fi s-saqāfa / ẓurūf kitīr / inna s-saqāfa lam takun ᶜaṣīr / dār al-kutub taḥta amr il-wāḥid / maktabti l-gamᶜa taḥta amr il-wāḥid / il-kutub rakhīṣa giddan

6

faḍlan ᶜala inn il- / bi-mugarrad il-insān / ḥatta ma dakhal il-gamᶜa itghayyarit / il-muᶜamla / min il-walidēn lil-wāḥid / taʾallabit liṣ-ṣadāqa waz-zamāla / u-baʾit ḥāga tanya khāliṣ / ul-gharība/ inni baᶜda kida bi-sinīn / yimkin kammil (il)asbāb illi dafaᶜitni liz-zawāg / inni kānit ḥaṣalitni fatrit / ḥukma(?) adabi / ba^c^d is-sawra / fa-^ɔ^ulti madām kida / il-wāḥid yitgawwiz ba^ɔ^a

7

kull il-ḥagāt di / ḥaḍartaha / u-ana sikirtēr barlamāni / u-shuft zu^c^amā zālika l-waqt / wa-smi^c^t kalamhum / u-^c^araḍathum u-qina^c^athum / u-kulli ḥāga di // ^ɔ^a^c^adti fi wuzart il-awqāf // u-hiyya wuzart . . . / il-wāḥid ^c^irif fīha kasīr mina l-aṣḍiqa(^ɔ^) / fīha nās ṭayyibīn giddan / il-wāḥid la yansāhum abadan

8

khallīna natazakkar su^ɔ^āl biyuṭraḥ ^c^ādatan / ayyuhum afḍal lil-adīb / an yakūn lahu ^c^amal / aw yakūn mutafarrigh / il-wāqi^c^ / inn il-adab mihna tastaḥiqq al-tafarrugh / wat-tafarrugh laysa ma^c^nāh il-farāgh / walla ma^c^nāh inna l-adīb yaq^c^ud fi maktaba / fi bētu / aw fi maktaba ^c^amma / wa-yi^ɔ^ra u-yikitb / innama.. lākin / il-mas^ɔ^ala mish mas^ɔ^alt ikhtiyār / fa-innu maḥkūm / ^c^ala l-adīb / fi biladna wa-yimkin fi bilād ukhra kasīra / an takūn lahu waẓīfa / taḍman-lu ar-rizq / yatafarragh lil-adab //

Notes

1. The series was suggested to me by Prof. Said Badawi, and Abbas al-Tonsi (both of AUC) kindly provided me with a copy.
2. Some linguists refer to register in the sense of style as defined here (Halliday, Saville-Troike), as a variety of speech related to specific contextually defined uses – while others (Trudgill) use register as a subcategory of style, restricted to specialized in-group styles, like occupational registers, characterized basically by specialized vocabulary.
3. Well-attested problems of speakers in producing the correct form of *i^c^rāb* in many instances should also be taken into consideration when trying to account for the relative value of these morphemes as stylistic markers.
4. I have elsewhere analyzed the occurrences of *i^c^rāb*-forms in different linguistic environments and functions in data of mixed style, and a hierarchical pattern of relative frequency seems to emerge from such analysis. (Unpublished working paper produced for a seminar for research fellows, Oslo 1987).

References

Allan Bell: "Language style as audience design", *Language in Society*, 13 (1984): 145–205.

Douglas Biber: *Variation across speech and writing*, Cambridge 1988

Penelope Brown and Colin Fraser: "Speech as a marker of situation", in Klaus R. Scherer and Howard Giles (eds): *Social markers in speech*, Cambridge 1979: 33–62.

Mushira Eid: "The Non-randomness of Diglossic Variation in Arabic", *Glossa* 16,1 (1982) 54–84.

—— "Principles for code-switching between standard and Egyptian Arabic", *Al- ᶜArabiyya* 21 (1988), 5–79.
Nils Erik Enkvist: "On defining style: an essay on applied linguistics", in John Spencer (ed): *Linguistics and Style*, Oxford 1964.
M.A.K. Halliday: "The Users and Uses of Language", in Joshua A. Fishman (ed.): *Readings in the Sociology of Language*, The Hague/Paris 1968.
Clive Holes: "Patterns of communal language variation in Bahrain", *Language in Society* 12 (1983): 433–57.
William Labov: "The Study of Language in its Social Context", 1970, reprinted in Pride and Holmes: *Sociolinguistics*, Penguin 1972, 180–202.
—— *Sociolinguistic Patterns*, Philadelphia, 1972.
Kanakri: *Style and style shifting in ESA of Jordan*, Unpubl. PhD. diss., Madison 1988.
T.F. Mitchell: "What is Educated Spoken Arabic", *International Journal of the Sociology of Language* 61 (1986), 7–32.
Jonathan Owens and Raslan Bani-Yasin: "The lexical basis of variation in Jordanian Arabic", *Linguistics* 25 (1987), 705–738.
Muriel Saville-Troike: *The Ethnography of Communication – an Introduction* (2nd edition) 1989.
Richard Wilbur Schmidt: *Sociostylistic Variation in Spoken Egyptian Arabic: A Re-examination of the Concept of Diglossia*, Unpublished Ph.D. diss., Brown University, 1974.
Werner Winter: "Styles as dialects", in I. Dolozel and R.W. Bailey (eds): *Statistics and Style*, N.Y. 1969, 3–9.

22

The Language of Ibn al-Mujāwir's 7th/13th Century Guide to Arabia, *Tārīkh al-Mustabṣir*[1]

G. Rex Smith
University of Manchester

Tārīkh al-Mustabṣir (*TM*) is a 7th/13th century text which has been readily available to the scholarly world since its publication by the Swedish scholar, Oscar Löfgren, Leiden, 195–4. The name of the author of the *TM* is undoubtedly Abū Bakr b. Muḥammad b. Masᶜūd b. ᶜAlī b. Aḥmad Ibn al-Mujāwir (IM), not the well known Damascene, also Ibn al-Mujāwir, whose full name appears on the title page of the printed version of the text. The true author hailed from the east of the Islamic world, not from Damascus. He appears to have had business interests, or at least he writes from the point of view of a businessman, and the *TM* is a description of the west and south of the Arabian Peninsula. IM begins by singing the praises of what he calls *fann al-tārīkh*, which I can only translate 'historical geography', and the basic layout of the work is a route list – from A to B is x parasangs (where, incidentally, a parasang, *farsakh*, is in all probability the distance that one can walk in one hour[2]). Fortunately, however, the text is much more than a route list, for it is frequently punctuated at some length with all manner of digressions. As we might expect from someone interested in business, prices, customs dues, taxes, coinage, weights and measures, commodities, agriculture etc., all these are dealt with, often in great detail. Also our author is interested in the people whom he meets on his travels: their dress, their food, their habits and mores – in particular their sexual mores – their houses, their water supplies, their rulers and their history – though he often falters on the latter – and all these pass under his scrutiny. The text too is replete with amusing and sometimes bizarre anecdotes, as well as with passages packed with information concerning the early 7th/13th century Arabian Peninsula. I have elsewhere discussed other aspects of the work: the author's treatment of Dhofar and the island of Socotra,[3] the humorous and the bizarre in the text,[4] the eastern connection of the author,[5] an interpretation of some 'anthropological' passages[6]and more recently concerning the author as a story-teller.[7]

IM's description of western Arabia begins, not surprisingly, in the Holy Cities. He travels south through Tihāmat al-Yaman, round on to the southern coast, right along the southern coast, though also mentioning inland towns such as Ṣanᶜāᵓ and even, further north, Ṣaᶜdah and Najrān, round Raᵓs al-Ḥadd into the Gulf and up, calling in on one or two islands and returning to the east overland through Iraq.

This then is the text in question. Without doubt written in the early years of the 7th/13th century when the Ayyubid relatives of Saladin in Cairo ruled over much of southern Arabia on his behalf, it is a veritable mine of information concerning the social and economic history of the area in particular and throws much light on its anthropology, and also on its history and geography. It was known even before Löfgren's edition in the 1950s, for as early as 1864, Sprenger used the text extensively in his *Post-und Reiserouten des Orients* (published in Leipzig) and historians of mediaeval Yemen have made full use of the important material it provides, in particular that concerning historical geography. The text comes to us in several MSS, although the oldest, Istanbul, Aya Sofya 3080, dated 1003 (= AD 1595), is disappointingly late, having been copied nearly 400 years after its composition. The remainder, the most important of which is that of Leiden (University Library Or 5572), all date from the 19th, one or two perhaps even later from the 20th, century. As fascinating as the contents of the text is, its language has been completely ignored by those who know the text. It is high time, I think, that this should be addressed and that the Arabic of this 7th/13th century easterner (probably Khurāsānī), so much influenced by the usages and dialects of the area he himself highlights, as well as by those of his own background, should be put under the microscope, albeit rather briefly here. Before such a discussion, however, something needs to be said about the subject of so-called Middle Arabic (MA), since the main conclusion is that this text belongs in this category of Arabic.

What then is MA? I must make it clear from the outset that I am using the term to mean *that literary form of the Arabic language which is a mixture of non-classical Arabic elements and pure classical Arabic elements* – by classical Arabic (CA), incidentally, I mean the language of the classical grammarians. Joshua Blau, whose name immediately comes to mind in the context of MA, expounds definitions in this regard much more complicated than that, and his definitions actually change over the years.[8] MA is not then a chronological term. The earliest examples which occur in quantity are the Arabic papyrus texts which date from the

1st/7th century.[9] These are particularly valuable examples, being as they are, original documents, uncorrupted by later scribes, and what is more written *before* (for the most part) the writings of the classical grammarians. Examples of MA texts can be traced right through the centuries down to the 19th, even the present, century.

The majority of MA texts by far were composed by Jews – Judaeo-Arabic (JA) – invariably written in the Hebrew script – and by Christians – Christian Arabic (ChA) – and Blau has produced comprehensive grammars of both.[10] Complete MA texts written by Muslims, however, are much thinner on the ground. Since the early 1970s when it was the subject of a detailed study by Schen,[11] only one is cited with any frequency, Usāmah Ibn Munqidh's *Kitāb al-Iᶜtibār*, produced at the end of the very long life of the Syrian author about 584/1188.[12] I shall return to the *Iᶜtibār* later.

There are two extremely interesting questions, it seems to me, which concern the writing of MA. What is the process of composition? How do MA texts come out as this mixture of non-CA and CA in various blends?[13] An attempt to answer this question is made in the conclusions of this paper. The second, much more difficult, is why would one want to write in MA as opposed to CA? The answer is more confidently given in the case of JA and ChA. Jews and Christians, it is argued, had no particular loyalty and emotional attachment to CA as the language of the Qurᵓān and might well in any case have no formal training in CA, even if they spoke Arabic as their first language. An argument such as this is difficult to contradict, but where does that leave us in the all too rare cases of MA composed by Muslims? In particular, why did Usāmah Ibn Munqidh compose the *Iᶜtibār* in MA after already having completed at least half a dozen other works, including a *dīwān* of poetry, in perfect CA?[14] Perhaps now is the time to turn to the 7th/13th century text written by an easterner, which, I hope to show, has clear signs of having been written in MA, and, there can be no doubt, was composed by a Muslim – the *TM* of IM.

There follows a list of 87 examples from the text of the *TM* which illustrate its non-CA features. The list is but a brief representation of these features. I use the headings 1. *Lexical peculiarities*, 2. *Morphology* and 3. *Syntax*. The reader should note that it had originally been my intention to include a section on orthography, but that would have been of doubtful value since the oldest, Istanbul, MS, from which all these examples are taken, was copied about 400 years after the composition of the work and thus opportunities for corruption were many. This being the case, the examples merely represent the 11th/16th century scribe's orthographic peculiarities. The examples of the first category, *Lexical peculiarities*, also include one or two expressions of such idiomatic interest that I determined to record them as I scanned the text and came across them. It should also be noted that some examples contain more than one non-CA feature and that it is therefore difficult in some cases to keep any one example under the appropriate linguistic heading. Finally it should be noted that the numbers after the number of the example represent the page and the line on which it begins in the Löfgren printed text, but that the example is written exactly as it is found in the 11th/16th century Istanbul MS. References are given to Hopkins 1982, based on the papyri, and to Schen 1972–3, which documents the non-CA features of the *Iᶜtibār*.

EXAMPLES OF THE NON-CA FEATURES IN THE TEXT OF THE *TM*

1. *Lexical peculiarities*

Example 1.1 Page 8.3

فيرجع بروكها علي وركها عاده

'So her kneeling on all fours becomes normal practice.' *rajaᶜa* with the meaning 'become'.

1.2 41.11

والنخل رجع الان سلطانى

'The date-palms now belong to the sultan.' I.e. for the first time.

1.3 12.4

فلما رجعت الدوله لال ايوب ضربوا الدراهم الكبار

'When the Ayyubids assumed control, they struck "large" dirhams.' I.e. 'assumed control' for the first time.

1.4 68.17

ولا زال علي حاله الي ان رجعت الخلق يستجير به

'He continued as he was until the people sought/began to seek his protection.' NB *lā* with the perfect verb (see below, Syntax, C – negatives) and cf. Wright 1951, ii, 2 D. The perfect of *raja^ca* is here used with an asyndetic imperfect with or without the meaning 'begin' – the context is not sufficiently clear. *Khalq* is IM's commonly used word signifying 'people'.

1.5 45.9

انفذ صاحب مكه الي شيخ التجار بجده
وطلب منه حملاً حديداً

'The lord of Mecca sent a message to the shaykh of the merchants in Jeddah, requesting a load of iron.' *anfadha* (derived form IV) is invariably used in the *TM* with the meaning of *arsala* – cf. *I^ctibār*, where it is *naffadha* (II).

1.6 37.7

وهو سوق يلتام فيه الخلق

'It is a market which people frequent.'[15] *iltāma* for *ilta^ɔama* is very frequently used in the *TM*.

1.7 112.3

فبينما هم في لا ونعم اذ سمع بخبرهما

'While the two of them remained undecided, he heard what they were doing.'

1.8 117.7

ولم يبق احد في زماننا يعلم مجري القوم
ولا كم كيف كانت احوالهم وامورهم

'There is nobody left now who knows what happened to these people, nor how many they were, nor how they were and what happened to them.' NB also *lam* with the apocopate negating present time (see below, *Syntax*, C – negatives); cf. Hopkins 1982, 86.

2. *Morphology*

A – verbs
2.A.1 23.15

الا ترى انا قد اضرينا بهذا الرجل

'Do you not realise that we have done this man harm?' NB *aḍraynā* (cf. Hopkins 1982, 76–7, but see Schen 1972–3, 69–70).
2.A.2 36.15

ونام عند النصاري وتعشى عند اليهود

'Sleep at the houses of Christians; sup at the houses of Jews.' NB *nām* and *ta*ᶜ*ashshā* for the imperatives of *nāma* and *ta*ᶜ*ashshā* (Hopkins, 85 and Schen, 71).
2.A.3 48.2

ولم يعاد بناه

'It has not been built again.' NB *yu*ᶜ*ād* after *lam*. (Hopkins, 83 and Schen, 71).
2.A.4 63.10

فلما زرع بها وحصد قلعه القوم من الاصول

'When [the crops] were sown there and came to maturity, these people pulled them out by the roots.' NB *ḥaṣada* (Hopkins, 73 and Schen, 67).
2.A.5 117.12

وكان طالبا كلوه فارسي بعدن

'He was making for Kilwa, but anchored in Aden.' NB *arsā* (IV) (Hopkins, 73 and Schen, 68)
2.A.6 124.7

ارسوا تحت جبل صيره وانفذوا رسولهم
الي بني زريع

'They anchored beneath Jabal Ṣīrah and sent their envoy to the Zurayᶜids.'

2.A.7 125.2

فلما ارست الجاشو مرسى عدن انفذ . . .

'When the Jāshū anchored in the anchorage of Aden, he sent . . .'

2.A.8 225.14

فقامت المراه غسلت يد السقا ورجله بماءٍ حار وادفته

'So the woman got up and washed the hands and feet of the water carrier in hot water and warmed him up.' NB *wa-adfat-hu* (Hopkins, 80 and Schen, 70). Note also the use of *al-mar^ʾah* when a specific woman is intended and also the asyndetic *ghasalat*.

2.A.9 45.12

وينفذ اليّ بحمل {بحمل} ثاني من حديد هذا العين

'. . . and sending me a second load of iron of this best kind.' NB *thānī* (Hopkins, 86 and Schen, 72).

2.A.10 58.16

وهو جبل عالي عاصي علي الملوك باليمن

'It is a high mountain which is in rebellion against the kings in the Yemen.' NB *ʿālī* and *ʿāṣī*.

B – nouns

2.B.1 5.11

وما بقى من اهلها قرشيين على مذهب
الامام زيد بن علي

'Its remaining inhabitants are Quraysh who follow the rite of Imam Zayd b. ʿAlī.' NB *Qurashiyyīn*, oblique case (Hopkins, 106 and Schen, 76).

2.B.2 54.2

فاذا اصبح خرج وترك نعلاه في بيت بنت عمرو

'When morning comes, he goes out, leaving his sandals behind in the house of ᶜAmr's daughter.' NB *naᶜlā-hu*, nom. (Hopkins, 101 and Schen, 75).

2.B.3 66.6

ان الامام ابو جعفر المنصور . . . ضرب
عنق سليمن بن هشام

'Imam Abū Jaᶜfar al-Manṣūr cut off the head of Sulaymān b, Hishām . . .' NB *Abū*, nom., after *inna*.

2.B.4 5.13

لان جلة مناكحهم الجوار السود من الحبش والنوبة

'. . . because most of their partners are black slave girls from Abyssinia and Nubia.' NB *al-jawār*.

2.B.5 290.15

واشتري الجوار البكور وقدم بهم الي الملك

'He bought the virgin slave girls and brought them to the king.' NB *al-jawār al-bukūr*; also *bi-him*, masc. pronoun, referring to the slave girls.

2.B.6 21.2

بير عظيم عميق

'A huge, deep well.' NB *bīr* is here masc. (Hopkins, 87 and cf. Wright 1951, i, 183 B).

C – numerals

2.C.1 12.7

ثمان عشره درهما

'Eighteen dirhams.' NB *thamān ᶜashrah*. (Hopkins, 117, Schen, 77 and Wright, i, 256 C).

2.C.2 12.9

ثمان فلوس

'Eight fals '.

D-prepositions

2.D.1 7.6

يقدمه قدام العروس كل علي قدر حاله

'. . . brings it forward in front of the bride, each one according to his financial circumstances.' NB *quddām* is rare in CA. (Hopkins, 128 and Schen, 78).

3. *Syntax*

A – imperfect verb
3.A.1 13.12

ويبيعوه طاقات بالعدد

'They sell it in layers by number.' NB *wa-yabīʿū-hu*. (Hopkins, 134 and Schen, 79).
3.A.2 48.18

فحينئذ يخرجوا المغاربه من الصهاريج

'Then they drive away the Maghribīs from the water tanks.' NB *yukharrijū* or *yukhrijū* and also that *ḥīnaʾidhin* invariably has the meaning of 'then', 'next'.
3.A.3 79.14

ويقيموا الناس في النخل مدة شهرين او ثلاثه
ويكون غالب اكلهم الحموضات والملوحات

'These people remain in the date groves for two or three months and most of their food is made up of sour and salty plants.' NB the following:

yuqīmū; the plur. verb standing before an expressed plur. subject, very common in the *TM* (see below, B – concord); the use of the imperfect of *kāna* to express the present time (see below, G – auxiliary verbs).

3.A.4 23.3

واتوه نصيب من الزبيب يكون فيه قدر
مكوك على نطع

'They brought him some raisins, the amount of a *makkūk*[16] on a leather mat.' NB also the use of the imperfect of *kāna* to express the present tense. Note also *naṣīb*, rather than *naṣīban*.

3.A.5 37.16

ويكون اهل القريه محتاطين بالقصر من
اربع تربيعه

'The villagers are surrounded by the castle on all four sides.'

3.A.6 81.12

لانه يكون في ايام موسم سفاره الجاوه
الامطار كثيره

'. . . because, in the season of travel to Java, the rains are many.'[17]

3.A.7 121.1

يقولون له تشتري منا حشيش البحر
يعنون به العنبر

'They say to him, "Buy sea-grass from us," meaning ambergris.' NB the use of the 2nd pers. imperf. for the imperative. This is quite common in the *TM*, although not as common as in the *Iᶜtibār*. (Schen, 79 and also Hopkins, 136).

3.A.8 291.7

فقال الملك تردهم الى جزيرتهم

'The king replied, "Send them back to their island".' NB the use of the imperf. for the imperative. The masc. pronouns here refer to females, a common feature of the *TM* and indeed of MA in general. (Hopkins, 147).

3.A.9 127.13

فقال له صاحب الدار يصعد

'The master of the house told him to come up.' NB *yaṣᶜad/yaṣᶜadu*, meaning literally 'let him come up'; cf. CA *fal-yaṣᶜad/li-yaṣᶜad* or possibly here . . . *an yaṣᶜada*.

B – concord

3.B.1 5.4

ويسمونها التجار عروق الذهب

'The merchants call them the golden dunes.' NB the plur. verb standing before the expressed plur. subject. (Hopkins, 138 and Schen, 80).

3.B.2 7.6

وكذلك يفعل النساء

'The women do thus.' NB masc. sing. verb before the fem. plur. expressed subject.

3.B.3 19.16

فاقبلت الناس يهرعون اليه

'The people hurried to him.' NB the fem. sing. verb before the masc. plur. expressed subject, followed by a masc. plur. verbal *ḥāl*.

3.B.4 31.10

فصارت اهل هذا الزمان يدخلون كبب غزل الوبر

'The people have now begun to introduce balls of animal fur thread.' NB the fem. sing. auxiliary followed by the masc. plur. main verb.

3.B.5 95.17

فصارت الحبشه تخوض البحر بالخيل والرجل

'The Abyssinians began to wade across the sea on horseback and on foot.' Cf. 3.B.5 above. Here the auxiliary verb is fem. sing. and the main verb remains fem. sing. See Wright 1951, ii, 39 A.

3.B.6 111.10

ويوجد حول البير حجارة مكسرات وافاعي
نايمات وحيات قايمات

'Around the well broken stones, sleeping vipers and rearing snakes can be found.' NB the inanimate subject (*ḥijārah*) in the plur. has a masc. sing. verb and the participle qualifying it is fem. plur. Similarly, the other inanimate nouns in the plur. having qualifying participles in the fem. plur.

3.B.7 25.11

فجعلن النوايح للناس كلهم يقلن واحرباه

'The keening women began to say of everybody, "Alas, my grief for Ḥarb!"' NB the fem. plur. auxiliary verb standing before the fem. plur. expressed subject, followed by the fem. plur. main verb.

3.B.8 43.4

وفيهم اثنان احدهما يسمى سيار والثاني مياس
فسكنوا جده

'Among them are two, one of whom is called Sayyār and the other Mayyās, and they settled in Jeddah.' NB *fa-sakanū*, a masc. plur. verb refers to the two men named above.

3.B.9 95.6

فقلت له فاي الجبال هم

'I said to him, "Which of the mountains are they?"' A masc. plur. nom. pronoun referring to an inanimate object in the plur.

3.B.10 253.15

وتظفر النسا روسهم في اوسط روسهم ترجع
تشبه الهدهد

'The women plait their hair in the middle of their head which makes them look like a hoopoo bird.'[18] NB the pronoun of *rūsa-hum*, although masc., refers to the women. Note also that the auxiliary *tarji*ᶜ*u* is asyndetic (see below, I – asyndetic clauses).

3.B.11 290.17

وجدهم رجع علي نسق واحد

'He found them in the same state.' NB the attached masc. plur. pronoun refers to females. *Rujja*ᶜ (a nom. *ḥāl!*) is the plur. of *rāji*ᶜ. For *raja*ᶜ*a* with the meaning 'become' or simply 'be', see above, 1.1 ff.

3.B.12 128.3

وهذه الف دينار تنفقها ما دمت فى بلادنا

'Here are a thousand dinars which you can have to spend as long as you are in our town.' NB *dīnār* is correctly sing. after the numeral *alf*, but both the demonstrative *hādhihi* and the attached acc. pronoun are fem. sing., presumably referring to an inanimate object in the notional plur. (See Schen, 72).

C – negatives

3.C.1 81.9

لم ينعقد ورده إلا من برق البرق

'Its flower only flowers after the flashing of lightning.' NB here and very frequently in the *TM lam* plus the apocopate gives a *present* negative meaning.

3.C.2 82.2

اما ورد الكادي فلم يكن في ساير المشمومات
الذ منه رايحه

'As for the fragrant screwpine, it is the most sweet-smelling among all odiferous plants.' See 3.C.1 above.

3.C.3 101.10

قلت واين الوادي قال في اعمال ترن ولم تمت
الي يوم القيمه

'I said, "Where is the wadi?" He replied, "In the regions of Taran/Turan and she will not die until the Day of Resurrection".' NB *lam* with the apocopate with a *future* negative meaning. Note also *qiyāmah* without the *alif*.

3.C.4 20.17

ولا زال القوم في بنائه الى ان حاذي البنا ذروة
الجبل

'The people continued to build it up until it came level with the summit of the mountain.' NB *lā* with the perfect verb. (See Hopkins, 151 and Schen, 82).

3.C.5 65.12

ولا زال يسالهم ويخبروه حتي عدد القوم خمسة
جماعه

'He continued to question them and they to give him information until they counted up to five persons.' Note also *wa-yukhbirū-hu* and the use of *ᶜaddada*, II, presumably for *ᶜadda*, I.

D – cases

3.D.1 7.17

وليس هذا الفن عندهم عار

'This practice is not regarded among them as a disgrace.' NB *ᶜār* without *alif al-tanwīn*. (See Hopkins, 160 and Schen, 83).

3.D.2 21.8

وبقي الحصن خراب الي الان

'The fortress has remained in ruins until now.' NB *kharāb* without *alif al-tanwīn*.

3.D.3 80.2

وما ياخذونه نقد بل تمر

'But they took it in dates rather than in cash.' NB *naqd* and *tamr* without *alif al-tanwīn*; also the *mā* with the imperfect.

3.D.4 81.10

فاذا برق البرق طلع منه كثير بالمره

'When the lightning flashes, it grows in great abundance.' NB *kathīr*; also *bi-al-marrah* = *marrah wāḥidah* = 'very'.

E – numerals

3.E.1 12.3

اربعة وعشرين علوي

'24 *ᶜalawī* dinars.' NB *ᶜalawī*, without *alif al-tanwīn*.

3.E.2 12.15

ثمانمايه درهما

'800 dirhams.' NB *dirhaman* after *miᵓah*. Note also *thamānmiyah*.

F – prepositions

3.F.1 127.11

فدار عدن

'So he took a turn around Aden.' NB the absence of the preposition after *dāra*.

3.F.2 236.2

فحينيذ اعطي سيف الدين سنقر له حيس

'Then Sayf al-Dīn Sunqur handed over to him Ḥays.' NB the direct object and the preposition *li* – after *a*ᶜ*ṭā*. Ḥays is the name of a place.

G – auxiliary verbs

3.G.1 13.10

هذا في اليمن ونواحيها يكون يسوى كل مايه من بخوارزم . . . . سبعين دينارا

'This is in the Yemen and its various regions, but every hundred *mann* in Khwārizm . . . is the equivalent of 70 dinars.' The imperfect of *kāna* is used as an auxiliary verb with the imperfect of the main verb to give a present meaning.

H – isolation

3.H.1 31.18

كثير من الرعاة ممن يحمل الذئب على غنمه فيقوم الراعي يطارد الذئب يريد يقتله

'Many shepherds of those who have had their flocks attacked by wolves hunt down the wolf with the intention of killing it.' An interesting example of the isolation of the subject of the sentence. Note also the use of *qāma* as an auxiliary verb, though here with no noticeable force of meaning, and the subordinate asyndetic clause after *yurīdu* (see below, I – asyndetic clauses).

I – asyndetic clauses

3.I.1 20.13

وليس هذا من عمل العرب لا يتدبر لهم فيه عمل

'This is not work that the Arabs do, [since] no such work occurs to them.' (Hopkins, 228 and Schen, 90).

3.I.2 101.1

وتزوجت رجلا من وجوه العرب اسكنها العربي
ارض ترن

'She married a prominent Arab [and] he settled her in the land of Taran/Turan.'

3.I.3 107.19

فقال لاعوانه اغدوا ابصروا هذا الجبل

'He said to his supporters, "Go [and] have a look at his mountain".'

3.I.4 116.1

فحينيذ قاموا فتحوا له فما مما يلي جبل عمران

'Then they went [and] opened up a mouth for him near Jabal ᶜImrān.' (See Schen, 90, suggesting a semi-auxiliary role for *qāma* in such sentences).

3.I.5 17.11

وقد جري مركب من القمر الي عدن بهذا المجرى . . .
اقلع من القمر

'A ship from Madagascar made this same run to Aden . . . [and] set sail from Madagascar.'

3.I.6 127.19

خفت من المطر وقعت تحت الميزاب

'I was afraid of the rain, [but] fell under the water spout!' This adage is found as follows: *farra min al-maṭar wa-qaᶜada taḥt al-mīzāb*. See Maydānī 1955, ii, 90.

3.I.7 191.14

واقدم الي السوق الفلاني فانها تتوعد به شاهدها

'Go to such and such a market, for she goes there every week,[19] [and] have a look at her.'

3.I.8 20.16

وبنوا حول الجبل الحجر المنقوش المربع طول
كل حجرمنه سبعة اذرع

'Around the mountain they built up hewn, rectangular stones, the length of each of which was seven cubits.'

3.I.9 33.1

لم يقدر الانسان يعبره

'No one can cross it.'

3.I.10 86.2

ان ما قدر زوجها يخرجها من عنده إلا بمهرها لقلة
رغبته فيها

'Her husband could only get rid of her, since he had such little desire for her, by paying her a dowry.' Note also the word order after *inna*.

3.I.11 86.3

فاذا اراد رجل يتزوج امرأة يجون نسا الحافه

'When a man intends to marry a woman, the women of the quarter come.' Note also the masc. plur. verb standing before the fem plur. subject.

3.I.12 191.13

اريد اشاهد جمال كريمتك

'I want to see with my own eyes your daughter's beauty.'

3.I.13 120.11

واخذوا ثمنه بني به جامع عدن

'They took the price of it with which the mosque of Aden was built.' An asyndetic relative clause with a definite antecedent? (See Schen, 91).
3.I.14 128.8

فلما خرب ادير عليه سور ثاني من القصب شبك

'When it fell into ruin, a second wall was put round it made of canes, one inserted inside another.'

J – conditionals

a) *in* conditionals (relatively rare in the *TM*)
3.J.a.1 66.13

فان كنت تقتلنا بذنب فلم ننزع يدا من الطاعه

'If you kill us for some transgression, we shall not withdraw our obedience.' NB the auxiliary *kāna* in the perf. with the imperfect of the verb in the conditional clause, with *lam* and the apocopate in the main clause.
3.J.a.2 290.7

ان يفترش كل ليلة جارية نوبيه بكر يزول ما به
من العرض والمرض

'If he had sexual intercourse every night with a virgin Nubian slave girl, his illness and symptoms would disappear.' The verb in the conditional clause could be an apocopate, but the main verb *yzwl* must be *yazūlu*.

b) *idhā* conditionals (very common, both with a genuine conditional meaning, and with a temporal meaning)
3.J.b.1 8.4

اذا تخاصم رجل وامراته واغتاظت المراة منه غايه
الغيظ تقول المراة لزوجها . . .

'If a man and his wife get into an argument and she gets extremely angry with him, she says to him, . . .' The main clause would appear to be imperfect indicative. This is possible in CA; see Wright 1951, ii, 10 A & B.

3.J.b.2 33.8

اذا تاه بعض الحجاج بطريق مكة ووصل الي القوم
فبعضهم يقتله واخرون يقبلونه

'If one of the pilgrims goes astray on the way to Mecca and finds his way to these people, some of them will kill him, others will receive him [as a guest].' Two apparently imperfect indicative verbs in the main clause. Note also the nominal sentence in each case.

3.J.b.3 41.16

واذا قل الماء في حده فمنها يستقي الماء اهل حده

'When water is scarce in Ḥaddah, the inhabitants draw water from [the well].' NB the word order of the main clause: *fa-* with a prepositional phrase, followed by an imperfect indicative verb, the direct object and finally the subject.

3.J.b.4 65.13

اذا مات هذا فيتولي من بعده الثاني

'When this one dies, the second will take over after his death.' NB the *fa-* introducing the main verbal clause, the verb being imperfect indicative.

3.J.b.5 85.19

فاذا رجع الامر الي ذلك تقل رغبة الرجال فيها

'If it comes to this, the men have little desire for her.'

3.J.b.6 101.6

فاذا رويت الارض واستغنت الناس عن ماء السيل
فتقوم حينيذ من مقعدها

'When the land is watered and these people have no need of the flood water, she then rises from where she was sitting.' NB *fa-* prefixed to an imperfect indicative verb in the main clause.

c) *law* conditionals (usually orthodox)

3.J.c.1 105.3

لانه لو اتفق بهم لكان يستظهر علي اخذ المراكب

'Since, if he were to connect them together [i.e. the mountain and the fortress], he would be in a position to capture the ships.' NB the auxiliary *kāna* with the prefixed *lām jawāb al-sharṭ* and the imperfect of the main verb.

CONCLUSIONS

1. *The* TM *is written in MA.*
Although it is not always possible to find exact parallels in the language of the Arabic papyri, JA, ChA and the *Iᶜtibār* representing Muslim MA, there is, I think, sufficient linguistic evidence to argue that the language of the *TM* is MA and that it should be added to the *Iᶜtibār* as another example of a complete MA text written by a Muslim.

2. *The* TM *was composed containing more non-CA features than we observe in the text we now have before us.*
What has been an extremely interesting exercise in recent years has been to compare in detail both texts which can be identified as Muslim MA texts, the *TM* and the *Iᶜtibār* of Usāmah. Not only have the linguistic differences and similarities been studied, but also it is clear beyond doubt that the non-CA element in the *Iᶜtibār* is greater than that in the *TM*. The unique MS of the *Iᶜtibār* was copied from the original MS which bears the date 610 (= 1213), 26 lunar years after the death of the author,[20] whereas the earliest Istanbul MS of the *TM* dates from about 400 years after its composition. Again comparing the 11th/16th century Istanbul MS of the *TM* with the 19th century Leiden MS, while we note clearly that the two represent a common recension, the latter has undergone a major 'correcting' operation, with most, though not all, non-CA features of the former having been rendered into good CA.

It seems to me that the above permits the conclusion that the *TM* began its existence much more heavily laced with non-CA features which were 'corrected' by successive scribes who were unwilling to tolerate these 'incorrect' features. Since the text has been 'corrected', as we can see with our own eyes by observing Löfgren's excellent *apparatus criticus*,[21] between the 16th–19th centuries as it passed through the hands of scribes, we can safely assume that a similar process was going on between the 13th, when it was composed, and the 16th, centuries, when the earliest extant MS was copied.[22] The tentative suggestion can then be made that the same process has happened to a greater or lesser degree to all MA texts. The Arabic papyrus texts remain as originally composed and, sure enough, contain a very high level of non-CA elements.[23] The *Iʿtibār* similarly has a large quantity of such linguistic features. We have only one MS of the text, and that a copy of a MS dating from a time very close to the original composition, hence there has been little opportunity to 'correct' its language. Whether the same can be said for JA and ChA is possible. In these cases, of course, there would not be the same desire on the part of the scribes to 'correct' and perhaps the speculation should go no further, since I have not personally made comparisons with these texts.

We are no nearer, I fear, to answering the question why a Muslim, presumably – in the case of Usāmah, certainly – well versed in CA, would produce a text written in MA. Schen's endorsement of Landberg's suggestion[24] that Usāmah dictated the *Iʿtibār* as he lay, old and sick, remains reasonable. Is the fact that the reminiscences of this great warrior and huntsman are unique in the history of Arabic literature and outside any classical literary genre relevant?[25] We know nothing of IM except what the *TM* tells us. He may have been a businessman, and thus perhaps neither a man of letters nor of deep religious conviction. However, he quotes not infrequently from well known classical texts, including poetry, some of which he says he has composed himself. That he may have been a native Persian speaker (he also quotes Persian poetry, some of which he says he has composed) certainly does not mean that he was incapable of writing CA. His literary genre, historical geography, albeit with much more to offer, is well represented in Arabic literature and this would appear to suggest that the genre does not significantly effect the CA versus MA question. Without the discovery of more Muslim MA texts, the question why Muslims have written in MA may, alas, never be satisfactorily answered.

Notes

1. I am extremely grateful to Professor M. Yasir Suleiman and to Dr Avi Shivtiel, both of whom read this article in its entirety and who made suggestions for its improvement.

2. Steingass 1930, 918, is the only source to my knowledge which suggests that the Persian word means 'hour'. Payne Smith 1903, 463, gives the meaning 'an hour's journey' in Syriac.
3. Smith, G. Rex 1985.
4. Smith, G. Rex 1988.
5. Smith, G. Rex 1990.
6. Smith, G. Rex1993.
7. Smith, G. Rex forthcoming.
8. In Blau 1965, it is clear that he interprets MA as being the non-CA elements in an Arabic text (pp. 24–5). In Blau 1981, however, 187–203, he writes, 'It seems, however, more expedient to reserve the use of the term Middle Arabic for the mixed language of mediaeval texts, containing Standard Arabic, Neo-Arabic, and, as we shall see later, pseudo-correct features, and to call the vernacular component of Middle Arabic Neo-Arabic (or more exactly, the early layer of Neo-Arabic, its later layer being the language of modern Arabic dialects).' Schen 1972–3 writes of 'MA elements' and adopts Blau's 1965 definition of MA (pp. 218–9). See also Shivtiel 1991, 1441, where he suggests the term 'standard Arabic' rather than MA.
9. The grammar of which is examined in Hopkins 1982.
10. Blau 1961 and Blau 1966–7.
11. Schen 1972–3.
12. The text was originally edited by Derenbourg 1886. A much more reliable text was produced by Hitti 1930. Hitti 1929 is the text translated into English. Other translations include Miquel 1983 and Witkam 1986.
13. See Blau 1965, 25.
14. See Usāmah 1953. Other works include Usāmah 1935 and Usāmah 1965. See also Derenbourg 1893.
15. Dozy 1967, ii, 508.
16. See Hinz 1970, 44–5.
17. For *saffārah*, plur. of *saffār*, see Dozy 1967, i, 658.
18. Reading *taẓfiru* for *taḍfiru*.
19. See Serjeant & Lewcock 1983, 189, note 175; Piamenta 1990–1, 527.
20. Hitti 1929, 17.
21. See e.g. *TM*, 12, notes 2, 11, 12, 16; 108, notes 3, 6, 8; 151, notes 4, 5, 7 etc.
22. Schen, 233, is surely correct to reject the suggestions of Nöldeke, Landberg and Hitti that the text of the *Iᶜtibār* was composed in good CA and the amanuensis and/or scribe corrupted the text, turning much of it into MA.
23. It seems to me that Blau 1965, 123, underestimates the amount of non-CA elements in the Arabic papyrus texts. Cf. Hopkins, xlvii.
24. 1972–3, 228; Landberg 1888, 30.
25. See Nöldeke 1887, 237 ff.; Schen 1972–3, 228–9. Blau 1981, 191, note 23, rejects the idea of dictation in favour of the argument that the *Iᶜtibār* did not fall 'within one of the recognized categories of "literature" and so did not require an elevated style.'

References

Blau, Joshua 1961. *A Grammar of Mediaeval Judaeo-Arabic* (in Hebrew). Jerusalem.

Blau, Joshua 1965. *The Emergence and linguistic background of Judaeo-Arabic*. Oxford.
Blau, Joshua 1966–7. *A Grammar of Christian Arabic, based mainly on South Palestine texts from the first millennium* (Corpus Scriptorum Orientalium 27, 28 & 29). Louvain.
Blau, Joshua 1981. 'The State of research in the field of the linguistic study of Middle Arabic'. *Arabica* 28: 187–203.
Derenbourg, H. 1886. *Ousâma ibn Mounḳidh* . . . Paris.
Derenbourg, H. 1893. *Anthologie de textes arabes inédits par Ousama et sur Ousama*. Paris.
Dozy, R. 1967. *Supplément aux dictionnaires arabes*. 3rd edit. Leiden & Paris. 2 vols.
Hinz, Walther 1970. *Islamische Masse und Gewichte*. Leiden.
Hitti, Philip K. 1929. *Memoirs of an Arab-Syrian gentleman or an Arab knight in the Crusades: memoirs of Usamah ibn Munqidh*. Columbia.
Hitti, Philip K. 1930. *Usāmah's memoirs entitled* 'Kitāb al-Iᶜtibār' *by Usāmah ibn Munqidh*. Princeton.
Hopkins, Simon 1982. *Studies in the grammar of early Arabic*. Oxford.
Ibn al-Mujāwir 195–4. *Tārikh al-Mustabṣir*. Ed. Oscar Löfgren. Leiden. 2 vols.
Landberg, C. de 1888. *Critica Arabica II: H. Derenbourg, Ousâma ibn Mounqidh*. Leiden.
al-Maydānī, Aḥmad b. Muḥammad 1955. *Majmaᶜ al-amthāl*. Ed. Muḥammad Muḥyī al-Dīn ᶜAbd al-Ḥamīd. Cairo.
Miquel, André 1983. *Des Enseignements de la vie* . . . Paris.
Nöldeke, Th. 1887. 'H. Derenbourg: Ousāma ibn Mounqidh'. *Wiener Zeitschrift zur Kunde des Morgenlandes* 1: 237 ff.
Payne Smith, R. 1903. *A Compendious Syriac dictionary*. Oxford.
Piamenta, Moshe 1990–1. *A Dictionary of post-classical Yemeni Arabic*. Leiden. 2 vols.
Schen, I., 1972–3. 'Usama Ibn Munqidh's memoirs: some further light on Muslim Middle Arabic'. *JSS* 17/2 &18/1: 218–36 & 64–97.
Serjeant, R.B. & Lewcock, Ronald 1983. *Ṣanᶜāʾ, an Arabian Islamic city*. London.
Shivtiel, Avihai 1991. 'The Maze of Arabic'. In Alan S. Kaye (ed.), *Semitic Studies. In honor of Wolf Leslau*. ii. Wiesbaden.
Smith, G. Rex 1985. 'Ibn al-Mujāwir on Dhofar and Socotra'. *Proceedings of the Seminar for Arabian Studies* 15: 79–91.
Smith, G. Rex 1988. 'Ibn al-Mujāwir's 7th/13th century Arabia – the wondrous and the humorous'. In Irvine, A.K., Serjeant, R.B. & Smith, G. Rex (eds.), *A Miscelleany of Middle Eastern articles. In Memoriam Thomas Muir Johnstone 1924–83*. Harlow.
Smith, G. Rex 1990. 'Ibn al-Mujāwir's 7th/13th century guide to Arabia – the eastern connection'. *Occasional Papers of the School of Abbasid Studies* 3: 7–89.
Smith, G. Rex 1993. 'Some "anthropological" passages from Ibn al-Mujāwir's guide to Arabia and their proposed interpretations'. In Andre Gingrich *et alii* (eds.), *Studies in oriental culture and history. Festschrift for Walter Dostal*. Frankfurt am Main etc.
Smith, G. Rex, forthcoming. 'Ibn al-Mujāwir as a story-teller – some examples

edited and interpreted from his 7th/13th century guide to Arabia'. In Farida and Jarir Abu-Haidar (eds.), *Classical and popular medieval Arabic literature: a marriage of convenience?* Festschrft for Professor H.T. Norris.
Steingass, F. 1930. *A Comprehensive Persian-English dictionary*. London.
Usāmah Ibn Munqidh1935. *Kitāb Lubāb al-ādāb*. Ed. Aḥmad Muḥammad Shākir. Cairo.
Usāmah Ibn Munqidh1953. *Dīwān Usāmah Ibn Munqidh*. Eds. Aḥmad Aḥmad Badawī & Ḥāmid ᶜAbd al-Majīd. Cairo.
Usāmah Ibn Munqidh1965. *Kitāb al-Manāzil wa-al-diyār*. Ed. al-Arlaʾūṭ. Beirut.
Witkam, J.J. 1986. *Wat anders dan vechen en jagen? Memoires van een Syrisch edelman*. Amsterdam.
Wright, W. 1951. *A Grammar of the Arabic language*. 3rd. edit. Cambridge.

For Product Safety Concerns and Information please contact our EU
representative GPSR@taylorandfrancis.com
Taylor & Francis Verlag GmbH, Kaufingerstraße 24, 80331 München, Germany

www.ingramcontent.com/pod-product-compliance
Lightning Source LLC
Chambersburg PA
CBHW071152100726
47908CB00002B/347
* 9 7 8 1 1 3 8 9 8 5 8 8 9 *